THE SPORTS ILLUSTRATED
BOOK OF BRIDGE

THE SPORTS ILLUSTRATED
BOOK OF BRIDGE

by Charles Goren

AND THE EDITORS OF SPORTS ILLUSTRATED

A Chancellor Hall Book

TIME INCORPORATED • NEW YORK

TIME INC. BOOK DIVISION

EDITOR Norman P. Ross

COPY DIRECTOR *ART DIRECTOR*
William Jay Gold Edward A. Hamilton

CHIEF OF RESEARCH Beatrice T. Dobie

**"The Sports Illustrated Book of Bridge"
was produced under the direction of**

EDITOR Norton Wood

RESEARCHER Danuta Dorozynski

•

PUBLISHER Jerome S. Hardy

GENERAL MANAGER John A. Watters

SPORTS ILLUSTRATED MAGAZINE

MANAGING EDITOR *PUBLISHER*
Andre Laguerre Sidney L. James

FOREWORD

Charles Henry Goren has probably brought more people together in friendly anguish than the June moon.

Strictly speaking, this is not attributable to Charlie's natural capacity for sentiment, which is considerable, nor to his missionary zeal, which is awesome, but to the simple fact that he has ruled for more than a dozen years as *the* bridge authority. By standardizing the game through his very own point count system and his tireless advocacy of it, Goren has made it possible (the wildly improbable is always possible in Goren's world) for a pipefitter from Nebraska to sit down to a hand of bridge in London, say, with that grand old party Somerset Maugham, and feel right at home.

The story of how Goren rose to his present eminence is detailed in lively fashion by Jack Olsen in the Introduction beginning on page 10. Long before 1957 Goren had won every honor and every trophy bridge has to offer. Yet by his own reckoning it was in that year that he *really* arrived—for it was then that *Sports Illustrated* asked him to write a weekly column for its pages. He recalled to the editors at the time that he had once been a sports reporter as an undergraduate at McGill University, and it had always troubled him that by U.S. newspaper tradition bridge, which he considers the greatest sport of all, was not to be found on the sports page. Its recognition by *Sports Illustrated*, he felt, was vindication of his views at last. (And it has, indeed, come to pass that bridge is today a sports-page feature in some newspapers.)

Goren takes a remarkably sporting attitude toward the poorer players in the game he has dominated for so many years. "In the early days of my career," he writes on a later page of this book, "I became indignant with bids that I felt were bad. But I soon mellowed. It dawned on me that bad bids—that is, bids *I* wouldn't have made—frequently made good drama. Without them, a bridge script could be dull, like errorless baseball, which can become distressingly mechanical. Not infrequently the ball team that wins is one that uses tactics which are so daring that at first they appear suicidal. Similarly in bridge, seemingly unsound procedures may succeed because they also surprise."

Sports Illustrated readers who follow Goren's column in the magazine have found it never dull and very often packed with surprise. No professorial graybeard, his sense of humor is as sharp as his intellect. And he has a rare talent for dispensing the hard lessons of bridge technique under a sugar-coating of metaphor and wit. The best of Goren's weekly essays— an even hundred of them—have been drawn together in this book, beginning on page 48, to provide a fine library collection for reading and rereading with continued enjoyment. On subsequent pages are quizzes to challenge the resourcefulness of every player, and a complete presentation of the Goren System itself to serve as a primer for the bridge beginner or a refresher course for the more advanced player. There are pictures, too, of notable personalities in the world of bridge and interesting aspects of the game—including a series of reproductions in color of some of the world's rarest and most beautiful playing cards.

Maugham, who calls bridge the "most entertaining and intelligent card game the wit of man has so far devised," could have been more swayed by the writing of his friend Charlie Goren than that of any other contemporary when he said: "I am an ardent reader of the books that are written on this fascinating game. They make excellent bedside reading. They are both exciting and soothing. They enable you to bear a bad cold in the head with patience and a peremptory demand for income tax with fortitude."

It is our fervent hope that *The Sports Illustrated Book of Bridge* will do all that for its readers and more. Not the least to be expected is that it will make each of you a better bridge player.

Sidney L. James
Publisher
Sports Illustrated

CONTENTS

DOWN THE YEARS FROM WHIST

JACK OLSEN, *the* SPORTS ILLUSTRATED *associate
editor who wrote the introductory essay which
follows, began playing bridge as a young reporter
covering the federal courts in Washington, D.C.
All the other reporters played while waiting
for something to happen, he says, and he had to
learn the game "in self-defense." In this
company his very first rubber was at a penny
a point. Since then, Olsen has written often and
entertainingly about bridge and its practitioners—
most recently in his book,* The Mad World of
Bridge, *published by Holt, Rinehart and Winston
in 1960. On the following pages he conducts
a light-hearted investigation into the nature and
origins of America's favorite card game.*

OF ALL the manifold human contests by which the world finds amusement, the game of contract bridge may well be the most ubiquitous. The British have their cricket; the French love bicycle racing; the Russians are chess fanatics; the Americans call baseball the national game. But *all* nationalities play bridge.

What Alexander the Great and Caesar and Napoleon failed to do, bridge did. It brought into being a universal language among adherents everywhere. It crossed national boundaries faster than a new jazz tune on short wave. It took over the leisure time of Arabs and Alabamans, Irishmen and Filipinos, kings and world bankers, taxi drivers and taxi dancers. Go into a baseball locker room after a big game and, like as not, there will be a razzle-dazzle bridge game taking place on an upturned footlocker in the corner. Bridge was played in the foxholes of two world wars, in command posts, in the bellies of bombers on long-range missions, in assault craft churning toward enemy-held shorelines. Bridge enlivens the commuting trips of thousands of Americans; it brightens the afternoons of matrons in exurbia; it fills the off-duty hours of delegates to the United Nations.

It is safe to say that the inventor of bridge would be venerated as an international hero (though scorned by a few) if anybody knew who he was. One can think of baseball and Abner Doubleday, basketball and Dr. James Naismith. But there is no one individual (and no country) that can lay claim to the invention of bridge.

The great cartoonist, H. T. Webster, had as good a theory as any for the murky ancestry of bridge. In a 1930 drawing in the New York *World,* he pictured two devils sitting at a card table in the acrid smokes of hell. One is explaining, "It's a game for four. Everyone has to bid and I've thrown in a lot of conventions to make it more confusing. I call it bridge, and if it doesn't get results I've got another variation that's sure-fire. This will be known as contract, and I'll bet my pitchfork it will demoralize the human race."

Says the other devil: "It's genius, Big Bo, sheer genius."

One thing that can be stated with some certainty is that bridge derived from whist—a game as much like twentieth-century contract bridge as the Wrights' airplane is like the X-15. In whist, 52 cards are dealt to four players and trump is decided willy-nilly by turning up the last card. The simple little game was played by just about everyone in England for three centuries. Charles Cotton wrote in 1674 that "every child almost of eight years old hath a competent knowledge in that recreation." Whist was the subject of hundreds of books, including several by Edmond Hoyle. The game popped up repeatedly in eighteenth-century literature, even as bridge does nowadays. Dr. Samuel Johnson praised it as a force for "kindness." A British ambassador to France, Lord Granville, was so enamored of the game that he lost $95,000 in a single sitting at Graham's Club in London. Lord Chesterfield dropped $1,000,000 at Crockford's in one week, and Beau Brummell walked off a $100,000 winner in a night. There was even a game called "duplicate whist," in which boards were replayed as they are in duplicate bridge. Then, as now, the attempt was to strip all possible elements of luck from the game.

But exactly how did whist become bridge? Here the historian leaves the broad highway of recorded history and enters the backwoods area of chauvinistic claims and counterclaims. Russia claims bridge, as do Turkey and France. The Soviets argue that bridge was an amalgam of whist and the popular Russian game of *Vint,* and they claim that the word "bridge" derived from their original name: *biritch.* The Turks argue, not without apparent justification, that bridge was played in Constantinople in 1860. The French claim that it was played on the Riviera as *khedive.* An American admiral, Douglas E. Dismukes, said that bridge was invented by a British steamship captain, who introduced it at a British club in the Barbados in 1890. The name of the place where the admiral maintained he had seen that first Western Hemisphere game being played: *Bridge*town.

Whatever its specific origins, bridge came in like a fissioning explosion, promptly blasted a swath through British and American card-playing circles, and all but leveled whist in its path. The documented arrival of bridge in England occurred in 1894, and the instrument of its introduction was a prominent Londoner, Lord Brougham. He had just returned from the south of France, where he had learned bridge, and he was dealing a hand of whist at the staid Portland Club, the traditional headquarters of whist. His mind still on the Riviera, Lord Brougham neglected to turn up the last   *11* card for trumps and was pounced upon by his fellow players. "Oh," he apologized, "I thought I was playing bridge." This piqued the curiosity of the other players; Lord Brougham was asked to spell out the rules, and a rubber was played. Soon other members became interested, and within months there was more bridge than whist being played at the Portland. Anguished screams went up. The famous "Cavendish," the lord high plenipotentiary of whist, said bridge was ridiculous and a bore, refused to go to the Portland Club, and announced: "It is disgusting to find the temple of whist thus desecrated." (To his great credit, history records that Cavendish relented after a few years and observed that there was "no game of cards in the world wherein skill, sound judgment and insight into the adversary's methods will meet with more certain reward than they will in bridge.")

Almost simultaneously, bridge had been introduced into the United States by a player who learned the game in Paris. As in England, it quickly bowled over other card games and caused terrible rows and laments over the fanaticism and downright mania it induced in its practitioners. The *New Republic* described the game as a "fierce concentration on a petty end," and charged all bridge players with "a drunken attempt to escape from realities." The *Fortnightly Review* complained that social conversation was being destroyed; "the tables are filled by occupied, interested players, and one is left to one's reflections on the futility of hopes and expectations." For such sufferers from the onslaught of the new game, one admirer of bridge suggested a way out: "suicide."

The church hurled accusations that homes were being broken up, men were being turned into ne'er-do-wells, and souls were being lost over the new "fad." These criticisms were about as effective as beaver dams would be on the Mississippi. In later years Elmer Davis was to sum up the case for the defense: "Most of the complaints about bridge boil down to this, that it is sometimes played by the wrong people. Too much liquor brings out your true nature, whatever that may be; and so does a bad bid, a disastrous take-out, a stupid play by your partner. People who crack under such a strain would crack under whatever strain might be imposed upon them, and I do not see that bridge can be blamed for it."

The bridge introduced into America in 1893 and England in 1894 is now called "bridge-whist," to differentiate it from the new games that slowly evolved. In bridge-whist, it was up to the dealer to name trumps; but he could decline if he wished and allow his partner the privilege. In a word, he "bridged" the decision to his partner. The game was stilted and formal, and met the social needs of a stilted and formal age. One would never lead without asking permission of one's partner: "Partner, may I lead?" And partner would say, "Pray do." One would as soon arrive at a bridge game in one's underwear as to omit these little niceties.

The first new hybrid to grow out of "bridge-whist" had its origins in a remote part of India, where three members of the British civil service found themselves one day without a fourth. They hit on the idea of bidding for the fourth hand, and playing it face-up. The London *Daily Mail* wrote up the game as a "good pastime for four players," and auction bridge was born. This was about 1905, and the new game flourished. It grew so fast that hardly anyone could believe it was anything more than a fad. One observer noted: "Auction has invaded, seemingly, every grade of society, and has, like a devastating fever, laid low the rich and the poor, the believer and the skeptic, the proud and the humble. In Washington, the throne of empire has itself been threatened." In England, whips often had difficulty holding quorums in the Houses of Parliament; the honorable members would be off in the anterooms playing auction.

Many students of human behavior thought the craze would burn itself out. Wrote one in 1909: "The fever of bridge in America has just about reached its height, and I am curious to see if there will be a gradual diminution of interest. Ping-pong lasted a year, diabolo two, bicycling five; bridge has lasted 15 years. How much longer will it endure?" That is *one* question which history has answered.

In the early 1900s the principle of contract began slowly to be absorbed into the theory of bridge. The basic idea of contract—that the bidder only gets toward game what he "contracts" to make—came from *plafond,* a French game which was well established by 1915. Auction fans who visited France returned home and attempted to adapt the contract system to their favorite game, but without much success. The main trouble was that it added more digits and arithmetic to an already frightfully complex scoring system.

In 1917 and again in 1920, members of the New York Whist Club's Card Committee, the grand panjandrums of auction bridge in the U.S., toyed with the thought of incorporating the contract principle into bridge's by-laws, but both times vetoed the idea because it would make the game too "difficult." Then Harold S. "Mike" Vanderbilt went on a long cruise from San Francisco to Havana on the liner *Finland,* and boredom became the mother of invention.

It was 1925. Vanderbilt and his three companions on the cruise ship had wearied of long years of auction, and they set about jazzing the game up. Vanderbilt decided that the contract principle offered the best possibility for improving bridge. He devised a new, simplified scoring table which *13* included large bonuses for slams and heavy penalties for undertricks. He decided that teams which had already won one game toward rubber should reap extra benefits for slams and overtricks, and be penalized extra heavily for failures. What to call a team in such a position? "Vulnerable," said a young lady observer, and the word was added to the lexicon of bridge.

The new game of contract bridge caught on so quickly that only two years after Vanderbilt's famous cruise the New York Whist Club published the official "Laws of Contract Bridge." Auction was swept off the tables just as quickly as auction itself had knocked off bridge-whist and bridge-whist had displaced whist.

Now began the "golden age" of bridge (if a game which has always been exceedingly popular can be said to have had a golden age). Everybody, it seemed, began writing books on bridge. There were almost as many systems as there were players. Conventions were invented on Tuesday and discarded on Wednesday. Berton Braley lamented poetically:

> Does a three-bid signal strength,
> Or a lot of measly length?
> Is my partner on the job or getting drowsy?
> There are sixty bridge conventions
> Which will signal your intentions
> And every single one of them is lousy!

The passage of time has served as a thorough weeding process in the garden of bridge, but many of the present-day systems and techniques go back three and four decades to that era when players were trying everything. For example, the "takeout" double. One night Major Charles Lee Patton, president of the Knickerbocker Whist Club, was playing against R. F. Foster, one of the early experts of bridge. Foster had an annoying habit: whenever he dealt, he would automatically bid "1 No Trump." This seemed to Major Patton to make no sense, and it completely muddled the subsequent bidding. Finally the major stopped the game and announced to his partner: "The next time Mr. Foster bids 1 No Trump and I have strong cards I am going to double. If you have a five-card suit, you bid it. If you haven't, pass, because you will know that I have the No Trump set in my own hand." The tactic worked, and other players in the club began using it. Throughout the East it was played as the "Patton Double." Years later Wilbur Whitehead and Briant McCampbell refined the technique into what is now known as the takeout double.

Other systems and conventions, however, were somewhat less than valuable. One such was the 1-under-1 bid, in which a bid of 1 Diamond actually meant 1 Club, a bid of 1 Spade actually meant 1 Heart and so on. The player evaluated his hand and bid one unit higher—this to confuse the enemy. But the system, in addition to being illegal in most tournament play, was too complicated for all but the most diabolically clever minds. Before long, those who attempted it found themselves so puzzled by their own bids that they gave it up.

Bringing order to the multiple-system chaos became the job of the bridge experts, who in their anxiety to write successful books and gain commercial followings only succeeded in compounding the confusion. The contract player of that time, sitting in a strange bridge game, had to choose among the Vanderbilt Club, the Barton Club, Pochabo System, Losing Trick Count, Sims System, Simple System, Direct System, Four Aces System, Chronological Order System, Bulldog System, Power Control System, Eighteen System, Picture Echo Calling, Acol and a couple of thousand others. He could even buy bridge systems in rhyme:

> Guarded King in each array,
> With an Ace; No Trump's the play.

Conflicting systems found their way into jurisprudence. Mrs. Ethel Harrington, of Berkeley, Calif., sued for divorce, charging that her husband was cruel. "Why, he even demanded that I change the bridge system I used to one he preferred," she told the court.

Said the judge: "Opposing bridge systems are not grounds for divorce."

"Well," said the embittered wife, "he deserted me after I refused to change systems."

The *Saturday Evening Post* observed in 1930: "Conflicting conventions have changed what was once the basis for a nice friendly evening into an inferno of disagreement. No two people, it seems, bid contract alike."

Outlook and Independent accused the bridge experts: "What a boon their books have been to the lagging publishing business. . . . How cleverly they change the rules for contract as soon as the playing public becomes familiar with one set of laws! Parisian stylists are no more astute in contriving new fashions than are the masters of cards in inventing bridge conventions."

George S. Kaufman, the gentle needler, suggested that bridge partners be permitted to sit side by side on a bench, so that they could study each other's hands. Thus "a great deal of folderol about bidding systems could be scrapped immediately." In another lampoon, Kaufman invented a complex convention, the entire aim of which was to show partner how many deuces and treys one holds. Arthur "Bugs" Baer established several systems—one in which dummy is permitted to point out cards in the enemies' hands; another, called "the leaping finesse," allowing the declarer to reach over and play cards from his opponents' hands.

To help the neophyte bridger through this morass of conventions, serious and satirical, F. E. Bruelheide suggested "a series of buttons or badges for the use of the players to avoid the lengthy discussions as to which method is to be followed. . . . Names need not be mentioned; symbols could be used. Three fingers would indicate the player was playing the Vanderbilt Club, a big stick would indicate the Two-Club convention, etc."

Especially irked by the surfeit of systems and conventions were the British. To them, it smacked of chicanery to try to communicate information to one's partner. When an American, John L. Balderston, played in a London club in 1926, he attempted a perfectly informative and useful take-out double of a 1 No-Trump opening bid. His partner was silent, the opponents made 2 No Trump, game, and rubber. "Why didn't you respond to my take-out double?" Balderston asked. Said the Englishman: "I consider that to double, without belief in your ability to defeat the contract, constitutes cheating." When club members dared to post descriptions of new systems and conventions on the Portland Club's bulletin boards, other members would rip them down and burn them. One ranking British player advised his fellows:

"When you sit down to play, your partner may say, 'I'm playing the big Club.' The best thing you can do is look blank. He will then conclude that you do not understand bridge. Probably his next question will be, 'Do you play a Club?'

"A suitable answer to this is, 'Yes, when I've got one.' Ridicule is the only means by which this nonsense will be eradicated."

By 1930, there were two clearly different styles of bridge: British type, *sans* systems, and American type, replete with artificial systems. Now two problems had to be resolved: first, which of the many American systems was best; and second, which over-all style, British or American, produced a better game of bridge. Waiting in the wings to answer both questions, his hands trembling with eagerness and his eyes flashing dollar signs, was a young, sleek-haired half genius and half necromancer named Ely Culbertson.

A historian who finds the exact origins of bridge puzzling would find the exact origins of Ely Culbertson a total enigma. It is not that there is too little information available; there is too much. And almost all of it came from the fertile minds of Culbertson and one of the world's most successful press agents, Benjamin Sonnenberg, who gave Culbertson his initial impetus. Not that Culbertson needed much help. Most public personalities who hire press agents do so because they have an inbred shyness or dullness or inability to get the invaluable "mentions" in the newspapers. Culbertson was the opposite. He needed only a push from Sonnenberg to soar to new heights of publicity, and it wasn't long before Sonnenberg quietly dropped out of the picture, a totally unnecessary appendage.

Culbertson had dash, verve, gall, conceit, bravado, a sharp tongue, a riverboat gambler's heart and a powerful flair for card-playing. He checked in one day, with his pretty Irish-American wife, Josephine, at the Chatham Hotel in New York, and proceeded to run up a huge bill. With Sonnenberg's help, he explained that he was the son of an American engineer and a Cossack chieftain's daughter, that he was born in Romania and grew up in the Caucasus, that he learned to play cards to make money for a group of revolutionaries, that his sweetheart had been murdered and he was imprisoned after trying to kill the local governor, that he flunked out of Yale and Cornell, fought in a Mexican revolution, studied at the Sorbonne, and finally settled down in the United States to play bridge for a living in Greenwich Village. He let it be known that he liked only frozen meats, smoked imported cigarettes worth seven cents each, had fifteen relatives in the Caucasus who were dependent on him, and was the world's greatest practitioner of contract bridge. In this entire farrago of fabricated and semifabricated information, there was only one incontrovertible fact: he *was* a first-class bridge player. And he did not hesitate to prove it.

It was early in 1930, and Culbertson was leafing through *Reflections of a Bridge Player,* a book by the bridge editor of the London *Daily Telegraph,* Lt. Col. Walter Buller. Culbertson's opportunistic heart pounded as he read: "I feel sure that a good [British] four could be got together to take on the Americans, and that, while not necessarily the best available, they would beat them 'sky-high.' Even at duplicate bridge I would lay heavy odds on them beating any team from America."

At the time, Culbertson was promoting his own "approach-forcing system," which was little different from, and little better than, a dozen other systems going the rounds. Mrs. Madeleine Kerwin, a well-known bridge expert, charged that she had codified the same system three years earlier than Culbertson. "Mr. Culbertson has appropriated it and given it his name," she claimed. "He is the racketeer of the bridge world." Replied Culbertson: "She is a local teacher unknown outside a limited circle. I will not dignify her charge by answering it."

Now Culbertson had signed a contract to write a huge tome on his "great new system," but he had not yet set pen to paper. What could he do to make a big splash and guarantee the success of the book? He thought about Colonel Buller and the British claims to bridge superiority. Culbertson was the proprietor of a magazine called *Bridge World,* and he wrote in its columns:

"Certain American players are prepared, if necessary, to go to England and play a series of matches either for love or for any other stake within reason with any four British experts. Furthermore the American players are prepared not to postpone this sporting event to a remote 'some day,' but to play during the coming summer. An opportunity is now offered our British friends to transfer the discussion from generalities to actual practical basis—a showdown."

Right here is where the serious student of bridge must pause and pay homage to the skinny, acerbic, nettling Culbertson, despite all the phony claims and sharp practices and downright lies he had lofted on the four winds. There were a dozen bridge experts fighting to make the public accept *their* bridge systems and buy *their* bridge books and make *them* rich. Many were better known than Culbertson, and several were regarded as his superiors in play. But of that entire group of ambitious men, Culbertson was the only one with the courage to lay his system and his talents right on the line where the whole world could judge. And in the last analysis, it was this—and not merely the three-ring circus of phony publicity—which made Culbertson the undisputed king of the world of bridge.

Culbertson was overjoyed when the equally eager Buller cabled: "CHALLENGE FOR LONDON MATCH THIS SUMMER ACCEPTED." An American team was formed of the two Culbertsons, Waldemar von Zedtwitz and Theodore Lightner; the British chose Buller and three others who shared his strong prejudice for "pure," unsystemized bridge. In September the Americans sailed for England. Culbertson, holed up in his cabin, finished writing the last chapters of his *Contract Bridge Blue Book,* which would not be worth a nickel a copy if his team lost. It was a daring gamble.

The match was held under conditions which were perfect for pubicity. London dailies ran full articles on each day's progress across Page One; American newspapers demanded full coverage from wire-service reporters on the spot. The game was the toughest ticket in town. Bobbies shoved gatecrashers back; lucky kibitzers sat in ringside seats, as at a boxing match, and watched in awed silence.

By the end of the first morning's play, the British were 960 points ahead. Matters went along almost evenly in the evening session, and by 1 A.M. the players were ready to go to bed. Someone said, "Let's have one more," and Col. Buller made an awful mistake; he accepted. In an incautious moment the courageous but bumbling Buller made a sacrifice bid of 5 Clubs. Von Zedtwitz held K Q J 5 of Clubs, by itself enough to set the contract. In addition, the American team held two Aces, a King, two Queens and a Jack. Buller went down to a demoralizing set of 1,400 points. In the other room, Culbertson held the same hand as Buller, allowed his opponents to play 4 Hearts, and set them one. The net swing was 1,500 points, and hearts were heavy all over England.

The shaken British players, doubtless cursing Buller under their breaths, played "dogmeat" bridge the next day and went behind by 4,450 points. The Americans won the match by a wide margin, then trounced two more British teams for good measure.

Culbertson claimed a victory for his system, not for his play. Buller screamed out in his newspaper column: "It wasn't the system. It was the fact that the Americans had played together for many years, and we had never before played duplicate. Mr. Culbertson, having 'stolen' every natural device known to good card-players, comes here and announces the whole thing as his 'system.'

"It is suggested that we lost because we were not playing 'Culbertson.'

"We were, and he and his team were playing 'Buller.'. . . Roughly speaking, Mr. Culbertson did what I did, but whereas he said it was his system, I said nothing. So among those trying to find something wrong with the British team, Mr. Culbertson has got away with it."

Could a man about to publish a book of expertise ask for a better build-up? It went on and on. London newspapers attributed the victory to the "machine-gun relentlessness" of the American bidding. A ranking British bridge expert charged that anybody who would believe Buller "will believe anything." Culbertson jumped in and announced that the British play had been "lousy." Buller's laments, said Culbertson, were a "loser's squeal," and "music to my ears," whereupon *Punch* suggested that it would be nice if "Ely Culbertson, painted green, were drowned in the village pond."

Returned to the United States, Culbertson used the pages of his own publication, *Bridge World,* to trumpet demands for a bridge book by—of all people—Culbertson. Long into the night, he would sit in his tiny office writing letters to the editor, himself. And one day, unable any longer to ignore the "public" clamor, he released the book for which the nation's bridge players had been primed—and every other bridge system began a slow swirl down the drain.

The other experts put up a fight, but they were up against a *winner*. People demanded the book of "that fellow who beat the British," and soon the Culbertson book was outselling all the others put together. So the foremost experts on American bridge joined forces to fight Culbertson, calling themselves Bridge Headquarters, Inc. Great names like Sidney Lenz, Wilbur Whitehead and Milton Work agreed to sacrifice their own systems to devise a universal bidding system for everyone. Five experts resigned from the staff of *Bridge World* to join the new organization. Culbertson laughed publicly at the whole panicky operation. Bridge Headquarters, Inc., he said, is a "purely commercial proposition," thus conveying the impression that "The Culbertsons', Inc.," was some sort of eleemosynary organization dedicated only to the public weal. He called the new group "a merger of ex-authorities," and said there was no need for a universal system since 90 per cent of bridge players already used the Culbertson method. "I do not deny this merger might work out a fairly acceptable system for people who never played bridge before," he said. "Each has had a great deal of experience. For instance, this will be Mr. Lenz's system No. 5. . . . Mr. Work's No. 4."

Soon the merged forces produced a blend of the best features of all their systems, and dubbed it, naturally, the "Official System." Said Culbertson: "It's the official bunk." Cockier than ever and now king of the hill, he began firing salvos of insults toward the enemy camp. He selected Sidney Lenz, the previous king, for special treatment; Lenz, a gentle man of advancing years, refused to become annoyed. But one day Culbertson laid down a public challenge which could not be ignored. He announced that he and Josephine would play Lenz and any partner a match of 150 rubbers. The Culbertson team would put up $5,000, the Lenz team $1,000, and the bets would be paid to charity. Lenz, prodded by his fellow members of Bridge Headquarters, Inc., accepted, and named the brilliant Oswald Jacoby as his partner. Thus began "The Bridge Battle of the Century."

To the front at the Chatham Hotel rushed Damon Runyon, Heywood Broun, Grantland Rice, Ring Lardner, Robert Benchley, H. Allen Smith, Lucius Beebe, Henry McLemore, Westbrook Pegler, and dozens of other reporters. Three telegraph rooms were set up next to the Culbertson apartment, and all during the match an average of 85,000 words a day were dispatched. Press photographers fitted their cameras through tiny cracks cut in a screen for the benefit of reporters. Movietone News was on the scene. The players were attired in formal wear, and referee Alfred Gruenther, then a lieutenant and an instructor at West Point, was a colorful figure in his formal uniform with gold epaulets, red stripes and tight trousers.

The match had hardly begun before it was clear who was going to reap the biggest publicity harvest, win or lose. Culbertson titillated the press with his comments and his airs. How fascinating it was that his two children were nicknamed "Fifi" and "Jump-bid!" What good copy it was when Culbertson sat down to play with a steak in front of him! ("My God, Ely," said Lenz, "you're getting grease all over the cards. Why don't you eat at the proper time, like the rest of us?" Answered Ely: "My vast public won't let me.")

Culbertson left no ploy unturned. He would jump up and down on real and imagined errands. He would study his hand for what seemed like days, often causing Lenz to doze off. Once Lenz was set two tricks on a cinch contract; he explained, "I fell asleep while waiting for Ely to bid, and I dreamed that Diamonds were trumps, and I woke up and played out my dream hand."

The play was often mediocre, sometimes downright sloppy. On the opening hand, Jacoby bid 3 No Trump and was set one. On the next hand, the Culbertsons bid 5 Diamonds and went down four. Lenz, on a 2-Heart bid, was set 1,800 points. Mrs. Culbertson forgot to draw trumps on a small-slam bid, and was set. Ely bid 5 Diamonds on a hand containing six certain losers and went down 1,400 points. The Lenz team held almost every honor in the deck, failed to bid slam, and made 7. For the nation's "dogmeat" bridge players, watching avidly, it was a fiesta.

After 27 rubbers, Lenz and Jacoby had taken a 7,000-point lead, but the Culbertsons fought back, drew even, and inched ahead. Now the Lenz-Jacoby partnership began to show the strain of playing against the world's champion of bridge and aggravation. One night Lenz blurted to Jacoby: "Why do you make such rotten bids?"

Jacoby sat stunned. Culbertson said, "Shall we play another rubber?"

"Not with me, you don't!" Jacoby snapped, and stood up. Gruenther told him to sit back down. Jacoby speared Lenz with a poison-arrowed stare, and said, "Sidney, in a hand in the second rubber tonight you made an absolutely stupid defensive play, and then you criticize *me*. I'm resigning right now as your partner."

Lenz stammered, "Well, well sir. Well, sir. All right, sir." Jacoby's place was taken by a retired Navy officer, Commander Winfield Liggett Jr. The last card dropped on the night of Jan. 8, 1932, four weeks after the match had started, with the Culbertsons the victors by 8,980 points. That was the end of Lenz and the "Official System."

Meanwhile, an enormous hulk of a man named P. Hal Sims was beating everybody who came across his path. The leading player on a fine team which called itself "The Four Horsemen," Sims set his sights on succeeding Culbertson as the king of bridge. He invented a system, won tournaments, and invited the bridge greats to his 21-room mansion in Deal, N.J., there to trounce them at 25 cents a point. He was a master of psychology and what Albert Morehead later described as "sly glances, self-conscious smirks and quasi-fearful tremors." He was, in a word, a large, economy-sized Culbertson. It was inevitable that the two should meet. When Culbertson, sensing that his publicity was waning, issued a public challenge to "anybody" in 1935, P. Hal Sims came roaring into battle with a letter:

"For years, you have been subtly instilling into the minds of a more or less unsuspecting public the idea that you and Mrs. Culbertson are the leading pair of the world. After listening to your most recent boastful claims in the press and over the radio it occurred to me that you might be in a frame of mind to accept a challenge from Mrs. Sims and myself. Contract is really a fascinating game, and I am sure that if you found the time to take it up, you would eventually derive tremendous enjoyment from it."

Answered Culbertson: "Your challenge is accepted with pleasure. All these years I have been itching to lay my bridge hands on you."

Sims moved into the Molly Pitcher Hotel in Red Bank, N.J., and began roadwork and shadow boxing. Curfew rang at 11 P.M. There were long daily bridge workouts against fine players like Sir Derrick Wernher, Barbara Collyer and E. M. Goddard. Culbertson, meanwhile, went about business as usual, which consisted largely of the counting and depositing of money.

The terms called for 150 rubbers in 21 days, a substantial side bet, and a forfeit of $5,000 for quitters. Gruenther was referee. The match began March 25, 1935, and it was almost a rerun of the Bridge Battle of the Century. Culbertson kept calling Sims "Maestro" and "Petronius," while Sims burned inside. Culbertson would show up late, explain that he was delayed by "my public." Early in the match, the Simses began to quarrel. "Darling," said Sims after a disastrous hand, "must I tell you every time that a King and one in a suit I've bid three times is worth a raise?"

"But Hal," Mrs. Sims replied. "I thought—"

"Thought!" roared Sims. "How many times have I told you not to think? Just do what I tell you!"

After 113 rubbers, Mr. Sims asked Mrs. Culbertson what was taking her so long. "I'm thinking, Dorrie," said Josephine.

Culbertson broke in: *"Cogito, ergo sum."*

Snapped Sims: "Speak English, professor, when you play bridge with me."

"The referee understood me," said Culbertson.

"Well, I'm playing this match, not the referee, and I prefer English."

When matters quieted down again, Culbertson made a formal complaint that the Simses' feet were crowding him. "It's all right for Dorothy's feet to get into my quarter," he said, "but now *those* big feet." He ordered an usher to mark off the four quarters in chalk. "If there's anything I don't like," he said with a straight face, "it's having other people's feet on top of mine. It's a complex with me."

The match ground on, spiced by constant bickering, all of which was dutifully reported in the press and on the radio, and finally the Culbertsons came out ahead by 16,130 points. Sims claimed he had had poor hands, but box-scorers pointed out that the Sims team had held substantially more honors. Never mind, said Sims, his team had had poor fits. He challenged Culbertson to a return, but it was never held. Both men had had enough. Culbertson was now making huge profits from columns, books, radio, bridge schools and endorsements, and he sensed that the public needed a rest from his needlings. Already the New York *Post* had announced on Page One that Ely Culbertson had won another victory: he had been elected New York City's No. 1 bore.

Now better players began to come along. A team which called itself the "Four Aces" (and included Jacoby) was so certain it could handle the Culbertsons that it issued a Culbertsonesque challenge. The Aces offered Ely and Josephine a handicap of 5,000 points in a match of 300 boards, and promised to pay $10,000 to a milk-fund charity if they lost. Culbertson need put up nothing.

As always, there was a commercial motivation behind all this; the Four Aces were about to publish a book on their "system." Culbertson refused to be drawn into the publicity-seeking match, and public disinterest made the Four Aces' book a failure. Culbertson claimed loudly that he was the only person to make any money off the book; he had bet one of the Aces $1,500 that it would not sell 10,000 copies.

IN 1936, the American Contract Bridge League devised its system of rating bridge players according to "master points," which are awarded for victories in major and minor tournaments across the country. Twelve Life Masters were named automatically at the start. From then on, no one could become a Life Master until he racked up a total of 300 master points—a requirement which seems astonishing when one considers that many a competent bridge player plays a lifetime without getting so much as a single master point. But hardly had the rule been laid down when a saturninely handsome young man from Philadelphia turned up with the required number of points, and quickly became the 13th Life Master. He was Charles Henry Goren, an earnest and unpretentious ex-lawyer, a bridge champion as totally unlike Ely Culbertson as could be imagined.

In contrast to Culbertson, Goren made no effort to keep his origins a secret. His father was a cabinetmaker: the family lived in a poor, tough section of Philadelphia, and the two sons, Charles and Edward, had to bang their way out of many a street battle. Edward Goren, now a successful Philadelphia businessman, recalls: "Charlie had blond curly hair but he fought like a tiger. He was not afraid of anything in the world." The young Charles Goren also manifested a remarkable indifference to pain, and an ability to concentrate on whatever interested him for consecutive hours on end. He had, in a word, *endurance*. And there is no single characteristic more important than endurance in the grueling world of tournament bridge. Add intelligence and an aggressive, competitive spirit, and the sum is a bridge champion.

Charles Goren, now mellowed and polished, no longer shows the competitive drive of his youth, but he is aware that far underneath his present urbanity the drive remains. "That was the main lesson I learned from childhood," he says. "It was important in our community to do things better than the other fellow or you'd never be noticed."

At first, fighting was what Goren did better than the other fellow, but soon he learned a more positive way to stand out. Year after year, with monotonous regularity, he led his class in scholarship. But college was not in the cards. He went to work as a furniture salesman, where his prodigious memory was an asset. A customer would stay away for six months; on his return, Goren would rush up, call him by name, and another sale would be set up. After a year, a cousin who owned a business in Montreal asked the family how young Charlie was doing. "What?" said the cousin. "Working in a furniture store? Send him up here to me and I'll put him through college."

24   Goren enrolled at McGill University, selecting law because "it had the

easiest hours." He led his class for three years, and just before graduation met a girl who played bridge. "She said to me, 'Do you play bridge?'" he recalls. "And I knew that girls play bridge in the afternoon, So I said, 'Sure,' and I sat down to play and made a complete ass of myself. She laughed at me like nothing you ever saw. I liked this girl. For her to laugh at me was like putting a knife through me. So I took an oath then that I was never going to sit down at a card table again until I knew how to play bridge."

He went back home to Philadelphia and bought Milton Work's *Auction Bridge*, "and I read that thing for six or eight months. If they had destroyed the plates, I could have reconstructed the book from memory."

When he went back to McGill the following year to visit, the girl wouldn't play with him. "But I wouldn't call the time wasted," Goren says wryly.

As a lawyer, Goren was no champion. He quickly found out that Pennsylvania law bore little resemblance to Canadian law. "I bluffed my way through the bar exam," he recalls. "I didn't really know enough to pass the bar. But I was able to sling the language around by that time. So whenever the question revolved around Pennsylvania law, I bluffed it through by citing decisions. I'd say, 'Well, in the case of Hotspur vs. Hotspur, the House of Lords decided so and so, from which we draw the following principles. . . .' I spoke with such authority that the examiner thought, 'Well, this fellow must know what he's talking about,' and I passed."

From 1923 until 1936, Goren practiced law. He never made more than five or six thousand dollars a year, and by the time his name began to be worth money in bridge circles, he was happy to get out. "I should say that the law gave me up, not that I gave up the law," he says.

By the early 1930s, he had begun playing tournament bridge (using the Culbertson system) and had worked his way through a list of partners. Then one night at a tournament in Atlantic City, N.J., he spotted a redheaded ex-showgirl named Helen Sobel playing her cards with the guile of a fox and the aggressiveness of a wolverine. Goren liked her style, and asked her hand in partnership (though not in marriage; Goren remains the perpetual bachelor). The new partnership flourished; it was—although no one knew it at the time—a bridge union of the best male player and the best female player in the world. Soon Goren's walk-up apartment at 1408 Spruce Street in Philadelphia began to overflow with trophies.

It was in 1932 that Goren got up the courage to send analyses of ten bridge hands to the king, Culbertson. To Goren's gratification, the hands popped up in Culbertson's syndicated column, and a check for $30 came through the mail—$3 a hand. Then Milton Work asked Goren to try a few analyses for him, and offered $5 a hand. "So Ely got no more of my business," says Goren.

Milton Work, one of the great teachers of bridge, was then an old man —worn out by time, and worn out by a long series of bitter, futile struggles against Culbertson. It wasn't long before Work was using seven columns a week from Goren. They were brightly written, in marked contrast to the typical bridge commentary of the day, and the newspaper syndicate began complimenting Work on his new, colorful style. Emboldened by these ghostly successes, Goren tried a book under his own by-line: *Winning Bridge Made Easy.* The book appeared to have little chance of succeeding. Ely Culbertson had conned the public into believing that "if it isn't Culbertson, it isn't bridge." A publisher could have set the St. Louis telephone book in type, marked "Ely Culbertson" on the cover, and sold 100,000 copies. But in the face of this powerful image, Goren's book did well—simply because it was clear, it was helpful, and most of all it was bright. Goren did not believe that a book on bridge had to be written pompously; he larded his text with anecdotes and humor.

The young expert kept piling up points in tournaments, and before long began meddling around with the idea of a new system. As he saw the Culbertson system, it had several glaring defects, not the least of which was that it involved fractions. "People have a natural aversion to fractions," Goren says, "and I became convinced that a whole-number system would have a special appeal." Milton Work had devised a system for evaluating No-Trump hands. It was based on a value of 4 for Aces, 3 for Kings, 2 for Queens, and 1 for Jacks. Goren liked the idea, but it too had big drawbacks, and it was only usable for No-Trump bids.

For a total of fifteen years, Goren tried and rejected new ideas. One of his problems was that he was not good at mathematics; he would lay out a system, only to run into trouble evaluating the subtleties—such as how to count an unprotected Queen. One day he met William M. Anderson, an insurance executive and brilliant mathematician who now is president of the North American Life Assurance Company. Anderson found himself intrigued by the complex problems laid before him by Goren. Applying a busy slide rule and the laws of means, probability and chance, Anderson set about solving the problems the way one solves a puzzle, and for the same reason. By the time he had finished, Anderson had taken the final question marks out of the Goren system. And Goren, unlike Culbertson, has never lacked the grace to give the other man full credit. "I could not have done it without him," Goren says. "He studied and studied, and he wound up even getting *me* interested in mathematics. He was the one who suggested adding a point for all four Aces, and subtracting a point for Aceless hands, and he helped me a great deal in raising dummy points. I was never quite sure what point allotment to make under varying conditions."

Now Goren had a system, and he had a national reputation, but he still had Culbertson to contend with. It had become a firm axiom of the bridge world that only one man could make any real money out of the game at any one time. The public had had a bitter taste of variegated systems back in the early 1930s, and it wasn't having any more. Goren figured he would handle the problem directly. He and Mrs. Sobel accepted one of Culbertson's all-encompassing public challenges, and a match was scheduled. But at the last minute Culbertson pleaded the press of business and ducked out. Goren, today a businessman as well as a bridge champion, observes dryly: "He was using good judgment." For a while Culbertson would remain kingpin by sheer momentum, declining matches with superior players, staying aloof, playing the role of the elder statesman of bridge.

Goren's first real break came in the early 1940s. He was writing a bridge column in Philadelphia and, with Mrs. Sobel, winning everything in sight. Culbertson was writing a column for the Chicago *Tribune* Syndicate, and dabbling in international politics. When Marshall Field started the liberal Chicago *Sun*, Culbertson left the conservative *Tribune* for what he thought would be greener pastures. Goren, by this time nationally known for his master-points accumulation, took over for the *Tribune*.

Now Culbertson's popularity began to wane. Goren was writing books, and his newspaper readers grabbed them up. One success led to another, until eventually he authored a total of 25 bridge books. (*The Sports Illustrated Book of Bridge* is No. 26.) Goren's *New Contract Bridge Complete* was on the best-seller lists for weeks, and to date has sold a staggering 200,000 copies—just as Culbertson racked up huge sales in the 1930s and once sold more copies of his basic book in a single year than the other best-seller, *Anthony Adverse*.

But the difference was that Goren offered his readers a more natural system, a system which could penetrate the minds of average and expert players alike. One by one bridge players abandoned the old fractional point count of Culbertson ("two and a half to open, one and a half to respond") in favor of the Goren system. Added to the natural appeal of simplicity was the wry and warm style of Goren. He would not hesitate to tell the reader that there were certain hands that should be dropped on the floor and redealt, or that sometimes it paid to slip a Heart in among one's Diamonds and pretend the hand had been misread. Culbertson took himself too seriously to write suggestions like that.

The Goren system brought bridge roaring back into prominence after it had dipped a little in the years following World War II. People who had never assayed a single game of bridge could learn enough of the Goren system in a few nights to play passably well, and within a few weeks could be good enough to play in local tournaments. The effect was to draw in new players, and the result may be seen in the fact that there are an estimated 35 million bridge players today. They play "Goren," and one can play "Goren" any place in the world and find partners who understand one's bidding and play. As a friend of Goren said recently, "You know, there's no such thing as a *bad* player any more. Charlie raised the whole level of bridge in this country. Anybody who can add two and two can play Charlie's system, and they all do."

Part of the reason for this phenomenon is Charles Goren's work schedule, and his own personality. He hustles the road as an ambassador of bridge and the Goren system. He serves as an arbiter in international disputes, and thinks nothing of flying across the ocean to settle a matter which requires the hand of bridge's senior citizen. He writes a bridge column for *Sports Illustrated;* he keeps up his seven-times-weekly column for the *Tribune* syndicate; he lectures; he writes books; he rules over an organization of bridge teachers; he has a television program and assorted other activities. But most of all, he plays bridge.

Goren is the kind of bridge nut (there is simply no other way to put it) who will fly to Denver in the middle of the night at a friend's invitation because he hears there is a good game going on. He still trumps an Ace with the inner delight of a rookie pitcher striking out Mickey Mantle. He has learned how to relax at the bridge table, and how to make his partner relax. Sometimes he finds himself partnered with a sweet grandmother from Boise who forgets trump, doesn't count cards, and in general qualifies for the "dogmeat" description. "I try to put her at ease," says Goren. "I like to be nice to people. Why not? They're my customers."

He once was paid what must be the perfect tribute by one of his "customers." Answering letters sent in by readers, he had begun noticing an occasional "well-phrased" letter on subtle points of bridge from Leonard Goldberg of Louisville, Ky. "Then there was an interval of several months," Goren recalls, "and finally a letter came in and I recognized the handwriting and I said, 'I haven't heard from him for some time. This is Leonard Goldberg.' And I opened the letter and it was signed 'Leonard Goren.' "

Later a friend from Cincinnati solved the mystery for the baffled Goren. "Oh, didn't you know about that?" he said. "He decided he wanted to change his name and he was such an admirer of the stuff you had written that he changed his name to Goren." One day Goren found himself playing against his namesake in a Louisville tournament. Leonard Goren finished first; Charles Goren finished fourth; and the Louisville *Courier-Journal* headlined: WRONG GOREN WINS.

Charles Goren is now 60 and slowing down a little, although he still puts in a working day which would tire many a younger man. He finds it almost impossible to take a vacation; bridge hands keep running through his mind, and he is apt to spend an entire day alongside the swimming pool doing double-dummy problems. He has a prodigious memory for cards, but he may forget the simplest things away from the bridge table. Once he sat down on a Monday morning and, on a bet, reconstructed the exact holdings of every player on every hand of 140 played in a weekend tournament. On the other hand, he once asked a friend, "When was Pearl Harbor?"

Goren tells a story on himself about the time he went with Victor Kwong, an Arizona hotel man, to pay a call on Chinese Ambassador to the United States Wellington Koo, and to autograph a copy of his latest book for His Excellency. En route, Goren pulled out his pen and said, "Let's see, Victor, how do you spell it again?"

"E-X-C-E-L-L-E-N-C-Y," said Kwong.

"No, I mean his name," said Goren.

"Which one can't you spell?" Kwong asked, enjoying his friend's discomfiture, "Wellington or Koo?"

At the bridge table, Goren plays the pure Goren system; a bridge expert once kibitzed him for six hours and announced afterward, "He didn't make one bid all night that didn't come right out of his book." He tends toward a logical game and away from trick conventions which may baffle partner and opponent alike. In tournaments, players are required to give their opponents a list showing what conventions they play. Goren and Sobel have gone through dozens of tournaments with blank sheets.

Goren takes a charitable view of tricky new systems, like the Italian system, partially because he knows his own system is too solidly entrenched to be in jeopardy, and partially because he knows the artificial systems can never supplant his natural doctrine for the average bridge player. "Some of the new systems are fine," he says, "but I have the feeling that they are only fine for the very advanced player. There are new systems in which an opening bid of two shows a weak hand, or jump shifts on a low level may show weakness. This can be a boon for the tournament player, but it is likely only to confuse the others." For his own part, Goren says: "I am neither conservative nor spectacular. I aim for soundness. In sound play, you have to take certain calculated risks and I'm not averse to taking them—but that doesn't make me a reckless player. You have to make decisions, sometimes unilateral decisions, and unless you're willing to make drastic decisions you're at a disadvantage. Now a drastic decision may be something that appears to be on the conservative side. You take that course of action which is more calculated to produce points. Sometimes this takes guts. It takes guts to bid 7, but sometimes it takes guts to pass."

He likes to recall how he found out that super-safety sometimes loses. "I was playing against Josephine Culbertson's team and I was playing with three unknowns and we had them lashed to the mast. At the end I was defending against 5 Diamonds, redoubled. I had a choice to make, and I thought we had the match bagged already. So I decided to play safe to beat them. My safety play beat them one; I could have beaten them two, and that made the difference. While I was playing that hand, our team had been having some very bad luck at the other table. We lost the match and I couldn't sleep the whole night."

Goren always goes out of his way to accuse himself when his partnership loses. Says Howard Schenken: "If anything goes wrong, he takes the blame." When an unfamiliar partner errs, Goren looks the other way. "I don't even notice it," he says. "If they make a mistake on a hand they should have made, I say, 'I'm sorry, partner, I did bid too much, but I'm in a gay mood now and we'll make up for it next time,' or something like that." In one tournament, his partner held two spot Spades and gave Goren a Spade response to Goren's own Spade opening. Goren went to 4 Spades and somehow eked out the contract. Afterward, his only comment was, "Partner, your Spade bid was one of the nicest compliments I have ever been paid." He is the perfect loser, and more importantly, the perfect winner. When he and Oswald Jacoby trounced the President and Vice-President of Notre Dame, Goren said, "God seemed to be testing the fathers' patience with each deal. They played very well, but they really had no cards at all. There's a moral there someplace. Virtue is not always rewarded."

Inevitably Goren meets with some criticism from his peers, many of whom have a vested interest in toppling Goren from his perch so that the money will be spread around a little more. Only one man can stand at the top of the bridge world, and he is the one to whom the public will turn. He is also the one at whom all the other "experts" will aim their barrages. One hears remarks from the top bridge players designed at deprecating Goren's talents. His close friend, bridge champion Dick Frey, says, "Every player is jealous of the one at the top of the heap. When Culbertson was at his height they said he wasn't a good player. But he was. Now some of Charlie's contemporaries say he never was any good. The record will show that's sheer nonsense."

The record Dick Frey talks about can be described in a legal phrase Charles Goren and every other young lawyer had to learn: *res ipsa loquitur,* "the thing speaks for itself." He has amassed almost 6,500 master points. He has won 37 national championships, and as recently as 1958, with Mrs. Sobel, won the Masters Pairs Championship, the World Series of bridge, for the second time. He has made millions of dollars and millions of friends, has given a lucidity and form to bridge that it never had in the past, and more than any other man has brought the sweet comfort of a fascinating game to interested people all over the world. Charles Goren is all at once the Babe Ruth, Mahatma Gandhi and Walter Lippman of bridge. The record is clear, and *res ipsa loquitur.*

Jack Olsen
ASSOCIATE EDITOR
SPORTS ILLUSTRATED

A CAVALCADE OF BRIDGE

TO THE VACATIONER *who whiles away a rainy summer afternoon at the card table, bridge is one kind of game. To the commuter on the 6:15, slapping down five cards at a time as he deals to his frenetic nightly foursome, it is another game altogether. To the expert who follows the big-time tournament circuit in pursuit of master points, bridge is a proposition far removed from the concept of the game held by anyone else at all. But one thing on which bridge players of every variety and every degree of skill could quickly agree is this: there is no other pastime that offers the same combination of companionship, intellectual stimulus and competitive excitement. Here is a look at the phenomenon of bridge in pictures.*

BRIDGE BATTLE OF THE CENTURY

The most celebrated of all bridge contests pitted Ely Culbertson (left) and his wife Jo against Sidney Lenz (with glasses) and Oswald Jacoby, in 1931. Referee of the showdown match was Lieut. Alfred M. Gruenther (standing). After four weeks of play, during which Jacoby dropped out, to be replaced by Winfield Liggett Jr., the Culbertsons won by 8,980 points—establishing Ely Culbertson as the dominant figure in U. S. bridge of that era.

A GAME WITH HAROLD VANDERBILT

*The father of modern bridge, Harold S. Vanderbilt,
who worked out the theory of contract in 1925, is
shown in a recent photograph by Toni Frissell at
his winter house in Manalapan, Florida, where,
after a morning's swim, he settles down to a
card session with friends who are expert players.*

*At a table in the patio, Vanderbilt (right) has
Waldemar von Zedtwitz as his partner. The other
players are William Root and Mitchell Barnes
(back to camera). Bridge games like this at the
Vanderbilt house often begin after lunch and last,
with a break for dinner, until well past midnight.*

35

The shrine of bridge in Great Britain is the
venerable Portland Club, on Charles Street near
London's Berkeley Square. The earliest version
of the game was introduced here from the Continent
in 1894. Today the club represents British players
in formulating the international laws of bridge.

In a rare interior view of the club, steward
Arthur Plumley is shown recording the stakes of
members in his ledger. No money changes hands in
this gentlemen's retreat. Scores are turned in
for each table after an evening's play, and the
results are then posted to the members' accounts.

36

*The steward arranges tables in the comfortable
playing rooms of the Portland Club, whose roster
of 100 members includes many prominent Londoners.
Although by tradition the Portland is Britain's
official bridge organization, it does not make up
teams, and no top tournament player is a member.*

Row upon row of bridge tables above an endless expanse of flowered hotel carpeting mark the typical regional tournament in which players who feel they have graduated from rubber bridge compete avidly for master points.

This picture shows a recent Knickerbocker, for which 4,500 people filled the ballroom space of the Statler-Hilton Hotel in New York City. Some 250,000 compete almost every week in events of this kind across the U. S.

*Watching over a student practice session, Edgar
Kaplan, one of five bridge professionals who run
the fashionable Card School in New York, stops at
a table to talk over the bidding. At this bridge
academy, players in an average group pay $60 for
eight two-hour lessons plus eight practice periods.*

*A pretty student puzzling over her hand gets some
expert advice from Kaplan. Bridge teaching in the
U.S. has boomed in recent years, partly because of
the prestige attached to winning master points in
tournaments. Aspiring amateurs often retain famous
players to be their partners in national events.*

In a classic tournament scene, Charles Goren is surrounded by anguished kibitzers at Fleming's Hotel in London as he frowns over a hand in one of the world's toughest bridge meets, the London Masters' Pairs. The problem

*facing Bridge Master Goren and company at this tense moment was whether
to try for a slam with relatively weak cards. Seconds later he gambled on
the big bid and won, to bring relieved smiles to a score of anxious faces.*

BALM TO THE COMMUTER

The first man to the smoker saves the seats, the conductor supplies the pack, and most of the car listens in. The cards are never shuffled, slams come up every second deal, and the game is boisterous in the extreme. They call it "ghoulie" bridge, and it makes the hour-long evening ride from New York to Westport go by so fast that the players are nearly always reluctant to leave the train.

Commuter bridge fanatics were often caricatured by the late H. T. Webster, whose notable series of cartoons on the special trials of bridge players appeared in the New York Herald Tribune and 80 other newspapers between 1931 and 1952.

100 MEMORABLE HANDS

BRIDGE BUFFS HAVE *long found amusement and solid instruction in the columns by Charles Goren that appear regularly in* SPORTS ILLUSTRATED. *In each of these the Bridge Master discusses the bidding and play of some provocative hand that makes a point for improving one's game— a private lesson from the man who has won more bridge tournaments than any other player in history. For this book, Mr. Goren has selected an even 100 hands from his columns recently published in the magazine. They are the hands that to him best illustrate the principles of modern play. Readers will find it a challenge to study the cards in each case, decide how the hand should be played, and then compare technique with the world's leading expert.*

Good saws need teeth

As the coiner of an occasional maxim—for example, "An opening bid facing an opening bid equals game"—I have no wish to depreciate my own currency. But a maxim cannot be more than a general guide. Thus it may be true, as the aphorists say, that "All roads lead to Rome," but it does not necessarily follow that everyone wants to go to Rome.

In bridge there are enough bidding maxims to pave several roads. On the one side are the old-line players who quickly bid what they think can be made, leaving the opponents as much in the dark as possible. On the other are the scientists who are so explicit in laying the groundwork for their contracts that they sometimes bar themselves from fulfillment. Both camps bolster their arguments with all the saws you would care to come by.

Somewhere in between, however, lies the sensible course. Let me illustrate with the hand shown at right.

South won the Diamond opening, drew trumps, and lost his Spade finesse without being unduly concerned. East returned a Club, but this attack on South's vulnerable spot came too late; the Spade suit was set up.

A victory for the "old school"? Yes and no. North bid the slam without knowing whether or not it could be made, and at the same time he closed the door on the possibility of reaching a grand slam.

This hand was played in a practice team-of-four match, and at the other table the result was a dud for the scientific bidders when their auction went:

NORTH	EAST	SOUTH	WEST
1 ♠	Pass	2 ♥	Pass
4 ♣	DBL	4 ♦	Pass
5 ♥	Pass	6 ♥	Pass
Pass	Pass		

North's choice of the cue bid in Clubs gave East the chance to double, announcing his strength in that suit. This so affected slam chances that North contented himself with bidding only 5 Hearts. But South went on to slam.

Even against the Club lead—which, of course, West made as a result of his partner's double of that suit—South could have made the slam if the Spade finesse had succeeded. But it didn't, and down he went. The total swing was 1,030 points (980 for making the slam and another 50 at the other table for defeating it).

Actually this was not a defeat for the scientific method *per se*. If the scientists wished to exchange complete information, North, instead of leaping to 4 Clubs, could bid 4 No Trump (Blackwood) and after hearing about South's Ace, could continue with 5 No Trump, asking for Kings. South's announcement of only one King would dampen North's fire to some extent and leave him content to settle for a small-slam contract. And since East would never have the chance to double Clubs, the scientists would get the same favorable Diamond lead that was made at the first table.

EXTRA TRICK   When you have every reason to envisage a slam contract, don't let the opponents get into the act to communicate with each other about facts that will be helpful in the selection of a damaging opening lead.

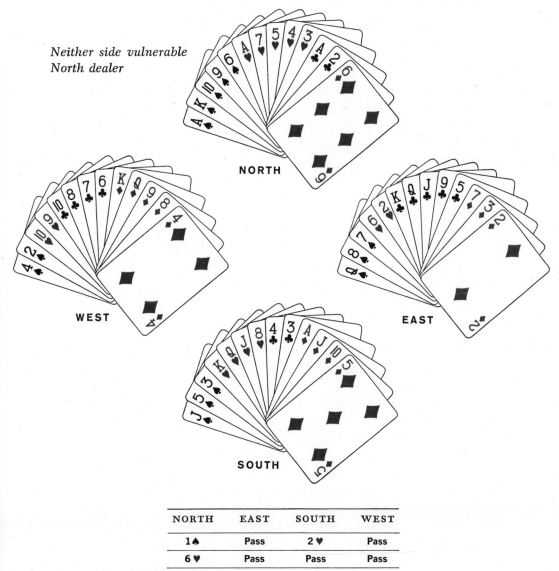

Neither side vulnerable
North dealer

NORTH	EAST	SOUTH	WEST
1 ♠	Pass	2 ♥	Pass
6 ♥	Pass	Pass	Pass

Opening lead: Diamond King

Quicker than the eye

OCCASIONALLY I like to dig into my personal archives for an unpublished hand of the nature of the one shown at right. It was dealt to the late Hal Sims who, despite his 300 pounds, could afford to play high-stake golf in a foursome with three professionals, provided they would afterwards play a few rubbers of high-stake bridge. I had filed the story under the heading, "The Hand Is Quicker Than the Eye," and the title is still apt.

To a bridge player there is just one thing more frustrating than bidding a grand slam in No Trump lacking an Ace. That is to hold an Ace against a No-Trump grand slam and never win a trick with it. In this remarkable deal, which was played during a national championship at Asbury Park, N.J., East was victimized by Sims's neat bit of hocus-pocus.

Perhaps South's cue bid in Spades was unwise—especially in view of his partner's subsequent weird leap to 6 in that suit, and his unrealistic push to a grand slam after Sims bid 6 No Trump in an effort to extricate himself from 6 Spades.

East was guilty of avarice when he doubled 6 Spades. He was to pay dearly for it. From the sound and fury of East's doubles, West's lead of a Spade was entirely logical.

Sims counted twelve tricks: five Hearts, five Clubs and two Spades. A successful Spade finesse would produce the thirteenth—but it was impossible to believe that the Spade finesse could succeed. Sims had to find another way of pulling a rabbit out of the hat.

He took dummy's Ace of Spades and King of Spades, discarding Diamonds from his hand. Then, playing swiftly as he always did, Sims cashed his five Club tricks, discarding a low Spade and the lone Diamond from North's hand. Now he was ready for the hocus-pocus. He cashed his Heart Ace, "accidentally—on purpose" playing dummy's 4. He played his Heart Jack, overtaking with dummy's Queen. And he continued leading down the Hearts until dummy remained on lead with the lowly 3.

East knew that South had another Heart. He knew, too, that South did not have a Spade. So he threw away the Queen of Spades in order to hold his Ace of Diamonds, expecting South to win the last Heart trick.

But East had been hoodwinked. When South produced his last Heart, instead of being one that would win the trick and force him to surrender a Diamond to East's Ace, it was the lowly deuce—small enough to crawl under dummy's 3. So North, not South, won the twelfth trick. And North, not East, won the vital thirteenth that brought home the grand slam.

50 EXTRA TRICK It would be an appalling task to remember all 52 cards in

every deal, and it is seldom necessary to do so. On this hand, for example, after the very first trick East could forget about the Spades, except for those he could see in North's hand, because South had already shown out. The next three tricks eliminated his concern about Clubs. And from South's discards on tricks one and two, it was obvious that the only Diamond of any consequence to East was his own Ace.

That left his mind free to concentrate upon Hearts. The reason he was led astray, of course, was that Hearts did not seem important to him—since he did not have one of them in his hand.

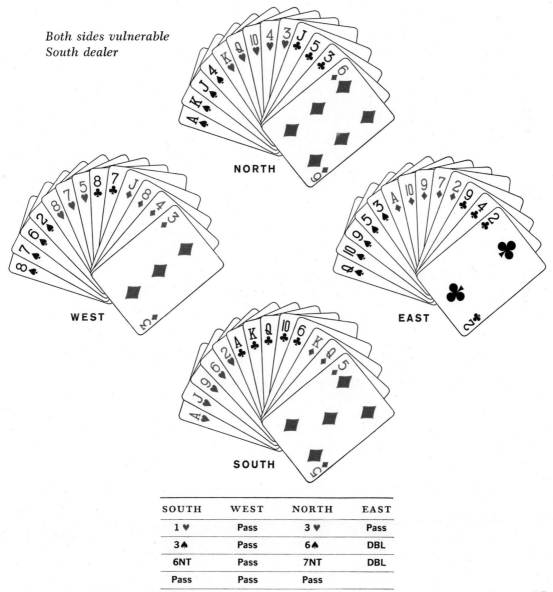

Both sides vulnerable
South dealer

NORTH

WEST

EAST

SOUTH

SOUTH	WEST	NORTH	EAST
1 ♥	Pass	3 ♥	Pass
3 ♠	Pass	6 ♠	DBL
6NT	Pass	7NT	DBL
Pass	Pass	Pass	

Opening lead: Spade 2

Depressed by the angels

IT IS one of the great charms of bridge that all the science in the world can become impotent when it is working against a certain magic which the beginner will sometimes fall heir to. The deal shown at right was played in a tournament some time ago, and the West hand was held by the writer, who, let it be known, does not look upon this as a sound diet. North and South were a pair of charming ladies who professed to be readers of mine. The bidding leads one to suspect they were not very close readers. Believe it or not, it actually took place.

The opening bid, the response, and the rebid of 3 Clubs were right out of the book. North's bid of 3 Diamonds was certainly the best available. It provided partner with an opportunity to bid for game at No Trump if she had Spades guarded. This seemed much more desirable than trying for eleven tricks with such an evenly balanced hand.

South's next call of 3 Hearts is a choice an expert might have made. It can hardly denote a genuine Heart suit, which would have been shown long before. It simply throws the choice back to North to try No Trump, if she has some sort of Spade stopper, or to bid for game in a minor suit if she thinks sufficient values are held. However, North had got into the swing of raising partner and went to 4 Hearts. South at this point got tired of bidding and passed.

The 8 of Spades was opened by West and two tricks were cashed in the suit. On the Spade continuation, South ruffed with the 4. This was over-ruffed with the 5, but there were no more tricks for the defense. It will be noted that a 5-Club contract would have been doomed to failure, because on the third round of Spades South would be obliged to ruff high and thus establish a trump trick for West.

At the conclusion of the hand, South turned to me with the comment, "I tried to bid the hand the way you do. I remembered that you don't like any of the conventions, but show your Aces on good hands. Did I bid it well?"

I was too depressed at the contemplation of our score to think up any witticism of my own, so I borrowed one from Sidney Lenz: "Angels could have done no more."

EXTRA TRICK As some of my more persevering readers may have figured out, there is a way to defeat the 4-Heart contract. West must lead either a Diamond or a Club at the start, and the suit must be continued each time the defense gets in. In order to cut the opponents' line of communication, declarer is obliged to keep playing Spades before touching trumps.

When East gets in with the second Spade, a third round of Spades promotes the overruff for West, and now East can trump whichever minor suit West originally led.

Neither side vulnerable
South dealer

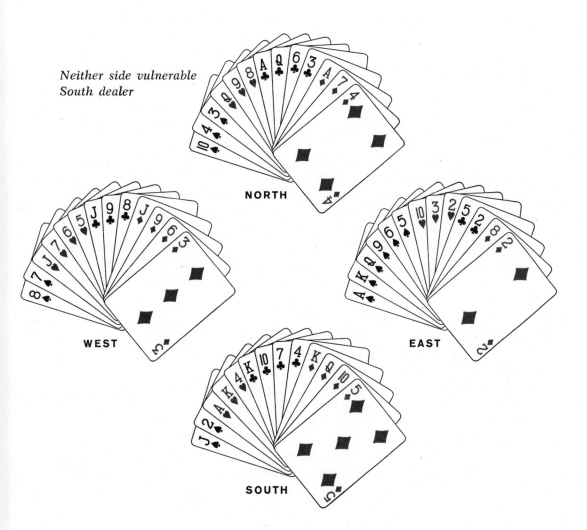

NORTH

WEST

EAST

SOUTH

SOUTH	WEST	NORTH	EAST
1 ♦	Pass	2 ♣	2 ♠
3 ♣	Pass	3 ♦	Pass
3 ♥	Pass	4 ♥	Pass
Pass	Pass		

Opening lead: Spade 8

The greatest crime in bridge

TRADITIONALLY, trumping your partner's Ace is the most heinous crime in bridge. A tolerant expert, however, is inclined to regard this mortifying lapse as a minor misdemeanor, punishable by no more than a rap on the knuckles. (This to insure that partner stays awake during the next few deals.)

No, the capital offense, according to the most experienced players, is failure to trump partner's high card when doing so might save the day. East narrowly escaped arraignment for this misdeed in the curious deal set forth at right. It was only by trumping partner's Ace that he was able to redeem himself.

West hoped his partner might be able to trump the very first Heart and be inspired to return a Diamond. So he led the Queen of Hearts instead of the King. At the next trick, West was tempted to lead a low Heart but feared that this might present declarer with a vital trick, so he continued by playing the Heart King.

This reversal of the usual order of play should have alerted East to the expediency of trumping the trick and making the desired return of a Diamond. But East remained blissfully unaware of his obligation, and discarded the deuce of Diamonds. Next, since he had to protect East's natural trump trick if that player happened to hold three Spades including the Jack, West led the Ace of Hearts.

Suddenly a great light dawned. East realized that his partner had wanted him to trump the previous leads, so he tried to make up for lost time by trumping this one. Fortunately, he elected to ruff with the Jack of Spades—the uppercut play. Normally, South could have evaded the uppercut by discarding his losing Club. Recognizing the danger of a Diamond ruff, however, declarer covered with the Spade King. This promoted West's Queen into a third trick for the defenders. When East also collected a trick with the King of Clubs, the contract was torpedoed—thanks to East's commission of "the greatest crime in bridge."

EXTRA TRICK All bridge precepts are designed to assist the player in coping with the problems that arise at the table with the greatest frequency. However, situations sometimes occur that must be worked out on a common sense basis even though a general rule is violated in the process. Observe that West could have accomplished his goal in the hand shown here by a bit of unorthodox strategy. The normal lead from a holding including the Ace-King of a suit is the King; therefore, when a player leads the Ace, it denies possession of the King.

Since West wanted to put his partner on lead early via a Heart ruff, he could have opened the Ace of Hearts in the hope that East either was void of the suit or had a singleton. Now at trick two West can continue with the Queen of Hearts, which serves a double purpose. East will ruff in the expectation that declarer has the King of Hearts. And, since partner has presumably played his highest Heart, the Queen will serve as a suit-preference signal requesting the return of the higher-ranking side suit, Diamonds.

Both sides vulnerable
South dealer

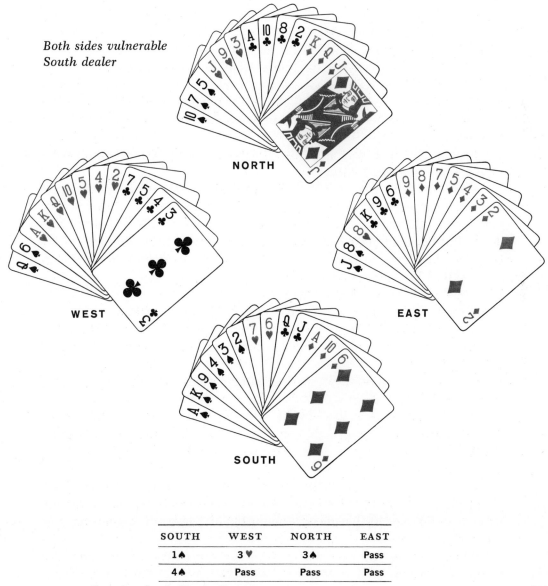

SOUTH	WEST	NORTH	EAST
1♠	3♥	3♠	Pass
4♠	Pass	Pass	Pass

Opening lead: Heart Queen

Better than a peek

"ONE peek is better than two finesses," runs the cynical bridge adage—a mistaken doctrine that quite overlooks such factors as astigmatism and opponents who do not properly sort their cards.

Entirely aside from the question of ethics, most experts prefer opponents who hold their cards close to the chest. This is more than a matter of pride. The truth is that a good player would rather trust his insight than his eyesight. To clear up this seeming paradox and illustrate how much surer it is to see with the mind's eye, here's a hand with a history.

The deal was played in a tournament at a convention of bridge teachers. North and South were among the famous experts who had been invited to give the teachers a taste of topflight competition. East and West were a pair of teachers whose bidding could be trusted to be exemplary, as indeed it was.

There is a fifth character in this little drama—the kibitzer, South's wife, seated at the southeast corner of the table.

After taking her Ace of Hearts, West led the 8. East won with the King and returned the Jack, forcing South's Queen, West and North discarding low Spades. Obviously, if he lost the lead once more, declarer would be down. But he could make nine tricks and the game if he could bring home six tricks in Clubs. So South led the Club 9, agonized only briefly when West played low, and played the Ace from dummy, causing East to lose her singleton King and her temper.

Turning upon the kibitzer, she accused: "You kicked him."

"I resent that," South put in, full of injured pride. "You must think I'm very naïve. I hardly had to be kicked into knowing you had the King of Clubs."

Indeed, it was more obvious than either a kick or a peek could have made it. West had already played the Ace of Hearts. She could not have held the King of Clubs as well, or she would have given no thought to passing her partner's opening bid. East must have the King of Clubs, and South's only chance to make his game was to find it unguarded.

EXTRA TRICK   Don't stop counting points when the bidding is over. Point count can be of considerable help during the play. As in this hand, the opponent who passes his partner's opening bid of 1 in a suit cannot have as many as 7 points.

When a player who passed initially turns up with an Ace and two Kings, you can be sure he does not have another Ace, and it is most unlikely that he holds another King.

If declarer's opening bid was 1 No Trump, count his points, and at some stage during the play you will know exactly what cards he has and what your partner must have. If he bid correctly, his hand includes not less than 16 points and not more than 18. Thus, if you know 15 of his points, he cannot have a missing Ace; if you know 16, he cannot have another King. You may plan your defense as confidently as if you actually saw these missing cards in your partner's hand.

Both sides vulnerable
East dealer

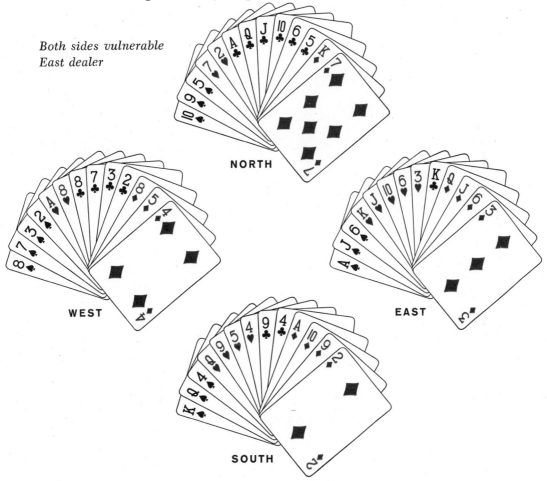

EAST	SOUTH	WEST	NORTH
1♥	Pass	Pass	2♣
Pass	2NT	Pass	3NT
Pass	Pass	Pass	

Opening lead: Heart Ace

Bad luck or bad judgment?

HAVE you noticed how many bridge players have a tendency to emphasize their hard luck? It is a distinct form of hypochondria. The player who suffers from the disease appears to take great pride in claiming that he is always the victim of misfortune. It is strange how easy it is for him to forget the many good cards that come his way. Take the story of the hand that follows. It was told at a hypochondriac's clinic where despondent bridge players had assembled to relate their most unlucky experiences at the card table. Only a bridge hypochondriac could find bad fortune in holding such a huge hand as South's.

The brief but bizarre auction as set forth at right requires some explaining; actually, this was only the official part of the bidding that took place. What really happened was that South became so excited by his glorious hand that he overlooked the minor detail that the hand had been dealt to him by East. Without waiting for that player to speak, South launched into a bid of 2 Spades—out of turn!

The rule book having been duly consulted, South's bid was canceled. East's right to bid first was restored and, as the penalty for South's mistake, North was barred from taking any part in the bidding.

"So," as the narrator of this supposed example of hard luck described it, "after East passed, of course I bid 7 Spades. This was doubled by my left-hand opponent. He led the Ace of Diamonds and then the Ace of Clubs. I was down one. But if he had led the Ace of Clubs first, I would have made the hand."

A certain amount of humor, of course, lies in the confidence with which South contracted for a grand slam despite his three losers—referring to the incident as nothing more than a case of hard luck.

Yet there was pathos, too, in this situation, because the man really was the victim of a bad break. The fate of South's grand-slam bid depended entirely on which of his two Aces West selected for the opening lead. Had I been on lead with West's hand, I would have produced the Ace of Clubs. Obviously, declarer must have a void somewhere; since I had only three Clubs and five Diamonds, there was a better chance that the Club Ace would live.

Against me, South would have made his 7 Spades, and I would have had the hard-luck story to tell at the next meeting of the moaners' club.

EXTRA TRICK Should such penalties as afflicted the declarer on this hand be invoked in a "sociable" game? Players who write to ask similar questions find me firmly on the side of law and order. Through long experience, I have learned that the only way to keep a game sociable is by impartial observance of all the rules. The moment some laws are waived, all laws come into question. And that is when the real arguments begin.

Both sides vulnerable
East dealer

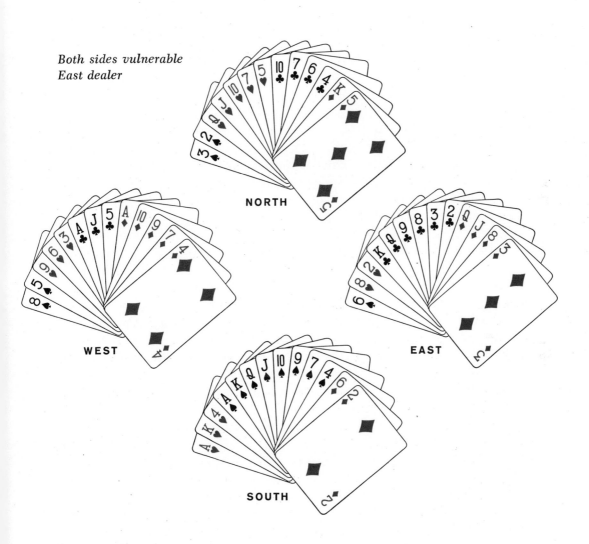

NORTH

WEST

EAST

SOUTH

EAST	SOUTH	WEST	NORTH
Pass	7♠	DBL	Pass
Pass	Pass		

The hand of adversity

I HAVE always subscribed to the maxim about the ill wind that nearly always blows somebody good. Thus, I am firmly convinced that the bad bidder, whether he gets that way from recklessness or ignorance, contributes unwittingly to the science of bridge. Many an inspired play, many a brilliant coup has been brought off because it was made necessary by some previous atrocity in the bidding—just as many of the finest golf shots are produced because of an earlier gaff.

There are few thrills comparable to the one experienced in bringing home an "impossible" contract, as in the deal shown at right.

West's double of 1 Heart was just one of those things. His enthusiasm may have come through a sudden misapprehension that he was playing a game of Kalabrias or perhaps gin rummy. His hand was well suited for either game, though not for bridge. Yet there is just a suggestion of method in his madness. His purpose—and I make it plain I do not admire his judgment—was to find a spot at which to sacrifice against the anticipated game contract of his adversaries. South's leap to game was based only partially on the merits of his hand. I should say that he was at least equally moved by a feeling of righteous indignation. East doubled, West led the Queen of Clubs, and the battle was on.

It was evident to South that his work was cut out for him. Several deductions had to be made at the start. From the apparent lack of high cards in West's hand, it was evident that the double of 1 Heart must have been based on distribution. In other words, West had either one or no Hearts. If he had none, the situation was hopeless, since East would then make two trump tricks. But if West held one Heart, and that one happened to be either the 9 or the 10, the trump loss could be limited to one trick. Declarer laid down the Ace of Hearts and was delighted to drop West's 9. West's probable distribution, then, appeared to be 4–4–4–1, which would place two Diamonds in the East hand. If one of them was the King, the contract could be made. Otherwise there was no hope.

A low Diamond was therefore led to dummy's Ace and a small trump followed. East played the 7 and the finesse of the 8 of trumps held. The Queen of trumps then drove out the King. Subsequently the lead of a low Diamond out of the South hand cleared the King of that suit and established the Queen. The losses were held to one Heart, one Spade and one Diamond.

EXTRA TRICK   When a contract appears to be virtually hopeless, the declarer should adopt an optimistic attitude and, no matter how desperate the prospect, look for a favorable distribution that will give him a chance to make the hand. He should then proceed on the assumption that the good break in cards exists. Many a lost cause has been salvaged because declarer didn't know when he was licked.

North-South vulnerable
West dealer

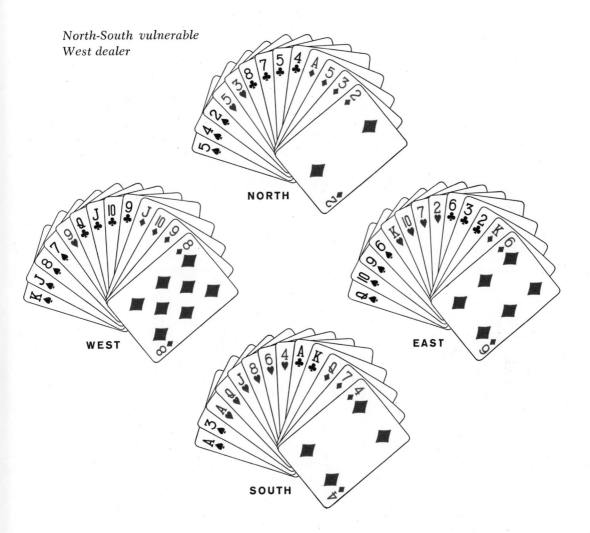

NORTH

WEST

EAST

SOUTH

WEST	NORTH	EAST	SOUTH
Pass	Pass	Pass	1 ♥
DBL	Pass	1 ♠	4 ♥
Pass	Pass	DBL	Pass
Pass	Pass		

Opening lead: Club Queen

61

A dashing little slam

INTERNATIONAL bridge matches have become so numerous that unless there are colorful sidelights to capture the public eye the tournaments receive little more attention than a good local event. Most people seem to be interested in one point, however: what language was used? The question is a good one. I am not a facile linguist and occasionally my difficulty with a foreign tongue has resulted in a miscall.

There was quite a different problem on the following hand, which I played in Buenos Aires in 1958, with Margaret Wagar as my partner. We lost the mixed pair championship in the waning minutes of the tournament to Peter Leventritt, my New York friend, and Mrs. Lewis Fremont of Buenos Aires. But before we did, Leventritt tried to bolster my sagging spirits after a succession of bad boards by telling me, "You really have a soft touch for the next round."

He pointed to a mild-mannered gentleman of obvious Latin extraction, who was to be our next opponent, and added: "He bids like a cowboy. I just got him for 1100 points."

As we took our seats for the final round, Mrs. Wagar and I were confronted with the hand at right.

The reader is at liberty to draw his own character deductions from the bidding sequence, the accuracy of which I will vouch for. South, the gaucho referred to above, had "Sin Triumphe" on his mind, and no amount of pleading by the fair señorita across the table, who presumably spoke the same language, was going to move him.

I was at West. It appeared that our bouncing boy in the South position was well prepared for a Spade lead, so I selected the 6 of Diamonds. Mrs. Wagar won with the Ace and returned the 4. Declarer took the King, then tried the double Heart finesse and succeeded. He next cashed the Ace and King of Clubs. Rudely ignoring probabilities, the cards broke 2–2. This provided him with an entry to his hand in the form of the 10 of Clubs, which permitted him to take another Heart finesse and claim the balance of the tricks when that suit broke.

The hand took him less time to play than it is taking me to tell it. Furthermore, he played with the confident air of one who is used to miracles. In the interests of inter-American relations—and with a sizable lump in my throat—I congratulated the gentleman. He accepted very graciously.

"I'm sorry, partner," spoke up Margaret Wagar in a soft voice, "I could have beaten it."

I was sure she was jesting and didn't pursue the subject further.

When we left the table she pointed out that if she had returned a Club on the second trick, declarer would have had only one entry to his hand and would have been unable to take two Heart finesses.

EXTRA TRICK   A 6-Club contract would have been a more legitimate commitment on this hand, for, granted an early entry to dummy, declarer need take only a single finesse in Hearts. If the King is onside, and both Hearts and Clubs break favorably, the Heart suit can be successfully established by ruffing the third round.

North-South vulnerable
South dealer

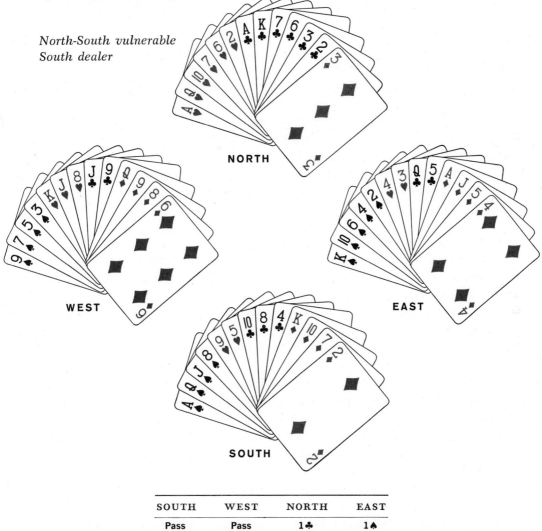

SOUTH	WEST	NORTH	EAST
Pass	Pass	1♣	1♠
2NT	Pass	3♥	Pass
3NT	Pass	5♥	Pass
5NT	Pass	6♥	Pass
6NT	Pass	Pass	Pass

Opening lead: Diamond 6

A dummy reversal by Lenz

IN writing about bridge, as in playing it, I am happy to acknowledge a debt to a gentleman whose long string of championship victories spanned three generations of the game—whist, auction and contract. I refer, of course, to my friend the late Sidney Lenz. He was the first to write about many of the plays that have become standard today. He was a sparkling raconteur, a high-ranking amateur at table tennis, and a bewildering parlor magician.

But the magic he produced as declarer in the play of the hand shown at right had nothing to do with his powers as a prestidigitator. You would have thought it did, however, if you had watched the thirteenth trick seem to materialize out of thin air.

The auction might suggest that clairvoyance was one of Lenz's many talents, since he bid the grand slam without an Ace in his hand. But North's bidding clearly revealed the three Aces he needed, and South himself, with his convenient void, could take care of the first trick in Hearts. So, when North got around to proclaiming his powerful Spade support at long last, South decided to go for all the marbles.

West opened the play with the Jack of Hearts. Lenz ruffed this trick and counted up the rest that could be easily won. The total came to twelve—five Spade tricks, six Club tricks and the Ace of Diamonds. The thirteenth card that stubbornly remained to be taken care of was that extra little Diamond in South's hand.

Obviously, the grand slam could be made only if one of dummy's trumps could take care of that losing Diamond. However, since the laws of contract bridge were no different for Mr. Lenz than for any ordinary player, he had to consider a rather sticky penalty to be paid for trumping a suit of which he was not void. At least three rounds of trumps would have to be drawn before South could safely discard dummy's Diamonds on his Clubs—and by that time dummy would have no more trumps to use for ruffing Diamonds. Nevertheless, Lenz did find a most useful and ingenious way to let dummy's trump take care of his Diamond loser.

No black magic was required. After ruffing the opening lead, a Diamond to dummy's Ace let declarer trump another Heart. Next, Lenz cashed the King of Spades and led a Spade to dummy's Queen. A third Heart was ruffed with South's remaining Spade, and dummy got back with a Club. Now, while the Ace of Spades drew East's last trump, it also took care of providing a parking place for South's remaining Diamond. The Clubs were good for the rest of the tricks.

EXTRA TRICK The play Lenz used to produce the thirteenth trick for his grand slam is called a "dummy reversal." It seldom pays to use trumps in the long-trump hand for ruffing; except as this may establish a long suit in dummy, the play normally will not add any tricks to the total you are otherwise able to win. The single exception is the case illustrated here, where you are able to bring the long-trump hand down to a holding of fewer trumps than the opposite hand began with, and thereafter use what started out as the shorter hand for the purpose of drawing the adverse trumps.

North-South vulnerable
North dealer

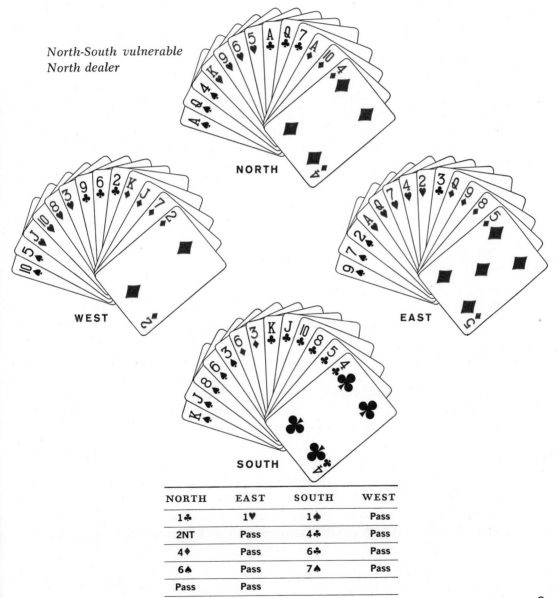

NORTH	EAST	SOUTH	WEST
1♣	1♥	1♠	Pass
2NT	Pass	4♣	Pass
4♦	Pass	6♣	Pass
6♠	Pass	7♠	Pass
Pass	Pass		

Opening lead: Heart Jack

A successful four-horse parlay

AS a fascinated kibitzer of the following deal, I found myself, at the conclusion of the play, deploring the absence of pari-mutuel facilities for wagering on the outcome of bridge hands. With my predilection for buying a $2 ticket on the longest shot in each race, I'm sure I would have "got down" on declarer in this contract of 4 Hearts, and in the process collected a record price when declarer brought his forlorn hope home under a smart ride.

The final contract of 4 Hearts is hardly sound, and the fault for reaching it is entirely North's. There was no justification for his raise with a hand so lacking in power.

The requirements for a single raise in a major suit are 7 to 10 points. This hand falls far short of that total. It was unlikely that a game would be missed by failure to keep the bidding open. Despite the powerhouse that South held, there was really no play for the contract—or so it would seem merely by examining the North-South hands. Even if the Club finesse succeeds, declarer has three losing Spades and a losing Diamond and, short of tearing up the cards, no visible way of getting rid of a single one of them.

Fortunately—or unfortunately, depending upon the player's point of view—West selected the only lead to give declarer a faint chance of running room. The preferred lead would be a trump, but on the actual lead of the Ace of Spades East dropped the Queen. When the suit was continued, East won with the King but could not reach partner's hand to cash the third Spade. He exited with the Queen of Diamonds. Declarer won, entered dummy with a trump and took the Club finesse.

Next, South drew the outstanding trumps, cashed the Ace of Clubs, re-entered dummy with a trump and ruffed North's remaining Club. Then he played the Ace of Diamonds, followed by the 9 and a prayer that East would win the trick. This East did. With nothing left but Clubs and Diamonds, East was obliged to make a lead that permitted declarer to ruff in one hand as he discarded the losing Spade from the other.

In order for declarer to win the hand, (1) the Ace of Spades had to be opened, (2) the Spade suit had to be blocked, (3) the Club finesse had to win and (4) East had to have all three of the high Diamonds. That's quite a parlay. But give South credit for spotting that glimmer of daylight along the rail.

EXTRA TRICK The player who passes a weak hand like North's rarely loses the opportunity to reveal his meager assets later on. Unless partner holds an opening 2-No Trump bid or better, nothing will be lost by playing at 1 Heart. But the opponents will seldom permit that.

In this situation, for example, it is permissible for East to shade a re-opening takeout double, and that is probably East's best course if North should pass. South might redouble to show his powerhouse, West would bid 1 Spade, and now a free raise to 2 Hearts exactly expresses North's hand. South might bid as high as 3 Hearts if pushed but, warned by partner's initial pass, he would avoid the "hopeless" game bid, which just this once wasn't hopeless.

Both sides vulnerable
South dealer

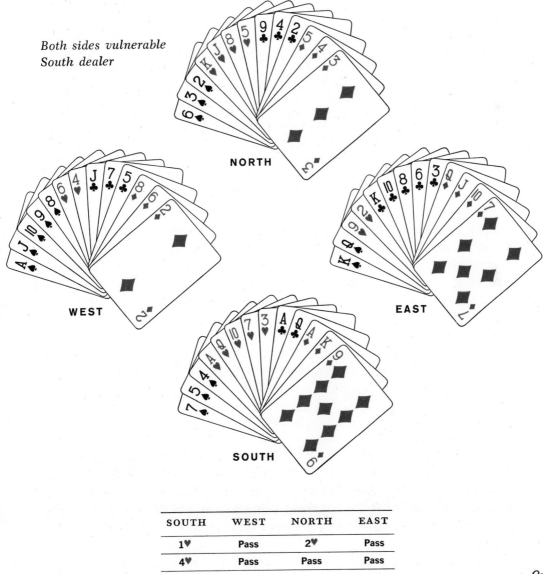

SOUTH	WEST	NORTH	EAST
1♥	Pass	2♥	Pass
4♥	Pass	Pass	Pass

Opening lead: Spade Ace

Post-mortem on a Heart case

DOCTORS are generally too busy tending patients to spare the time to play in bridge tournaments. However, they are trained observers. When they do play bridge they bring to the table a diagnostic skill that is an invaluable asset in both bidding and play. Many of the physicians with whom I have enjoyed a game have the potential to become fine players. But, fortunately for us all, they have chosen to bend their talents in another direction.

The following deal was defended by a pair of Long Island physicians, a radiologist and a general practitioner who more frequently team in medical diagnosis.

After dummy was put down, East studied the prospects of finding four tricks for his side. If South had as many as three Hearts, this would be no problem. If he had no more than one Heart there was unlikely to be an answer. So East assumed that declarer held two Hearts. A third trick was available to his side in the Ace of Diamonds. The only possibilities of winning a fourth trick were if West held a high trump or if East could somehow get a Diamond ruff.

For this ruff to materialize, East would have to overtake the 10 of Hearts with the Jack, cash the Ace of Diamonds, and underlead the three high Hearts in hopes that West held the 9-spot. If it turned out that West did not have the 9 of Hearts but did have a trump trick, East would be guilty of a gamble that threw away the setting trick.

Which should East play for? By training, doctors follow the conservative course, but desperate cases sometimes require desperate measures. Dr. West came to the assistance of his colleague and advised him how to proceed.

West didn't need his x-ray equipment to get the entire picture. When East overtook the Heart 10 with the Jack to lead the Ace of Diamonds into the teeth of dummy's long suit, it was clear that East held all the higher Hearts and only the bare Ace of Diamonds. So West followed suit with his highest Diamond.

It did not matter that the best West could give was the 6-spot; East got the message. If his partner held a sure trump trick and did not have the 9 of Hearts he could have no reason to play anything but a low Diamond. His signal that the Diamond continuation was the way to beat the hand must mean that West held a card that would let him get the lead to make the play.

So Dr. East led back the 8 of Hearts. Dr. West won the trick with his 9. The second round of Diamonds was led and trumped and that brought in the setting trick. With only three cards higher than a 5-spot, West had made each of them prove of vital importance.

South tried to express his admiration, but bridge-playing doctors don't have time for post-mortems. East cut the other deck, handed it to South to deal and said: "Next case."

EXTRA TRICK   Today most experts lead low from three to an honor in partner's suit; some lead low from any three cards. Had West lacked the 9, only a low-card opening lead could have saved game in this deal.

Neither side vulnerable
East dealer

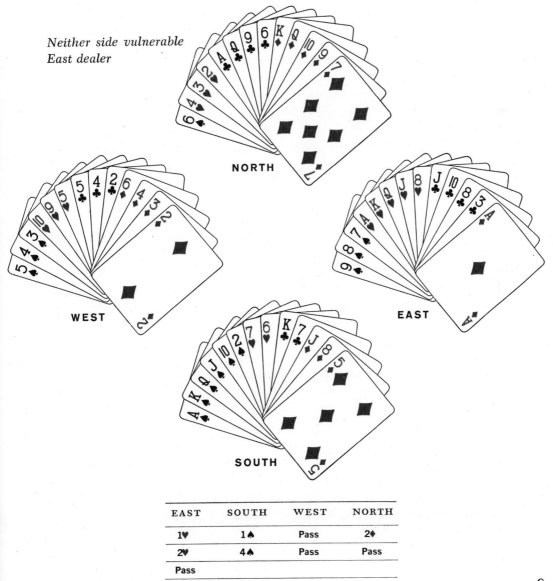

EAST	SOUTH	WEST	NORTH
1♥	1♠	Pass	2♦
2♥	4♠	Pass	Pass
Pass			

Opening lead: Heart 10

He tipped his mitt

EVERY once in a while you will find some mention of psychic bidding on these pages, but do not be misled. I am no great devotee of the psychic bid. Whatever dramatic value such bids may have, their practical advantages have been greatly exaggerated. In the following hand we are concerned with a bit of crime detection rather than a study of the crime itself.

West, for reasons best known to himself, opened the bidding with 1 Heart. Perhaps it was his purpose to talk the opposition out of the contract in which he believed they had their best chance for game. His tactics boomeranged in a most unexpected manner and, at least for the time being, left him with the impression that crime does not pay.

In the mistaken belief that the opposition had been led completely astray, and in the hope that the Club suit could be brought in with the loss of only one trick, West doubled the final contract of 3 No Trump. North's redouble, with a partner who had previously passed, was the act of one who was feeling his oats.

When the Club was opened and the dummy appeared, the psychic character of West's opening bid was exposed. It would seem that the fate of the contract hinged on bringing the Heart suit home without loss. East's raise made it evident that any length in the Heart suit lay with him. Declarer therefore played the Club Jack in dummy, to win the trick there. He returned the Heart Jack, and when East didn't cover, he played low. When West's 10 fell on the Jack, South successfully finessed the 7-spot on the second round of the suit. The Ace and King picked up East's Queen, and South made 3 No Trump redoubled with an overtrick.

Declarer's analysis proved entirely sound. Because of West's opening bid of 1 Heart, it was reasonable to suppose that the bulk of the outstanding Hearts would be found in East's hand. The remote chance that West would show up with the lone Queen of Hearts had to be risked, for if South's conclusion was correct, a first-round finesse was mandatory. West, in an effort to confuse the issue, had tipped his mitt.

EXTRA TRICK   When you don't hold sufficient strength for a legitimate bid, it is almost always better to leave the bidding to those who do. That way you will go down less often.

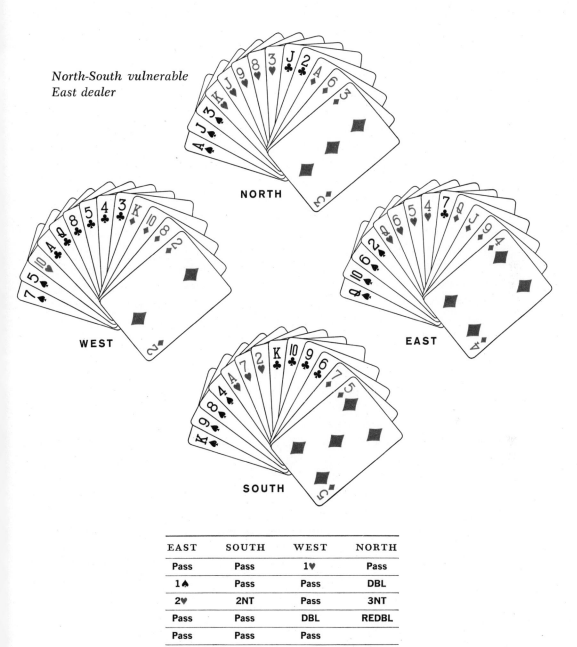

North-South vulnerable
East dealer

NORTH

WEST

EAST

SOUTH

EAST	SOUTH	WEST	NORTH
Pass	Pass	1♥	Pass
1♠	Pass	Pass	DBL
2♥	2NT	Pass	3NT
Pass	Pass	DBL	REDBL
Pass	Pass	Pass	

Opening lead: Club 5

A useful coffeehouse recipe

THE favorite games of the European coffeehouses, card centers of the Old World, are played with fervor and gusto. The moaning and the groaning, the gloating and the emoting are all part of the fun.

In bridge, such histrionics—called for obvious reasons "coffeehousing" —are tabooed by some four and one-half pages of laws. Under special circumstances, however, the subtle possibilities of the coffeehousing art have been explored by the experts.

In serious play, expert players are never guilty of coffeehousing, but they delight in taking advantage of inept coffeehousers. A favorite victim is the player who always hesitates when he does not have the honor with which to cover a lead. After this happens once, an observant declarer has a sure guide to all two-way finesses. The only problem is the opponent one meets for the first time. And sometimes one can successfully diagnose even a complete stranger. The following hand provides an example of one way this can be accomplished.

The bidding was commendably brief between opposing pairs of strangers. South opened with 2 No Trump, and North jumped right to 6. Declarer won the opening Club lead in his hand, knocked out the Ace of Diamonds, captured the Club return and found it necessary to locate the Queen of Hearts in order to make the slam.

Eventually he led the Jack of Hearts from his hand. West huddled briefly and played small. I am not going to tell you which opponent held the Queen of Hearts, but South guessed wrong and went down one trick. After the opponents had left the table, South apologized to his partner. "Sorry," he said, "I couldn't tell if West was a coffeehouse huddler or a double crosser."

"Lunkhead," his partner replied. "Your first play should have been the Jack of Spades!"

You see what North meant, of course. Suppose South leads the Jack of Spades. It does not matter what West plays, for declarer cannot lose the trick. However, the lead of the Jack lends the appearance that South is contemplating a finesse for the Queen of Spades. West's demeanor at this point may prove to be highly revealing. No matter what card he plays, declarer goes up with dummy's King of Spades. But when South returns to his hand with a Diamond and leads the Jack of Hearts, West is no longer a stranger.

If West huddled over the play of the Jack of Spades when he couldn't possibly have the Queen, declarer should know how to find the Queen of Hearts when he leads the Jack of that suit from his hand. If West huddles again, it is a sure thing that he does not have the missing Queen.

EXTRA TRICK An opening bid of 2 No Trump announces a hand with 22, 23 or 24 points in high cards. It takes a combined total of 33 points to justify a small-slam bid, so if responder has 11 to 13 points, he can safely jump to 6 No Trump. At the same time, he knows that a grand slam is out of reach. With more than 13 points, the responder should make some effort to explore grand-slam prospects. A combined total of 37 points is enough to insure that his side holds all four Aces.

Both sides vulnerable
South dealer

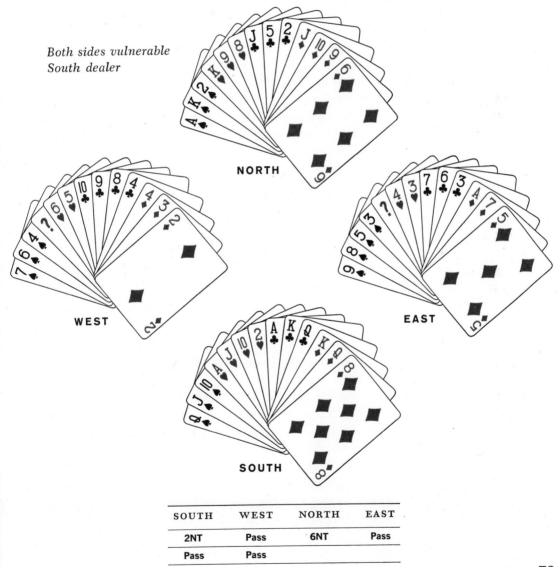

SOUTH	WEST	NORTH	EAST
2NT	Pass	6NT	Pass
Pass	Pass		

Opening lead: Club 10

Who is to blame?

INTERESTING hands sent to me by readers often leave me in a quandary. This is particularly so if my analysis of the bidding or of how the hand was played is in any way critical. If I mention my correspondent's name, am I not guilty of biting the hand that feeds me material? On the other hand, if I fail to identify him, do I not take advantage of his kindness without the common courtesy of properly acknowledging it?

Usually I compromise by mentioning my correspondent's initials and home town, and I will fall back upon that practice in discussing this grand slam. P. C. H. of Arlington, Va., may hide behind that anonymity or identify himself to his friends, as he wishes, after reading what I have to say in reply to his comment, "We didn't make it but, if psychic, could have."

The final contract was impeccable, although there is much to be said against the manner in which it was reached. South does not have a sound opening bid. He can muster up a skimpy 13 points with the aid of counting 2 for his singleton. Although 13 points carries an option on the right to open, South doesn't maintain his 13-point rating for any longer than required to deduct 1 point because his hand includes no Ace. When partner's jump-shift response sounded the warning that he might be headed for dizzy heights, South's courage in bidding his four-card Spade suit is of the kind that frequently results in a posthumous award.

North's skip response was amply justified—but duly punished, nevertheless. With suits of equal length, it is proper to bid the higher-ranking one first—especially when both are respectably endowed with top-card strength. The difference between A J 10 and A K Q is not a good reason for bidding Hearts before Spades. Had North observed this rule, he might have had the pleasure of playing the hand for the grand slam, and of being what my correspondent calls "psychic."

It is easy to guess that declarer first drew trumps so that neither opponent could ruff one of his precious winners. But in the course of protecting these winners, declarer left himself with only two trumps to take care of dummy's three losers.

This is one case in which "safe" play is dangerous. If an opponent can ruff the second Heart, the long Hearts will never be established, so South should ruff them himself. After winning the first Heart trick, he cashes a second high Heart, discarding his little Club. Then he ruffs dummy's small Hearts and third Club before taking more than a single round of trumps. Now dummy has nothing left but top trumps and the good Queen of Hearts to be cashed after the opponents' trumps are gone.

EXTRA TRICK Had North been declarer, the chances are he would have played the hand correctly, because declarer ordinarily trumps losing cards with dummy's trumps as a matter of habit. It requires a departure from the usual procedure to use your own trumps for ruffing and thus make dummy the master hand.

Neither side vulnerable
South dealer

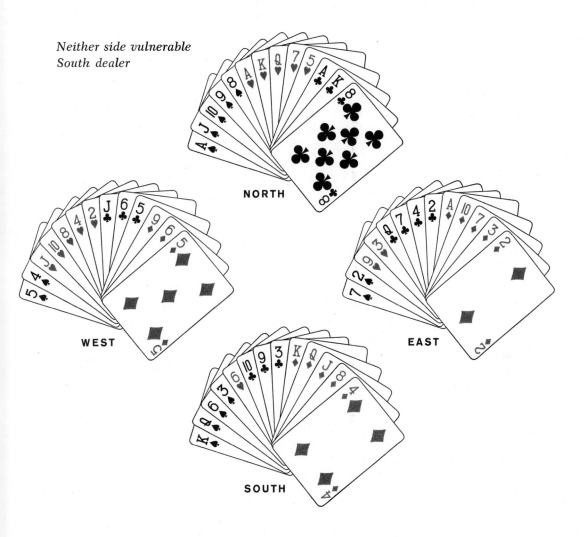

SOUTH	WEST	NORTH	EAST
1♦	Pass	2♥	Pass
2♠	Pass	7♠	DBL
Pass	Pass	Pass	

Opening lead: Heart Jack

Hooked by a low Heart

AMONG the Europeans whom we delight in welcoming to our shores is Adam Meredith, a gentleman of Celtic extraction who has been representing Great Britain in international competition for several years.

On his first visit to the United States, Meredith was invited by the American Contract Bridge League to participate in our Life Masters' Individual Championship, an event in which one faces a new partner on every set of deals. It was my good fortune to draw Mr. Meredith on a rather active set of boards.

On one of the deals Meredith departed from his usual swashbuckling manner to bid a hand with utmost delicacy, enabling us to reach a grandslam contract in No Trump. At the opening lead, as I made the gesture to claim all the tricks, a wail of disappointment was heard from Meredith. "I was rather hoping it would require a double squeeze," he complained. "If the hand is such a laydown the others will have the same score."

He need not have complained so strenuously. In the next deal, shown here, he and I were victimized by a play of outstanding brilliance.

Meredith, sitting East, considered North-South's vulnerability situation ideal to allow for muddying their communications. He therefore overcalled North's Club bid with 2 Spades. South bid 2 No Trump. My bid of 3 Hearts was perhaps doubtful strategy, but I knew it was my last chance to get into the act, and the call might have the merit of directing the defense. North went on to 3 No Trump and the bidding ended serenely.

I opened the 8 of Spades, which forced out declarer's Jack. Declarer realized that he must develop the Club suit for his contract, but also recognized the danger of giving up an early Club trick. From the bidding he concluded that West had a six-card suit, and from his failure to lead it he drew the inference that it was not solid. It appeared a certainty that East held a singleton honor, undoubtedly the King or Queen. If East won the Club trick and led a high Heart it would be apparent to West that he could safely overtake.

Declarer thereupon decided on a crafty strategem; he put out a false lure, and I went for it hook, line and sinker. His first play was a low Heart. I was beguiled into going up with the Queen, catching my partner's singleton King (though it would have made no difference had I played low). Now declarer had time to give up a Club to East and raked in ten tricks.

Reporting this deal would afford me a great deal more pleasure had I gone up with the Ace of Hearts, but it must go down in the records that I failed to rise to the occasion.

EXTRA TRICK The pre-emptive jump overcall can be an effective weapon when properly employed. But excessive usage can lead to a series of disastrous sets which will seriously damage partnership morale as well as the exchequer.

North-South vulnerable
North dealer

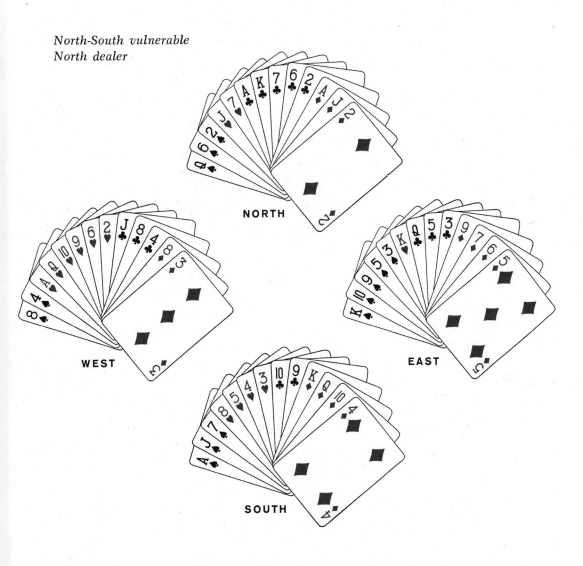

NORTH

WEST

EAST

SOUTH

NORTH	EAST	SOUTH	WEST
1♣	2♠	2NT	3♥
3NT	Pass	Pass	Pass

Opening lead: Spade 8

Collision at trick ten

A PLAYER who does well in a bridge tournament is rewarded by the American Contract Bridge League with a grant of master points. You can't spend them, but the total you amass goes on the record to indicate that you are a good player. Your total also decides whether you are qualified to play in master events.

The system works well enough when applied to American players. The trouble is that we do not have a system of foreign exchange whereby the exploits of a foreign star can be translated into an equivalent number of points. This would not be for the record but for the purpose of qualifying newcomers and visitors to the events in which they deserve to play.

There is something incongruous, for example, in labeling as a non-master the player who starred as declarer in the following deal.

South was Bela (Mike) Kassay—one of the leading bridge players of Hungary as well as one of the leaders in the anti-Communist revolt of 1956 (as a result of which he is now playing his bridge in the U. S.). Even though he brought with him all the skill that made him a great player in Hungary, Kassay ranked here as a non-master until he won 50 master points in American competition. Whether this was fair, either to Kassay or the lesser players against whom he had to compete, you may judge from what happened here.

The opening lead gave declarer a problem. With two top trumps missing, it appeared that the only chance was to win a Heart finesse. But East's takeout double and West's lead of Hearts convinced Kassay that the King must be offside, so he won the trick with dummy's Ace. He cashed the Ace and King of Clubs, discarding a Heart. Then he ruffed a third Club.

Returning to dummy by ruffing a Spade, declarer played a fourth Club and East discarded. (It would scarcely have helped the defenders for East to ruff with the Ace of Diamonds, for this would give South a chance to ditch his remaining Heart.) South ruffed the Club, got back to dummy with another Spade ruff and played the fifth Club, which now was high.

Once again, East realized that it would be futile to ruff with the Diamond Ace. When he discarded, South threw his last Heart. West ruffed with a low Diamond, but after declarer trumped the next Heart lead he played a trump, and East's Ace and West's King won this trick with a resounding redundancy. South lost tricks only to the 5 of Diamonds and the Ace, and so brought home his doubled contract.

EXTRA TRICK Although South deserves full credit for his fine play, East could have defeated the hand with a superbrilliant defense. Had he realized the situation, East could have discarded one Heart on the fourth round of Clubs and thrown the King of Hearts on the fifth Club. This would have enabled him to trump the second lead of Hearts with his Ace of Diamonds and would have spared his partner's bare King from the embarrassment that followed. I mention this, however, only to forestall those keen-eyed readers who will have noted the possibility and may already have taken their pens in hand. It would indeed have been a colossal play.

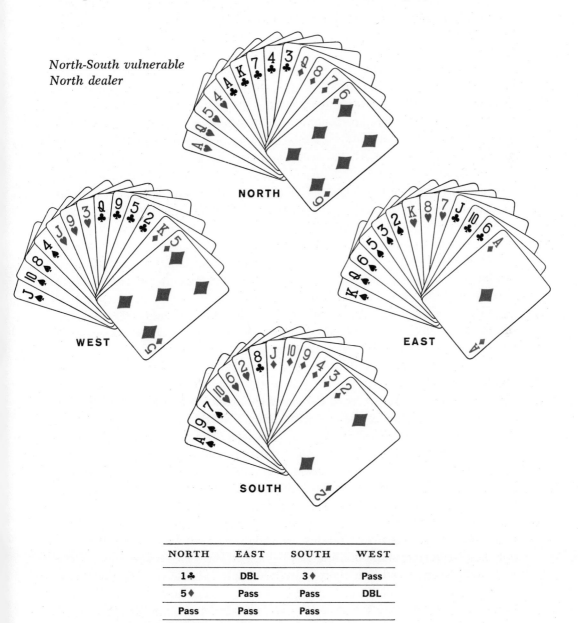

North-South vulnerable
North dealer

NORTH	EAST	SOUTH	WEST
1♣	DBL	3♦	Pass
5♦	Pass	Pass	DBL
Pass	Pass	Pass	

Opening lead: Heart 3

Rarely so happy an ending

ON a recent trip to the Riviera to play in a bridge tournament, I ran into an old friend, Captain Ewart Kempson, editor of Britain's *Bridge Magazine* and one of the finest players in England. After the play I accompanied Captain Kempson back to England, where we spent a profitable afternoon browsing through the files of the *London Times*. There we uncovered this choice hand, which had appeared in a London duplicate bridge contest.

A considerable number of the pairs playing in the tournament eventually committed themselves to making 6 Hearts. It is an entirely logical contract which can·be broken only by a four-one trump split.

The diagram shows the sequence of bidding that led to this unlucky contract at one of the tables. While the bidding was reasonably sound in its early stages, it appears to have been derailed a little later on. South eventually found himself in a spot where, in order to rescue himself from a three-card Diamond suit, he was bound to bid a slam in Hearts without the assurance that partner had even one supporting card in the suit.

There was another South player, however, who found this prospect completely distasteful. He, too, had cue-bid his Diamond suit and followed with a cue bid in Clubs. North decided to treat the Diamond response as honest and leaped to a slam in that suit. South was afraid to return to Hearts in the face of his partner's strong preference for Diamonds, and elected to brazen it out at the bizarre contract of 6 Diamonds. I leave it to the reader to decide whether the result was the just reward of courage or the unmerited good fortune of cowardice.

The 10 of Clubs was led, and the Jack held in dummy. The Ace of Spades was followed by a Spade ruff in the closed hand. Dummy was entered with the Ace of Hearts, and another Spade was ruffed with the Ace of trumps. With the fortunate Spade break, North's long suit was established. The 10 of Diamonds was then finessed, and declarer cashed dummy's top trumps. This left only one trump outstanding, and declarer proceeded to lead dummy's good Spades. West could ruff in whenever it suited him to do so, but any return he could make after that would permit declarer to cash the rest of the tricks in dummy.

After studying the account of this remarkable exploit, I walked back to my hotel, took out my own book on bridge, and with a firm hand ripped out the chapter on slam bidding.

It will be observed that there is no defense against the 6-Diamond contract. It is true that a trump opening makes it a little more difficult, but the hand can still be won. Two Spades can be ruffed in the closed hand, and the Club Jack must be finessed to obtain sufficient entries to dummy.

EXTRA TRICK This example points up the danger of promiscuous cue-bidding before it has become clearly established that there is available a contract at which the hand can play with reasonable safety. Remember, ending in the wrong suit will rarely produce so happy a landing.

Both sides vulnerable
North dealer

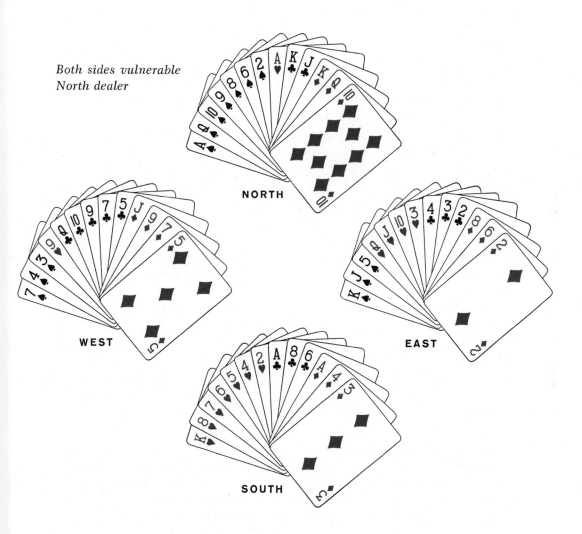

NORTH	EAST	SOUTH	WEST
1♠	Pass	2♥	Pass
3♠	Pass	4♦	Pass
4♠	Pass	5♣	Pass
6♦	Pass	6♥	Pass
Pass	Pass		

Opening lead: Club 10

The Gerber Club dinner

TALK is not as cheap as it sometimes appears to be. This was demonstrated by a little byplay in connection with the hand shown at right. It was played during the Mixed Team of Four Championship at a national tournament of the American Contract Bridge League some years ago. Ably fulfilling the role of kibitzer-in-chief at the tournament was John Gerber of Houston, inventor of the celebrated 4-Club slam convention. After this particular hand, Mr. Gerber promptly injected himself into the analysis at the post-mortem proceedings. But I'm getting a little ahead of my story.

East, apprehensive of an enemy attack in Spades, decided to pre-empt with a bid of 5 Clubs, a daring act when one considers the conditions of vulnerability. South, your reporter, who had mentally projected a pussy-foot campaign should East open with a bid of 1, had no choice but to over-call with 5 Spades, and East brazenly carried on to 6 Clubs. South, in the vague hope that North might be able to bid higher, made a forcing pass, and North, Helen Sobel, doubled. The defense cashed two Diamond tricks, and the minus-200 score (honors are not counted at match-point play) proved a gratifying result for East and West.

Crushed by the adverse strategy, your reporter, on a hasty analysis, announced that we had been euchred out of a small slam. Gerber, one of the quickest thinkers I have ever encountered at the card table, instantly volunteered that the Spade slam could be defeated by the opening lead of the Ace and another trump. Helen Sobel just as quickly asserted that 6 Spades was invincible, and a wager to cover dinner that night was promptly made.

The cards were spread again, and play proceeded with all hands exposed. The second Spade lead was won with the 6 in dummy. Then followed the King of Hearts, covered by East's Ace, which South ruffed. A low Diamond to the Jack held the trick, and the Jack of Hearts covered by East's Queen was ruffed by South. Then followed all the trumps, with the South hand reduced to Ace-7-4 of Diamonds and the North hand to King-5 of Diamonds and the 9 of Hearts. West, holding Queen-8-6 of Diamonds and the 10 of Hearts, could find no safe discard. But all this required less time than it is taking me to describe it.

Gerber conceded that he had spoken too quickly, but he was a charming host at dinner.

EXTRA TRICK The Gerber Convention uses a jump bid to 4 Clubs exactly as Blackwood employs the bid of 4 No Trump. Partner is required to show how many Aces he has by a series of "step" responses: 4 Diamonds, none (or all four); 4 Hearts, one; 4 Spades, two; etc. Thereafter, to learn about Kings, the Gerberite bids 5 Clubs where the Blackwooder would say 5 No Trump.

Gerber offers two advantages: information exchanged at a lower level, and no confusion when either partner has previously bid No Trump. Some players use Gerber after No Trump and Blackwood when only suits have been mentioned.

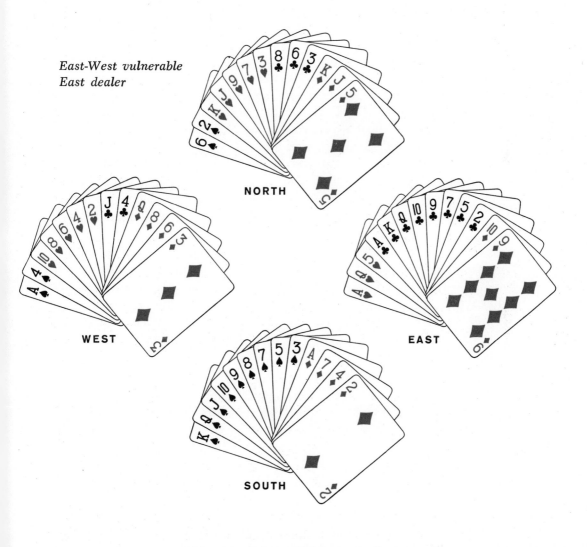

East-West vulnerable
East dealer

NORTH

WEST

EAST

SOUTH

EAST	SOUTH	WEST	NORTH
5♣	5♠	Pass	Pass
6♣	Pass	Pass	DBL
Pass	Pass	Pass	

A double escape route

WE HAVE seen numerous cases where slam bids were played by a declarer who held a singleton trump. It was not at all uncommon in the days of the Vanderbilt Club convention, when the player might respond artificially with 1 Diamond without a Diamond in his hand—subsequently to become declarer at 6 or 7 Diamonds. From time to time, even in these days, a hand finds its way into print in which, by reason of partner's sudden burst into Blackwood, a player finds himself playing at a slam in a suit in which he has one or none.

But to play a hand at a grand slam, with a singleton in a suit declarer has deliberately chosen as trump, is a rarity which demands attention. One such hand occurred in the Masters Pair Championship during a national tournament of the American Contract Bridge League. The deal is shown at right.

Under the terms of the convention employed by North and South, the opening call of 3 No Trump was a gambling bid based on a long, solid minor suit. This convention finds much favor in the eyes of British tournament players, who employ it to great effect. It has no distinct requirements as to stoppers or point count. Actually it amounts to a shot in the dark, relying for success upon faith, hope, and the luck of the opening lead.

North consequently chose this moment to open with 3 No Trump. South could count on his ability to produce six or more tricks, so he barged into a slam for his partner. East thought he had his fish in a barrel and might as well gain the extra points, so he doubled.

To South it now became apparent that East held the Ace and King of Hearts, because obviously North's opening bid was based on a long and solid Club suit. There could be no doubt of that at this point; so, with everything to gain and nothing to lose, South engineered a coup to transfer the opening lead to West. He escaped to 7 Clubs! There was a chance that West, burdened with choosing the opening lead, might guess wrong.

In point of fact, West chose to lead a Spade, and declarer ran off with thirteen tricks. We do not at this juncture wish to point a moral. We are only reporting the facts.

EXTRA TRICK I am reminded of the restraint of a lady whose tournament opponents reached a grand slam against her Ace of Trumps. A kibitzer inquired, "Why didn't you double?" And the lady explained: "You evidently don't know who that man is," referring to the Life Master at her right. "He redoubles at the drop of a hat."

The lady had the right idea, if for the wrong reason. The best advice about doubling a slam which good opponents have reached voluntarily is "don't." There are two exceptions. One is when your double is for the purpose of telling partner to make an unusual lead which would give you a chance to set the contract. The other—it occurs more rarely—is when you are certain that your double will be profitable no matter how it affects the opponents' bidding or play.

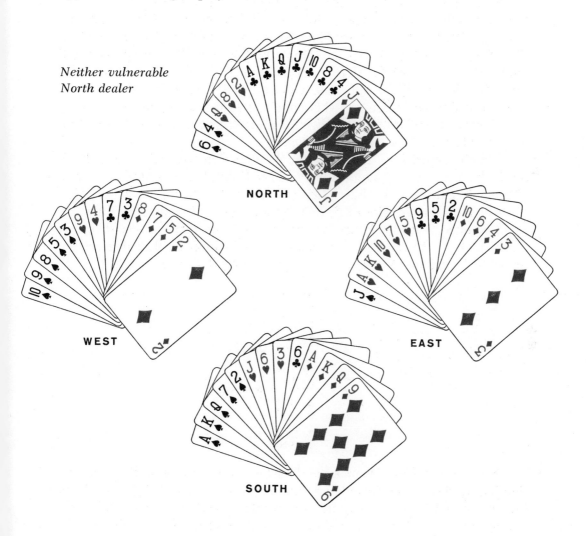

Neither vulnerable
North dealer

NORTH

WEST

EAST

SOUTH

NORTH	EAST	SOUTH	WEST
3NT	Pass	6NT	Pass
Pass	DBL	7♣	Pass
Pass	DBL	Pass	Pass
Pass			

You can't beat the cards

ON the last day of baseball at Ebbets Field, I went over to Brooklyn to play bridge with the Dodgers. We played on top of a trunk in the players' dressing room—the baseball man's card table. In the course of three rubbers Manager Walt Alston kept shuffling his lineup. I played with and against Pee Wee Reese, Gil Hodges, Gino Cimoli, Ed Roebuck, the manager himself and the then-coach Billy Herman. Duke Snider, Charlie Neal, Don Zimmer, Coach Jake Pitler and half a dozen other knowledgeable kibitzers left no doubt that bridge was this team's favorite card game.

How good is their bridge? Judge for yourself by the way I got caught in this double play. (*See diagram at right.*)

Cimoli opened the Club 10. Billy Herman won with the Ace and led back the Jack. The situation did not look hopeful. I was sure to lose a Diamond, and Herman (East) figured to have two trump tricks in order to justify his double. However, there was a chance I could trap Billy.

I planned to lead a Heart to dummy's Ace and trump a Heart in my hand, cash the Ace and King of Diamonds and trump another Heart, then cash the high Club. At this point I hoped to find the cards like this:

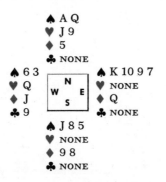

```
              ♠ A Q
              ♥ J 9
              ♦ 5
              ♣ NONE
♠ 6 3          N          ♠ K 10 9 7
♥ Q        W       E      ♥ NONE
♦ J            S          ♦ Q
♣ 9                       ♣ NONE
              ♠ J 8 5
              ♥ NONE
              ♦ 9 8
              ♣ NONE
```

Now I would lead a Diamond and East would have to win. With nothing left but Spades, his lead would let dummy make the Ace and Queen. Then dummy would lead a Heart and East would be caught in a pickle. If he trumped with the King, I would discard and make my Jack at the end. If he trumped with the 10, I would overruff. Either way, East could not prevent my Jack of trumps from winning the game-going trick.

The cards lay exactly where I hoped they would, but Herman got out of the trap with a beautiful fall-away. He dumped the Queen of Diamonds under my King. Consequently, the third Diamond was won by West's Jack and Cimoli cooperated by returning a trump.

It did no good for me to rise with dummy's Ace and lead a Heart. East trumped with the 9 to force my Jack, overruffed my play of dummy's Queen of Spades on the fourth Diamond, and won the last trick with his high 10 of trumps.

EXTRA TRICK   That night the Dodgers played their last home game in Brooklyn. They beat the Pirates. But they couldn't beat the Cards (baseball) for second place in the National League, and I couldn't beat the cards (bridge) or the Dodgers either. Moral: Never play out of your league.

Neither side vulnerable
North dealer

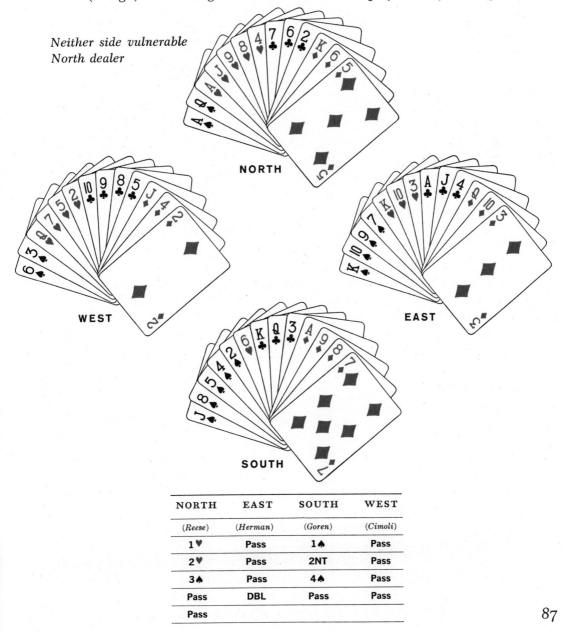

NORTH	EAST	SOUTH	WEST
(Reese)	*(Herman)*	*(Goren)*	*(Cimoli)*
1♥	Pass	1♠	Pass
2♥	Pass	2NT	Pass
3♠	Pass	4♠	Pass
Pass	DBL	Pass	Pass
Pass			

Always give a good answer

A GREAT many players have muddled through a lifetime of bridge without ever having acquainted themselves with one of the most important conventions of defensive play. The rule I am talking about covers the matter of selecting the proper card when returning the suit which your partner has led. If you originally held two or three cards of that suit, you return the higher of your remaining cards; but if you held four or more, you return the card which was originally your fourth best.

Observe how West was able to put this convention to use in order to read the distribution of the Spade suit in the following hand.

North's rebid of 2 Diamonds has the endorsement of this department. Players reluctant to make a minimum rebid might choose the call of 2 Clubs, but normally we do not approve of showing a four-card suit before rebidding a six-carder. Many players stand in fear of being dropped prematurely if their rebid has a slightly discouraging ring. Actually, if South subsides after North's 2-Diamond rebid, the combined hands will hardly rate to produce game. South, however, was strong enough to persist to game in spite of North's warning that he had a six-four distribution with nothing to contribute in Spades and Hearts.

West naturally opened the 4 of Spades, and East's King held the trick as South followed with the 6. East returned the 8. South covered with the 10, and West was called upon to make the decision that would make or break the defense.

He had the following data with which to work: South has the Queen of Spades, a fact which was established at once when East followed with the King at trick one. East did not have an original holding of four Spades, for then he would have returned his fourth best. The 8 could not be his fourth best, for the only higher card unaccounted for is the 10. The 8, therefore, is his remaining high Spade. East is marked with another Spade; otherwise South would have a five-card suit, which he surely would have mentioned at some time in the auction. This marks declarer with exactly four Spades and a sure stopper. Now if declarer has the King of Diamonds there is no hope to defeat the contract, so that sound defense requires mentally placing that card with East. Since it was indispensable to have East retain a Spade, West permitted declarer to hold the trick.

It was abundantly clear to South what West was up to, but what could South do about it? He could not make the game without the Diamond suit, and when he finessed for the King he lost the trick to East. The lead of East's remaining Spade trapped declarer's Queen, and the defenders collected four Spades and one Diamond trick to break the contract.

EXTRA TRICK South did miss a trick, although in this instance it would not have helped. If West had the King of Diamonds, declarer could well afford to make him a present of a trick, for the Spade Queen was safe unless East got the lead. Therefore, declarer's first lead should have been a Diamond to dummy's Ace! The forlorn chance that East held the blank King was well worth the possible loss of an unimportant overtrick.

Both sides vulnerable
North dealer

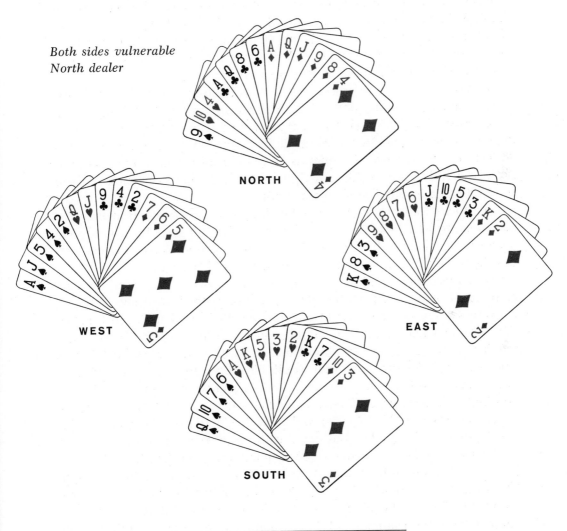

NORTH	EAST	SOUTH	WEST
1♦	Pass	1♥	Pass
2♦	Pass	2NT	Pass
3♣	Pass	3NT	Pass
Pass	Pass		

Opening lead: Spade 4

This lawyer could afford a King

EACH year the American Contract Bridge League selects from its roster of 75,000 players one honorary member. Past selections have included such historic names as Milton Work, Wilbur Whitehead, Ely Culbertson, Harold S. Vanderbilt and General Alfred Gruenther. And in one year, 1958, the choice was my good friend and frequent teammate, Lee Hazen. A successful attorney, Hazen is one bridge star who has achieved top rank while carrying on a full-time professional career.

The strenuous job of competing in a bridge tournament is doubly exhausting on top of a full day's work. Yet, during a national championship in Los Angeles recently, Hazen flew two round trips coast-to-coast, carrying on his business in New York while he competed in the California city.

Hazen owns a sense of humor as keen as his sense of timing in bridge. Both flashed brightly in his description of what happened when he held the East cards in the deal shown at right.

"Partner's lead of the Queen of Spades," said Lee, "was an unexpected pleasure. In fact, I became so enthusiastic that I gave him a really big come-on signal—one that he could not possibly ignore. Just to make sure that he wouldn't shift to some other suit, I played the King of Spades."

Of course, Hazen's play of the Spade King was not merely an extravagant signal; it was an essential play. Signaling with the 10-spot, although it expressed enthusiasm, would not have elicited another Spade lead for the very good reason that—as Hazen had instantly realized—West might not have another Spade to play. Declarer would have permitted West's Queen to hold the trick, and that would have been that. West would have had to lead another suit and, since he had plenty of stoppers in Hearts and Clubs, declarer would have had ample time to establish the Diamonds. The defenders would have taken only one Spade and two Diamond tricks, and South would have breezed home with an overtrick to boot.

East's overtake of partner's Queen, however, made South's hold-up of his Ace of Spades futile, for East could and did continue leading the suit. The 10 forced out South's Jack and, when he got in with the Queen of Diamonds, the Spade 9 knocked out declarer's Ace. South had no way to make game without the Diamond suit, and when East got in again with the Diamond Ace he still had three good tricks remaining and was able to put the contract down two.

EXTRA TRICK   When you give a come-on signal, the rule is: "Play the highest card you can spare." In this case, East could spare the King, and failure to play it would have been fatal. But in all cases, failure to play a higher card indicates inability to do so, and the information thus conveyed will frequently unmask declarer's attempt at deceiving by false-carding.

It must be pointed out, however, that more tricks are lost because a player signals with a card he cannot afford to yield than because the come-on signal is too low to be effective. Throw an Ace if you can afford to, but trust a 3-spot to do the job if you cannot spare a more encouraging card without danger of thereby setting up an extra trick for the enemy.

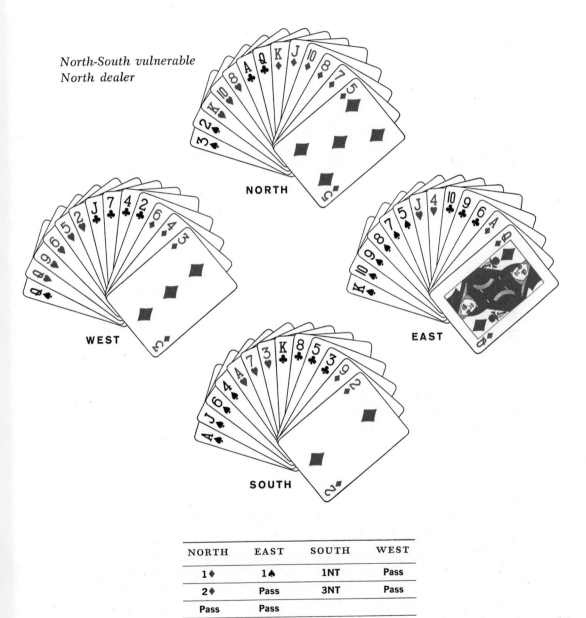

North-South vulnerable
North dealer

NORTH

WEST

EAST

SOUTH

NORTH	EAST	SOUTH	WEST
1♦	1♠	1NT	Pass
2♦	Pass	3NT	Pass
Pass	Pass		

Opening lead: Spade Queen

Actors should stick to the stage

STRICTLY from the standpoint of ethics and manners, any acting at the bridge table is bad acting. Generally, it is also unsuccessful. The would-be actor who hopes to gull expert opposition more than once is deluding only himself. If, despite all, he feels compelled to act, he would do better to imitate the dead pan of Buster Keaton rather than the expressive panto-mime of Charlie Chaplin. The scene is now set for East's ill-starred role in the hand which is detailed at right.

You might suspect that only an excess of timidity could account for South's rebid of 3 Clubs at his second turn. How could he risk the possi-bility of being passed out there with a hand that might easily produce a slam? You would know the answer if you were acquainted with East and had heard the pitiful sound of his passes. East is a ham actor who gives away the show. With a poor hand, he bids in a cheery voice; but when his passes groan like echoes from the sepulcher, beware. He's loaded!

South was Leland Ferer, a business associate of mine. He knew that North would probably keep the bidding open—but he counted on East's saving the situation even if North passed. Meanwhile, he could let the cautious tempo of the bidding suggest that he was stretching for game.

Given another chance—as he thought he would be—South chose to contract for game in No Trump. This is a nomination which fails to gain this department's vote. With a Heart lead clearly advertised, making 3 No Trump hinges on dropping the King of Clubs—whereas 5 Clubs breezes home even if a Club trick must be lost. However, South was playing to score a killing, and East obliged him by doubling.

West's lead of the Spade 7 assumed that partner's double called for the lead of dummy's suit. Nothing was to be gained by ducking, so declarer ran up with the Ace. He took the Club finesse and, when the King fell on the second Club, East's hand was subjected to the torture of having to make no less than six discards.

Dummy let go all four remaining Spades, both Hearts and the small Diamond. East peeled three Hearts and two Spades, but the final discard stretched him to the breaking point. A Diamond would establish North's entire suit; the Heart Ace would surely promote South's King. East's only hope was that West held the 6 of Spades, and he discarded the Spade King. But declarer cashed the Spade 6, winding up the debacle.

As South raked in all the tricks and recorded 1,250 points on his score, West offered a tongue-in-cheek apology. "Sorry, partner," he said to East, "I could have saved two tricks by leading the 2 of Spades instead of the 7. Charge 400 points to my account."

EXTRA TRICK East might have suspected that he held too much strength for his own good. East could be sure that South would be able to run an indeterminate number of Club tricks. His double offered the opponents a chance to exit to 4 Clubs, had they been out on a limb, while increasing their profit possibilities if they were willing to gamble it out at No Trump.

Neither side vulnerable
North dealer

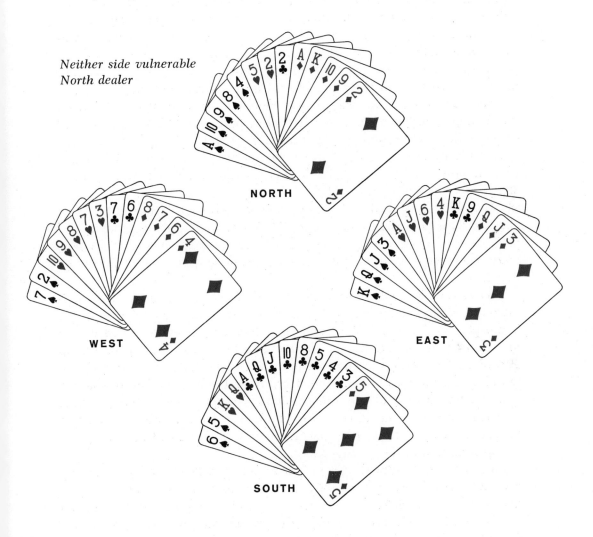

NORTH	EAST	SOUTH	WEST
1♠	Pass	2♣	Pass
2♦	Pass	3♣	Pass
3♦	Pass	3NT	Pass
Pass	DBL	REDBL	Pass
Pass	Pass		

Opening lead: Spade 7

The monster of the Midi

IN American bridge, the only recognized distinction between pro and amateur is that an amateur is described as one who plays ineptly. The American Contract Bridge League, which conducts all important tournaments in the United States and sanctions many local tourneys, frowns upon cash prizes and disapproves of betting among contestants. This is not the case in Europe, where cash prizes are offered in many tournaments.

The hand at right was played by Claude Reichenbach, star of the Swiss international bridge team and a frequent partner of mine. It occurred during a duplicate tourney at Monte Carlo, in which the grand prize was 400,000 francs and each day's top scorer got 100,000 francs. Reichenbach was the only declarer to achieve a plus score on the hand which I have called "the monster of the Midi."

The bidding method best geared to cope with such freaks is the now-obsolete Sims powerhouse opening 3 bid, which calls upon partner to display his Aces. On learning that North did not have the Ace of Diamonds, South would sign off at 6 Clubs—the only slam contract that could not be defeated.

Whatever West led, South could get rid of his six Diamonds by trumping one and discarding five on North's top cards. Unfortunately for all the South players, however, Clubs and Diamonds are lower than Hearts and Spades; no South could buy the contract at a bid of less than 6 No Trump or 7 Clubs. The latter was the contract when I held the East hand. Feeling grateful that the enemy had landed in my best suit, I did not double for fear North-South would find a more suitable stopping place. The 50 points we collected turned out to be nearly bottom on the deal. Reichenbach got his plus score by permitting his partner to play at 6 Hearts, fulfilled against the opening lead of the Diamond Ace.

All over the Eden Beach Casino the ax fell on 7-Heart and 7 No-Trump contracts. One North player, outraged that an opponent would dare to double such a rockcrusher, redoubled on his commitment to take all thirteen tricks at Hearts. East hit upon the devastating opening lead of a Club. Undoubtedly the most frustrated of the declarers, however, was the North who played at 7 No Trump doubled.

East's Ace-of-Diamonds opening set the contract at the go-off, but worse was to follow. East led another Diamond. North might have saved a trick by going in with dummy's Queen and later throwing East in with the fifth Club. But North assumed that the Clubs would break and tried to salvage something from the wreckage by finessing dummy's 8 of Diamonds.

West grabbed the 9 and surrendered his sure second trick in the suit by returning a Diamond to put dummy back on lead. After winning the Diamonds and the four top Clubs, the eleventh trick was lost to East's Club 10. It wasn't until the twelfth trick that North, with his powerhouse, was able to take a trick in his own hand.

EXTRA TRICK   The primary purpose of an opening 2 bid is to make sure you get another chance to bid. But a freak hand like South's can safely be opened 1 Club without fear it will be passed out.

Neither side vulnerable
South dealer

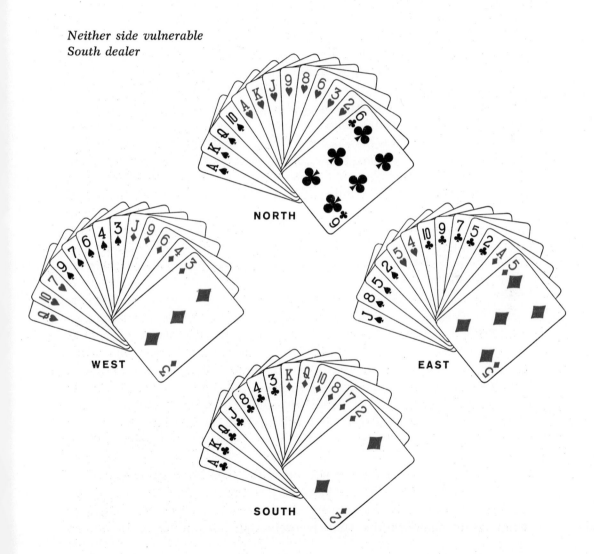

Mr. Blackwood demands obedience

IN THE proper application of the Blackwood Convention, the partner of the 4 No-Trump bidder must reply obediently to the asking bids, revealing the number of Aces and Kings held by him. Thereafter he has no further obligations and, what is more to the point, no further rights. The decision as to the final contract must be left to the 4 No-Trump bidder.

On the hand at right, however, things didn't work out that way. North struck out for freedom, and you might describe his last bid in the words of the boy who sees a giraffe for the first time: "There ain't no such animal."

When North made a jump raise of the opening bid, South had good reason to point toward a slam. He reasoned that if partner held two Aces, the small slam would be an odds-on certainty; and even with one Ace there might be an outside chance, if North happened to have some favorable Heart holding. How he was going to determine this last feature I don't know, but at any rate there is no quarrel to be picked on grounds of the inquiry. North denied any Aces and South, of course, signed off at 5 Spades. North, apparently totally swept up in a crusade for freedom, argued to himself that he had more than he might have had for his 3-Spade jump and went blithely on to 6 Spades. Mind you, South had already said, "Partner, if you have no Aces we cannot make a slam." But North in effect replied, "Partner, I don't think you know what you're talking about." Perhaps he was right.

West elected to open the 6 of Spades, and if South was emotionally affected, he gave no outward sign of it. He won in dummy and led a Diamond. Right or wrong, East ducked, hoping to put declarer to a guess of some kind. Declarer's choice of the card to play on this trick is noteworthy. He chose the Queen; this, he calculated, might create the impression in West's mind that he was taking a finesse with the holding of Ace-Queen. He then led the 7 of Clubs. West took with the Ace and in desperation led a Heart, hoping to find partner with a trick in that suit. Declarer was in and drew trumps, following with three Diamond discards on the good Clubs in dummy.

No brief is held for the defense, but a full measure of tribute must be given to South, who made his plays in just the sequence to provide him with a remote chance for success. As for North, he should donate his winnings to some worthy charity, preferably one interested in human rights.

EXTRA TRICK   The Blackwood 4–5 No-Trump Convention has several safe-guarding provisions that would increase its usefulness if only more players observed them. First: the asker must be safe at the bid to which his partner's response will force him. Second: the responder must do no more than his duty unless, by a bid of 5 No Trump, the asker releases the happy news that the slam-bound side holds all the Aces. Only then, freed of the possibility of losing a first-round trick, is the responder at liberty to make a decision regarding the final contract.

Neither vulnerable
South dealer

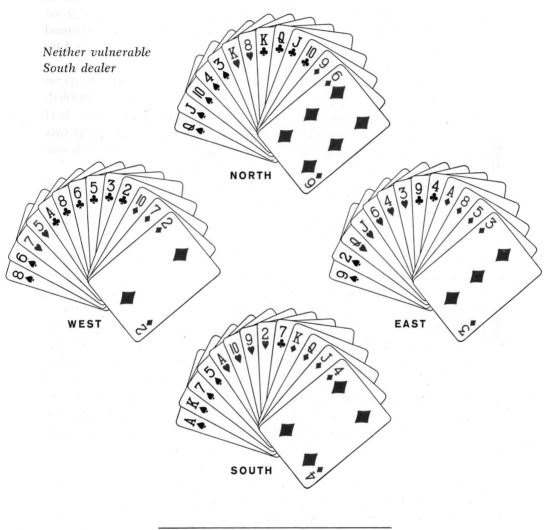

SOUTH	WEST	NORTH	EAST
1♠	Pass	3♠	Pass
4NT	Pass	5♣	Pass
5♠	Pass	6♠	Pass
Pass	Pass		

Opening lead: Spade 6

97

Make it up with psychology

IN TOURNAMENT bridge it is not only proper, it is often necessary to fall back on psychology to augment a small deficit in high cards. This is one way to get an edge over other pairs. The following hand is a good example. Helen Sobel and I played it during the 1958 Summer National Championships, and it figured prominently in our victory in the Life Masters Pair.

Our bidding performed a twofold mission. We arrived at a ticklish game contract, which might have been set by no more than 100 points if doubled. At the same time, we kept the opponents from getting to their own best spot, 4 Clubs, where they would have scored a 130-point profit (80 points for the trick score and 50 bonus for the partial). The next step in our campaign was to bring home the game contract.

I took the King of Hearts opening lead with the Ace and played a high trump. Now, if I led a high Heart through West, I could establish a trick for the discard of a Diamond—but not without permitting West to gain the lead. The danger would then become apparent, and West would shift to a Diamond at once. If the Ace-Queen were offside, as the bidding strongly indicated, I would lose one Heart, two Diamonds and one Club trick. I would be down one.

So I had to lull any fears my opponent in the West seat might have, and hope that East would win the Heart trick that must be surrendered. To attain this end, I led the 3 of Hearts from the South hand. West put up the 7, but it wasn't high enough. East was forced to win the trick with his 8 of Hearts. He cashed one high Club, but I ruffed the next Club and led the Jack of Hearts through West's marked Queen. West covered, and dummy ruffed. A Club ruff put me back on lead to cash the 10 of Hearts and get rid of one of dummy's two losing Diamonds. We lost only one trick in each of the nontrump suits and brought home game for a top score on the deal.

EXTRA TRICK   When the assistance of the defenders is required to fulfill a contract, the declarer should execute his "maneuver" as early as possible in order to avoid alerting the opponents.

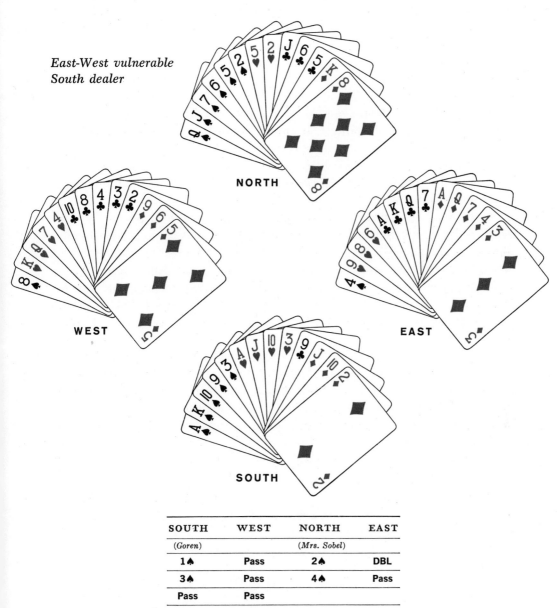

East-West vulnerable
South dealer

NORTH

WEST

EAST

SOUTH

SOUTH	WEST	NORTH	EAST
(Goren)		(Mrs. Sobel)	
1♠	Pass	2♠	DBL
3♠	Pass	4♠	Pass
Pass	Pass		

Opening lead: Heart King

A double revelation

IF given knowledge of the adverse holdings, would you care to play the hand at right at 7 Hearts doubled? The declarer in this little drama brought off the grand slam without benefit of a peek.

North decided to open with a forcing bid of 2 Clubs, though his hand contained more losers than we normally identify with a 2 demand bid. South, preparing for big things, was content to temporize for the moment with a response of 2 Hearts. North's leap to 3 No Trump will not be endorsed by the purists, particularly since North had already announced a super-powerhouse with his very first bid.

Convinced that precise scientific investigation would not reveal the exact trick-taking potentialities of the hand, South decided to jump straightway to 6 Hearts. North, obviously unmindful that it was he who had opened with 2 Clubs and jumped to 3 No Trump, went gaily on to 7.

East, knowing that the Club suit could not be established, and expecting to win a trick with the King of Diamonds, decided to double. This gesture proved of material assistance to declarer, for it marked beyond doubt the location of the missing King of Diamonds.

West opened the 9 of Clubs, which was taken by the King in dummy, South discarding a Diamond. Declarer played three rounds of trumps, throwing a Diamond from dummy. A Spade to North's King was followed by the Ace and another Club, verifying the fact that the suit would not break. South ruffed and played two more trumps, discarding a Diamond and a Spade from dummy.

At this point the holdings were:

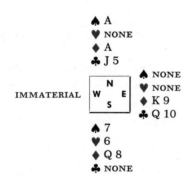

$$
\begin{array}{c}
\spadesuit \text{ A} \\
\heartsuit \text{ NONE} \\
\diamondsuit \text{ A} \\
\clubsuit \text{ J 5}
\end{array}
$$

IMMATERIAL

$$
\begin{array}{c}
\spadesuit \text{ NONE} \\
\heartsuit \text{ NONE} \\
\diamondsuit \text{ K 9} \\
\clubsuit \text{ Q 10}
\end{array}
$$

$$
\begin{array}{c}
\spadesuit \text{ 7} \\
\heartsuit \text{ 6} \\
\diamondsuit \text{ Q 8} \\
\clubsuit \text{ NONE}
\end{array}
$$

If South leads to dummy's Ace of Spades, East will find it impossible to discard. If he throws a Club, South will ruff a Club and establish the

Jack. If he throws a Diamond, declarer will cash the Diamond Ace in dummy, ruff himself in with a Club lead and produce the Queen of Diamonds for trick thirteen. This, of course, is what he did.

EXTRA TRICK   Against a slam bid, a double by the player not on lead is a convention. It calls for an unusual lead, most often the suit first bid by the dummy. So used, it helps the doubler's partner. Used otherwise, it is more likely to furnish aid and comfort to the enemy.

North-South vulnerable
North dealer

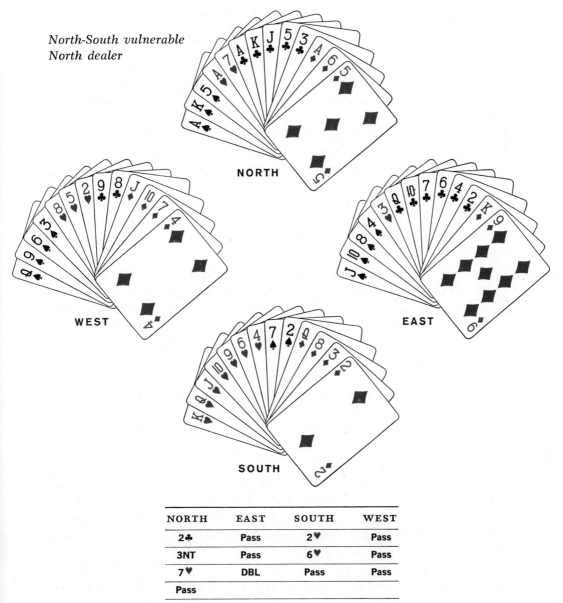

NORTH	EAST	SOUTH	WEST
2♣	Pass	2♥	Pass
3NT	Pass	6♥	Pass
7♥	DBL	Pass	Pass
Pass			

Opening lead: Club 9

Watch out for an early hoax

ONE of the many intriguing things about bridge is the number of opportunities it presents for engineering hoaxes. There is not space enough here to go into the numerous ramifications of the hoax, but I can at least assert a first principle: the essential ingredient is speed. You have to start fast if your intended victim is to be caught flat-footed.

It is by no means a rare experience to be faced with a contract that simply cannot be fulfilled unless at least one opponent is fooled. This is not to say that you should resort to coffeehousing (discussed elsewhere among these hands). A good hoax depends upon trapping your victim before he is aware of the nature of his danger. For example, consider the hand at right:

There was not much artistry in the bidding. The North hand is not easy to rebid and, as a consequence, many players would be reluctant to open. North's raise to 3 Hearts is also somewhat doubtful, even though in support of South's free bid. In cases of this kind, we usually prefer to rebid a nonrebiddable suit rather than offer partner undue encouragement by raising the level of the contract. South's subsequent leap to 6 Hearts was based somewhat on the expectation of finding a reasonably good Spade suit in partner's hand.

The opening Diamond lead was ruffed by declarer. Apparently two Spade tricks would have to be lost. Against perfect defense, South could make his contract only if one defender held the King and Queen of Spades unguarded. To this hope declarer added the chance of making contract against an adversary with the King and any smaller Spade. He gave the defense an opportunity for a slip by immediately leading a Spade to dummy's Ace.

This play was made before East was aware of the danger that lurked in his possession of the King.

After cashing the Ace of Spades, declarer ruffed dummy's remaining Diamond and then played one round of trumps. Fortunately, each opponent had to follow suit, else East might have had one more opportunity to get rid of his danger card. South then cashed his King of Clubs, crossed to dummy's Club Ace and trumped the last Club. A Spade play now imposed upon East the doubtful pleasure of leading. Whether East chose to lead a Diamond or a Club, declarer could ruff in dummy while discarding the losing Spade from his hand.

It is reasonable to assume that if declarer had gone about the business of stripping the hand before leading the Ace of Spades, East would have had time to collect his wits. Suspecting the trap, he would no doubt have unloaded the King of Spades on dummy's Ace. In the rehash of the incident, East contended that to drop the King of Spades at trick two would have required clairvoyance. We discreetly abstained from comment.

EXTRA TRICK   East was a late sleeper, deaf to the alarm. The very fact that declarer led a Spade, without drawing a single round of trumps, should have aroused his suspicion. Whenever a good player departs from the usual order of play, watch out. He may be a hoax engineer getting ready for the fast one.

Both sides vulnerable
North dealer

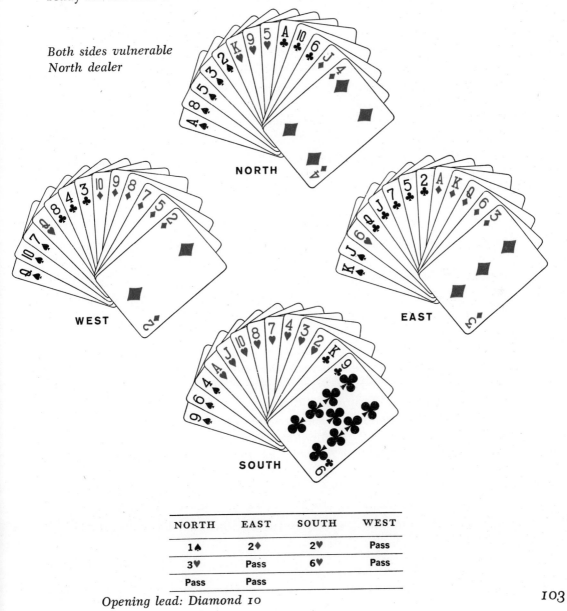

NORTH	EAST	SOUTH	WEST
1♠	2♦	2♥	Pass
3♥	Pass	6♥	Pass
Pass	Pass		

Opening lead: Diamond 10

Why ignore the evidence?

AS a one-time Philadelphia lawyer, I lend a sympathetic ear when attorneys complain about the effect of delays caused by crowded court calendars. Too often, by the time a case is called for trial, key witnesses have forgotten their testimony.

Yet brain surgeons have recently confirmed what psychiatrists have always held: nothing is really forgotten. Everything your five senses experience is recorded on an endless tape, available if you touch the right button.

In bridge the trick is not only to remember but also to make use of the information thus recalled. In the following case, East lost the verdict through failure to re-examine the testimony offered by the opposing side.

The bidding was laced with the competitive spice so often added when one side owns a part score. North might have denied himself the fleeting pleasure of doubling the 1-Spade bid. Somebody was sure to run out, whereas a raise to 2 Clubs—enough for game—might silence the Heart suit which North could be sure the opponents must command.

Later in the auction, North had no more stomach for the double of Hearts than his partner had showed for the earlier double of Spades. As it happens, the 4-Heart bid could be punished to the tune of 500 points. If North heeded the bidding and opened the Ace of Spades, South could ruff the next Spade and put his partner back on lead with a Club while he still had a trump to ruff the third Spade trick. But these two ruffs would be somewhat offset by the saving of a Diamond trick; declarer would be able to throw East's small Diamonds on his established Spades.

However, North and South found no fault with their profits at 5 Clubs. East won the Diamond opening and returned the suit. To his disappointment, West produced the deuce of Diamonds instead of the hoped-for trump. Declarer knocked out West's Ace of Clubs and was able to trump two losing Hearts in dummy and discard the third low Heart on North's Ace of Spades. The defenders collected only their two minor-suit Aces and North and South collected 750 for game and rubber.

West's opening lead was the only one that offered a chance to set the contract. If East had ducked the first Diamond, West would have won the first round of trumps with his Ace and then led the Diamond deuce. East's Ace would have won and a third Diamond, ruffed by West, would have put declarer down. "But your 3-spot was such a low one," East alibied. "How could I tell it was not a singleton?"

East had forgotten, or ignored, the testimony of his opponent's bidding. If West held only one Diamond, South must have five to the K-J. With such a holding, South would have opened the bidding with 1 Diamond, not 1 Club. So West is marked with two Diamonds, and East must realize that he can keep the entry he needs to give his partner a ruff only by holding the Diamond Ace to win the second lead of the suit.

EXTRA TRICK Unless you think the opponents are making a psychic bid in order to steal your suit, don't double a bid you know cannot be left in.

Both sides vulnerable
North-South 60 on score
South dealer

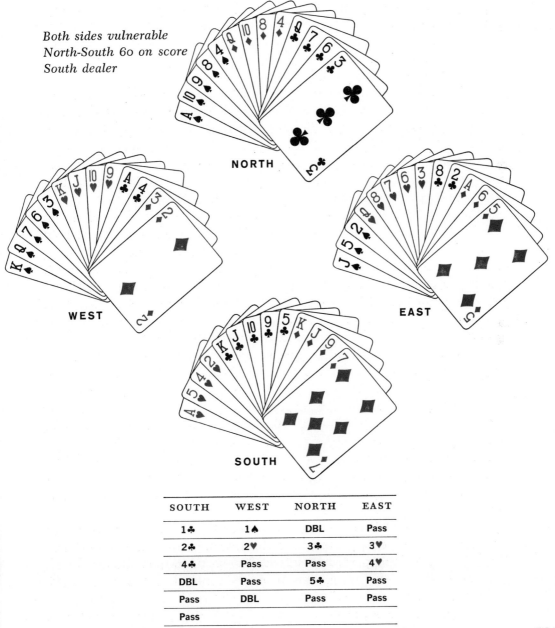

SOUTH	WEST	NORTH	EAST
1♣	1♠	DBL	Pass
2♣	2♥	3♣	3♥
4♣	Pass	Pass	4♥
DBL	Pass	5♣	Pass
Pass	DBL	Pass	Pass
Pass			

Opening lead: Diamond 3

The small Club incident

SOME hands are almost unbelievable. So is some luck. Both points were never better demonstrated than in the following deal which was watched at the Cavendish Club in New York by Sonny Moyse, editor of *Bridge World*. He reported to me: "I would write it up if I thought anybody would believe me. The trouble is, they wouldn't. But everybody accepts your writing as gospel. I think you ought to tell the story."

Thus challenged, how could I refuse?

The East hand meets many of the requirements for an opening 2 bid: game in hand, three suits with first-round control. It even has enough points—20—for a hand with an eight-card suit and a good five-card suit. Strategically, however, the 2 bid is not to be commended. There is no danger that this hand will pass out at a contract of 1 Spade. There *is* danger that partner will carry the bidding too high with the wrong Aces, or that the opponents will be warned of East's freakish distribution.

North's 3 No-Trump bid was the "unusual" No Trump—a call for South to choose between the two minor suits. When South found enough material to show the Diamonds in spite of the intervening 4-Spade bid, North knew that his partner held real Diamond length. East's 5-Heart bid confirmed North's suspicion that East had an extreme freak, and his pass to 6 Diamonds was further evidence of no Club or Diamond losers. So, when West went on to 6 Hearts, North decided that his partner would be short in that suit and that the finesses in Clubs or Diamonds would be "on."

I admire North's reasoning—but not nearly so much as I admire East's courage in allowing the double of 7 Diamonds to stand. He could hardly be confident that West's Clubs included the 5-spot! Yet it was upon just that lowly card that the grand slam depended.

The Heart opening was won with dummy's Ace. With a grand slam hanging in the balance, declarer took plenty of time to analyze his chances. Eventually, he reached the same conclusion that led North to bid 7 Diamonds although he was reasonably sure he could defeat 6 Hearts. He decided that East was void in both minor suits. So South did his best to put a fast one past West.

Dummy's Ace of Diamonds won the second trick, and a low Diamond put South in with the King. Here South led the innocent-looking 6 of Clubs. Had West put on the 5, declarer intended to let the 6-spot ride for the essential deep finesse that would have made the contract. But West is a well-known insomniac at the bridge table—especially when the contract is a grand slam. He covered the 6 of Clubs with the 7, forcing dummy's Jack. Thereafter, by covering each Club led by South, West established the 5 of Clubs as the thin little trick that saved a fat bundle of points.

EXTRA TRICK A 2 demand bid is best reserved for a hand which can be properly described in no other way, and with which there is a danger you will be passed out if you open with a bid of only 1. Without an over-whelming share of the high cards, a 2 bid is seldom necessary and rarely advisable.

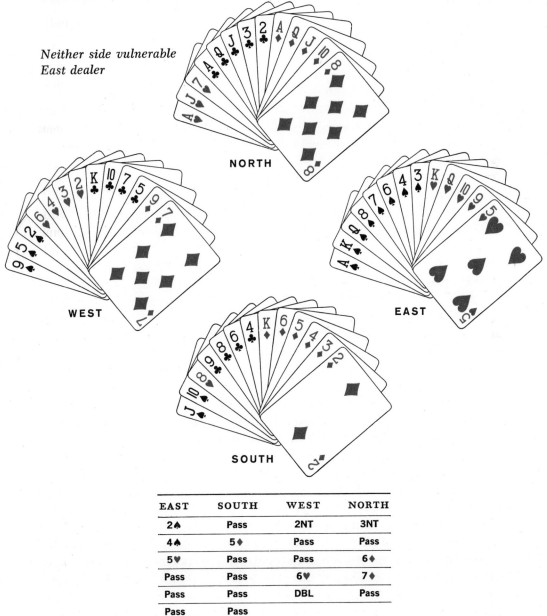

Neither side vulnerable
East dealer

NORTH

WEST

EAST

SOUTH

EAST	SOUTH	WEST	NORTH
2♠	Pass	2NT	3NT
4♠	5♦	Pass	Pass
5♥	Pass	Pass	6♦
Pass	Pass	6♥	7♦
Pass	Pass	DBL	Pass
Pass	Pass		

Opening lead: Heart 2

A good code can be cracked

BRIDGE is a game not only of intelligence but also of counterintelligence. The following episode of card-table espionage involves a double cross that should not have succeeded. The code in which the defenders were communicating was known to the declarer—and the defenders knew that their messages were being intercepted. On this hand, West should have looked for signs that his partner's communiqué had been tampered with.

No one at the table could have had the slightest doubt that West's Diamond opening was a singleton lead. East's only problem was to tell his partner what suit to return after West had ruffed the second Diamond; meanwhile, South laid his plan to scramble the enemy's communications. So, when East won the first lead with the Ace of Diamonds, declarer followed suit with the 5.

The code used by defenders in this situation is a simple one. The player who knows his partner is going to ruff chooses a high card for his lead if he wants to be put back with the higher of the two remaining side suits; he leads a low card if his re-entry lies in the lower suit.

But when East returned his low card—the Diamond 9—to suggest a Club return, South obscured the message by following with the Diamond 10. West trumped the trick and assumed that his partner held the missing 3-spot and had led his higher Diamond to signal that his re-entry was in Spades. West led the Queen of Spades and South easily made his contract, drawing trumps and discarding a loser on dummy's fifth Diamond.

While West was the victim of South's delicate counterintelligence work, his real guilt was in letting an ambiguous signal override everything that simple bridge intelligence should have told him. No matter what East's message seemed to say, that player simply could not hold the Ace of Spades. Unless South held that card, his bidding—enterprising enough as it was—would have been sheer insanity opposite a partner whose first response had indicated a weakish hand.

Without the Ace of Spades, South could not have bid as he did; but he might possibly have done so lacking the King of Clubs. Therefore, whether or not he fathomed South's ruse, West should have returned a low Club. The desperate possibility that East held the Club King was the only real chance the defense had to defeat the contract. And, as the cards were dealt, this low Club lead would have done the job. East would win with the King and give West another Diamond ruff for the setting trick. Thereafter, the fact that the Club Ace would not live was a blow the defenders could bear

without great suffering.

EXTRA TRICK   With length in the opponents' trump suit, a singleton is
rarely the preferred lead, especially a singleton lead into a suit the declarer
has bid. As the cards were placed, the singleton would set the hand with
perfect defense—because East held the King of Clubs. But against a Spade
opening lead, declarer, even if he held the King of Clubs, would have to
guess the Diamond situation in order to make his contract. And by not leading his singleton West would have made it difficult for declarer to guess the
distribution of the Diamond suit.

East-West vulnerable
South dealer

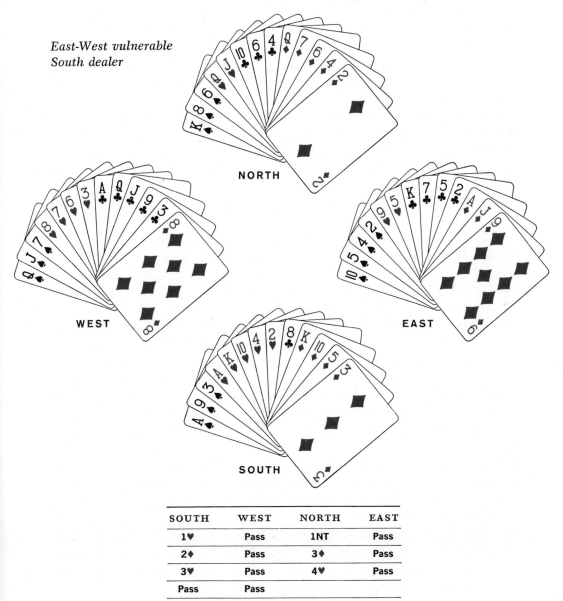

SOUTH	WEST	NORTH	EAST
1♥	Pass	1NT	Pass
2♦	Pass	3♦	Pass
3♥	Pass	4♥	Pass
Pass	Pass		

Opening lead: Diamond 8

The Heart that broke par

THERE is no better way to learn to play bridge than by sitting down in a game—preferably with better players—with a good teacher at your elbow. Among the most enthusiastic users of this method for improving their game are the bridge experts themselves.

Annually I have conducted a bridge teachers' convention in New York. The teachers are coached by me and my associates, Olive Peterson of Philadelphia and Paul Hodge of Dallas. They hear from perhaps a dozen of the finest experts. But the big moments of this three-day conference— and perhaps the ones from which the teachers learn the most—are the two evenings when they play a series of prepared hands that call for especially skillful bidding or play in order to achieve a par result.

This kind of game has always been popular among good players. The problem is to create hands that cannot go wrong. Like this one, for instance. (*See opposite page.*)

South's hand is just too good to settle for less than a 6-Heart bid, considering that the contract can be fulfilled if partner has as little as the Jack of Clubs.

Remember, please, that hands like this are deliberately concocted to demonstrate a point. West has a reasonably normal opening lead in the Jack of Spades. South wins the trick and takes inventory. Over in dummy there are two perfectly good tricks in Diamonds, on which declarer could discard his losing Clubs—but how can he get there? Is there any better play than to lead out all the trumps but one, cash the good Spades and the Ace of Diamonds, and then play Clubs, trusting that the King was doubleton, or that one of the opponents was unwise enough to unguard it?

With six Clubs outstanding, the odds are against finding a singleton or doubleton King. And with dummy's good Diamonds in plain sight, no sane defender is going to bother to hold on to Diamonds, so the chance of an opponent discarding a Club is not very bright. But South does have a fifty-fifty chance.

The winning play doesn't look like the usual finesse because you have to lead away from your high cards instead of toward them. But it's the same even chance that West, rather than East, will hold the 10 of Hearts.

The idea on this hand is for South to win the Spade, cash the Diamond Ace, then lead a low Heart. This makes West a present of a trick he isn't entitled to win—the Heart 10. But it establishes the Heart 9 as a re-entry to dummy. A second trump play puts North on lead, and declarer discards two Clubs on dummy's good Diamonds.

It happened that way at every table but one. There the iconoclast in the

West seat opened the 7 of Hearts. Oh, yes, North won the trick with the 9. But South hadn't yet cashed his Ace of Diamonds, so all this enabled him to do was to take a Club finesse.

Alas, I had not been foresighted enough to give East the King of Clubs. So the finesse lost, the slam went down, and once again I was convinced that it is hard to create a par that it truly foolproof.

EXTRA TRICK There are many devices available where cards are sold that enable you to play par hands. I suggest you try one of them when you feel the urge to test your game.

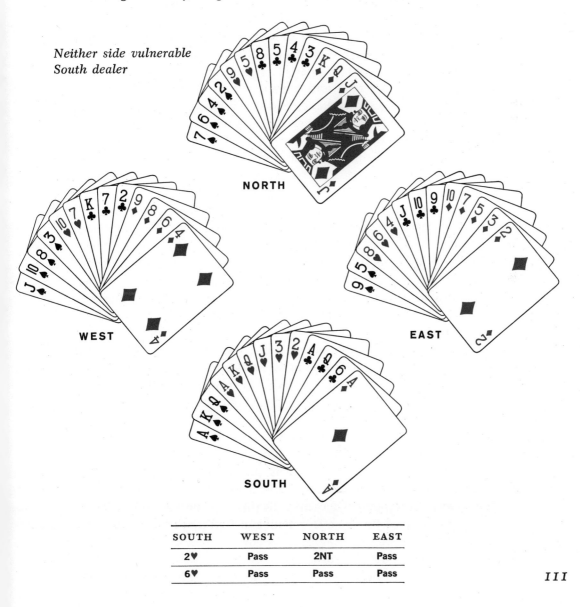

Neither side vulnerable
South dealer

SOUTH	WEST	NORTH	EAST
2♥	Pass	2NT	Pass
6♥	Pass	Pass	Pass

The odds are a man's best friend

WHEN a good golfer starts missing the fairway with his drives and finding the traps with his approaches, he does not waste time seeking locker-room sympathy. Instead, he consults his pro. Unfortunately, this simple remedy is not often followed by the unsuccessful bridge player. For one reason, many players are genuinely convinced that they are dogged by ill fortune. For another reason, it is not always possible to find a bridge "pro" who can tell the good player where he is slipping.

When no pro is available, the most reliable lessons are to be found in the results achieved by the field in a duplicate game where the same hands are played by a good number of players. A case in point is the deal shown at right, from a recent tournament.

A 5-Diamond contract could be made even by Aunt Matilda, but 3 No Trump was reached at almost every table. Not many declarers, however, managed to snaffle nine tricks.

One South player did make the contract, but not by his own efforts. He won the Heart opening, led a Club to dummy and played a small Diamond. East failed to rise with the King, so West's Ace was knocked out before the Hearts could be established. But at most of the tables where an attempt was made to set up the Diamond suit, East put up the King on the first Diamond lead and knocked out South's last Heart stopper while West retained the Ace of Diamonds. How many tricks South went down depended upon how many he cashed before trying to make his contract—either by finding East with the Diamond Ace or by a successful Spade finesse.

The particular luck-bemoaner who inspired this essay spoke with proper scorn of those who pinned their hopes on the Diamond suit. "Obviously," he explained, "with only one Heart stop remaining after the opening lead, it would take a miracle to bring home enough tricks in Diamonds. I didn't try any such nonsense. Instead, I gave myself a fifty-fifty chance by taking the Spade finesse. But with my luck, of course, it lost."

"That's strange," his listener remarked. "Against me the declarer took the Spade finesse and made his game."

"You mean you didn't take the Queen of Spades?"

"Oh, I won the Spade Queen," was the quiet reply. "But the bridge player I was up against took a first-round finesse with the 8-spot!"

Our hero got the point. Of course, in this deal he had only himself to blame. He had played for the even chance of finding the Queen of Spades with West; he could as easily have given himself the three-to-one chance of finding West with the Queen or 10.

Suppose East had been able to win the first Spade lead with the 10.

Declarer still had his fifty-fifty chance of a successful finesse for the Queen on the next Spade lead. But, as the cards were dealt, the 8 would have forced the Queen on the first round and South would have had the trick he needed for his contract.

EXTRA TRICK   When two important cards are out against you, there is a very good chance that they will be in different hands—not to mention the possibility that both may be in the favorable hand. At any rate, two chances are always better than one.

Both sides vulnerable
South dealer

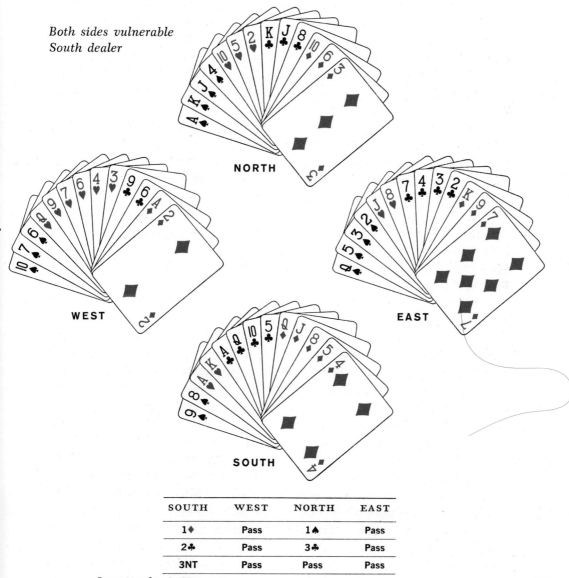

SOUTH	WEST	NORTH	EAST
1♦	Pass	1♠	Pass
2♣	Pass	3♣	Pass
3NT	Pass	Pass	Pass

Opening lead: Heart 6

The surprise attack in action

THE surprise attack has enjoyed great favor in love, war and sport. It is a particular help to the bridge player in making the opening lead.

To go back a step: there is some reason to fear that textbooks (including my own) have oversold the idea that certain card combinations provide ideal leads—for example, the King from K Q J or A-K; the Queen from Q J 10; and so forth. These, of course, are sound leads under normal circumstances, and they must be set down as preferred leads for the beginner and not-too-experienced player. But when the player reaches the stage where he can think for himself—when he can analyze and draw shrewd deductions from the bidding he has heard—he should not hesitate to jettison the conventional attack in favor of a boldly imaginative lead.

The following hand illustrates what I mean.

The bidding is given as it actually occurred at one of New York's leading bridge clubs. Some modern experts might frown on this bidding as not very scientific, but no serious fault can be found with the final contract of 6 Hearts, even though 6 Spades is ironclad. North felt that since his partner's Heart response was a 2-over-1 takeout, there was a strong probability that South had the top cards in the suit, in which case he could pull trumps and run the long Spade suit, ruffing one round of Spades if necessary. Even if South had made his bid on five Hearts to the A-J, with some Club strength as compensation, he might have made the slam with a little luck on the missing Heart King.

The truly interesting feature of this hand, however, is the opening-lead problem that faced West.

West's conventional lead was the King of Diamonds. He would then hope to set up a Diamond winner while retaining the Club Ace for entry and the setting trick. But this lead did not look attractive to West. He was sure that dummy would turn up with the Diamond Ace, because North certainly would not have bid a slam with losers in both minor suits.

West decided that the only hope of beating the slam depended on putting his partner on lead in a hurry so that he could return a Spade for West to ruff. This could be done if East had the Club King, or if dummy had the King, East the Queen, and declarer, holding the Club Jack, misjudged the situation and played low from dummy on a low Club lead by West.

Thus West led the Club 6.

East was merely going through the motions of following suit when he put in the Club Jack, but when, to his astonishment, he found himself in possession of the trick, he quickly snapped to attention. There could be only one reason for West to have underled an Ace against a slam contract:

he wanted a certain return, and it wasn't very hard for East to figure out what that return should be. He led a Spade, and West's ruff defeated the slam contract.

EXTRA TRICK In the final analysis, a player in West's position has to have full knowledge of his opponents' bidding proclivities in order to choose the best lead against a slam contract. It was because West knew that North, particularly, was a sound and even conservative bidder that he could properly make such a daring lead. Against different opponents and specifically the sort who are more or less slam-happy, the "normal" lead of the Diamond King would be preferred.

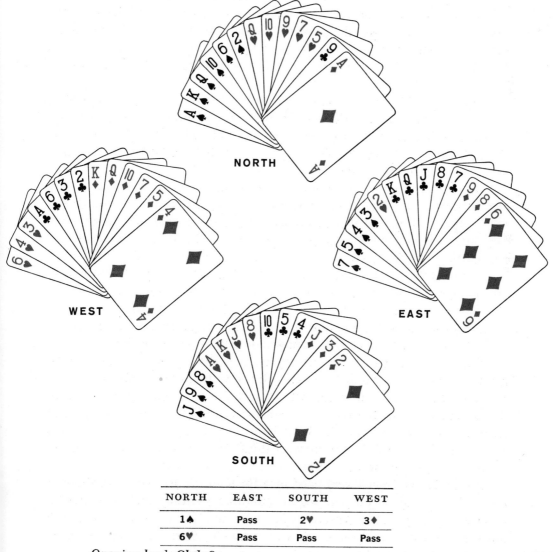

NORTH	EAST	SOUTH	WEST
1♠	Pass	2♥	3♦
6♥	Pass	Pass	Pass

Opening lead: Club 6

A nursery rhyme that works

THE fellow who hands out advice in any field is asking for trouble. The advice may be perfectly sound, but it becomes progressively less so as it is passed from person to person. Alexander Pope knew what he was talking about when he referred to a little learning, and he might have added that a little truth is equally dangerous.

Getting down to cases in bridge: I have been preaching for a long time that "an opening bid facing an opening bid will produce game." And so it will—with reasonable qualifications. On a recent occasion, however, this slogan of mine was tossed right back in my face by a friend who found that it did not apply in the case of the following hand. I sympathized with him but tried to convince him that it wasn't the slogan that was at fault.

Unfortunately for my friend, who was North—and for myself, sitting just behind him (at his request)—South went down one at his 5-Diamond contract. Whereupon North turned to me and said with some acerbity, "You and your nursery rhymes! I had an opening bid facing an opening bid—so why didn't we make game?"

I could have turned the other cheek but, for one thing, I'm rather fond of this "nursery rhyme." It has pulled in a lot of points for me through the years. So I told him that the slogan doesn't apply to minor-suit games needing eleven tricks, and that he might have considered the advisability of getting to 3 No Trump. Granted, I continued, it would not be proper for North to bid No Trump himself as a second-round response to South's Diamond rebid, because whatever strength South might have in Clubs should be led up to, not through. The wise thing for North to do was to underbid a shade, raising to only 3 Diamonds instead of 4, and his partner undoubtedly would have been happy to veer into 3 No Trump.

Another point—which I didn't discuss with my friend because his partner was a nice fellow and I certainly didn't want to embarrass him—was that the 5-Diamond contract, inferior though it was, could have been made. South actually won the first trick with his Heart King, drew trumps and tried to pass a Spade into the West hand. But he had no luck with this plan, and so he finally had to play for the Club Ace on-side. No luck there either, and down he went.

It would have been a very good idea for South to let West win the first trick. West could do no better than continue Hearts. South would win, pull the opposing trumps, discard a Spade on the Heart Ace, and then cash the King and Ace of Spades and ruff a Spade. With that suit breaking three-three, South would have a parking spot for a Club and would not have to worry about the position of the Club Ace. If Spades did not break, he could try for the favorable Club lie as a last resort.

But I still say that my friend should have bid only 3 Diamonds, not 4, instead of trying to fix me for writing nursery rhymes.

EXTRA TRICK   A raise from 2 to 3 in a major suit invites partner to bid game in that suit; but the same raise in a minor suit usually suggests that partner should choose between a 3-No-Trump contract and the minor-suit game contract.

Both sides vulnerable
South dealer

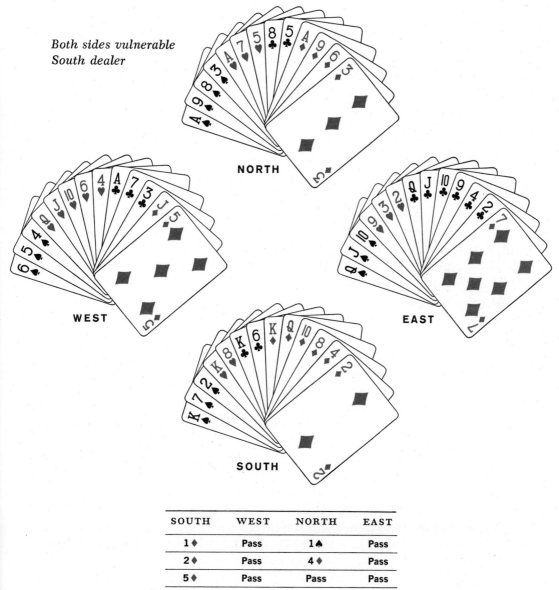

SOUTH	WEST	NORTH	EAST
1♦	Pass	1♠	Pass
2♦	Pass	4♦	Pass
5♦	Pass	Pass	Pass

Opening lead: Heart Queen

Lead on—but be careful

SINCE bridge experts are human (despite a formidable weight of opinion to the contrary), if they were granted just one wish they would probably ask for a generous portion of Aces and Kings. But if they couldn't have these, they would probably settle for the next best thing—a satchel full of good opening leads.

It is always something of a comfort to the opening leader when his partner has bid a suit. This obviously provides a clue which may be helpful. Yet it is not always a sure indicator of the correct opening lead. Sometimes it is better not to lead the suit partner has bid. In the current offering West made a wise decision.

Before we get around to the opening lead, let's take note of the fact that West first had a decision to make in the bidding. With his vulnerable partner going it alone up to the 4 level, against nonvulnerable opponents, there was some temptation for West to bid 5 Diamonds. But his evenly balanced distribution argued against such action.

We are aware, of course, that had West chosen to bid 5 Diamonds the contract might well have come safely home. It would have required a Club lead from South to break the contract, and there was a distinct likelihood that such an opening would not have been forthcoming. Against a red-suit attack, East would draw trumps and lead the Spade Jack. South would win, and would no doubt shift to Clubs—but too late. East would win, cross to dummy with a trump and take another Spade finesse. With the fall of the Queen, one of dummy's Clubs would go off on East's fourth Spade. If South's initial lead were a Spade, East would have his job done for him before he lost control in Clubs.

But let's get back to things as they were, with South the declarer at 4 Hearts and West on lead.

West had sound reasons for refusing to open partner's suit. East's unassisted drive to the 4 level marked him with considerable length in Diamonds. West's holding of four cards convinced him that there would be few if any defensive tricks in that suit.

Also, West knew that there was no need to establish Diamonds, for if a Diamond trick were available it could be cashed at leisure. He knew that he was not going to have many chances to lead, so it behooved him to take advantage of his one sure opportunity.

He therefore led the Jack of Spades, in a move that was very salubrious for the defenders. Declarer ducked in dummy, and East played the encouraging 7-spot. South won, drew trumps and knocked out the Ace of Clubs. But East now exploited his partner's good opening lead by underleading the Diamond Ace to put West in. A second Spade play through dummy's Queen now gave East-West the setting trick.

EXTRA TRICK Playing at a suit contract, if you have only one or two cards in the suit which has been mentioned by partner, it would appear that your choice of opening leads has been made for you. But when you have great length in his suit, a search for a more constructive lead is sometimes to be recommended.

East-West vulnerable
East dealer

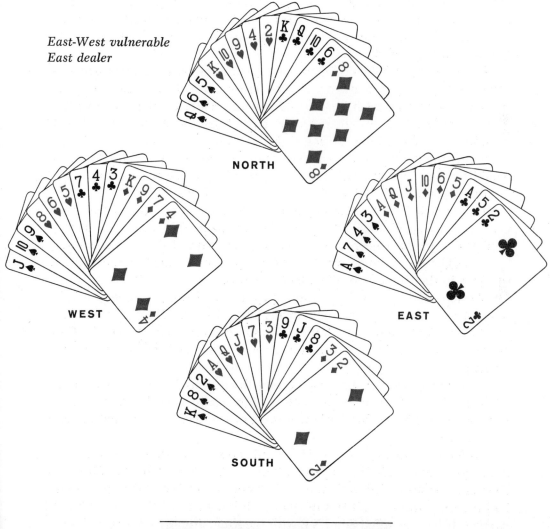

EAST	SOUTH	WEST	NORTH
1 ♦	1 ♥	Pass	3 ♥
4 ♦	Pass	Pass	4 ♥
Pass	Pass	Pass	

Smothering the untouchable

NOTHING infuriates contract bridge people so much as listening to someone say, "Let's play cards—bridge or something." When that happens the standard operating procedure is to draw oneself up, glare venomously at the speaker and stalk from the room. What kind of bridge can one play with an insensitive clod who doesn't appreciate the difference between a glorious semi-science and a mere card game? Could a pinochle player, for example, offer such an exhibition of legerdemain as was produced in the following bridge hand?

North, with 10 points in high cards, made the best response when he gave his partner a single raise; 1 No Trump would have been too discouraging. South might have proceeded with greater caution by rebidding only 3 Spades, but the effect would have been the same, since North would scarcely have hung a trick short of game.

When the dummy was spread, declarer could see at a glance that he would have to lose two Diamonds and a Heart, and so the contract obviously depended on the position of the trump King.

East signaled for a Diamond come-on by playing the 9, and South decided to hold up his Ace. West then led the Diamond Queen, South won and let the trump Queen ride through West, who of course declined to cover. Declarer continued with the Jack of trumps, planting the evil eye on West in the vague hope of inducing a cover.

West, confident of his position, saw no objection to engaging in a little pleasantry by announcing to declarer that the King was an "untouchable." South kept quiet but he did not give up hope. He led the Club deuce to the King and returned the small Diamond remaining in the dummy.

East didn't give the matter a second thought as he went up with the Diamond Jack. He then exited with a Club. South won, led to the Heart King, ruffed dummy's low Club with the 3 of trumps, and then led the Ace and 8 of Hearts.

To South's satisfaction, the Heart suit broke three-three and East was in on the third round. That defender had to return a Club or the thirteenth Diamond. South ruffed with the 8 of trumps—and West, though he still had the King and a small trump against dummy's blank Ace, was *hors de combat*. If he overruffed South's 8 with the King, dummy's Ace would overruff him and South's remaining trump would be high; and if West preferred to "discard" his last trump 6 underneath South's 8, that wouldn't do him much good either, since the Heart would be pitched from the table and the trump Ace would remain for the last trick.

South's moment had come. He turned to West and said sweetly, "It was a pleasure to introduce you to the smother play."

EXTRA TRICK   South certainly did a good job, but I'd better not leave any loose ends for eagle-eyed readers.

If South had known all about the hand, he could have brought off his smother play without help from the enemy by conceding his second Diamond loser before leading the second trump. As the play went, East could have beaten the hand by not putting up the Diamond Jack, letting his partner win with the 10 to knock out the then-blank Ace of trumps.

Both sides vulnerable

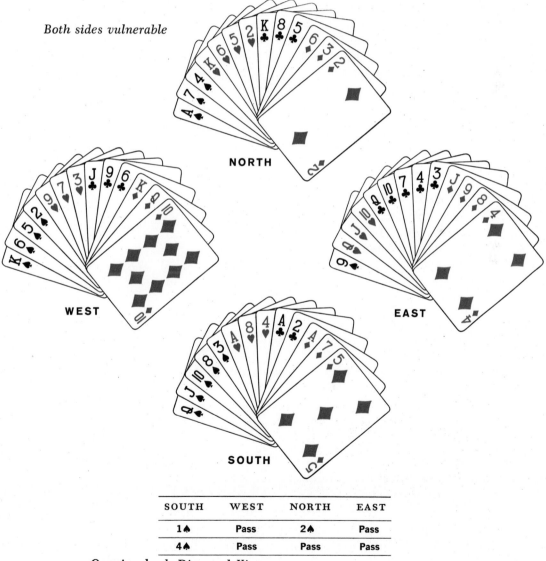

SOUTH	WEST	NORTH	EAST
1♠	Pass	2♠	Pass
4♠	Pass	Pass	Pass

Opening lead: Diamond King

Never trust a stranger

THE late Damon Runyon once told about the card-playing advice given to him by his father. Shortly before the old gentleman's death, he said to young Damon: "Son, sometime, somewhere, a stranger will come up to you and show you a brand-new deck of cards. The seal will be unbroken, and he'll offer to bet he can make the Jack of Spades jump out of this deck and squirt cider in your left ear. Son, do not bet, because sure as you do, you're going to have an ear full of cider!"

Which brings us to a bridge hand and the sad story about a friend of mine who had never heard this bit of advice.

"I was South," said my friend, "and though you may not approve of my bidding 4 Spades, you'll agree it was a fine contract."

"Yes," I said, "I'll have to agree to that."

"You'll also have to agree that it was horrible luck to find the three missing trumps bunched in the West hand, so that I had to lose a trump trick along with two Hearts and a Diamond."

I looked at the layout and said, "What happened?"

"What happened? I went down one, of course, but that wasn't the worst of it! When it was over, a kibitzer offered to bet me he could make the hand! So I took him up. And I lost! Can you believe it?"

"Oh yes, I can," I said. "I suppose West led the Queen of Clubs?"

He nodded. "That's right."

"So," I said slowly, "the kibitzer won with the Club Ace, laid down a high trump, and got the bad news about the trump break."

"Yes, just as I got it in the actual play."

"But then," I continued, "the kibitzer got smart. Obviously West didn't have a Heart—else he would have led it originally. So the kibitzer cashed the King of Clubs and then led dummy's little Club and passed it to West, throwing off a Diamond from his own hand. Right?"

"Yes," he said. "How did you know?"

Choosing to ignore that not very complimentary question, I continued, "And West made his best return—a low Diamond."

"Yes."

"The kibitzer won with the King, cashed the other high trump and the Diamond Ace and ruffed dummy's remaining Diamond. Still right?"

"Yes," he said sulkily.

"Then he threw West in with the trump Queen, and West had to give him, the kibitzer, a ruff and discard. That is, West had to lead a Diamond or a Club, and the kibitzer chucked a Heart from dummy while he trumped in his own hand. After that, he had only one Heart to lose. Still right?"

"Yes! Are you going to tell me I should have played the hand that way at the table? That double-dummy way?"

"Maybe not," I said. "But I will tell you not to stick out your ear for a squirt of cider!" He of course didn't know what I was talking about.

EXTRA TRICK   Sometimes you can overcome a bad break if you make it work for you instead of against you. The winning play is not quite as double-dummy as my friend would like to think. Declarer's only hope is to throw West in and to keep East out. When East fails to follow to the third Club he affords a sure way to accomplish this.

Both sides vulnerable
East dealer

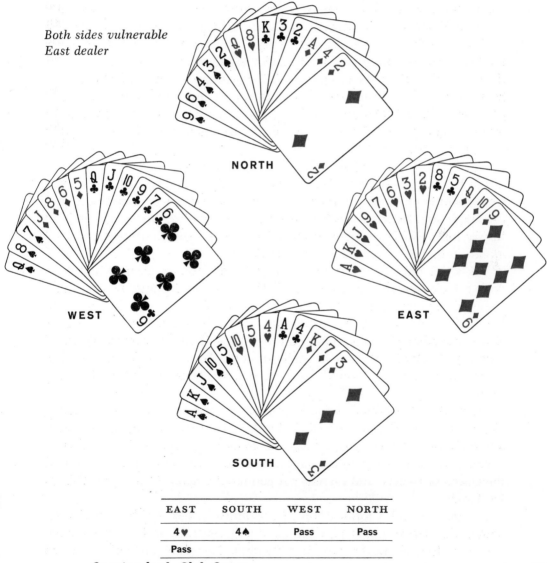

EAST	SOUTH	WEST	NORTH
4♥	4♠	Pass	Pass
Pass			

Opening lead: Club Queen

They play rough in Canada

AS AN alumnus of McGill University, an affectionate nostalgia grips me whenever I re-enter Canada. This lasts until I sit down at the bridge table. Then my Canadian friends proceed to put a severe strain on the affection by doing their best to beat my alleged brains out. And their best is very good indeed.

Rating high among the Canadian players are my good friends Eric Murray of Toronto and Douglas Drury, until recently of Vancouver. Both are Life Masters of the American Contract Bridge League, of which the Canadian bridge leagues are now a part. I remember very well—but not fondly—what they did to me in the following tournament hand.

I was West. Since I cannot cherish the memory of partners who have to pass out my 1 bids, I no longer recall the unfortunate player who sat East. Because of Drury's (South's) brilliant play, East never had a chance to get into the act, although I am still proud of the coup by which I attempted to bring him to life.

My opening lead was the Jack of Spades. Dummy played low, and East's 3-spot left me in no doubt that Drury's King was a false card. So, when I won the King of Clubs I could see that there would not be time to bring in the Spade suit. Declarer would surely win three Spades, three Clubs and—to justify his 2 No-Trump response—he must have the King-Queen of Diamonds, bringing his total up to nine tricks.

This left only the faint hope that my unfortunate partner had been dealt a Jack—specifically, the Jack of Hearts. So on winning the first Club, I shifted to the Queen of Hearts. As you will observe by referring to the hand, this wildcat venture struck oil in that East did indeed hold four Hearts including the Jack. After dummy's King of Hearts won my Queen, I would get back with the Ace of Clubs, cash the Ace of Hearts, then lead the deuce to partner's Jack—and East's remaining Heart would produce the setting trick.

However, that wasn't what happened. Drury could assure himself a Heart trick, no matter who held the Ace, by covering the Queen with dummy's King. If East took the Ace, his remaining 10-9 would be a certain stopper. But South resisted the temptation. He simply made me a present of the Queen of Hearts, and thereby cut communications between the defending hands.

There was still a forlorn hope. I continued by leading the 2 of Hearts, hoping that Drury might play me for the Queen-Jack and partner for the Ace. But declarer never gave it a thought. He came up with dummy's King to win the trick and bring home a handsome and well-earned game.

EXTRA TRICK The fourth dimension in bridge is the same as in Einstein's theory—though not as difficult to demonstrate. The three trick-winning forces—high cards, long cards and trumps—are strongly controlled by the time factor. In the deal just described, I could see, by reconstructing South's hand, that West did not have time to follow a normal defense. His play of the Heart Queen was an attempt to enlist time on his side; it was foiled by South's timing of the moment he chose to win his high card in Hearts.

North-South vulnerable
West dealer

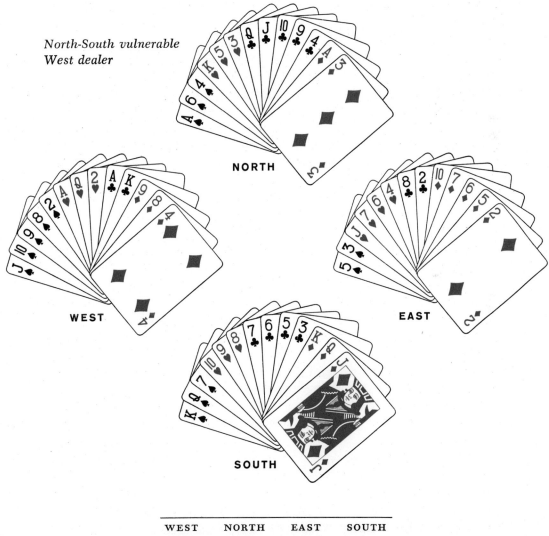

WEST	NORTH	EAST	SOUTH
1♠	DBL	Pass	2NT
Pass	3NT	Pass	Pass
Pass			

Opening lead: Spade Jack

Rules are made to be broken

EVERY time the postman gratefully unloads a substantial portion of his burden on my doorstep, it's a reasonable bet that the most anguished letter will read something like this: "My partner passed my opening 2 bid. Isn't that against the rules?"

Yes, it is against the rules. But it is not against the laws—a difference which isn't always clear in the mind of the average player. The official Laws of Contract Bridge declare how the game must be played. It isn't permissible to violate these laws, and if you do so, even unknowingly, you must pay a penalty. Rules, on the other hand, are simply guides to effective bidding and play. Some, like the rule about responding to a 2 bid, should be obeyed without exception, though there is no penalty save the loss of partner's esteem if you fail to do so. Others should often be ignored. Many a bridge player remains in the mediocre class through blind faith in such old wives' tales as: "second hand low," "never finesse against partner," and "always cover an honor."

At best, these rules are helpful only to the beginner. They cannot take the place of imagination in deciding what to do in a particular case. The following hand provides a simple illustration of what I mean.

West led his deuce of Spades, dummy played low, and East won with the 9. East could have been a hero by shifting to a low Club, thus setting the stage for West to get a Club ruff. (West would soon get in with his Ace of trumps, lead his remaining Club to East's Ace, and ruff the Club return.) But, not being clairvoyant, East returned his singleton trump.

West won and led another Spade, but declarer was now in full control of the situation. He ruffed, drew West's trumps, and still had a trump of his own after knocking out the Club Ace. He lost only to the two Aces and the Spade, and made the game and rubber.

Commiserating with his partner, East admitted he had thought about sacrificing at 4 Spades, and West agreed this would have been a good idea. But they were wrong. No sacrifice was needed. The 4-Diamond contract should have been defeated without any need for heroic measures by East.

The basic flaw in the defense was West's opening lead of the Spade deuce, stemming from blindly following a "rule" of play. Usually, it is correct to lead the lowest card from such a holding in partner's bid suit. But, in view of the bidding, West might have visualized the need to break the rule and lead the Spade Queen. North had bid No Trump after hearing the opposing Spade bids. It was virtually certain that he, not South, had a high Spade. If this was the King, it might be vital for West either to force it out or to hold the lead for a Spade continuation. Forcing declarer to use up a trump or two was particularly attractive because of West's own length in the trump suit.

It can be seen that this proper lead, the Spade Queen, would have scuttled declarer's chances completely—assuming a reasonably careful defense thereafter. Shortening declarer's trumps every time the defenders got in would have been fatal to the contract.

EXTRA TRICK   Never let a rule take the place of considering the individual situation that confronts you. The most important rule to learn is this: No rule is as valuable as knowing the proper time to break it.

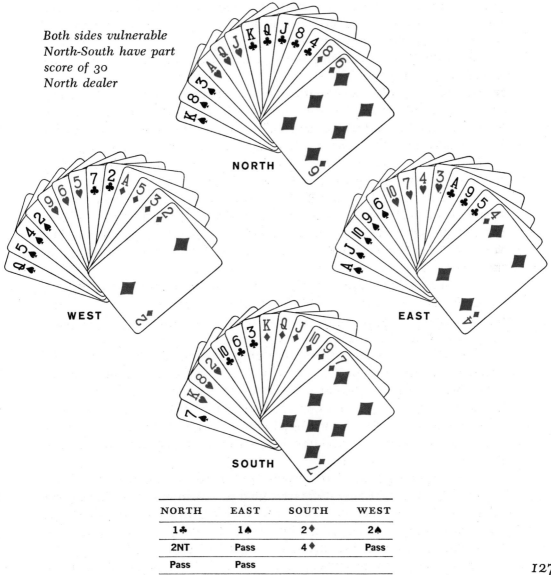

Both sides vulnerable
North-South have part
score of 30
North dealer

NORTH	EAST	SOUTH	WEST
1♣	1♠	2♦	2♠
2NT	Pass	4♦	Pass
Pass	Pass		

The General takes command

GENERAL Alfred M. Gruenther, widely known as "The Brain," is probably the best-qualified bridge player ever to come out of the military service. His connection with the game goes back to the early thirties, when he was a mere first lieutenant serving as an instructor at West Point and directed the most important bridge tournaments in this country. He set a standard with these tournaments which has not since been excelled. Although (or perhaps because) he was something of a martinet, Al Gruenther won for himself a measure of respect and affection among bridge players that has never been approached by anyone else.

As for the General's playing skill—well, I for one consider the following sample impressive.

General Gruenther was South. When his partner managed (by dredging rather deep!) to find the values for a vulnerable takeout double of the Spade bid, the General would have had to demote himself several ranks if he had failed to bid the slam in Diamonds.

East's nonvulnerable leap in Spades was, of course, a desperate effort to forestall drastic enemy action. It was bad bridge for West to double the slam, despite his feeling that he had three suits pretty well tied up. Far from hurting declarer, the double could only have a helpful effect by indicating the exact location of the outstanding strength. Still, it is only fair to observe that few declarers would be able to take full advantage of the information as General Gruenther did.

West led the Spade Queen and, when the anemic dummy was revealed, the General could not be very happy about what he saw. However, in the best tradition of his profession, he settled down for some long-range planning—with excellent effect.

Wasting no time or entries on trump-drawing, at the second trick declarer led the deuce of Hearts. West had to duck or surrender twelve tricks then and there. When dummy's Heart Queen held, declarer discarded his Heart King on North's King of Spades. Then he ruffed a Heart, starting the elimination of that suit. A trump to the 9 permitted the ruffing away of dummy's last Heart, and declarer then led to the trump King to play the Spade 9.

West's opening lead of the Spade Queen had strongly indicated the sequence Q J 10; the General's master plan had been based on that logical inference, plus the fact that West was marked with the King of Clubs. So declarer simply discarded a Club on the Spade 9, giving the trick to West. Now it was up to that defender to "get out" if he could.

Obviously, there was no escape for West. If he led a major-suit card, the

General would ruff in dummy while he got rid of his last Club loser. When West actually elected to return a Club, declarer ducked in dummy and won with his Queen. The only trick General Gruenther lost was one he did not need to surrender but which, when presented to the enemy, maneuvered the latter into a trap from which there was no successful retreat.

EXTRA TRICK   Contrary to the thinking of a good many players, drawing trumps is not always the first order of business. Declarer should give priority to consideration of how best to time his line of play and properly utilize his entries to dummy.

North-South vulnerable
West dealer

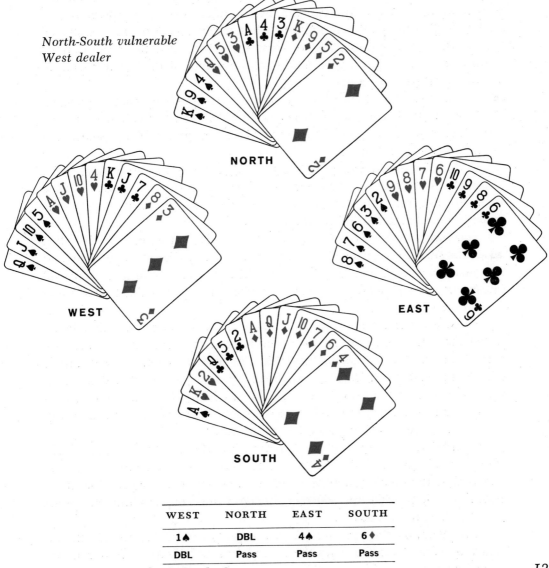

WEST	NORTH	EAST	SOUTH
1♠	DBL	4♠	6♦
DBL	Pass	Pass	Pass

Opening lead: Spade Queen

Bidding isn't the whole story

ITALY's bridge juggernaut, which has dominated world play during recent years, has stirred up a lot of arguments in bridge circles. The disputes are over the virtues of the "Italian System."

Confusion arises from the fact that there is no one Italian system. Italy's team plays two different systems and they are diametrically opposed in principle. Each features an artificial opening bid of 1 Club. But the Roman Club, used by Avarelli and Belladonna, is designed primarily to exchange distributional information, while the Neapolitan Club, employed by the others, has to do exclusively with high-card strength. If the Italians themselves cannot agree, then neither technique of bidding would seem to be the royal road to success.

In the following hand from a World Championship match between the U.S. and Italy, it is obvious that bidding skill can be evaluated only by what happens in the play. With the U.S. team sitting North-South, the auction went as shown.

It should be observed that South's 2-Spade bid was well calculated, although his Spade suit was none too strong. North recognized it as a forward-going bid, and his raise to 3 Spades, though rather aggressive, evoked the admiration of spectators.

Thus encouraged, South (Sam Fry) properly carried on to game. But when the dummy was spread, it appeared that the United States pair had not made a sound investment. Even allowing for a winning Diamond finesse, declarer faced the loss of a Club trick and the possible loss of three tricks in trumps.

Because communication problems were acute, declarer immediately led the Spade 6 from dummy in the vague hope that "something would happen." It should be mentioned here that Fry played extremely well during the championship matches, but with this gesture he abandoned the contract. East's 9 forced South's 10 and West's King. The Jack and Queen dropped under West's Ace, but West's 8-spot was good for a third trump trick, and the Ace of Clubs was the setting card.

I don't mind if you charge to system failure the lack of the Spade Jack, which would have provided a reasonable chance for the contract. Yet the fact is that the combination of cards as they stood, if properly handled, affords a valid play for the contract. Declarer must hope to find West with A J, K J or A K x in Spades.

After winning the opening lead with the Queen of Hearts, he should lead a low Club. East wins with the 10 and returns a Heart, won in dummy. Declarer ruffs a low Club, as the Ace drops from West. Now a low Spade is led toward dummy, and West wins with the King. No matter what he returns, the Queen of Spades will now topple the missing honors. And, since West has the King of Diamonds, he cannot avoid putting declarer into his own hand to draw the last trump. South makes 4 Spades for a plus of 420 instead of a minus of 50.

EXTRA TRICK   In rubber bridge it usually pays to bid all close games, even though the prospects for fulfilling the contract may be somewhat less than even. The reward for success is considerably greater than the loss incurred for going set–provided, of course, that the opponents don't double.

East-West vulnerable
West dealer

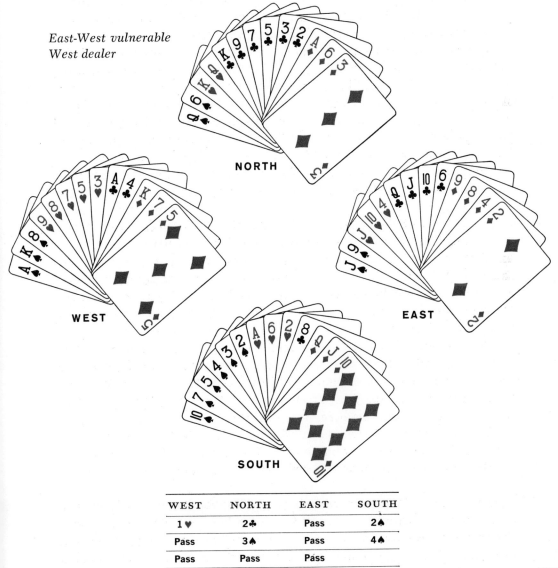

WEST	NORTH	EAST	SOUTH
1♥	2♣	Pass	2♠
Pass	3♠	Pass	4♠
Pass	Pass	Pass	

Opening lead: Heart 9

A museum piece in Spades

UNDERLEADING Aces against a suit contract has, through the years, boomeranged too often to be among the most favored of opening leads. Occasionally, however, a surprise attack of this kind will be successful, especially if the dummy hand has bid No Trump or taken some other action suggesting possession of the King in the suit under consideration.

But, if underleading the Ace is a rarity, underleading both the Ace and King of a suit should rank as a museum piece. With an uneasy feeling that I am about to cause the more adventurous among my readers to lose thousands of points, let me recount a deal in which West produced this rare gambit with spectacular success. I don't dare describe it without warning that the tactic should be used only in a dire emergency.

There was an "off key" note in the bidding. South opened with 1 Spade and North chose to respond with 2 No Trump, although he held four of partner's suit. Technically, he was 1 point short of the requirements, but his even distribution militated in favor of the short road to game.

South cheerfully accepted the No-Trump contract, for which his hand was best suited, and then North had a sudden change of heart and proceeded to 4 Spades—a bit of judgment which we regard as of doubtful soundness. With balanced distribution and all suits stopped, distinct preference should be given to No Trump, even with four of partner's suit.

With an ear tuned closely to the bidding, West concluded that the Queen of Hearts would be found in the dummy to provide dummy's stopper in that suit. He concluded, too, that on straightforward play the prospects for defeating the contract were not bright, for East could hardly be expected to produce two tricks.

West decided that drastic measures were called for—namely, a low-Heart lead—and it came forth accompanied by a prayer. The effect was spectacular. Declarer played the 9 from dummy in the hope that West had led from the King-Jack. This appears to have been the proper play. East won with the Jack and the defense cashed three tricks in the suit.

Then came the thirteenth Heart and East ruffed with the 10 of Spades, forcing declarer's Queen and promoting West's Jack to winning rank.

West's spectacular underlead had gained not just one trick, but two.

EXTRA TRICK Frequently with 4–3–3–3 distribution it is advisable to avoid offering partner a direct raise even when you have four trumps. Evenly balanced hands tend to play just as well at No Trump as in a suit. Remember that 4–3–3–3 should be considered a flaw whenever a hand is being evaluated as a potential dummy, and 1 point must be deducted.

North-South vulnerable
South dealer

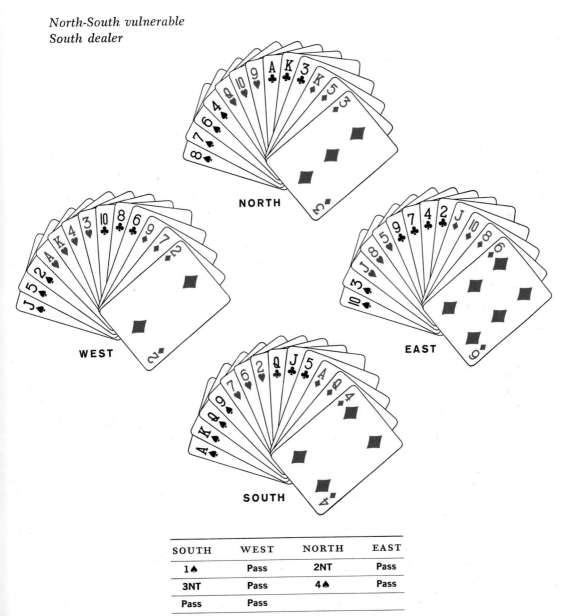

NORTH

WEST

EAST

SOUTH

SOUTH	WEST	NORTH	EAST
1♠	Pass	2NT	Pass
3NT	Pass	4♠	Pass
Pass	Pass		

Opening lead: Heart 3

Saved by a psychic

THE deal shown at right first saw daylight in a Florida State Championship, where the team play was at board-a-match. In this type of competition, each deal represents a match which is won, lost or tied, exactly as in match play in golf. Losing a board by 10 points or losing it by 2,000 costs the same—the loss of one match. Obviously the teams get all they can out of each deal.

All of which sets the stage for the story of this hand.

It will serve no purpose to recount how my partner and I got to a 2-Heart contract with the East-West cards, resulting in a three-trick set that cost us 300 points. It seemed impossible for our teammates to match this result by scoring 300 points against the more logical 2-Spade contract we assumed would be reached at the other table. A double-dummy opening of the Diamond Ace would have to be followed up by play that insured three Diamond ruffs by South and a Club ruff by North, in addition to collecting the two Aces and the King in the black suits. This was too much to expect, so we chalked up the board as irretrievably lost.

However, I had not counted on my irrepressible teammate, Harry Harkavy of Miami Beach. Holding the South hand against vulnerable opponents, he opened with a psychic bid of 1 Club, and the auction went as shown in the diagram.

West's 2-Spade bid was pre-emptive. North came in with 3 Diamonds, and West, when this was passed around to him, realized that South had perpetrated a fraud. His double was passed around to South who, in desperation, ran to 3 Hearts. This looked to East like money from home and he took appropriate action.

West opened the King of Spades. Harkavy won the trick with dummy's Ace and embarked upon a cross ruff. He played the Ace of Diamonds and ruffed a Diamond. He cashed the King and Ace of Clubs and ruffed a Club in dummy. He ruffed another Diamond in his own hand and then ruffed the fourth Club in dummy. This brought his total to eight tricks, and East, who had helplessly followed suit thus far, retained his five trumps headed by the three top honors.

South had left only three trumps headed by the 10, but a Diamond lead from dummy assured him of winning a ninth trick. If East trumped low, South would overruff; when East trumped high, South discarded a Spade and waited to make his 10 of Hearts on the third trump lead.

EXTRA TRICK Let me warn adventuresome readers that psychic and rescue bids seldom turn out as well as Harkavy's did here. Risking a big disaster is permissible only in board-a-match play where the biggest loss in any deal is a single point.

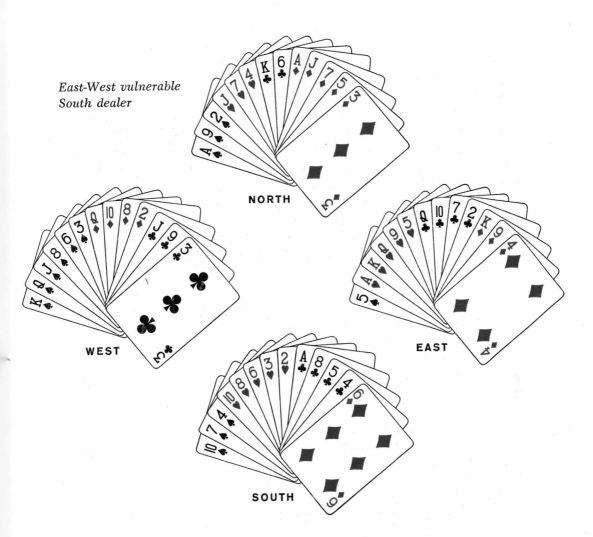

East-West vulnerable
South dealer

NORTH

WEST

EAST

SOUTH

SOUTH	WEST	NORTH	EAST
1♣	2♠	3♦	Pass
Pass	DBL	Pass	Pass
3♥	Pass	Pass	DBL
Pass	Pass	Pass	

Opening lead: Spade King

135

Getting off to a good start

AN extraordinary number of players appear to delight in doing things the hard way. I sometimes get the impression that they purposely start badly for the sheer pleasure of effecting a dramatic return from the dead.

A good or bad start at bridge often consists simply of the opening lead. It is generally agreed that some hands call for neutral leads. These are the hands on which one must take care to avoid the loss of a trick. There are other hands where time is the essential factor. Sometimes the bidding has suggested that declarer may be able to obtain discards on some good suit, so an attacking lead is indicated. There is still another type of lead, more difficult to classify, which is illustrated by the following hand.

It is our view that the bidding of all the players was above reproach.

It may seem odd that I have endorsed South's 4-Spade bid, since it could have been beaten 800 points. I do endorse it, however, for several reasons: (1) South had seven cold tricks in his own hand, and with North marked short in Hearts, South would not need much luck to make another trick or two by way of Heart ruffs, even if the dummy turned up without a face card. (2) It was likely, from where South sat, that the opponents would make their 4-Heart contract for game and rubber. Observe that they would have done just that if East had taken the Spade finesse for a Diamond discard. (3) The human element is not to be overlooked. Even though it is true that the bid of 4 Spades could, with ideal defense, have been soundly thrashed, in real life that caliber of defense is not always produced.

West, recalling only that partner had bid Hearts, opened the 6 of that suit—and for the rest of the play he might just as well have been sitting it out. South won with the Heart Ace, cashed the Diamond Ace and ruffed a Heart, then pitched his two Clubs on dummy's top Diamonds. A Club and Heart crossruff followed in close order, and declarer was quite gracious about giving West a couple of trump tricks. 4 Spades bid and doubled, with 5-odd made, gave North-South a very pleasing score.

In order to reap the maximum penalty, West had to lead Clubs (and East, of course, would return his singleton trump)—but such an opening lead must be regarded as double-dummy, and West is not open to criticism for being less than clairvoyant. But it was clear from East's pre-emptive Heart leap and South's 4-level overcall that freakish conditions might well be present, and so it was indispensable for West to get a look at dummy. The safe and sane way to do that was by laying down the Ace of trumps.

There is nothing second-sighted about this observation. Granted, few players even consider the lead of the Ace from an Ace-Queen-small combination, but that is because most players are creatures of habit. West had two Spade tricks, and he would still have them if he led the Ace. He would not be forced to continue the suit—he would do so only if the view of dummy made it advisable, as it would in this case. It would be logical enough to lead another trump even though it sacrificed the Queen; but even if West shifted to Clubs he would beat the contract one trick.

EXTRA TRICK   There should be no compulsion about leading the suit partner has bid. Sometimes it should actually be avoided.

Both sides vulnerable
West dealer

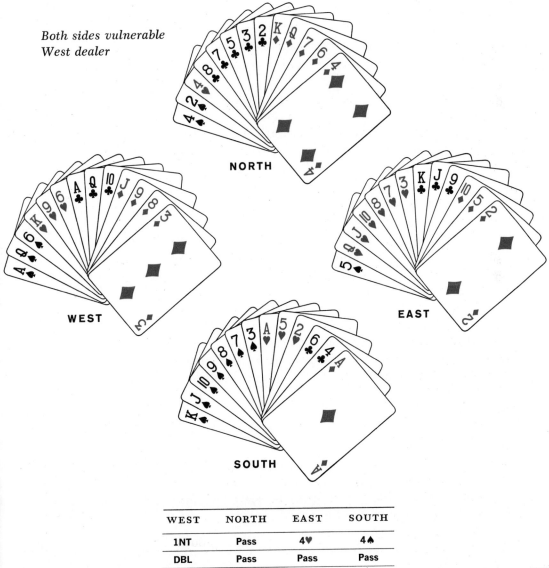

WEST	NORTH	EAST	SOUTH
1NT	Pass	4♥	4♠
DBL	Pass	Pass	Pass

Opening lead: Heart 6

Reserved for a convention

WHILE there appears to be a wide range between the modest bid of 1 Club and the ultimate high of 7 No Trump, there are, in fact, only 35 possible bids—excluding such calls as Pass and Double. To the average player this affords plenty of room for maneuver, and he is quite willing to fence off one of these bids—the one labeled 4 No Trump—as reserved exclusively for Mr. Blackwood. Any time the auction enters that particular area, it signals a call for Aces.

There is much to be said for this policy on grounds of both consistency and simplicity. To the expert, however, 35 notes is a none-too-ample bidding scale, and he is loath to surrender any one bid to a single use.

The following hand features the partnership employment of a 4 No-Trump bid, not as part of a convention requesting a display of Aces, but in its natural sense. Observe how North-South put it into operation.

North's opening bid of 1 Club elicited from South a bid of 1 Heart, a response as pleasant as it was unexpected. Obviously the hand had slam possibilities, and North replied with a jump shift. A jump in a new suit in this sequence of bids demands a game and at the same time suggests that a slam may be around the corner.

There is a certain risk attached to these fake bids in a higher-ranking suit, since partner may raise the second suit with distressing enthusiasm. North felt he could take the chance. If South raised Spades with any degree of violence, North's general strength assured a reasonably safe retreat into a high No-Trump contract. The important consideration was to make the slam suggestion before the game level had been passed.

On the second round South chose to return to 3 Clubs, intending to allay any fears partner might have about the complexion of his first-bid suit. North then jumped to 4 Hearts, and South's bid of 4 Spades, with Hearts definitely established as trumps, was an attempt to announce the King of that suit.

Then came the pivotal bid of the deal, North's 4 No-Trump call, which was not intended as a request for Aces. (Had North wished to ask for Aces, he would have done so on an earlier round.) It was meant to be a natural bid advertising a quick Diamond stopper.

North was unwilling to contract for slam himself, for fear that a Diamond opening through the King might yield two fast tricks to the enemy. Possession of the Queen of Diamonds made it clear to South that only one Diamond trick could be lost, since partner was marked with the King. So South contracted for 6 Hearts and won the slam handily.

EXTRA TRICK In long-established partnerships, it makes good sense to get maximum mileage out of every bid. Nevertheless, I make it a rule to treat every 4 No-Trump bid as Ace-asking unless I have positive knowledge to the contrary. In the rare cases where this assumption may be wrong, it will cost far less than those disasters where partner is left in a ghastly 4 No-Trump contract.

Both sides vulnerable
North dealer

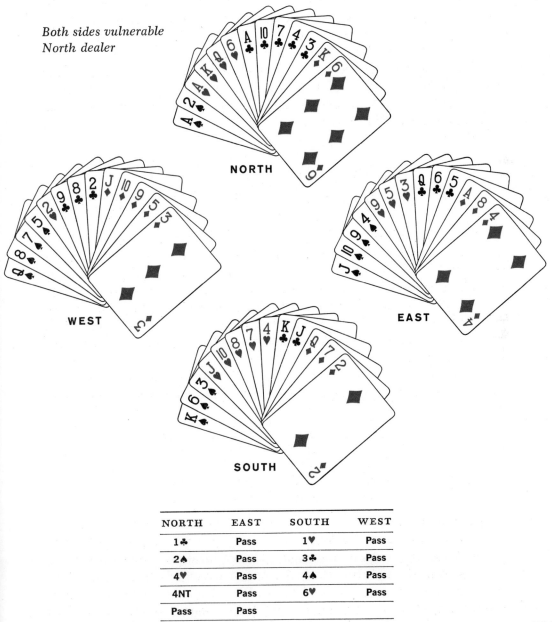

NORTH	EAST	SOUTH	WEST
1♣	Pass	1♥	Pass
2♠	Pass	3♣	Pass
4♥	Pass	4♠	Pass
4NT	Pass	6♥	Pass
Pass	Pass		

Opening lead: Diamond Jack

Pity the poor prognosticator

WHEN commenting on televised bridge matches, part of my role is to predict what I think is going to happen on every deal. It seems to me that the deals on which I issue storm warnings often turn out rather calmly, while those I forecast as rather routine turn out to be as tempestuous as the following combination, which produced a violent swing in a recent team-of-four match played without benefit of television.

If you looked over the layout at right and were asked to predict the result, you might with good reason forecast that either side could make some part score. How wrong you'd be. At the first table where the hand was played, the bidding went:

SOUTH	WEST	NORTH	EAST
Pass	1NT	Pass	2♦
DBL	3♦	Pass	3NT
Pass	Pass	Pass	

North opened his best suit, but unfortunately for him it turned out to be the best play for declarer. His lead of the 6 of Clubs brought out South's Queen and West's Ace. West cashed the Ace of Diamonds, went to dummy with the Diamond Jack and led back the 8 of Clubs. South covered with the 10 and West's Jack forced North's King. North shifted to a low Heart, won by South's Ace. But on South's low Heart return, West played the 6 and the suit was blocked. The contract could not be defeated after the Club opening.

As predictors, you and I are already discredited, but there's worse to follow when the hand is played at the other table. There the bidding goes:

SOUTH	WEST	NORTH	EAST
1♠	DBL	REDBL	2♦
2♥	2NT	DBL	3♦
Pass	Pass	3♠	Pass
4♠	Pass	Pass	Pass

Here the teammates of the players who had bid and made game with the East-West cards at the other table were now playing for game with the North-South hands. As the result of a beautiful play, they made it.

West won the first trick with the Ace of Diamonds. South ruffed the Diamond continuation, and led trumps, West winning the second round. South trumped the third Diamond and, before daring to draw West's last trump, took a Heart finesse to dummy's 10. When this succeeded he drew the rest of the trumps, incidentally exhausting his own, and ran the rest of the Heart suit. Now dummy, declarer and—fortunately for the success of the contract—West were left with nothing but Clubs.

This was where South made the winning play. Figuring West for the Jack of Clubs as well as the Ace, South led the Queen from his hand. If West ducked, declarer would simply lead next toward dummy's King. It did no good for West to win the first Club lead, however. He now had to lead away from his Jack, and declarer captured the last two tricks with his Club 10 and dummy's Club King. That "part score" hand of ours turned out to produce game both ways of the table and a swing of 1,220 points!

EXTRA TRICK   Notice the advantage of opening the bidding with a light hand that includes distributional strength and both majors. Much of the swing on this deal can be traced to South's pass at the first table.

Both sides vulnerable
South dealer

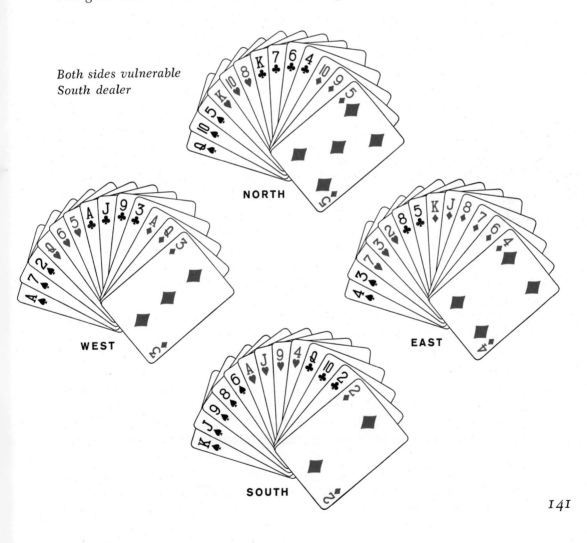

A good game of Hearts

I HAVE a good memory for faces—especially those on a deck of cards. But in the course of a few hundred thousand bridge tables, I must confess that I have encountered a host of temporary bridge companions whose identity remains cloaked behind the anonymity of such names as West, North or East. The following story was related to me by a Mr. South, and I'll try to tell it to you much as I enjoyed it at firsthand.

"You've played the game of Hearts, haven't you, Charlie?" South began. I admitted that I had taken an occasional hand in that pastime, where the object is to avoid winning tricks which include Hearts, because each one counts against you, and especially to avoid winning the Queen of Spades because that dark lady counts 13 all by herself. "Let me show you a bridge hand that is more like Hearts," he said.

"I had eight Hearts to the deuce," my friend began, as he took a deck of cards and laid out the deal at right.

When a player describes his hand as "eight to the deuce," it usually means that he came up with far less than his share of the world's goods. So I was surprised to see that Mr. South had been reasonably well endowed by whatever goddess directs the distribution of cards. His final contract of 4 Hearts was quite reasonable, though, as events turned out, it would have been profitable for East and West to sacrifice at 4 Spades. I am grateful that the opponents failed to do so, since it would have cost me this story.

"I haven't had so much fun on any hand since I played Hearts," he continued. "I let the opening lead of the Queen of Diamonds hold the trick and West continued by cashing the Ace of Spades. Then he shifted to the 6 of Clubs. Inevitably, I won with the Ace and faced the dark prospect of a dummy containing three good tricks but with no visible means of reaching them."

One thing was certain: West did not have another Diamond. Another inference seemed reasonable: since West had been dealt only one Diamond, it was not unlikely that he held three trumps. Cashing the Ace and King of Hearts turned that likelihood into a certainty. But West was evidently a player of some Hearts experience himself. He had no desire to win a trick with the Queen of Hearts when he would have no way to get out of his hand except by passing the lead to dummy—thus insuring that declarer would make his contract. So he dropped the Queen of Hearts under South's King.

Now you are able to see, as I did, why South began describing his hand as "eight Hearts to the deuce." I'll let South complete his own story.

"Here is where the fun came in," he said. "As they say in Hearts, I 'stiffed' him in with the deuce of Hearts and he was forced to give dummy the lead and let me win the rest.

"When West won a trick with his 3 of Hearts, he looked like a man who had just had to pay for the Queen of Spades. . . . And he did."

EXTRA TRICK   Sometimes the burden of leading may be fatal. In such cases you will find it more advantageous to give than to receive.

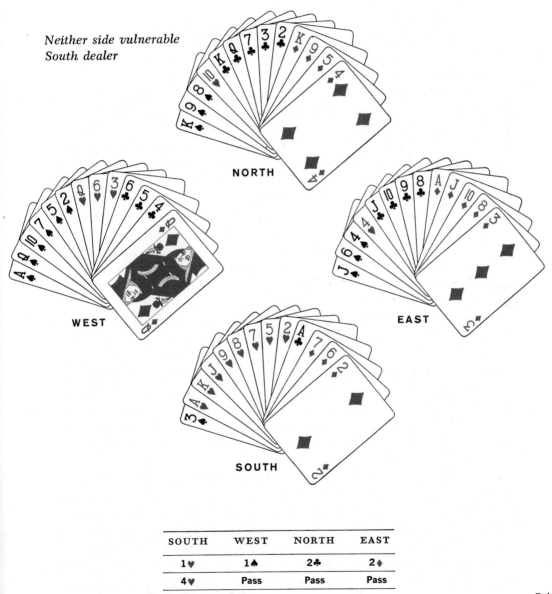

Neither side vulnerable
South dealer

NORTH

WEST

EAST

SOUTH

SOUTH	WEST	NORTH	EAST
1♥	1♠	2♣	2♦
4♥	Pass	Pass	Pass

Opening lead: Diamond Queen

Trapped by a winning trick

THE ordinary bridge table is something less than a square yard in area and has a surface that is reasonably flat and not too slippery. Sit down to play, however, and you soon discover the inadequacy of this description. The playing arena is actually honeycombed with pitfalls waiting to swallow up the gullible or the careless.

It wouldn't be easy to map all these pitfalls, but I can at least warn you against the apparently bottomless one into which Mr. and Mrs. Average Player drop a large proportion of their contracts. They vanish not into space but into the chasm of the fourth dimension—time.

Here's a typical case in which two players decided correctly what they had to do, but failed to take into account *when* they should do it.

Some of this country's experienced players would frown on South's 4 No-Trump bid in the sequence shown. In their personal style of bidding, this would not be a Blackwood call for Aces but merely a raise to No Trump. In my view, however, these players labor under a self-imposed handicap. While a bidder may occasionally wish to give a delicate, non-forcing raise in No Trump above the game level, in countless instances he wishes to find out about his partner's Aces and, sometimes, his Kings.

Thus, I am quite convinced that any 4 No-Trump bid which follows upon a previous display of great strength—e.g., South's 2-Spade jump response to the opening Heart bid—should be treated as part of the Blackwood Convention demanding information about Aces.

But let's move on from the bidding. The small-slam contract was a reasonably good sporting venture, though it could have been beaten by a Club lead. Lacking the benefit of second sight, West failed to open a Club. The Heart Queen appeared a safer choice, despite North's bid of that suit. And, with South's cooperation, this lead proved an effective thrust. Without hesitation, declarer reached for the Heart King. Then he drew trumps and led his remaining Heart to the Ace. Next, he ruffed a Heart in the optimistic hope that the suit would break. When that bubble burst, he ended up a trick short of his goal.

Since the odds were distinctly against the three-three break of the six missing Hearts, it should have been apparent from the outset that the line of play chosen was not the best way to establish the long Heart without which declarer had no chance to win a twelfth trick. In fact, South booted the contract at the very first trick when he captured the opening lead.

South's plan could succeed only if the Hearts were equally divided. By enlisting time on his side, he could have won the slam if the Hearts broke no worse than four-two. The winning play would have been to duck West's lead. Observe how easy the play is after that duck. Let West shift to Clubs; it doesn't matter. South wins, draws trumps, leads his other Heart to the Ace, and now his ruff of a low Heart sets up the suit.

EXTRA TRICK   Millions of bridge players are addicted to the same unfortunate habit: they play to the first trick before giving real thought to the over-all play. Form a plan when the dummy goes down—not when you have already made a play that wrecks the contract.

Both sides vulnerable
North dealer

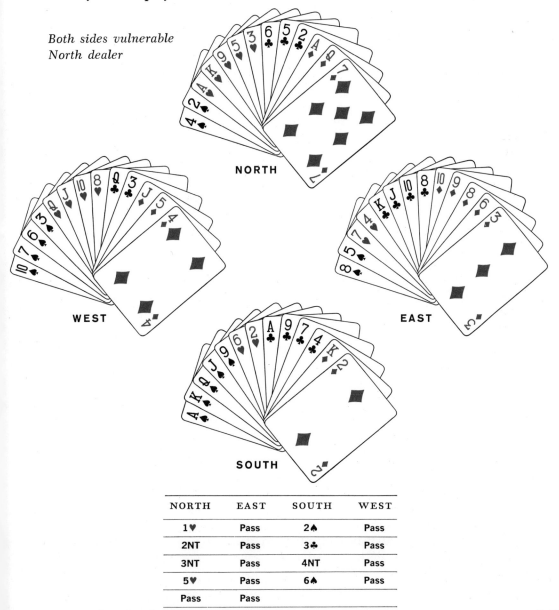

NORTH	EAST	SOUTH	WEST
1♥	Pass	2♠	Pass
2NT	Pass	3♣	Pass
3NT	Pass	4NT	Pass
5♥	Pass	6♠	Pass
Pass	Pass		

Opening lead: Heart Queen

I'd like some more

EUROPEANS, as no U.S. tournament player need be reminded, played exciting bridge during the 1950's. A fine example was this hand contested by the Italian and English teams in the European championship held at Oslo in 1958. Italy won the title for the third successive year, but only after a staunch fight by both France and Great Britain, whose teams were barely edged out.

It may or may not be significant that the British style is the very antithesis of the highly artificial methods then favored by the Italians. In the deal shown here, Britain was dumped by observing one convention and saved because it disregarded another.

In the room where Great Britain held the North-South cards, Alan Truscott, in fourth position, opened the North hand with 3 No Trump. Many British players use this opening bid as a strategic gamble with a hand that includes a long, solid minor suit. Without quarreling with this general strategy, I am not inclined to recommend it on this particular holding. Although partner has passed, the hand has great potentialities for slam, which may be investigated if he is offered an opportunity to participate in the discussion.

It may be argued that Mr. Truscott was the victim of an unkind fate—not because Diamonds were led, but because the East and West holdings were not reversed. Had East held West's six-card suit, the normal lead of the Diamond Jack would have given declarer enough tricks to leave several over for the next deal. However, East was on lead with the weaker holding in the suit. He led the 4 of Diamonds. West's Ace dropped North's King, the defenders ran six tricks, and Britain went set 200 points.

It was a fortunate thing for the British in the other room that they were not using—or rather abusing—the set of signals known as the suit-preference convention, enslavement to which (or rather a misunderstanding of which) has cost its users a great many points. In that other room the Italians, seated North-South, arrived at their proper slam contract—in Spades.

West opened the Ace of Diamonds, and East signaled with the 9. There is a certain group of convention mongers who would read this as a suit-preference signal, but I do not subscribe to that doctrine. The suit-preference convention, which provides that the play of a high card to partner's lead calls for a shift to the higher-ranking side suit, applies only when it is clearly indicated that a shift is called for. There are many times when third hand wishes his partner to continue the suit he has opened, and the natural way to effect that is by the play of a high card. In some cases, it will be plain that the third hand cannot desire a continuation, and then his discard *will* direct the shift.

In this case the defenders had a perfect understanding. East's play of the Diamond 9 called for more of the same suit, and when the 7 of Spades was used by dummy to ruff the Diamond continuation, East was assured of a trump trick to beat the slam.

Collecting their 100-point penalty halved the British net loss on this deal. Had the British players been suit-preference fanatics, West might have shifted to Hearts, which would have presented Italy with the slam.

EXTRA TRICK The most successful conventions are the simple ones. Outside of "top expert" circles it is enough, when partner leads a suit, to have your low card say "Stop" and your high card shout "I'd like some more."

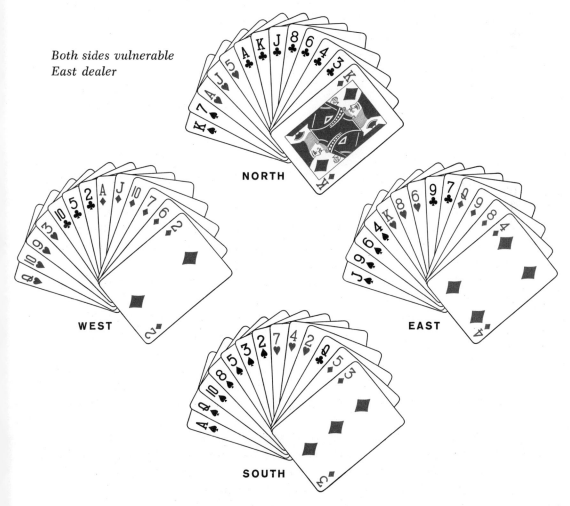

Both sides vulnerable
East dealer

NORTH

WEST

EAST

SOUTH

147

Now you see it, now you don't

ANY good professional thief knows that the easiest way to deceive an intended victim is to center his attention on any object other than the one to be stolen. This is the art of the magician, who attracts his audience's gaze to one hand while the other does its trickery. It is also the art of some good bridge players.

In the hand shown at right, South, the declarer, succeeded in focusing the opposition's attention on one suit to the complete neglect of the other.

The bidding is recorded as it took place. It will be seen that there are four top-card tricks "off" the hand, which immediately disqualifies the contract for a seal of approval. However, the hand is so constructed that it appears difficult to avoid gliding into the game contract.

The first round of bidding is normal, and South is justified, I think, in making one more try for game, despite his partner's indifferent response. Some players would show the Diamond suit in the hope that this might lead to a successful No-Trump contract, or at least help partner to determine whether or not there is a fit. However, South's choice turned out to be a happier one.

North should really pass the 3-Spade bid because he has so little playing strength. But the fifth trump has a strange psychological effect on most players, though it is plain to be seen that in hands like this it is just so much surplus.

West led the 10 of Hearts. East won with the Ace and returned the suit. Declarer went up with the King and immediately played the Jack of Hearts. It was clear that the contract was doomed to failure unless the enemy's attention could be diverted from the Club suit when the Ace of trumps was driven out. So, on the Jack of Hearts declarer discarded a Diamond from dummy.

When West took the Ace of trumps he was mindful of the speed with which declarer had disposed of one of dummy's Diamonds, and concluded that that was the weak spot in the hand. He therefore shifted to the 10 of Diamonds. This was taken by declarer with the Queen. The trumps were drawn and two of dummy's Clubs discarded on South's good Diamonds. West had been thrown off the scent. Whether or not he should have been is another story.

EXTRA TRICK The declarer's play on this hand illustrates, among other things, the psychological value of holding forth boldly even though the outlook is very dim. As in almost every other field, success in bridge often falls to the side that exerts the last extra bit of effort.

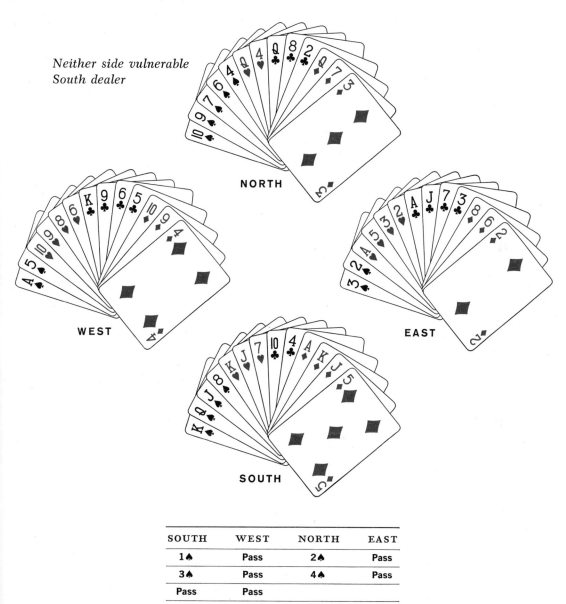

Neither side vulnerable
South dealer

SOUTH	WEST	NORTH	EAST
1♠	Pass	2♠	Pass
3♠	Pass	4♠	Pass
Pass	Pass		

Opening lead: Heart 10

149

Nice guys finish first

THE literature of every sport is replete with examples of trickery resorted to by players who will win at any cost. Fortunately for every such player, there are dozens who scorn victory unless it comes with honor.

In bridge it is not exceptional for nice guys to finish first. One who has —and often—is my good friend and frequent partner, Harry Fishbein of New York. Fishbein can always be counted on for a good story about a hand. This hand, which he played some years ago, is as fresh as when it was dealt to him and it proves an excellent point.

Fishbein, playing South, gave it everything he had during the bidding. After his modest 1-Diamond opening, he made a jump shift rebid of 3 Clubs. North then showed that his free bid in Spades included good support in Diamonds. Although South's cue bid then impaired the value of North's King of Hearts, he had sufficient values to justify showing his King of Clubs. Fishbein's leap to 7 exemplifies a kind of daring which is not foreign to his nature. Perhaps his two little Spades should have been a sobering influence. But then there would have been no story had he turned conservative.

If West had led the Ace of Hearts, declarer would have had an easy time. Dummy's Heart King would have provided the needed parking place for South's small Spade, and South's losing Club would have been ruffed in dummy. The 9 of Spades lead made matters much more difficult. But it, too, helped to guide declarer to the winning play.

Normally, Fishbein's hope would be to find West with the Queen and Jack of Spades as well as the Ace of Hearts, and to squeeze him out of his possessions. But, since the 9 of Spades lead marked East with the Spade honors, Fishbein projected his squeeze in that direction. By reversing dummy—making the dummy the long-trump hand—he was able to discard his losing Spade on dummy's long trump and cash twelve tricks without trumping a Club.

He won the Spade opening with dummy's Ace and trumped a Heart with the 9 of Diamonds. A low Diamond to dummy's 8 enabled South to ruff another Heart with an honor. Declarer went back to dummy's Queen of Diamonds to play North's King of Hearts and ruff it. He then cashed his high Diamond and high Spade.

Declarer's remaining cards were the Spade 3 and his four Clubs. Dummy held two Clubs, the 6 of Diamonds and the 10–8 of Spades. East held four Clubs and the Queen of Spades, and was ripe for the pressure play. South led a Club to dummy's King and cashed North's remaining trump. East had to hold the Queen of Spades to cover dummy's 10-spot, so was compelled to yield a Club. Fishbein discarded his last Spade and won the three remaining tricks with the Ace, Queen and 5 of Clubs, to make his daring grand slam.

EXTRA TRICK If the dummy has a reasonably good trump holding, declarer will sometimes find it profitable to visualize himself as sitting across the table. In that case he will strive to establish partner's hand and treat his own as dummy.

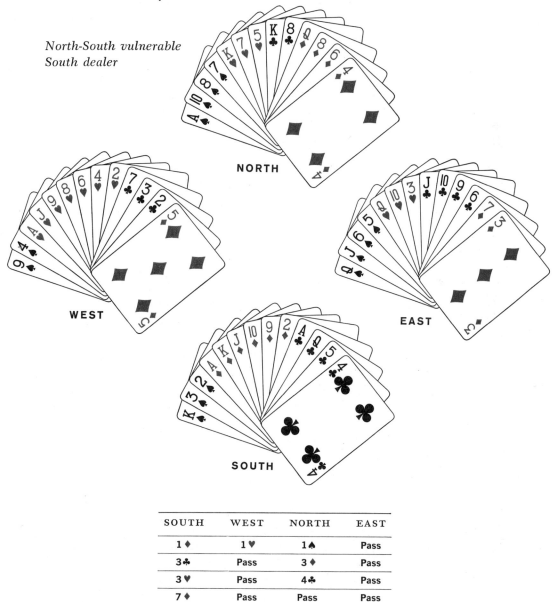

North-South vulnerable
South dealer

NORTH

WEST

EAST

SOUTH

SOUTH	WEST	NORTH	EAST
1 ♦	1 ♥	1 ♠	Pass
3 ♣	Pass	3 ♦	Pass
3 ♥	Pass	4 ♣	Pass
7 ♦	Pass	Pass	Pass

Opening lead: Spade 9

151

He didn't heed his own advice

THE switcheroo is a device that makes an old story new. For example, there's the bewhiskered tale of the chap who wanted to unload some stock and started a rumor that the company had struck oil. His rumor traveled fast and far. He heard it so often that instead of selling he bought more.

The switcheroo would go like this. The company actually does strike oil. But this person says, "No chestnut like that catches little ol' me. I'm the guy who started the rumor." In a way, that is what happened to East in the deal at right when, having convinced his partner that desperate measures were required, he began to doubt his own advice.

A delicate touch characterized the bidding up to the point where North made his slightly overenthusiastic commitment. South's modest bid of 1 Club and North's response of 1 Spade gave no hint of the oncoming fury. South's rebid of 2 Diamonds is a reasonable choice. With a somewhat touchy holding in both majors, he elected to describe a strong hand containing nine cards in the minors. (Strong, because he had bid a higher-ranking suit at the 2 level; nine cards, because when a player reverses in touching suits he always shows that the lower-ranking is longer.)

North clung to the delicate treatment with a rebid of his six-card Spade suit. South then thought it high time he contracted for game, and North decided to stop fencing. The reverse bid of 2 Diamonds, coupled with the jump bid in No Trump, was sufficient to incite him to drastic action. While he could not place his fingers on 33 points, he was influenced by the value of a six-card suit opposite a strong hand.

It seems to me that the character of his six-card suit might have induced a more cautious attitude. The bidding had shown South to hold at most two Spades. (He needed at least two Hearts to hold a stopper in that suit, since North knew he didn't have the Ace, and he had already announced five Clubs and four Diamonds.) East had two good reasons for doubling the 6 No-Trump bid. His holding in Spades guaranteed the contract if that suit were led, and his double of a slam bid called for the lead of dummy's suit, which was exactly what East wanted.

West dutifully led a Spade. East won the trick and began to suffer the twin onslaughts of doubt and greed. Maybe the Spade lead hadn't been necessary after all. Maybe partner had an honor in Clubs. Even if he didn't, South's five Club tricks, three Diamonds and three Hearts would total only eleven tricks. So, ignoring his own warning, East returned a Club.

But East had been absolutely right in the first place, as he soon discovered. When declarer ran five Clubs and three Hearts, East could not find two discards. He could spare one little Diamond, but on the next trick he could not give up either a Diamond or a Spade without simultaneously giving up the ghost. For, when East parted with a Diamond on the third Heart, South discarded his Jack of Spades and his Diamonds were high.

EXTRA TRICK   Observe that it takes the Spade lead to sink the contract. With any other lead East succumbs to the same squeeze. If he lets go a high Spade, declarer establishes a Spade trick. If he bares down to three Diamonds, declarer has twelve tricks without winning a Spade.

Neither side vulnerable
South dealer

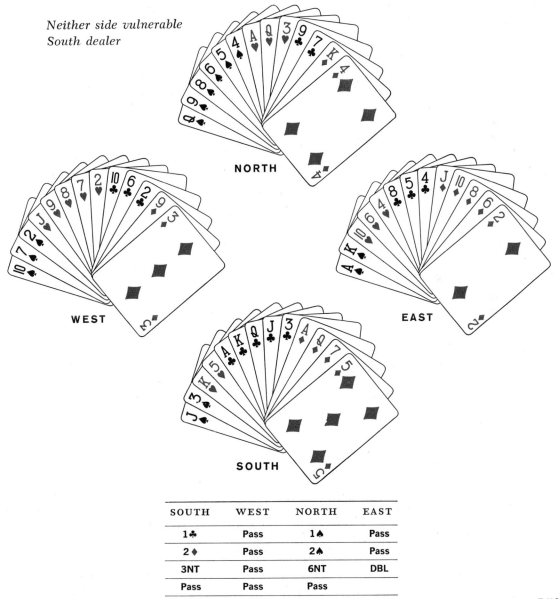

SOUTH	WEST	NORTH	EAST
1♣	Pass	1♠	Pass
2♦	Pass	2♠	Pass
3NT	Pass	6NT	DBL
Pass	Pass	Pass	

Opening lead: Spade 2

How to bet a tossup

THE origin of many popular terms is cloaked in mystery, but there can be little doubt why an even chance is often referred to as a tossup. But is the toss of a coin ever really a strictly even chance?

Consider, for example, the case of the penny that comes up heads on twelve consecutive tosses. How would you bet on the thirteenth toss? If you are with the majority, you would bet on tails, figuring it was about time for the tide to turn. But if you are a realist (or cynic) you would bet on heads again, figuring—until convinced otherwise—that there might just happen to be a bit more weight on one side of the penny.

The expert's edge at the bridge table does not need to be much more than the ability to sense which side of the tossup happens to be carrying that little bit of extra weight—as in the following hand.

If there were flaws in the bidding, it would have required the perfect opening lead—a Diamond—to point them up. Assured of a 10-point minimum in North's hand by the response of 2 Clubs, South was amply justified in his forcing jump rebid in Spades. North, on his part, had too much over that minimum to bid merely 4 Spades, so he made a raise beyond game to invite a slam. And South, with three Aces, had the control cards North's bid seemed to be asking for.

West briefly toyed with the thought of opening a trump, but he discarded that idea for an excellent reason. The bidding warned him that North's Club suit would furnish a flock of discards once the Ace had been driven out. It was necessary, therefore, to find the setting trick in a hurry.

But as it developed, the Heart suit was not the place to find it. South won the first lead with his Jack of Hearts, drew trumps, knocked out the Ace of Clubs and got rid of his Diamond loser on dummy's Jack of Clubs to bring home his slam.

"I guessed wrong," apologized West. "It seemed a tossup whether you had the King of Hearts or the Queen of Diamonds, and there was a slight advantage in the Heart lead because it would not throw away a trick if you had the Jack of Hearts instead of the King."

West's reasoning was true as far as it went. But it would have done him no good merely to save a trick; South, you'll observe, could have made his contract even if he didn't have the Jack of Hearts. West needed to find a defensive trick in a hurry.

Therefore, the only cards that mattered, assuming that the opponents held three Aces, were the King of Hearts and the Queen of Diamonds.

From a strictly mathematical view, there was as good a chance that East had been dealt one of these cards as the other. But West should have figured that there was a little extra weight on one side of the coin.

Why? Because the opponents had reached a slam lacking the 9 high-card points West could see in his own hand and—if that slam could be defeated—another King or Queen which East must hold. To put it simply, there was more chance that partner held a Queen than a King.

EXTRA TRICK   To decide which of two cards your partner is more likely to hold, visualize the strength of declarer's hand lacking one card or the other. The holding that best fits his bidding should give you the answer.

Both sides vulnerable
South dealer

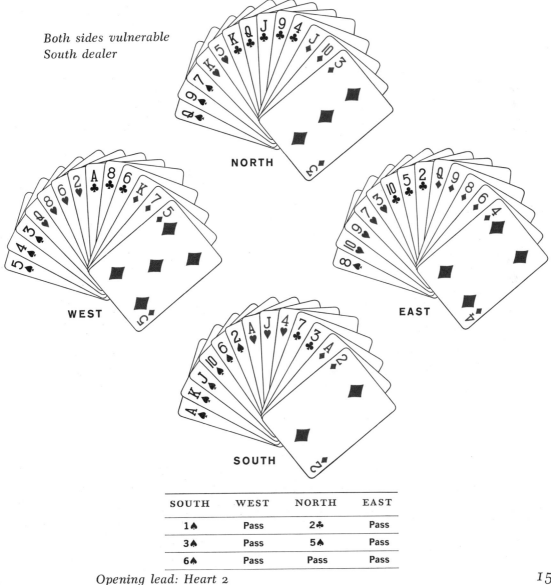

SOUTH	WEST	NORTH	EAST
1♠	Pass	2♣	Pass
3♠	Pass	5♠	Pass
6♠	Pass	Pass	Pass

Opening lead: Heart 2

It's only a question of time

A GOOD many viewers of my TV bridge matches have questioned our style of play. Obviously, in half an hour of telecasting—minus a few minutes for that important angel, the sponsor—only a limited number of hands can be shown. So, even though rubber bridge conditions prevail, the players must adjust their strategy to resemble the style of the sudden-death games enjoyed on commuter trains. When time runs out, we are concerned only with "who's ahead" and the margin of difference is not considered.

Here is a hand from a practice match between show contestants played under these sudden-death rules.

South, Arthur Glatt of Chicago, and his partner, Harold Ogust of New York, were some 400 points behind and the clock made it clear that this was going to be the last deal. Glatt figured that his side could not earn enough points against a 4-Diamond contract (he was right). So, in a do-or-die effort, he stabbed at 4 Hearts. West did not expect a big profit; his double served as a warning to partner not to make a sacrifice bid.

East overtook his partner's Queen of Diamonds and led a second round of the suit, which South trumped. Declarer was sure that the Heart finesse would succeed and not at all certain about the Spade finesse. Yet it was essential for him to play the Jack of Spades before he led trumps.

To see why, let's suppose that Glatt led a Heart immediately, finessing dummy's 10. After cashing the Heart Ace, how would he get back to his hand? A Club lead would allow East to get in with the Queen and return a third round of Diamonds to wreck the contract. The play of the Ace and a low Spade to the Jack could be countered by a low-Club return from West that would force out North's King or else allow East to get the lead at once for the killing Diamond return. Declarer could get one discard on dummy's Spades, but he would be left with two losing Clubs.

But Glatt foresaw this difficulty and met it by leading the Jack of Spades—not a Heart. If West did not cover, declarer would abandon the suit temporarily to cash the Ace and King of Hearts. Then he would repeat the Spade finesse, discard a Club on the Ace of Spades and trump a small one to establish the suit. Declarer could then afford to concede the Queen of Hearts and the Ace of Clubs.

West actually did cover the Jack of Spades when it was led, but it did him no good. North won with the Ace and South now abandoned the trump finesse, which he was certain would win. Instead, he cashed dummy's Ace of Hearts, led the 10 to his King and played the Spade 7. A successful finesse against West's 10-spot permitted South to discard one Club on dummy's Spade Queen, and he was able to set up another discard by trumping the fourth Spade to establish the suit.

By yielding to the pressure imposed by time, Glatt made the winning bid and brought home the contract.

EXTRA TRICK Desperate gambles, while sometimes proper strategy for sudden-death play, are not recommended in ordinary rubber bridge. The big loser in the long run is the player who tries to get even today by bidding as if there were no game tomorrow.

Both sides vulnerable
South dealer

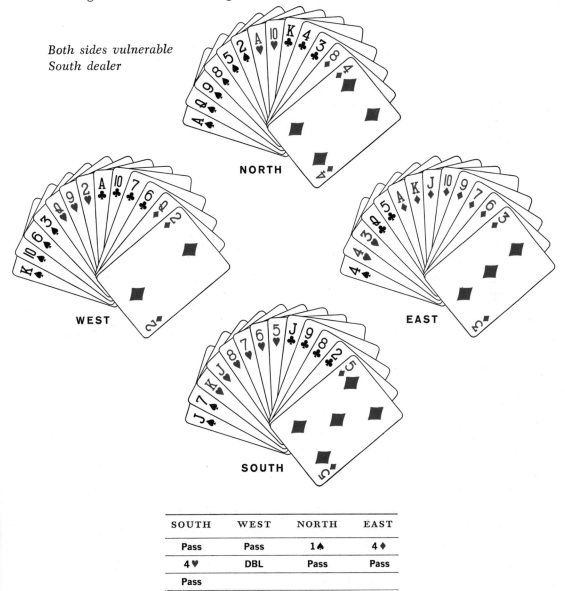

SOUTH	WEST	NORTH	EAST
Pass	Pass	1 ♠	4 ♦
4 ♥	DBL	Pass	Pass
Pass			

Opening lead: Diamond Queen

He forgot to duck

THIS episode in "The Perils of Bridge" might properly be termed a canard. Probably more people would recognize the word canard as meaning a hoax than would know its specific meaning in French as a duck. The following hand qualifies for the designation either way.

The duck is as familiar to bridge players as to ornithologists and French chefs. With a single stopper in the opponents' suit, most declarers know the value of holding up as long as possible. More advanced players recognize the need to hold up with a double stopper. But perhaps it is too much to expect any declarer to recognize that museum-piece rarity of a hand which calls for holding up with a triple stopper. The South player in the deal shown at right didn't wake up until after he had forgotten to duck.

Some players will look scornfully at East's opening bid of 1 Spade, but we have no fault to find with it. South's overcall of 1 No Trump is routine; it announces a balanced hand of 16 points or more, with adequate protection in Spades. North's raise to 2 No Trump is fully justified. While he has only 7 high-card points, his intermediate cards are worthy of note and his five-card suit is probably establishable.

West opened the Spade 6 and East played the Queen. South took the trick; then, naturally, started to clear the Diamond suit, leading low from his own hand. West grabbed the King, to lead another Spade. South won and knocked out East's Diamond Ace. But a Spade continuation removed declarer's third and last Spade stopper, and the upshot was that declarer came out with only eight tricks. He took three Spades, three Diamonds and two Clubs but, as is plain to be seen, he had no time to establish a Heart trick. When East got in with the Heart Ace he had two good Spades to cash, and the contract went down a trick.

Sound analysis will no doubt reveal that against a perfect defense South could not avoid incurring a loss. But he could have made matters much stickier for his adversaries.

Suppose that South, despite his three stoppers in the Spade suit, had ducked the first trick, permitting East to win with his Queen!

It is true that East could shift to Hearts and beat the contract, even though by doing so he would present South with an extra Heart trick. East must win the first Diamond lead and continue Hearts; West must save his King of Diamonds so that he has a long Heart when he gets the lead. Neither have we overlooked the fact that a Club shift by East at trick two, if followed by the perfect defense thereafter, also defeats the contract.

But do you consider that there is any real likelihood East would make either shift? The spots in the Spade suit were such that the inducement to continue Spades would be well-nigh irresistible. Declarer would win and lead a Diamond. Now, however, if West took the trick he would not have another Spade to return. And if East won the first Diamond, the result would be no better from the defensive standpoint.

EXTRA TRICK When you must decide whether to win or concede a trick, put yourself in your opponent's place and try to figure out what he is apt to do if he is allowed to hold the lead. Remember, he must make up his mind what to do looking at his hand—not yours.

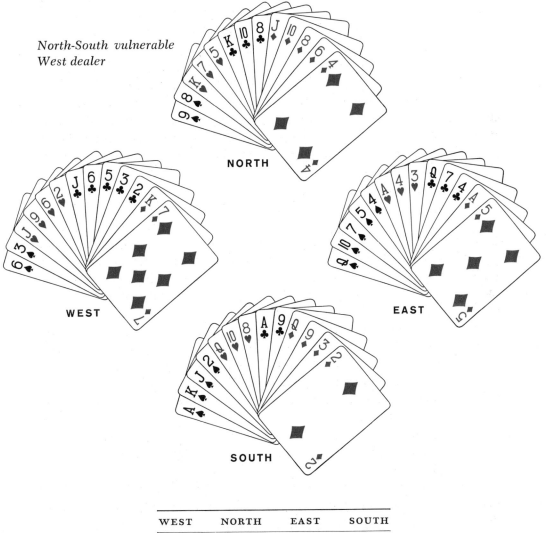

North-South vulnerable
West dealer

WEST	NORTH	EAST	SOUTH
Pass	Pass	1♠	1NT
Pass	2NT	Pass	3NT
Pass	Pass	Pass	

Opening lead: Spade 6

"I love mathematicians, but . . ."

ALTHOUGH they are becoming scarcer, I frequently meet persons who confess they are not bridge players. Strangely enough, the excuse I hear most often simply isn't valid: "I'm no good at mathematics," people tell me. Well, I have never found arithmetic to be the important element in bridge.

I will not say that I prefer partners who don't know how to add or subtract. But sometimes a little knowledge of mathematics can prove disastrous. The following hand, I think, is a case in point.

You could not ask for more dramatic bidding. Declarer's voice was heard but twice during the auction. His first bid was unorthodox, his second bid unorthodox and self-contradictory. His pass as dealer was made with the intention of launching a surprise attack later, though it is doubtful if he had in mind anything quite so surprising as what he finally produced. However, his pass was the means of eliciting information which should have helped him fulfill his contract—if only he had been less wedded to his mathematical theories.

In spite of North's opening Club bid, how did South know he could make a slam in Hearts? The answer is, he didn't know. But South's knowledge of the odds does not make him averse to taking an occasional chance. In view of the silence of both opponents, South was willing to risk that partner's opening bid included two Aces. If they were not the right ones (that is, if one of them proved to be the Ace of Clubs) there was, nevertheless, the chance that the opening lead might be favorable and afford him a chance to discard his Diamond loser.

However, North did hold the right two Aces, so South wasn't a bit disturbed that his opponent won the first trick by cashing the Diamond King. West then shifted to a trump. Pressing his luck, declarer casually drew trumps—all of them, in fact—but West clung to his four Spades. Consequently, when declarer got around to playing that suit, the defenders took the last two tricks.

"I could have saved a trick, of course, partner," South admitted readily. "But by pulling all the trumps, I tried to get anybody who might have four Spades to discard one."

"That wasn't what I was thinking about," North said. "You could have made the hand by putting the King of Clubs through and playing East for the Ace."

"Double dummy," snapped our mathematical South. "The odds favor a three-two division of five outstanding cards in a suit, whereas a finesse is only even money."

What South failed to take into account was the fact that West, known from the opening lead to have held the Ace-King of Diamonds, had failed to open the bidding, and further had failed to double an apparently blind 6-Heart bid. It was almost a certainty that East held the Ace of Clubs.

South should have won the second Heart in dummy and led the King of Clubs. East no doubt would have played the Ace; in any case, South could have created two sure discards for himself and made the contract without worrying about the division of the Spades.

EXTRA TRICK   Odds are abstract figures; they apply to the average deal, but may not have application in certain hands where the bidding has already proved that the odds are wrong.

Both sides vulnerable
South dealer

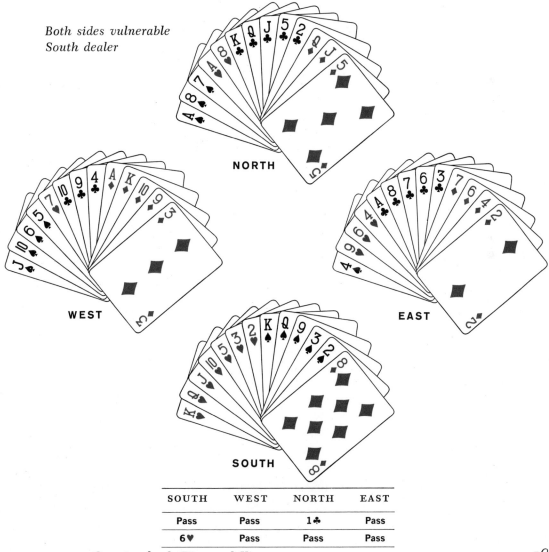

SOUTH	WEST	NORTH	EAST
Pass	Pass	1♣	Pass
6♥	Pass	Pass	Pass

Opening lead: Diamond King

License to kibitz

CUSTOMARILY, I have few opportunities to kibitz. In my television shows, however, not only am I cast as a kibitzer, but by the very nature of things I am expected to comment on every hand instead of maintaining a dignified and, I might add, difficult silence.

When the series was filmed I had the fun of watching far more hands than are shown on your TV screen. There were practice matches before the camera started rolling. There were hands played to while away the time when the electricians, stagehands and cameramen were performing essential chores. And, of course, there were the hands played after the show.

Naturally, some of the hands played off-camera were better than those we filmed. The following hand, played by Kay Rhodes with Margaret Wagar, the partners who set the all-time record by winning four straight National Women's Pair Championships, is a good example of what a TV show is forced at times to miss.

Sitting behind Kay Rhodes in the South position, I felt that she held herself well in check during the auction. Margaret Wagar, however, had suddenly burst into a grand-slam bid with the North hand, despite a Spade holding that made such an undertaking extremely hazardous. I must agree, however, that Miss Wagar's optimism had some points to commend it. When South jumped in Diamonds and then showed Club support, North hoped that her partner's holding included no more than one Spade. If she held two Spades, there was still the finesse to try if the Club suit failed to provide a discard.

West opened the Queen of Hearts, and when dummy was put down I, as kibitzer, figured out my line of play. My idea was to win the Heart, come off dummy with a trump, ruff a low Heart with a high Diamond in North's hand and continue trumps until the opponents had no more. Next, I would cash three top Clubs, ending with the Queen in South's hand. If the Club suit did not split, I would take the Spade finesse.

As you will see, I would have been defeated. The Clubs didn't split and the Spade King was offside. But Miss Rhodes made the hand easily.

She came to her hand with a trump and ruffed a Heart in dummy; then came back with a trump and drew another round to exhaust West. Next she led the Jack of Spades.

When West failed to produce the King, Kay went up with dummy's Ace, cashed the Ace of Clubs and came back to her hand with the Queen of Clubs. Next, she cashed her two good trumps and the King of Hearts, discarding the remainder of dummy's Spades.

East was hooked. He could see that it would be fatal to discard a Club,

162

so he let go the King of Spades and hoped that partner would hold the 10-spot. But Kay produced that card to win the twelfth trick, and dummy's high Club won the thirteenth and the grand slam.

EXTRA TRICK The first mention of the fourth suit to be bid by a partnership (in this case, North's Heart bid) can usually be read as forcing—even when made at the game level. With a real Heart suit North would have bid it over 2 Diamonds, instead of her bid of 3 Clubs.

Both sides vulnerable
North dealer

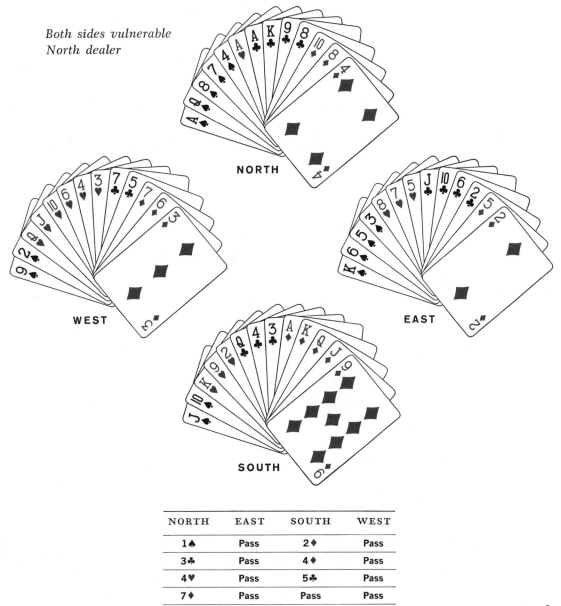

NORTH	EAST	SOUTH	WEST
1♠	Pass	2♦	Pass
3♣	Pass	4♦	Pass
4♥	Pass	5♣	Pass
7♦	Pass	Pass	Pass

Opening lead: Heart Queen

1959's king of swing

SOME time when Univac has a few minutes to spare, it might be possible to discover how many bridge deals are played in the course of a year. With some 35 million players in this country alone, many playing several times each week, I am sure the number would be staggering—so huge that one should be chary of claiming that any particular hand was the most remarkable of the year. However, here is one that, if not the most remarkable, surely was the biggest swing hand in a national tournament during 1959. It produced 2,980 points for the Philadelphia team against a team representing Houston, Texas.

With Philadelphia playing North-South in one room and the bidding as shown at right, the excitement was over as soon as the auction ended. West's Ace of Diamonds was the only trick his side could win. There was no way to prevent declarer from winning twelve and scoring 1,210 points (500 for the slam bonus, 300 for the game, 360 for the trick score and 50 for fulfilling a doubled contract).

In the other room, the Philadelphia team was playing East-West, and the excitement lasted considerably longer. The bidding:

WEST	NORTH	EAST	SOUTH
1♦	2♦	2♥	2♠
3♠	6♠	Pass	Pass
7♥	Pass	Pass	DBL
Pass	Pass	Pass	

In case you are wondering why South doubled when North held all the high cards for his side, it was because he (South) read his partner's pass to 7 Hearts as forcing—that is, requiring him to bid 7 Spades or double. Since South couldn't see any real hope of making 7 Spades, he chose the latter course.

Then he also had to choose the opening lead, and here the earlier cue bids led him astray. West had cued the Spades, suggesting no loser in that suit. North had cued the Diamonds, suggesting that he was void or held the Ace in that department. However, nothing but a Spade opening could set the grand slam, and South decided in favor of a Diamond. East then had no difficulty in taking all the tricks. After drawing trumps, he was able to discard both his losing Spades on West's long Diamonds. Bidding and making the grand slam, doubled, was worth 1,770 points and brought the total gain for the Philadelphia team on this single hand to 2,980 points.

Impressive as that sounds, perhaps the real swing is better expressed in the number of tricks won. In this one deal the Philadelphia team took twenty-five tricks!

EXTRA TRICK   There is no sure way to the correct bid on potential swing hands. With the inferior suit, Hearts, West's slower approach via the 3-Spade bid at the second table has much to recommend it. Even more commendable was his bid of 7 Hearts. Aside from the possibility of making that contract, it was safer to bid it than to risk the enemy's making 6 Spades. The best rule for such freaks: when in doubt, try to buy the contract.

Neither side vulnerable
West dealer

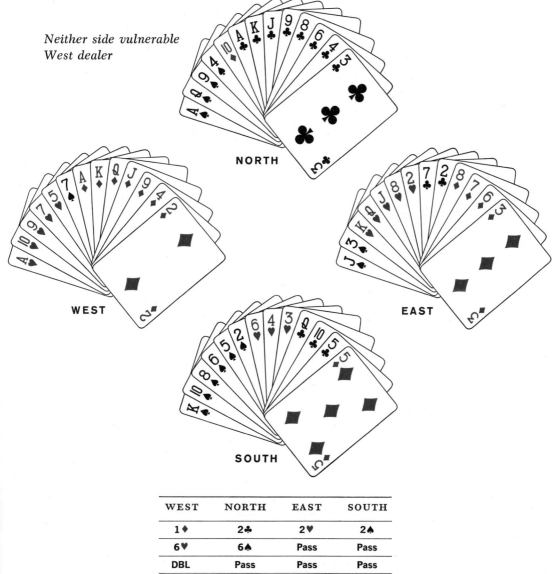

WEST	NORTH	EAST	SOUTH
1♦	2♣	2♥	2♠
6♥	6♠	Pass	Pass
DBL	Pass	Pass	Pass

Opening lead: Diamond Ace

He Aced his partner's trump

IN most of the world people fasten a rope at the top and climb down. In India, however, fakirs are said to be able to toss a rope into the air and climb up. But gravity isn't the only thing they turn upside down in that country. Whereas in other parts of the world a bridge player trumps his partner's Ace, in India a player once Aced his partner's trump.

Our hero was Shri D. V. Gore, a member of a Bombay team in a championship match played in Calcutta. The similarity in our names is such that I am tempted to claim at least a cousinship to the author of this play, but I must confess I have been unable to trace any branch of my family to the East. The hand was reported in the *Indian Bridge World* magazine.

North's 2 No-Trump response rates an award for bravery, though hardly for accuracy. However, a more seemly response of 1 No Trump would not have affected the final contract. South probably would have jump rebid to 3 Hearts, and of course his partner would have raised to 4. But even if South were to rebid only 2 Hearts, North would find another bid and South would then carry on to game.

Fortunately for the defenders—and for this story—West hit upon the essential opening lead of the Club Ace. Then he made the equally essential shift to a trump, in hopes of preventing declarer from ruffing a Spade loser.

Dummy's 9 of Hearts took the trick. Declarer saw three discards readily available—two on dummy's good Clubs and one on the Ace of Diamonds. But three discards were as good as none at all, for this would still leave South with three losers in Spades unless East held both the Ace and King or unless he could trump one round of the suit in dummy. So declarer led dummy's 6 of Spades.

East, Shri Gore, played low and North's 6 was allowed to ride around to West's 10. Continuing his plan of trying to kill the threat that dummy would ruff a Spade, West returned another Heart—and it was this trump which his partner Aced.

He didn't come up with the play in a hurry. Indeed, it needed a long, long huddle to muster up the nerve to make such an unusual discard. But East finally decided it was hopeless to set the contract if he kept the Ace of Spades, so he threw it away.

As a result, when declarer led another Spade toward his hand, West was able to win the trick and return the third Heart which swept the dummy bare of trumps. Winning in dummy and getting rid of three Spades on the available discards didn't do declarer a bit of good. He still had to surrender a Spade trick, and that was the trick that set the contract.

Observe what happens if East keeps the Ace of Spades. He is forced to win the second Spade lead and can neither lead a trump nor put his partner in to do so. South can trump any return, ruff a third Spade with dummy's last Heart and, after ruffing himself back in to draw the last adverse trump, the rest of South's Spades will be high. The defenders then will win only three tricks.

EXTRA TRICK   It isn't always easy to recognize the situation—and it takes a great deal of courage to make the sacrifice—but if winning a trick in your hand is sure to give the declarer his contract, get rid of the card that will ruin you. Trust that partner will be able to win the trick and then make an effective return lead.

Both sides vulnerable
South dealer

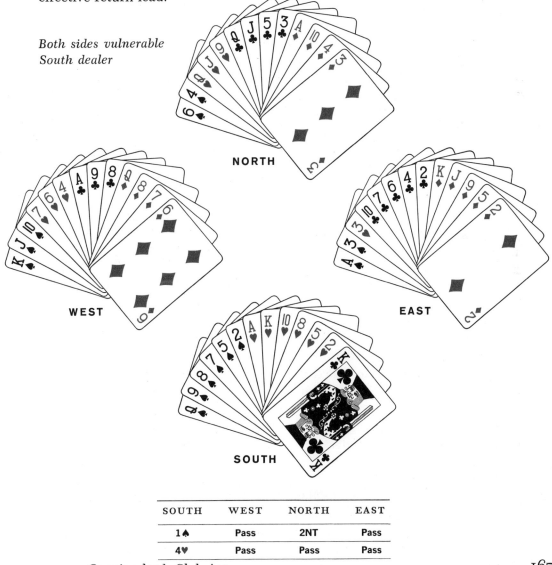

SOUTH	WEST	NORTH	EAST
1♠	Pass	2NT	Pass
4♥	Pass	Pass	Pass

Opening lead: Club Ace

The road to ruin

WATERLOO for Napoleon, according to Victor Hugo's legend, might have meant glorious victory instead of total defeat if his maps had disclosed the gulley that swallowed the flower of his cavalry—a sunken road meandering across the battlefield. The road broke the charge before it reached Wellington's famous squares.

As I see it, one of the principal effects of so-called scientific bidding is to give aid and comfort to the opponents and to permit them to learn as much as possible about declarer's hand before they are called upon to attack. In the current deal, for example, South furnished a clear warning that should have served as a blueprint for the defense.

East played the deuce of Hearts on the first trick, and South's Jack warned of his singleton. Nevertheless, West continued by leading the Queen of Hearts and South ruffed. Declarer played the Ace of trumps and when West showed out, the play of the hand became an open book.

Dummy's Club 10 was thrown under South's Ace. Declarer then led a Spade to dummy. After discarding his little Diamond on a second round of Spades, dummy's Club 3 was led through East for a finesse against the Jack. Picking up East's trumps, declarer showed his hand, conceding a trick to the Ace of Diamonds and chalking up the game and rubber.

Though South had furnished West with a complete guide, West's defense was considerably less potent than it might have been. Clearly, South must have a great Club suit, proof against anything but the bad break which West knew about but which South could scarcely foresee until he had led one round of trumps.

A Heart continuation was scarcely likely to embarrass the kind of trump suit South must hold. A Diamond lead would be into the teeth of his bid suit. The situation cried for a shift to Spades. No matter what Spades declarer held, a Spade lead could not help him, but it might have the advantage of robbing dummy of a much-needed later entry.

That is exactly what would have happened. Dummy would win two high Spades, permitting declarer to discard his little Diamond. Then a trump would be led—and South, who had no reason to foresee the four-nought distribution, would be entirely correct in playing for the adverse trumps to fall in three leads.

Once he played a high card on the first trump lead, the contract would be gone beyond recall. With no way to get back to dummy, declarer would have to lose a trump in addition to a Heart and a Diamond.

That West did not come up with this killing defense was in no way to South's credit. He did everything he could to help the defenders when he bid 4 Diamonds. Prospects of a good fit in that suit were quite remote once North failed to bid Diamonds over South's bid of 3 Clubs. South should have jumped directly to 5 Clubs, keeping the opponents as much as possible in the dark about his hand.

EXTRA TRICK   A four-card suit will rarely be a better trump suit than a seven-carder unless partner can bid the shorter suit on his own. Furthermore, telling partner as much as possible about your hand can be called good bidding only when partner can make better use of the information than the opponents.

Both sides vulnerable
South dealer

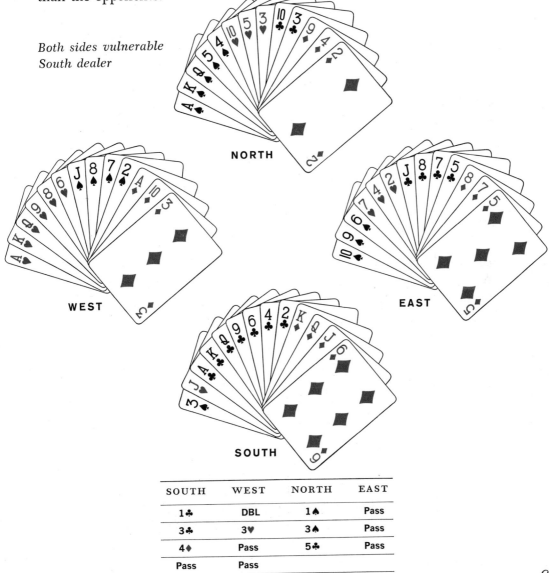

SOUTH	WEST	NORTH	EAST
1♣	DBL	1♠	Pass
3♣	3♥	3♠	Pass
4♦	Pass	5♣	Pass
Pass	Pass		

Opening lead: Heart King

A time to finesse

FROM the moment a bridge neophyte learns how to win an additional trick by finessing, his progress toward expertness may be charted on a graph recording the frequency of his finesses.

For a while, like a child with a new toy, he takes every finesse in sight. Sooner or later he learns to avoid the dangerous finesses which are not necessary to his purpose. Later still, he is able to sidestep finesses which on superficial analysis appear to be necessary but actually are not. Finally he comes to recognize the situation when an "unnecessary" finesse is the only way to make his contract. At that moment he has graduated to the high rank of expert.

How can an essential finesse be labeled "unnecessary"? To illustrate, let me cite this historic deal, played by my good Dutch friends the Fritz Goudsmits. It occurred in the international bridge matches held at Scheveningen, Netherlands, two decades ago.

I am unable to explain the Goudsmits' bidding system. Obviously, North's 2 No-Trump response was intended to describe a much stronger hand than it would today. However, the slam contract was reasonably sound. With a trump split, twelve tricks would have been available, regardless of the location of the Spade King. But declarer ran into a bad break in trumps.

Dummy won the Heart opening, and the Queen of Spades was led. East covered with the King, and South won with the Ace. Now if either opponent had started life with a doubleton 10, declarer would make a grand slam. But West showed out on the next Spade lead, leaving East's 10–8 as the major tenace.

To avoid conceding two trump tricks, South had to find some way of reducing his own hand to only two trumps and then getting dummy on lead at the crucial moment, so that East would have to play a trump from his 10–8 ahead of declarer's 9–7.

South led to his Diamond Ace, returned to dummy with a Heart and trumped a Diamond. Next he cashed the Ace of Clubs and led the 4. West played the 9 and, although declarer could win all the Club tricks without a finesse, he was forced to take the "unnecessary" finesse of dummy's 10-spot to gain an extra entry to dummy.

When the Club 10 held the trick, another low Diamond was trumped. Dummy was re-entered with the King of Clubs to lead the King of Diamonds. East had to play his Diamond Jack under the King, and South discarded his good Queen of Clubs.

On the next lead from dummy, South held the 9–7 of Spades behind

East's 10–8. No matter which trump East used, he could not prevent South from scoring the twelfth trick. Making the slam helped the Netherlands defeat Norway and finish second to the great Austrian team that dominated European bridge from 1933 to 1937.

EXTRA TRICK   Without detracting from Fritz Goudsmit's fine recovery, I should point out that his own haste had made the "unnecessary" finesse essential. It could have been avoided if he had cashed the Ace of Diamonds before leading a second Spade.

South dealer

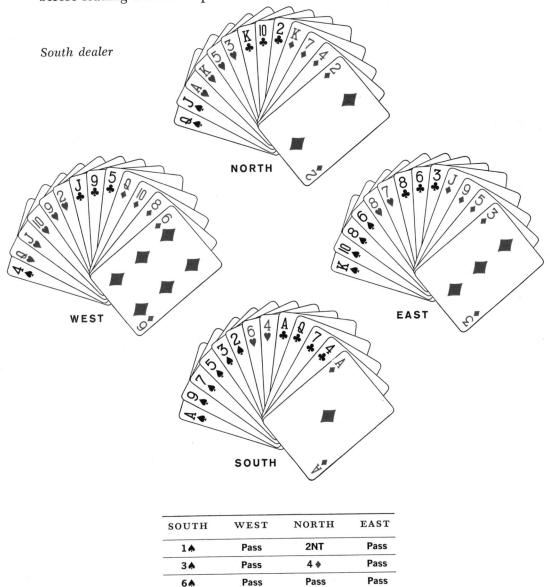

SOUTH	WEST	NORTH	EAST
1♠	Pass	2NT	Pass
3♠	Pass	4♦	Pass
6♠	Pass	Pass	Pass

Opening lead: Heart Queen

The uses of losing a trick

ANTIBRIDGE, the trick-losing game developed by some "advanced" California thinkers, is not an entirely new idea. In the early days of auction bridge you could bid "nullos," which, like antibridge, was a contract to lose tricks. The difference was that in nullos a bid was generally played without a trump suit; in antibridge you may make a minus bid in a suit. Nullos would be virtually forgotten today if it were not for the occasional caustic reference to a partner's miscue: "I thought you were playing nullos."

Yet there are some deals where the only way to win the game is by losing a trick. Consider the hand shown at right.

South's bid of 1 Diamond immediately over a take-out double promised no great strength. His forced rebid of 2 No Trump was also a weak call. But it seemed to North that his partner would need little more than the secondary strength in the red suits which South's bids promised, so he contracted boldly for the game.

The resulting duel of wits was worthy of the experts who made up this table. Dummy won the Club opening, and South studied carefully before he decided on his play. He recognized that if he started the Diamond suit, the defenders would simply duck one round of Diamonds and would then have little difficulty in keeping his hand from gaining the lead. So he made the excellent decision to try to establish two tricks in Hearts.

When dummy led the Queen of Hearts, it was East's turn to ponder. He won the trick and made the only return that would foil declarer's plan. He led a low Diamond. This beautiful maneuver prevented declarer from establishing the Hearts and then winning a Diamond lead in his own hand, when cashing two Heart tricks would insure making his contract.

Dummy won the Diamond trick with the Queen and continued Hearts. East took his Heart Ace, cashed the Ace of Diamonds and then led a low Spade. Declarer did his best to decline this Greek gift. He won the trick with dummy's Queen and cashed the Ace and King. But East refused to accept the return of the trick he had given away. He dumped his Jack under dummy's Ace and stranded the lead in dummy.

When West discarded his last Heart on dummy's 10 of Spades, South made the best of a bad bargain. If he had cashed the high Club, he would have had to surrender the last three tricks to West, going down two. Instead, he led dummy's deuce of Clubs up to his 8. West won with the 9 and continued with the Jack. Declarer held his loss to a one-trick set by letting the Jack win. This left North with the Ace–5 against West's 10–4, so North was able to win the last two tricks.

The strange part of this trick give-away contest was that if declarer had started his giving sooner he could have saved his contract. After East returned the low Diamond, letting dummy win the Queen, declarer should have cashed dummy's top Spades and high Club before leading another Heart. Then it would have done East no good to drop his Jack of Spades.

EXTRA TRICK Sometimes the only way to save a game is by giving up a trick. If having to lead later will be embarrassing, be sure to get out of your own way by cashing your winners first or getting rid of them by dumping high cards under your opponents' higher ones.

Neither side vulnerable
North dealer

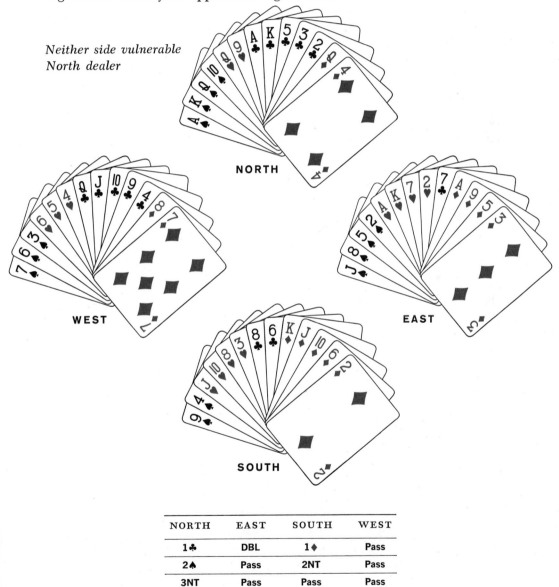

NORTH	EAST	SOUTH	WEST
1♣	DBL	1♦	Pass
2♠	Pass	2NT	Pass
3NT	Pass	Pass	Pass

Opening lead: Club Queen

173

Who makes up those hands?

ALMOST everyone who has read a report of a tournament wants to know: Who makes up the hands? The answer is nobody. The tournament hands you read about are usually dramatic because of the way they are played or the way they are bid, not because they have been prearranged. In most tournaments, every hand being played for the first time has been dealt at random. The identical hand, of course, is passed on later to other pairs to test their skill with the same cards.

There are special occasions when the deals are stacked. I use pre-arranged deals in my seminars for bridge teachers and advanced pupils. Here is a hand from a past teachers' convention in New York which illus-trates the kind of problem they have to cope with.

South's opening 1 No-Trump holding is an absolute maximum for that call, 18 points in high cards. North has 8 points in high cards plus a five-card suit, amply justifying his raise. No matter what bidding system is used, there is no problem in getting to the right contract—one of the prime considerations in making up the hands to be played in a stacked-deal game, for every deal includes a built-in point in the play. If the wrong contract were to be reached or the opening lead came from the wrong side of the table, the whole idea of the deal would be spoiled.

With South the declarer, West's normal opening lead is the Heart King. As declarer, how would you play for your 3 No-Trump contract?

If you are blessed with only a little knowledge, you know that there is a standard hold-up play when the King is led at No Trump and declarer holds Ace-Jack-small. Declarer ducks the first lead; then if the suit is con-tinued by the player on his left, he has two stoppers in the suit.

But this is a case where a little knowledge is dangerous. If you use the standard hold-up in the Heart suit, you run the risk that West will shift to Diamonds, and a Diamond shift will beat you. If you take the first Diamond trick, when the Club finesse loses, West will have another Diamond to return. If, instead, you hold up your Ace of Diamonds, East will shift back to Hearts and West's Hearts will be established before you can set up your Clubs.

Count your tricks and you find that you don't need to win two in Hearts; you have four Spades, one Heart and one Diamond for sure, and you can certainly win three in the Club suit without losing the lead to the dangerous hand—which will be East if you take the first Heart trick.

So you throw away the standard bridge rules you have learned, win the first Heart trick with the Ace, and go to dummy with a Spade to lead the Queen of Clubs. The finesse is wrong, but that doesn't matter. The defenders cannot prevent you from winning four Club tricks which, added to your six sure tricks in the other suits, brings you a comfortable ten tricks and an easy game.

EXTRA TRICK   Discover for yourself the reasons you are taught to play according to certain rules. If you know, for instance, why you hold up the Ace when you have Ace-Jack-small, you will readily recognize the occasion when it is necessary to make an exception to the general rule.

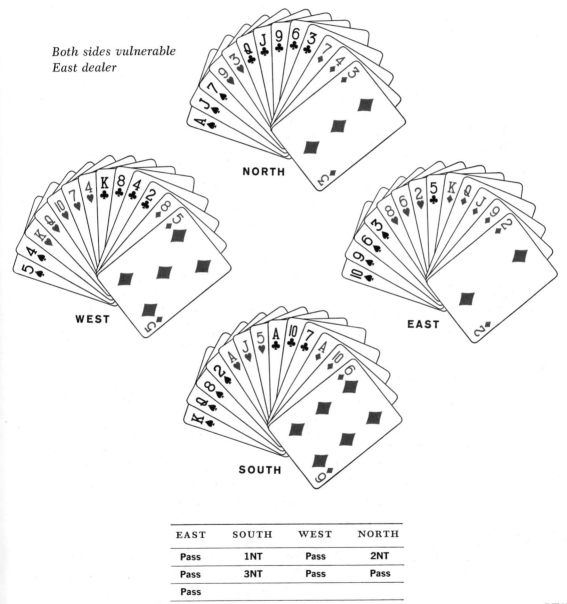

Both sides vulnerable
East dealer

EAST	SOUTH	WEST	NORTH
Pass	1NT	Pass	2NT
Pass	3NT	Pass	Pass
Pass			

Opening lead: Heart King

The "feel of the table"

ALONG with those who share my given name, I suffered through the hey-day of Jack Pearl. "Vas you dere, Sharlie?" the comedian asked, and all Charlies everywhere had to answer with that same helplessness of tall men asked to describe the exotic weather around their heads. Eventually, I turned annoyance to advantage by asking the same question of myself when I failed to profit by what I should have seen at the bridge table.

In chess it is possible to take in everything that went on in a given game simply by studying a diagram of the moves. No diagram of a bridge game can convey the same complete picture. There is a certain something —a perception which experts call "feel of the table"—that decides the fate of many bridge matches. And the only sure way to share that feel is to be there—very much there—when the hand is played. Rarely is that certain something as evident as it is in the following deal.

If South's bidding seems weird, allow me the storyteller's privilege of explaining why at the proper time.

I was reminded of this deal by the recent TV appearance of my old friend Percy Sheardown of Toronto. He was my partner, holding the West hand, when we played it against opponents who had wined as well as dined just before the evening tournament session.

"Shorty," as all his friends call Sheardown, opened the Queen of Diamonds. Declarer won and laid down the King of Spades. His hand hovered over the table in a way that indicated unmistakably that he expected to win the trick. He did a double-take when I produced the Ace of Spades; he transferred an incredulous stare from my Ace on the table to a card in his hand; then he moved that card from one end of his hand to the other.

It is now almost unnecessary for me to provide the promised explanation of the bidding. Obviously, South had thought his hand included the Ace of Spades, giving him an impregnable trump suit and making his Blackwood call for Aces a very logical bid. He thought he possessed the Ace of Spades and a singleton Queen of Clubs.

It was entirely apparent that South must hold the Ace of Clubs, but no better return suggested itself. On my Club return, South took his Ace and played the Queen of Spades. To his delight, and our disgust, both missing honors dropped. With dummy's Hearts readily available to take care of South's losers, the slam became a laydown.

While the opponents were sheepishly totaling up their score, Shorty cheered me up by shouldering the blame. "Sorry, Charlie," he said. "I could have beaten the hand." When I looked blank, he explained, "I should have led the King of Clubs!"

Had you been there, you would have known what he meant. There is little doubt that Shorty would have taken the trick from South's "singleton" Queen with his Club King before declarer discovered that his cards were not properly assorted. Later, when South found that he lacked the Ace of trumps, it would be too late for him to go back and win the first Club lead.

EXTRA TRICK   It is unethical to get information from your partner other than that conveyed by his bids and the fall of his cards. But there is no taboo against making the most of what you learn from the actions of your opponents, although you do so at your own risk.

Both sides vulnerable
South dealer

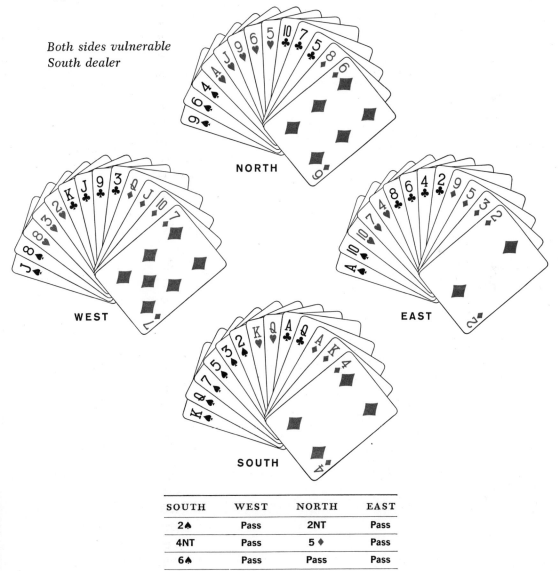

SOUTH	WEST	NORTH	EAST
2♠	Pass	2NT	Pass
4NT	Pass	5♦	Pass
6♠	Pass	Pass	Pass

Opening lead: Diamond Queen

Dramatic performer: bad actor

COFFEEHOUSING, which I have already mentioned, is perhaps too lightly dealt with in that section of the bridge laws which is concerned with the proprieties. Yet the law plainly says, "A player should refrain from . . . an unnecessary hesitation, remark, or mannerism which may deceive the opponents." Clearly, the genus Coffeehouse is on slippery ground. But that does not stop him from taking a strange sort of pride in his crafty work. He is found all over the world, as witness the following deal reported by Fred Gulliver in a contract bridge newsletter published by the New South Wales Bridge Association.

Mr. Gulliver does not amplify on the bidding sequence, which includes a slightly questionable jump rebid to 2 No Trump by North with no Heart stopper and only 18 points. However, he has admittedly a difficult choice and, at any rate, the final contract would have been made with ease but for the bad break in the trump suit.

West cashed a Heart trick "while the shop was open," as Mr. Gulliver described it. Declarer trumped the second Heart, played the Ace of Spades and led to the King, discovering that he was in trouble. South had to execute a Grand Coup, shortening his trumps by ruffing once again; he needed to win all the tricks and to wind up in dummy to lead through East at the right time.

Declarer saw that the percentage was against his being able to cash three Diamonds—yet this was essential to his success. To prevent the loss of the slam through East's trumping a third Diamond, South staged a performance which should have won him an Oscar.

Exhibiting no dismay at the bad break, declarer returned to his hand (and incidentally reduced his trumps to East's length) by ruffing another Heart. Then he went into his act. He led a Diamond toward dummy and, after deep thought, hesitantly played the Queen. When East produced the Diamond 2, South released a pent-up sigh at the success of his "finesse." Next, he cashed dummy's Ace of Diamonds and then led a low Diamond, meanwhile glaring at East with a triumphant air.

Convinced that South would be able to overruff, East discarded a Club and South's dramatic production became an assured success. He won the trick with the Diamond King, entered dummy with a Club and continued leading good Diamonds. Now, whenever East trumped, South could indeed overtrump, so the slam came home.

In Mr. Gulliver's tale, they found South's body in a back alley later that evening. In spite of South's conduct, I am not sure that the homicide was justified. East should have figured that if South really held only two Diamonds, he would have taken the Diamond finesse and ruffed a Diamond earlier—not a Heart. Otherwise he had no chance of keeping as many trumps as East and would have had to lose a trump trick.

EXTRA TRICK   I recommend two methods for making even an incurable coffeehouser see the error of his ways. Either stop playing with him or learn to turn his play-acting to your own advantage.

Both sides vulnerable
North dealer

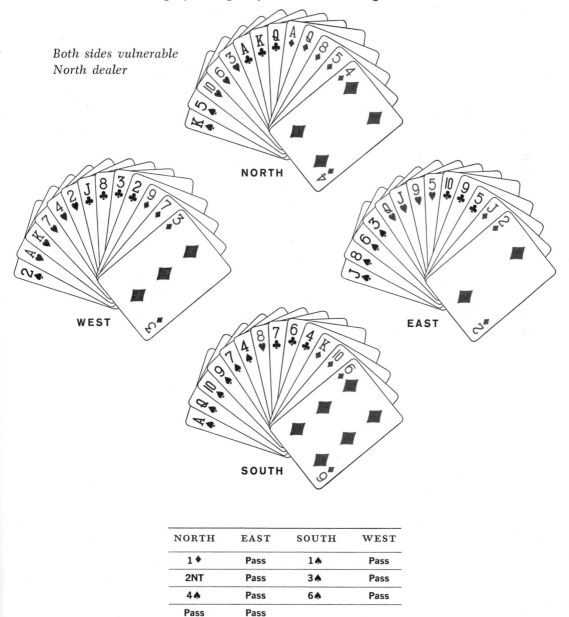

NORTH	EAST	SOUTH	WEST
1 ♦	Pass	1 ♠	Pass
2NT	Pass	3 ♠	Pass
4 ♠	Pass	6 ♠	Pass
Pass	Pass		

Opening lead: Heart King

179

Detective story

ALERTNESS of the first order is sometimes required when a defender inserts a well-placed bluff bid, more popularly known as a "psychic." The South in the following hand was put under extreme pressure by his crafty left-hand opponent, but came through with flying colors.

West overcalled the opening Heart bid with 1 Spade, guessing that that was the suit in which the opponents had their best chance for game. He hoped, too, that South might be induced to contract for No Trump if he held the Spades protected—in which case he would produce his secret weapon in the form of a seven-card Club suit. If doubled, he had, of course, a reasonably safe escape.

North naturally made a penalty double of the 1-Spade bid and West escaped to 4 Clubs. This placed North in a somewhat awkward position, for there was no clearly indicated course of action open to him. Having already doubled 1 Spade, he felt constrained to pass the next bid around to his partner, though there was a distinct temptation to try 4 Spades. There was little doubt that West had made a bluff bid in that suit, but here was the rub: While West almost certainly did not have Spades, East might have. North therefore passed, in the hope that somehow the air would clear.

It was at this point that South made a daring but sound bid. The routine call would have been 4 Diamonds. Had South chosen to make this bid, it would have had the effect of accenting North's fears that the balance of the Spade suit was held by East; for if South showed length in both Hearts and Diamonds, it would seem more than ever likely that he was short in Spades. South concluded that North must have extreme length in Spades in order to have doubled the suit at the level of 1, when it was apparent that North was not especially well equipped with high cards. South therefore chose to bid 4 Spades and all hands passed.

As anticipated, the declarer found a highly acceptable dummy and had no difficulty in fulfilling contract with an overtrick.

EXTRA TRICK It will be observed that a contract of 4 Hearts could not be fulfilled, and a contract of 5 Diamonds could be defeated by a lead of the singleton Spade.

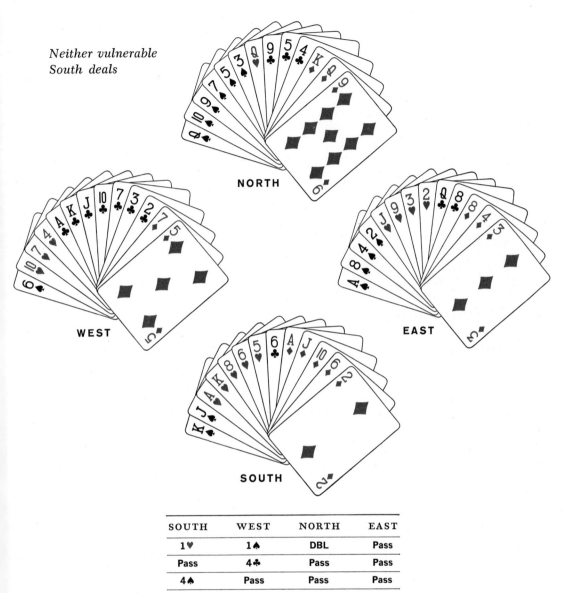

Neither vulnerable
South deals

NORTH

WEST

EAST

SOUTH

SOUTH	WEST	NORTH	EAST
1♥	1♠	DBL	Pass
Pass	4♣	Pass	Pass
4♠	Pass	Pass	Pass

Opening lead: Club King

A hand with a punch

THE nomenclature of contract bridge is full of colorful terms borrowed from other sports. For example, the play that makes an opponent surrender a trick because he cannot guard two suits at the same time was named the squeeze by Sidney Lenz. It reminded him of the baseball maneuver which sometimes is used to deliver the winning run from third base.

Baseball also furnishes the force. In bridge, this describes the play that compels declarer to use his or dummy's trumps. Punching, a word from boxing, is used by bridge players to describe the same force action.

The ring, of course, has many different punches. There is an equal variety of jabs and biffs at the bridge table. Take, for instance, this blow, which I was lucky enough to watch. It was brought up from the floor in order to make the declarer expend a high trump, and I called it an uppercut. The term still strikes me as apt, for in bridge, as in boxing, you have to set yourself for the uppercut before you can deliver it.

With 10 points in high cards, North had a good free raise in spite of holding only three trumps. But the trump suit was not as solid as it appeared. Its weakness lay in its vulnerability to the uppercut.

West took the King of Diamonds and then the Ace, with East echoing to show he wanted the suit continued. West knew that a third lead of Diamonds would not produce a ruffing trick for East, so he toyed briefly with the idea of shifting to a Club. But the high cards in plain sight clearly indicated that South must have the King of Clubs and probably other honors in that suit as well, so a Club lead could only help declarer.

Another possibility was for West to underlead the Ace of Spades in hopes that East held the Queen. But the bidding had marked West for the missing strength, so even if declarer did not have the Queen of Spades there was little chance of his failing to play dummy's King.

Obviously, the strategy was to develop a trick in the trump suit. If East held the 10 of Hearts and used it to ruff a third round of Diamonds, he could force South's Ace or King and leave West with a sure trump trick.

Having reasoned thus far, West led the 8 of Diamonds: not the highest one, because he wanted to be sure East would ruff, but a higher one than necessary as a warning that South could overruff, so that if East held two trumps he would ruff with the bigger one.

East dutifully trumped the trick with his 10 of Hearts—and the knockout punch was on its way. If South had stood still and taken the punch, overruffing with his King or Ace, he could not have escaped losing a trump trick and the Ace of Spades, to be set one trick.

But West's timing was a trifle off, and South was able to roll with the punch and escape the knockout. Instead of overtrumping, South simply threw off his Queen of Spades. That took the sting out of the punch and preserved the solidity of declarer's trump suit. He ruffed the Spade return, drew trumps and claimed the balance.

West could have scored the knockout. Since he had no hope of winning more than a single Spade trick, he should have cashed the Ace of Spades and then launched his uppercut.

EXTRA TRICK Before you try an uppercut, be sure to take the necessary side tricks so that declarer will catch the full brunt of the blow.

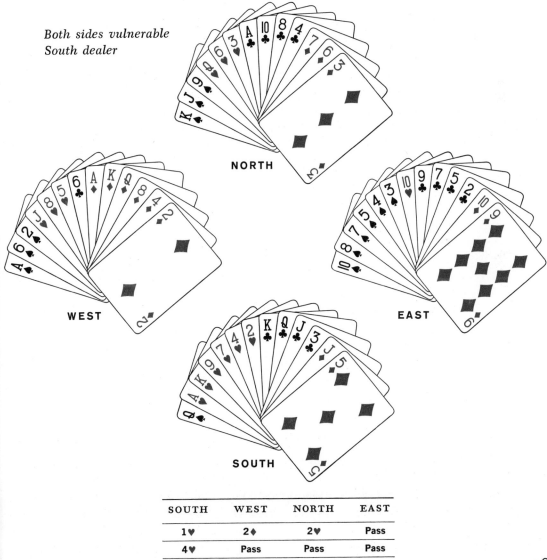

Both sides vulnerable
South dealer

NORTH

WEST

EAST

SOUTH

SOUTH	WEST	NORTH	EAST
1♥	2♦	2♥	Pass
4♥	Pass	Pass	Pass

Opening lead: Diamond King

Double trouble

OBSERVERS and players still talk about this remarkable deal during a recent national championship event, in which the defender had what appeared to be a sure set, with five Spades to 100 honors behind the 4-Spade bid. Yet the Spade game was brought home at nearly every table.

At several tables, the opening lead was the King of Spades—a play which both revealed the bad break in trumps and helped declarer to make his contract. But even without the help of that lead, the double had already alerted South to the likelihood that all five of the missing trumps were behind him. Declarer had to find a way to make one of West's four apparent tricks disappear—and without the aid of legerdemain.

Here is how it was made against the Queen of Clubs opening.

Declarer won the first trick with the Club Ace and led another Club to the King. When the Jack appeared, it helped give South a count on West's hand. Dummy's Ace and King of Hearts were taken, and South cleverly discarded the good 10 of Clubs. Next, he took the Ace and King of Diamonds and ruffed a Diamond in dummy. A Heart return was trumped by South. All this time, West had helplessly followed suit, and now the situation was:

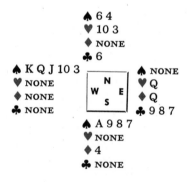

South led the 4 of Diamonds. If West trumped low, dummy could overruff and South's Spade Ace would provide declarer's tenth trick. So West had to trump with the Spade 10. Now, in order to prevent South from winning the next trick with a low Spade, West had to lead another honor. South won with the Ace and remained with the 9-8-7 against West's Queen-Jack-3. West got two more tricks, but South made his contract.

Only one West player was able to restrain the impulse to double 4 Spades. Harold Ogust was the declarer who played the hand at that table.

He could not foresee that trumps would be bunched against him, but he did make a safety play against a four-one break. His first lead after winning the Ace of Clubs was the Spade 9. West won the 10 and could have defeated the contract by leading back a trump honor, but he returned the Jack of Clubs.

EXTRA TRICK   Sometimes the only way to gain a trick is to throw a good card away. In this deal, if South had saved his good 10 of Clubs he would have lost his contract.

Neither side vulnerable
South dealer

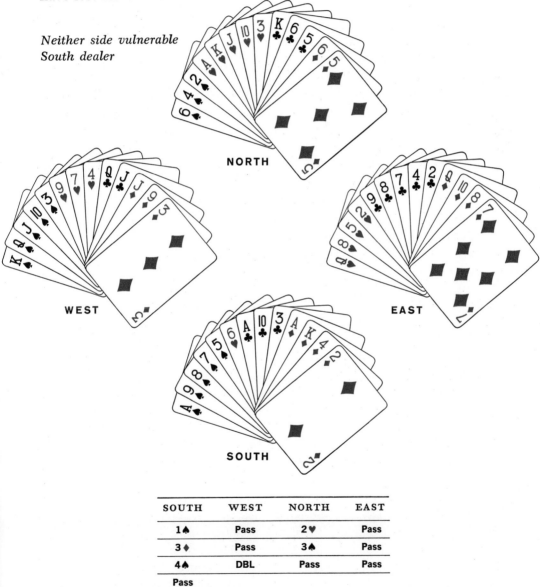

SOUTH	WEST	NORTH	EAST
1♠	Pass	2♥	Pass
3♦	Pass	3♠	Pass
4♠	DBL	Pass	Pass
Pass			

Opening lead: Club Queen

A waiter's dividend

SOONER or later almost every successful player publishes a bridge book. Harry Fishbein postponed his debut as an author until nearly a generation after he had introduced his well-known convention for coping with pre-emptive bids.

It is rare that a sexagenarian can stay at the top of his game; yet at 61, Fishbein captained the U. S. team in the 1959 World Championship Match. Outside of his convention, flashy berets are his trademark; he has more than 200 of them. He is one of the world's best bridge players, and if you don't believe me, study the following hand.

The bidding is straightforward enough to require little explanation. South's (Fishbein's) opening 2 bid of course showed a powerful holding. North, possessed of a six-card suit and two Aces, was amply justified in making a positive response.

Fishbein was quite uninterested in North's Hearts, which he did not expect to be solid, but he assumed that North would furnish a trick somewhere that would enable him to bring home a slam in Clubs.

Look at it from North's viewpoint. His partner, by leaping to 6 Clubs, had contracted to lose no more than one trick. And North had in his hand the one card which South surely must be figuring to lose—the Ace of trumps. So North allowed that one card to nudge him into the grand slam.

The Heart opening presented Fishbein with the opportunity for an immediate discard. His hand was solid with the exception of the Jack of Spades and the 10 of Diamonds. Which would you discard?

Mathematically, the choice is clear-cut. There is a better chance of dropping the Jack of Diamonds in three leads than of dropping the Queen of Spades or of winning a finesse for that card. So if you discarded the Jack of Spades on dummy's Ace of Hearts you would apparently be playing percentages. But you would also be losing your grand slam.

Fishbein made the contract by postponing his decision until he had acquired a little more information and given himself that vital extra chance which the shrewd performer constantly seeks. He didn't play the Ace of Hearts on the first trick. Instead he played the deuce of Hearts from dummy and ruffed in his hand in order to cash the Ace and King of Spades immediately. This play ran the slight risk that an opponent could trump the second round of Spades. But if one opponent actually held six Spades, that fact would increase the danger that Diamonds would not break, and the grand slam would probably be doomed to failure anyway.

The extra chance paid a big dividend. East's Queen of Spades dropped. So when Fishbein went to dummy with the Ace of trumps, he knew what he had to discard on the Ace of Hearts. He pitched the 10 of Diamonds and returned to his hand with a Diamond lead. After he drew the rest of East's trumps, the grand slam was a laydown.

EXTRA TRICK   If you are reasonably sure that you are taking few chances in waiting, postpone a crucial decision. You may then be able to obtain more information about the location of key cards.

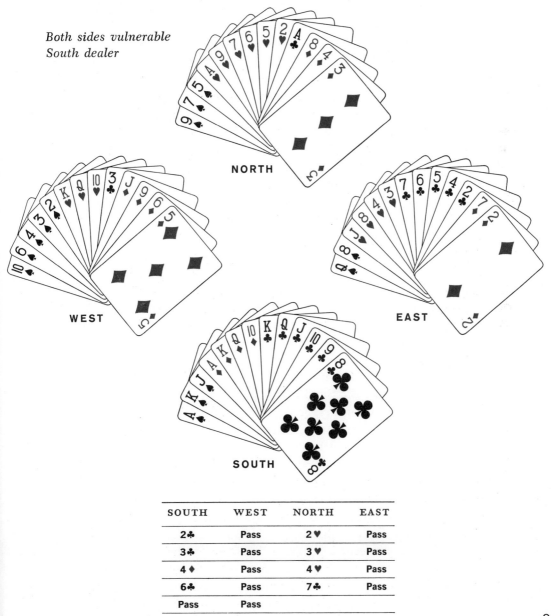

Both sides vulnerable
South dealer

NORTH

WEST

EAST

SOUTH

SOUTH	WEST	NORTH	EAST
2♣	Pass	2♥	Pass
3♣	Pass	3♥	Pass
4♦	Pass	4♥	Pass
6♣	Pass	7♣	Pass
Pass	Pass		

Opening lead: Heart King

Pierre Albarran

EUROPE lost her most widely followed bridge authority early in 1960 when Pierre Albarran died in Paris. American tennis fans will recall Albarran as a member of the French Olympic tennis team of 1920 and the Davis Cup team of 1921. Bridge followers will remember him as the star of the French team that won the European Bridge Championship in 1935.

Nineteen times a champion of France, Albarran originated the "canape" theory (bidding the shorter suit first and longer suit second, so that partner may pass the second bid with a weak hand) which is much followed by Europe's experts. He was the author of several successful bridge books, and shortly before his death submitted to me the manuscript of a book which we were to publish jointly in the United States. This hand is from that book. It is one that we played as partners when we were teammates at Cannes only a few years ago.

Albarran chose this hand to make an important point: watch your opponents carefully. His bidding, at South position, was reasonable enough, and gave him the outside chance that the opposition might decide to make the sacrifice bid of 4 Spades.

It seemed to Albarran that if he trumped a low Spade in dummy and gave up one trump, one Diamond and one Club, he could make his contract. But West had chosen to lead into the teeth of South's Spades, and East, a somewhat demonstrative type, far from looking displeased, had squared himself comfortably in his chair with a tranquil and satisfied look on his face. So Albarran deduced that East could twice overruff dummy—which would place with him the King and 10 of Hearts.

So far, so good. But how to make the best use of the deduction? South won the first trick with the Spade Jack, cashed the Ace and led the King, discarding a Club from dummy. East ruffed as Albarran expected, and back came a Club. Albarran rose with his Ace, led his losing 8 of Spades, and once again discarded a Club from dummy—the loser-on-loser play which he used to call the "Nameless Coup."

South still had a sure Diamond loser; but, by having discarded two Clubs while surrendering two Spades, he was able to trump his low Club in dummy. This gave him back a trick he had given away, and also provided the essential entry to dummy with which to take the Heart finesse. When that finesse succeeded, Albarran had brought home an "impossible" contract—the kind that always gives the expert the greatest pleasure. For Albarran, who delighted in guessing from their actions what his opponents held, the hand was doubly satisfying. As he often said, "The advantage of a poker face is not confined to poker."

EXTRA TRICK I never had the pleasure of playing with Albarran in his halcyon days, but they must have been something. When we played together at Cannes, Albarran was supposedly past his prime, but he was still the master. He temporarily abandoned his system and did me the honor of playing mine. This didn't ruffle his game in the least. He played with the grace and judgment of a man who had been born into the method, and left the gallery fully persuaded that we were a partnership of long standing. His courtesy must have won him many a tournament.

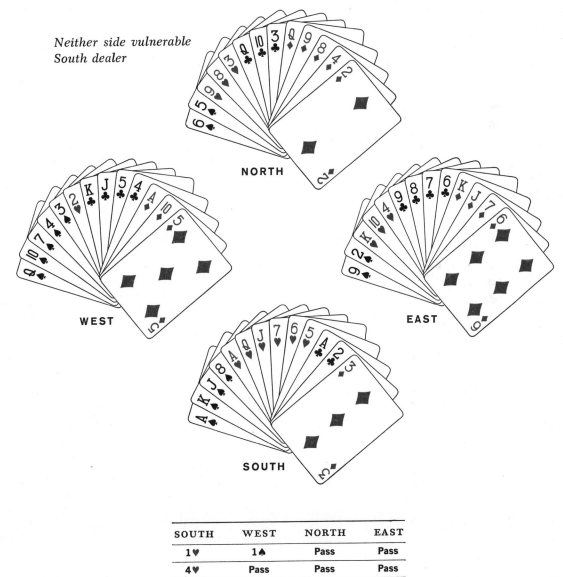

Neither side vulnerable
South dealer

SOUTH	WEST	NORTH	EAST
1♥	1♠	Pass	Pass
4♥	Pass	Pass	Pass

Opening lead: Spade 4

IMPs in the cards

WHEN a bridge session suddenly explodes in a series of wild distributions, players say, "The devil has got into the cards." To beat the devil, an increasing number of championship tournaments are scored in International Match Points, which are awarded in accordance with a table designed to minimize the chance that a single freak deal might decide an entire championship. Using IMPs, it is possible to gain more by scoring 560 regular bridge points than by scoring 4,100. For instance, if you should make 70 points in each of eight deals, you would be entitled to 16 IMPs (*see chart*), while 4,100 points on a single deal would be worth only 15 IMPs. Steady play, in other words, would net you more points than one big, lucky hand.

Following are International Match Point equivalents to bridge points totaled under the usual method. Note that IMPs are calculated after each deal, not after match

POINTS	IMPS	POINTS	IMPS	POINTS	IMPS
0–10	= 0	350–490	= 5	1,500–1,900	= 10
20–60	= 1	500–740	= 6	2,000–2,490	= 11
70–130	= 2	750–990	= 7	2,500–2,990	= 12
140–210	= 3	1,000–1,240	= 8	3,000–3,490	= 13
220–340	= 4	1,250–1,490	= 9	3,500–3,990	= 14
				4,000 or more	= 15

How is it possible to score more than 4,000 points on a single hand? The way this was once done in a match in Stockholm is shown at right.

East's leap to 4 Diamonds was an asking bid of a type long obsolete in this country but still used in Europe. The bid asked if partner held first- or second-round control of Diamonds. West ignored the intervening double to bid 5 Hearts, showing second-round Diamond control and the Heart Ace. East's 5 No Trump asked partner to bid 7 of the agreed suit (by inference, Hearts) if he had two top honors. When West bid the grand slam, South "sacrificed" at 7 Spades.

South ruffed the Heart opening and led out his trumps. On the last one, West had to find a discard from the Ace of Hearts and the K-10-9 of Clubs. When West discarded a Club, declarer threw the Queen of Hearts from dummy, saving the A-J-6 of Clubs.

A successful Club finesse, followed by the Ace to drop West's King, let South score all the tricks and 2,470 points—substantially better than setting 7 Hearts one trick.

But his team's gain was to be greater still. At the other table, a teammate bought the contract at 7 Diamonds doubled, and South selected the

Queen of Clubs for his opening lead. West's King covered, forcing North's Ace, and East trumped. After two rounds of trumps, a Heart lead revealed North's uncapturable Queen. So East led dummy's 10 of Clubs and finessed. He led another Club; North played his Jack, and declarer trumped. He returned to dummy with a high Heart and discarded his Heart losers on the Clubs. He too made a grand slam, adding 1,630 points to his team's score.

EXTRA TRICK When bidding warns of freakish distribution, it is usually sound practice to buy the contract at any price.

North-South vulnerable
West dealer

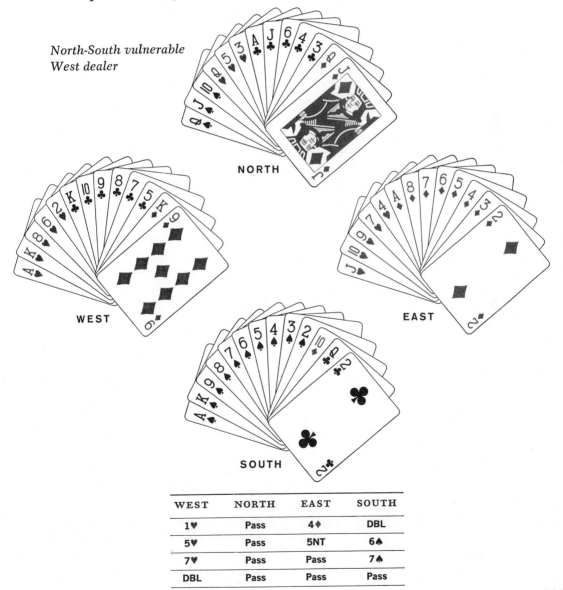

WEST	NORTH	EAST	SOUTH
1♥	Pass	4♦	DBL
5♥	Pass	5NT	6♠
7♥	Pass	Pass	7♠
DBL	Pass	Pass	Pass

Opening lead: Heart King

It's simpler in slow motion

KIBITZING a touch-and-go bridge hand can be like watching a duel. In bridge, however, the lunges, parries, feints and delicate maneuvers for position are in slow motion. Yet the kibitzer may go away shaking his head over the miracles performed by the experts. He shouldn't be that impressed. Often, as in the hand at right, victory is simply a matter of counting tricks and points. You do that every time you bid a hand.

First let me describe the play without any explanations. East put the Heart 10 on the first trick, and South let him keep the lead. East shifted to the Spade Queen and won the trick when the others played the 3, 2 and 4. East continued with the Jack of Spades, and dummy won with the Ace, returning a low Heart. East climbed up with the Ace of Hearts and led the 5 of Clubs. Declarer let this run to the board's 10, but West won with the Club Jack and got out with a Spade.

The defenders had won four tricks; declarer could take his King of Hearts, and four Diamond tricks, but the Club finesse had to succeed if he were to win a ninth trick. West's King of Clubs won the setting trick.

Why did South play as he did? How did East know he should abandon his best suits and shift to the Club? Here is the hand in slow motion.

To begin, South knew he could count on eight tricks, including the King of Hearts. With a Club finesse, he could make nine. But his problem was to make sure he could make nine, even if the Clubs fell badly. Thus, when East played the 10 of Hearts in hopes he could force South's King, South ducked. This insured that if East continued the suit and knocked out declarer's King, West would not be able to lead Hearts if he won a later trick. East, undismayed, shifted to Spades, probing for a weak spot. His partner's deuce was discouraging. Obviously, South held the King, but East hoped West might hold four Spades, and he continued that suit.

When the second Heart lead put East in with the Ace, it was time for him to do some figuring. South's No-Trump overcall showed the same as an opening No-Trump bid—16 to 18 points. His high cards in three suits were known because he would have led Diamonds at once had he not held the Ace. So East counted 10 points and knew that South must hold at least 6 points in Clubs. It was unlikely that these were K Q J, or South would have tried to knock out the Ace immediately. If he had Ace-King, he had nine tricks regardless. So it was right to assume that he had the Ace-Queen—but not the Jack, else he would have taken a Club finesse. This is the way East figured the hand—and set the contract.

What would have happened had East not shifted to Clubs? Assume that he continued Spades. South would win, cash his King of Hearts and run four tricks in Diamonds. Then he would lead the 10 of Clubs from dummy and let West win the trick. With nothing left but Clubs, West would have had to yield the last two tricks to South's Ace and Queen.

EXTRA TRICK Even the most erratic players usually stick to the required points when they bid No Trump. When declarer has opened or overcalled in No Trump, at some point in the play you will be able to picture his exact hand simply by counting up the value of what he has already played.

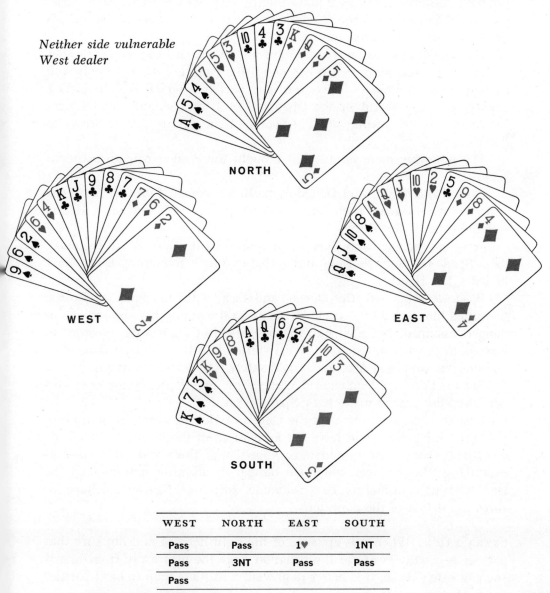

Neither side vulnerable
West dealer

NORTH

WEST

EAST

SOUTH

WEST	NORTH	EAST	SOUTH
Pass	Pass	1♥	1NT
Pass	3NT	Pass	Pass
Pass			

Opening lead: Heart 6

London bridge

DURING my life I have spent an incredible number of hours getting to bridge games—some of them embarrassingly short. My record, I believe, came at the beginning of the jet age. On a weekend I flew from New York to London and back just to play three sessions of bridge. These were no ordinary sessions, however. I played with Boris Schapiro against the best players in England for the Waddington Cup, emblematic of the British Masters Pairs Championship.

The Waddington is an invitation event, restricted to 22 pairs. Besides myself there were only two other non-British players, C. Delmouly and G. Bourchtoff of France. They won, and shortly afterwards helped their country take the World Bridge Olympiad in Turin. Schapiro and I were top in the second session but did poorly in the first and were lucky to finish ninth.

The following hand is one that brought the French pair an excellent score.

Even if Bourchtoff and Delmouly had been defeated on this hand (as Schapiro and I were), their 5-Spade contract was well judged; 5 Hearts was unbeatable. But things happened.

West opened the Club Queen and continued the suit. South trumped, led a Spade to dummy's King and ruffed dummy's remaining Club. Next he led a low Heart.

West went up with the Queen, and East, with mistaken generosity, permitted him to hold the trick. West, never dreaming that the set was in danger, assumed that East had the blank Ace of Diamonds. In order to leave partner with an exit card, West shifted to a Diamond, so that, after winning the supposed Ace, East could safely return another Heart.

But the Diamond lead caused West to lose an otherwise sure trick and permitted declarer to make his 5-Spade contract.

East should have overtaken the Queen of Hearts. Surely if South had the Heart King, he would have led a Heart from the dummy toward his own hand. Thus East should have known that there was no danger in overtaking West's Queen but great danger in allowing him to hold the lead. A Heart continuation or a Diamond shift from East would have insured the defeat of the contract.

EXTRA TRICK When you are sure of the right defense and not sure that partner is equally aware of the situation, take the play away from him if you can safely do so. It is better to prevent a mistake than to bawl partner out for having made one.

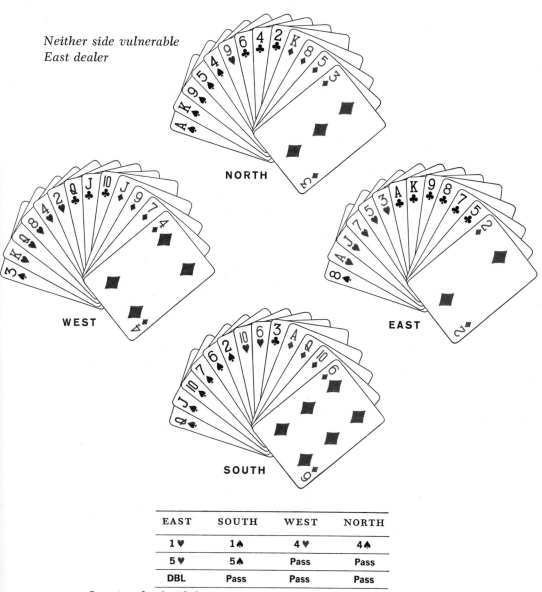

Neither side vulnerable
East dealer

NORTH

WEST

EAST

SOUTH

EAST	SOUTH	WEST	NORTH
1 ♥	1 ♠	4 ♥	4 ♠
5 ♥	5 ♠	Pass	Pass
DBL	Pass	Pass	Pass

Opening lead: Club Queen

A tricky accident

IN THE bridge player's anthology of alibis, few are so often heard as the one that goes, "Sorry partner, I misplaced a card." Dr. Leon Altman of Reading, Pa., a favorite partner of mine in the early days of contract, told me about a partner of his who had opened with a vulnerable bid of 2 No Trump. Although Altman had sufficient values in his hand to raise to 4, he contented himself with a single raise. The game contract was doubled and promptly redoubled. When the loss of 1600 points was recorded, he gazed quizzically at his partner. "I'm sorry," came the explanation. "I had a card misplaced." "Only one card?" queried the innocent victim.

Another familiar alibi is, "I'm sorry, partner, I pulled the wrong card." And that bring us to the following hand.

As the bidding is reviewed, I shall ask the reader to refrain from raising scornful eyebrows in my direction. I am merely the reporter in the case. Actually, the bidding started off reasonably enough. The 2-Diamond bid will pass muster, although some players are reluctant to open with a demand bid on freak hands where the minimum high-card requirement is held. There is always the danger that partner will have high cards in the void suit, on the basis of which he may decide to bid an unmakable slam.

Over the 4-Diamond bid, North is justified in bidding 4 Hearts. Common sense suggests that this is an Ace-showing bid, since North could hardly be trying to play the hand at Hearts, knowing that his partner held rafts of Diamonds and Spades. South's leap to 6 No Trump with a void in partner's suit is a monstrosity. Actually 6 Clubs would not be a bad contract, and could be defeated only because East can lead a singleton Spade.

West doubled the 6 No-Trump bid and led the Jack of Spades. Declarer won with the Queen and saw that to make the hand he would have to bring in dummy's Club suit; it was evident that Spades would not break well enough, and it was unlikely that the Diamonds would either. But to make the Clubs good, two entries to dummy were required. The double suggested that West held the King of Hearts, so prospects were bright.

The deuce of Hearts was led and the King of Hearts fell from West's hand, to the accompaniment of a gasp of horror. "Omigosh, I pulled the wrong card," said West. "Oh, we don't enforce the laws strictly. Take it back," South volunteered magnanimously. But West was sporting about it and refused the offer. The King had to be played. From then on, declarer had no hope. He went about setting up the Diamonds and eventually succumbed to a two-trick set.

East woke in time to say to West: "Partner, that was the most inspired fumble in the history of cards."

EXTRA TRICK   While declarer is reasoning out his plan of campaign, the defenders should be thinking too. When declarer leads a small Heart from his hand rather than a Club, it should be apparent to West that his opponent is void in Clubs. The need to kill dummy's entries will then become clear, and West can make the King of Hearts deliberately rather than by accident.

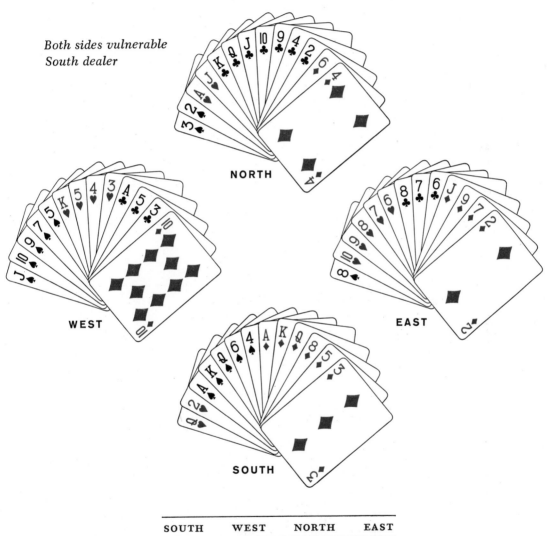

Both sides vulnerable
South dealer

NORTH

WEST

EAST

SOUTH

SOUTH	WEST	NORTH	EAST
2♦	Pass	3♣	Pass
3♠	Pass	4♣	Pass
4♦	Pass	4♥	Pass
6NT	DBL	Pass	Pass
Pass			

Opening lead: Spade Jack

The giveaway

EVER since the Greeks parked their wooden horse outside Troy's gates, unexpected gifts have carried an implied warning to beware. Nevertheless, the giveaway remains a highly successful device in bridge when, by deliberately giving an opponent a trick, you leave him no alternative but to go wrong. The slightest hesitation will give you away along with the trick. In the following deal, West proved himself a master of the tactic.

We do not approve of North's bid of 4 Hearts. In our methods the 4-Heart bid would normally be taken to indicate possession of the Ace.

After North's encouraging responses, South used Blackwood to check for controls. When he found North with an Aceless hand, he took the gamble that partner had some sort of Club fit—either the Queen or a short suit—or that he could furnish enough trick-taking material in the red suits to dispose of a possible Club loser. It was not an unreasonable gamble, and when dummy's cards were put down it appeared that the gamble would pay off. And it would have, against a less astute defense.

West elected to open a trump, and dummy's 8 of Spades won the trick. Declarer led a low Club from dummy, planning to cash his Ace and King and ruff one or, if necessary, two Clubs with dummy's remaining trumps— a plan that would have succeeded admirably if declarer had pursued it. After ruffing the third Club, declarer would return to his hand with the Ace of Diamonds and trump a fourth Club with dummy's Queen of Spades. Getting back to his hand by trumping a Diamond, South would draw West's remaining trumps. His last Club would be good, and in the end he would concede one trick to the Ace of Hearts and make his slam.

But then West trotted out a Trojan horse. On the very first Club lead, he dropped the Queen!

Put yourself in South's place. He had to assume that if he led another Club, West would trump dummy's Jack. Then the defenders could also cash the Ace of Hearts to set the slam. On the other hand, if South drew the trumps he would prevent West from getting a ruff. Then if the Hearts were favorably placed, that suit might be developed to furnish declarer with two Club discards, and he'd be home free.

So South drew trumps and played his Heart. West followed with a low Heart, and after agonizing over whether to finesse against the Jack by permitting the 9 to ride, South decided to put up the Queen. East won and returned a Diamond, which South won with the Ace. Two more rounds of trumps squeezed no one. Declarer then led to dummy's Club Jack and discovered West's deceit. He took one Club discard on the King of Hearts, but that left him with the Ace and 9 of Clubs while West held the 10–6.

West eventually won the setting trick with the 10 of Clubs—a feat that would have been impossible had he not sacrificed the Queen.

EXTRA TRICK   A trump, usually a poor lead against a slam bid, is often a good lead when you hold strength in the second suit declarer has bid. Note that if West had opened a Heart, declarer could have allowed the lead to run around to his 9 and later taken a ruffing finesse against East's Ace.

Both sides vulnerable
South dealer

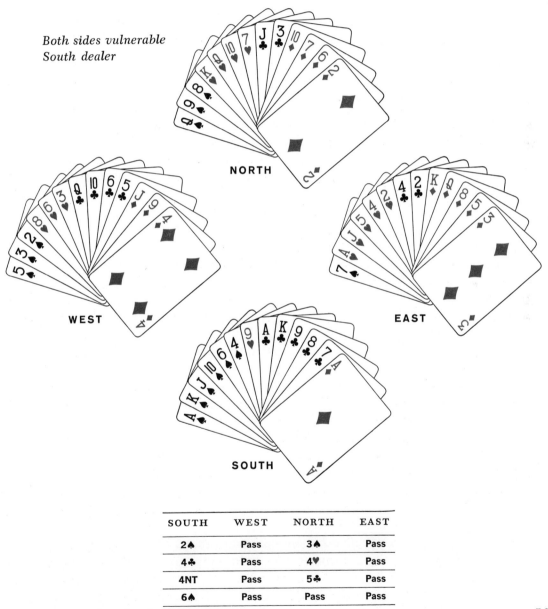

NORTH

WEST

EAST

SOUTH

SOUTH	WEST	NORTH	EAST
2♠	Pass	3♠	Pass
4♣	Pass	4♥	Pass
4NT	Pass	5♣	Pass
6♠	Pass	Pass	Pass

Opening lead: Spade 2

Q & A improves your play

BRIDGE experts are curious people—and you may take that in both senses of the word. After a grueling session of tournament bridge, it is not at all uncommon to find them relaxing in general quiz games that last into the early hours of the morning.

One would think that they had had enough quizzing under the normal demands of play. "What is my partner trying to tell me?" or "Why didn't declarer lead trumps when he had a chance to?" or "Where can we find the tricks to set this contract?" These are the questions a good—and curious— player always asks himself at the table.

Even with an apparently hopeless hand, you cannot let your curiosity flag. It would have been easy for East to go to sleep on this deal. But see how fortunate it was that he remained inquisitive.

No Trump appears to be a superior contract. But South elected to rebid his six-card suit, and North, feeling too insecure about his Club holding to persist with No Trump, raised the Spades to game.

In spite of East's encouraging signal with the 8 of Diamonds on the opening lead of the King, West shifted to the 2 of Hearts. Dummy's Jack was covered by East's Queen and won by declarer's Ace. South led a Diamond, won by West's Ace. East completed his echo when he followed with the Diamond 6. However, West continued with the 6 of Hearts, which was won by dummy's King.

Declarer led dummy's Queen of Diamonds. Of course he knew that East could ruff, but he hoped that this would resolve the trump situation. If he could avoid a trump loser, he would give up only two Diamonds and one Club trick, and his game contract would be assured.

It looked like the moment for East to make use of his otherwise worthless trump. Had he done so, South would have overruffed, cashed the King of Spades and, when East showed out, West's Queen would have been as completely revealed as an ecdysiast after a dozen encores.

But East asked himself some questions. "Why didn't partner give me a Diamond ruff?" The obvious answer was that South held only two Diamonds and would overruff. "Can declarer have a losing Heart?" The answer must be "No," for West's lead of a low one followed by a higher one indicated he held at least three.

Next came the payoff question. "Knowing that I have only two Diamonds, why didn't South draw trumps before playing the good Diamond Queen?" Evidently, South didn't need a discard and was fishing for information about the trump suit. Having answered his own questions, East held on to that "worthless" trump. He discarded a Club and so did South.

East's refusal to ruff must have struck declarer as an effort to protect a trump holding. So he cashed dummy's Spade Ace. But when he led the next Spade, East proved to be out of Spades and declarer out of luck. East had indeed protected a trump holding—his partner's. West's Queen of Spades and Ace of Clubs set the contract.

EXTRA TRICK Even when you hold a seemingly hopeless hand, playing the question-and-answer game may help you to turn one of your worthless-looking cards into the straw that breaks the enemy's back.

North-South vulnerable
South dealer

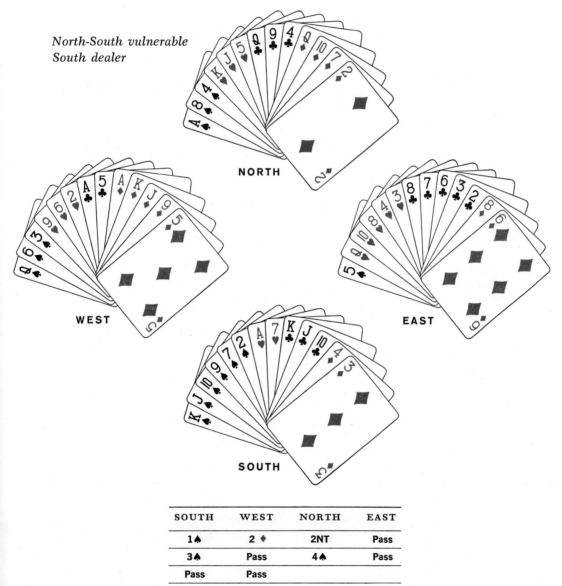

SOUTH	WEST	NORTH	EAST
1♠	2♦	2NT	Pass
3♠	Pass	4♠	Pass
Pass	Pass		

Opening lead: Diamond King

Teacher holds the high cards

IN my early days it was popularly held that "Those who can, do, and those who can't, teach." Whatever merit this may have had as a punch line, it most certainly has little validity as a practical guide.

From the teaching profession have come some of my favorite partners, the most notable of them Peter Leventritt, of the Card School of New York City. A seasoned instructor, he stresses the importance of preserving one's high cards for capturing adversely held honors. Yet in the hand shown here, Leventritt, defending with teammate Harold Ogust, by-passed the opportunity to capture a high card—and to good effect.

The bidding sequence is more or less forced. North opened with 1 Diamond, and South had little choice but to respond with 2 Clubs. North rebid 2 Diamonds. His suit was not, strictly speaking, rebiddable, but a rebid of 2 No Trump is not to be considered with a holding of only 13 high-card points. South showed the nature of his hand by calling 2 No Trump, and North carried on to game.

Leventritt, sitting West, opened the deuce of Spades. Declarer played low from the dummy. East won with the Queen and returned another Spade. Dummy won and led a low Diamond. East played the 9, declarer the Queen and, without the slightest hesitation, West let the Queen hold the trick.

Put yourself in South's place. Apparently East had the Ace of Diamonds. If so, the best chance to set up the suit with only one loser was to take a finesse against West for the Diamond Jack. When declarer led a low Diamond to dummy's 10, Leventritt naturally played low again, and East's Jack won the trick. Back came a third Spade, knocking out dummy's last stopper. Another round of Diamonds lost to West's Ace, and by this time the long Spade had been established. West proceeded to cash that card for the defender's fourth trick.

East's first discard had been the deuce of Hearts, so West shifted to the 8 of Clubs, and East's Queen forced the Ace. A Heart to dummy's King permitted North to cash the two established Diamonds. It was clear to East that if declarer held the Ace and Queen of Hearts, his opponents had the rest of the tricks. So he discarded his Hearts and held the King of Clubs to win the setting trick.

Why did Leventritt duck the first Diamond? If he took the Queen with the Ace, was it not likely that declarer would still take a losing finesse for the Jack and lose two tricks in the Diamond suit?

The answer is that West had to preserve the Ace of Diamonds as a re-entry. If he won the first Diamond he would never get in to cash the fourth

Spade. By playing in such a way that East took a Diamond trick while he still held a third Spade to return, Leventritt kept the timing advantage with the defenders instead of surrendering it to the declarer.

EXTRA TRICK   Usually a defender cannot do better than capture one of declarer's high cards with a higher one. But winning a trick at the right time is sometimes more important than killing an opposing honor. The privilege of leading at the crucial moment may be valuable enough to make it worthwhile that you run the risk of losing the trick altogether.

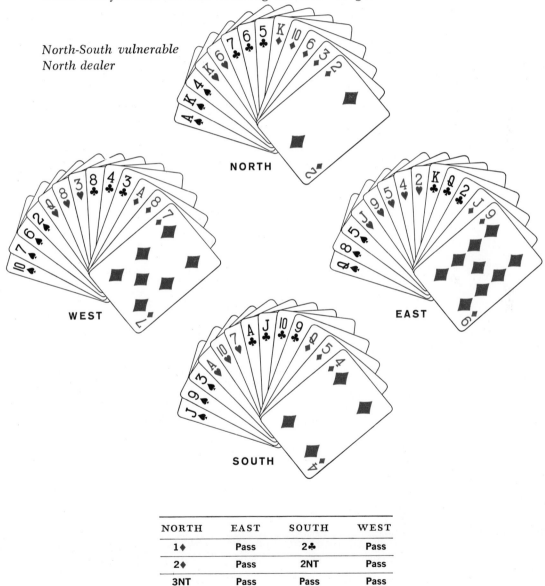

North-South vulnerable
North dealer

NORTH	EAST	SOUTH	WEST
1♦	Pass	2♣	Pass
2♦	Pass	2NT	Pass
3NT	Pass	Pass	Pass

Opening lead: Spade 2

Special island magic

HAITI, that magic-loving island republic, is playing high-class international bridge these days, and no legerdemain about it. Although the Haitians are short on experience, their play in team-of-four and pair competition is surprisingly rugged. I found this out during a trip to the island in 1960. Several companions and I had gone to Haiti to encourage and promote bridge there. I am not sure that our mission was necessary. It might even have proved embarrassing were it not for some bridge magic on our side — such as this demonstration put on by Harry Harkavy of Miami during a deal in the team-of-four contest. (*See diagram at right.*)

At the other table, where my partner and I held the East-West cards, our opponents and hosts settled in a comfortable contract of 3 Clubs, making 4 when declarer lost a trick in every suit but Spades. North-South scored 130 points (in tournament play a bonus of 50 points is awarded for fulfilling a part-score contract). To everyone at our table this appeared to be a normal result, with small prospect for any great swing. But with Harkavy in action, there is virtually no such thing as a swing-proof deal.

At his table, North's 1 No-Trump rebid designates a fair to middling hand. Harkavy (South) counted on finding perhaps 15 high-card points and a couple of Spades in his partner's hand, which would have made the 4-Spade contract a reasonable gamble.

When West opened the King of Hearts and the dummy was put down, it seemed that South would have to lose at least one trick in every suit. But with the kind of juggling for which he is famous, Harkavy made one of these tricks disappear.

After his King of Hearts held, West switched to a low Diamond. Dummy's 9 was covered by East's Jack and won by Declarer's Ace. A trump to dummy's Ace permitted South to ruff a Heart. Harkavy next led a Diamond to the 10, forcing East's King. East returned a Diamond to dummy's Queen and South discarded a Club. Another Heart was ruffed and West's Ace fell.

After a successful finesse of dummy's Club Queen, the Club Ace was cashed. Declarer did not make the mistake of discarding his losing Club on the good Heart. West would have ruffed, led a Diamond to be trumped by East's Queen, and after South overruffed, would have held the setting trick with his still-guarded 10 of Spades.

Instead, declarer led dummy's last Diamond. East ruffed with the Queen and South overruffed. This play stripped West of all his cards except the 10 8 4 of trumps. So, when South led the losing 8 of Clubs, West had to trump the trick. This not only cost East his Club trick; it also cost West a trump trick. For at the twelfth trick West had to lead from his 10–8 of Spades into Harkavy's J–9.

EXTRA TRICK A declarer who is faced with too many losers will often find it to his advantage to reduce his trump holding down to the level (or even below that) of his opponent's. In the end this can lead to a situation where the opponent has to trump his partner's good trick and then present declarer with a trick.

North-South vulnerable
North dealer

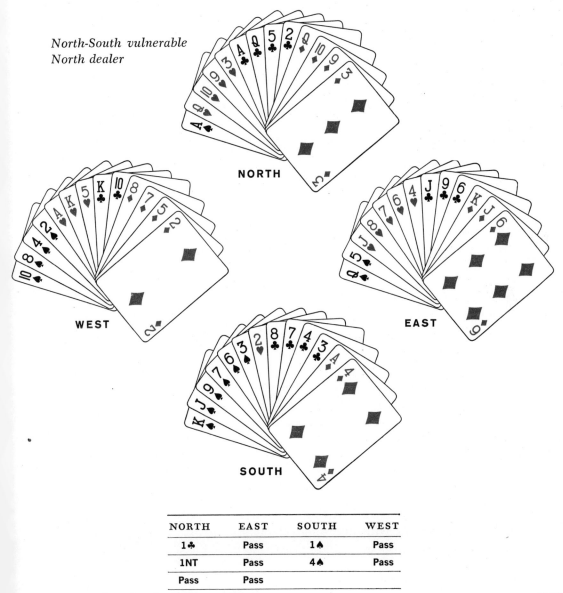

NORTH	EAST	SOUTH	WEST
1♣	Pass	1♠	Pass
1NT	Pass	4♠	Pass
Pass	Pass		

Opening lead: Heart King

A non-political convention

WHENEVER a new and better way to play a hand of bridge is developed, there are bound to be long, if subdued, protests by those players we have met who prefer to muddle through in their old-fashioned way and to trust to their upturned noses rather than to the findings of the experts. They have gotten along reasonably well through the years, and in their outmoded practices they find contentment.

Perhaps such players would do well to imitate the milk vendor who told his patrons, "My cows are not contented; they are anxious to do better."

A hand on which one of the old-timers who decries "these newfangled ideas" was unable to muddle through is shown on the page at right.

Against the 3 No-Trump contract, West chose the natural lead of the 4 of Spades. East's Queen was permitted to hold. The Spade 6 was returned and again declarer ducked. West won with the Jack. Now the only important Spade outstanding was the Ace, and West could drive it out with any of his three remaining Spades with equal effect. Since it made no difference to him, he chose to do so with the 2.

Declarer won and took a Club finesse, which lost to East. East's aim now was to put partner in to cash the setting tricks. Mindful of South's original Heart bid, he chose to return a Diamond. Thus declarer scampered off with nine tricks—four Diamonds and four Clubs in addition to his Ace of Spades.

Should East, as his partner contended, have smelled out the killing Heart return because dummy discarded a Heart on the third Spade? Maybe, but there is a convention which makes such guesses unnecessary.

When a player who has opened a suit is about to establish it finally, he can use a simple device to suggest to his partner the suit in which his future re-entry will be found. The clue is the size of the card he uses to drive out declarer's last stopper. If he leads his lowest card, he announces that his entry is to be found in the lower-ranking of the off-suits (in this case, Diamonds). If he establishes his suit by leading his highest card—in this case, the King—the suggested return is the higher-ranking of the off-suits (in this instance Hearts).

EXTRA TRICK One beauty of this convention is that it does not interfere to any great extent with any long-established theory. It is an additional refinement which may be employed with no added cost.

East-West vulnerable
South dealer

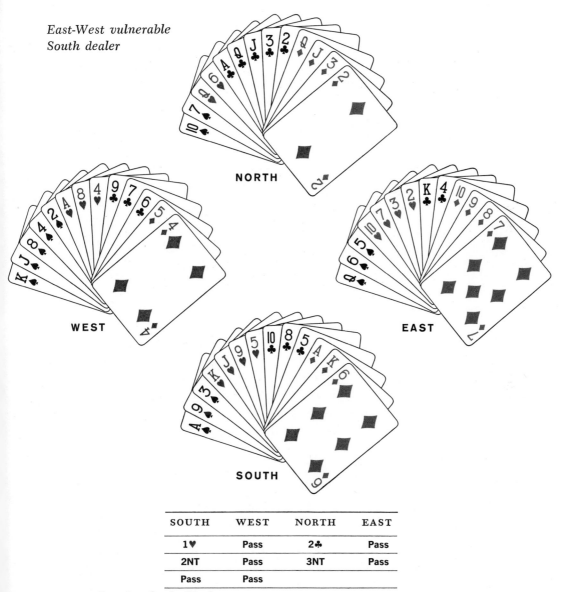

NORTH

WEST

EAST

SOUTH

SOUTH	WEST	NORTH	EAST
1♥	Pass	2♣	Pass
2NT	Pass	3NT	Pass
Pass	Pass		

Opening lead: Spade 4

The power of Kings

FOR the world's monarchs, these are perilous times. Even in a pack of cards, where one might assume that a King's power would remain constant, he is obliged to settle occasionally for something less than his accustomed authority. In the game of "KLOB," for instance, the King of trumps ranks lower than the Jack and 9.

In bridge, fortunately, a King is still a potentate. He can force out an Ace; he can stop the run of an adverse suit; and he can, of course, win any card of lower denomination. Seldom, however, has His Majesty played so many roles as in the following deal, which came up in a practice game between Mr. and Mrs. Howard Schenken and Mrs. Edith Kemp and John Gerber before my TV show.

The defense of this hand was so spectacular that I am both glad and sorry it was not played before the cameras; it would have been a splendid hand for the TV audience to watch, but the deal was so unusual that the viewers might have charged we had rigged it.

The bidding was governed somewhat by the conditions that usually apply in a TV match. Because of the pressure of the time limit, the team that is trailing must hope that it will become lucky fast in order to win.

On West's opening lead of the King of Diamonds South dropped the 7, trying to make East's 8 look like a come-on signal. But West wasn't tempted to lead another Diamond because he knew that his partner would have played the Jack on the trick if she had held it.

Dummy's Spade suit looked threatening, especially with the Ace of Clubs as an outside entry, so Schenken's second lead was the King of Clubs, thus killing dummy's entry to the Spades.

It would not have helped declarer to duck this card, since a Club continuation would force dummy's Ace on the next lead. So the Club Ace was taken and South came to his hand with the Queen of Clubs to lead the 8 of Spades.

Once again it was necessary to sacrifice a King. If West played low, declarer would pass the trick. And if East took her Queen, declarer would try another finesse at his next opportunity and bring in four Spade tricks and his game. By playing the King on the first lead, West killed the Spade suit. Declarer could have ducked the trick, hoping that West held the King and Queen, but Gerber preferred to hope that two Spade tricks would be enough. He took the Ace and led the Jack. Not being sure that South held only two Spades, East ducked this trick as Declarer had hoped she would.

Now Gerber shifted his attack to the Heart suit. He finessed the Queen, and West made a more prosaic use of his fourth King to capture the trick and lead his third Club, knocking out South's remaining stopper. Declarer still had hopes of a Heart break or a Diamond end play, but neither of these prospects materialized. South took only three Clubs, two Spades, two Hearts and one Diamond before East got in to win the rest of he tricks and put the contract down one.

EXTRA TRICK   Remember that the King has powers other than the mere winning of a trick. Sometimes, by sacrificing that potential, you can get back several tricks in return.

East-West vulnerable
South dealer

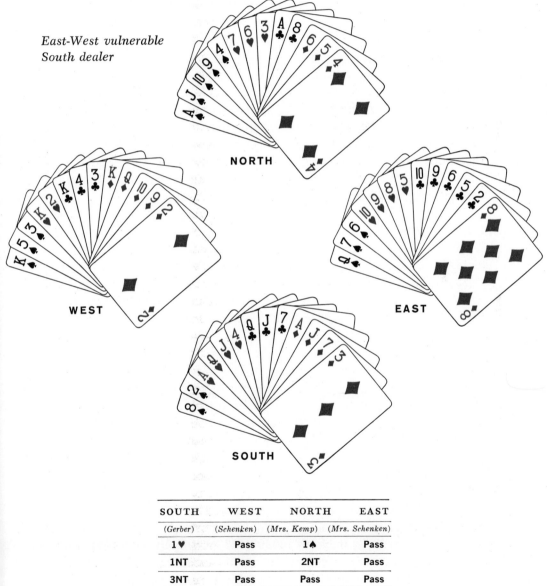

SOUTH	WEST	NORTH	EAST
(Gerber)	*(Schenken)*	*(Mrs. Kemp)*	*(Mrs. Schenken)*
1♥	Pass	1♠	Pass
1NT	Pass	2NT	Pass
3NT	Pass	Pass	Pass

Opening lead: Diamond King

IN TOURNAMENT bridge there is only one way for a player to pass his chance to bid; that is simply to say "Pass." Anything else, even "No bid," once quite acceptable, is frowned upon generally and banned in international competition.

Bidding wasn't always so strictly governed. In the early days of the game, one of the politer forms of accepting the last bid was to say, "Content." This suggestion that partner remain quiet was banished for obvious reasons, but there are occasions today when a player might like to revive the quaint bid. Present-day bidders have the penalty double with which they can convey the same "keep quiet" message to partner. But the bid is not always satisfactory, as West discovered unhappily in the following deal—which was told to me by my frequent teammate, Boris Koytchou.

Only a player with a pronounced aversion to being excluded from the auction would have ventured a raise to 5 Clubs with the hand South held. But this particular South was the kind of competitor who is easily ignited by such pre-emptive tactics as East's jump to 4 Spades.

And West, on this occasion, was a player who would have preferred that call, "Content," had it still been available. He was so pleased with the 5-Club bid that he wanted nothing to disturb it. Therefore he felt he had to double in order to warn partner not to rebid his Spade suit.

Left undisturbed, the 5-Club contract would have been set, if only for the reason that East would have been on lead. After cashing two Spade tricks, a third round of Spades would have permitted West to overruff dummy for the setting trick.

However, West's double of 5 Clubs had given South a chance to escape. So, uncertain of the quality of his partner's Club suit (the opening bid could conceivably have been made on as few as three to the Ace or King), South discreetly retired to 5 Hearts. The only thing that justified West's double of that contract was his conviction that South was firmly in a trap.

Dummy won the opening Club lead, cashed the Heart Ace and led a Heart to declarer's Queen. The Jack of Clubs was finessed, and another Club lead established the suit. West's last trump was drawn with dummy's Heart Jack, and South's losing Spades were discarded on the long Clubs. In the end, declarer lost only one Diamond trick.

Why didn't North redouble? Would East have gone on in Spades if West hadn't doubled? Or if North redoubled? At 5 Spades doubled, would East have gone down two tricks? (This would have required a perfect defense, with North overtaking the Jack of Clubs opening, cashing the Ace of Diamonds and underleading the Heart Ace, to allow South to return a

Diamond for North to ruff.) All of these questions are academic—and un-answerable, which is probably just as well.

South did volunteer to answer one question, however. "The ice-cold slam was not biddable," he contended, "because West refused to tell us in advance that he didn't have a Spade to lead."

EXTRA TRICK When you think that you can set the opponents, don't double if this call will enable them to escape to something better or safer. Just say "Pass."

East-West vulnerable
North dealer

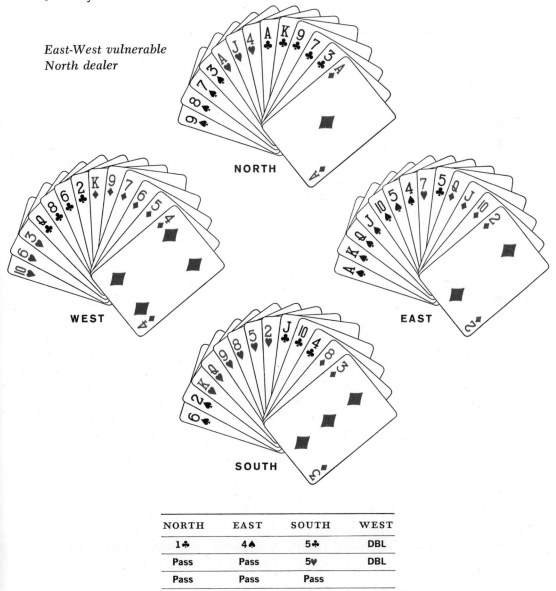

NORTH	EAST	SOUTH	WEST
1♣	4♠	5♣	DBL
Pass	Pass	5♥	DBL
Pass	Pass	Pass	

Opening lead: Club 6

The man who likes to lose

ALEX DREIER, my good friend with whom I share duties in the commentators' booth during my TV show, is a man who likes to lose—but not at the bridge table. Dreier is a huge man who not long ago weighed well over 300 pounds. He has lost 80 pounds but not a bit of the good nature that makes it such a pleasure to work with him.

Dreier represents the average player. The questions he asks on the show sometimes make him seem less than the adept player he is. Do not be deceived. Here is one of the hands he played in a warmup game with the stars a few minutes before they went on camera.

The bidding was a bit optimistic, which is not unusual in TV bridge or in any game where a short time of play often encourages bidders to shoot for good scores on every hand. Playing South, Dreier bid the Diamond suit after rebidding the Clubs, hoping that North might be encouraged to try 3 No Trump. But, even after North had raised Diamonds, South returned to his seven-card Club suit. However, North's preference was too decided to leave the Club bid in, despite South's having made it obvious that there was a great disparity in the length of the two suits. Dreier accepted his partner's final judgment, and then proceeded to vindicate it.

After winning the first trick with the Ace of Spades, West continued the suit on the theory that it would do him less harm than a shift. Dreier won with the Spade King and led the 2 of Diamonds. West played the 7—a troublesome false card—and dummy's 8 was won by East's 10. East returned the 3 of Hearts, and South, having already lost the only two tricks he could afford, trumped this trick, cashed the Ace of Clubs, and trumped a low Club with dummy's Diamond 6.

Now Dreier had to play so that he would not lose another trump trick. In view of the fall of the 7 from West on the first lead of the suit, it was tempting to play the Queen through, hoping that East held the King-4 and West the blank Jack. If that were the case and East covered the Diamond Queen with the King, and the Jack dropped, dummy's 9 would be high.

The trouble with this line of play was that in order to draw East's supposed remaining Diamond, declarer would have to play another round of trumps. This would leave the lead in dummy and South would have no way to get back to his hand. Thus there was really only one way the Diamonds could lie that would let the 5-Diamond contract be made. Dreier accordingly led a low Diamond, East played the King, and Dreier's faith was justified. He won the trick with the Ace and abandoned trumps, leading out good Clubs. Whenever West chose to ruff, dummy could overruff, and South's hand remained with the 5 of trumps—the only one outstanding—as an entry to the good Clubs.

EXTRA TRICK   When there is only one possible distribution that will permit you to make your contract, play the hand as if that distribution existed. You will be surprised how often the cards will fall into line for you.

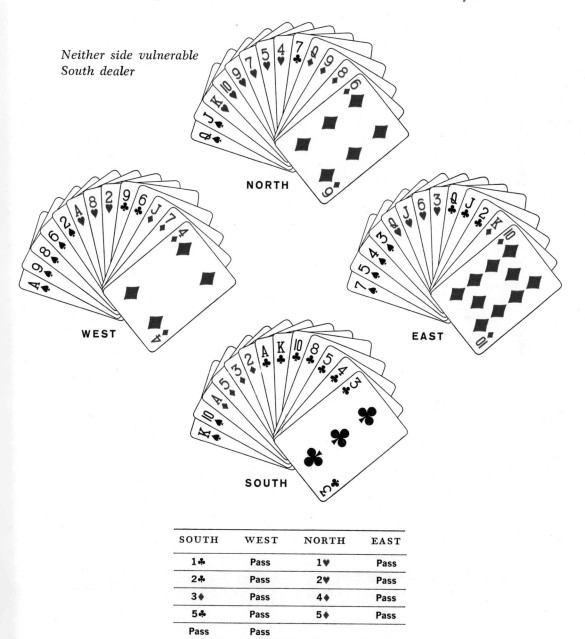

Neither side vulnerable
South dealer

NORTH

WEST

EAST

SOUTH

SOUTH	WEST	NORTH	EAST
1♣	Pass	1♥	Pass
2♣	Pass	2♥	Pass
3♦	Pass	4♦	Pass
5♣	Pass	5♦	Pass
Pass	Pass		

Opening lead: Spade Ace

Tricks with No Trump

"AS the inventor of the 'unusual No Trump,'" an indignant correspondent writes, "you are hereby beseeched to purge the miserable . . . ! The thing has become a booby trap." Her husband, she reports, has given the convention a brisk workout—and their losses have been on the spectacular side. "Please, Mr. Goren," she pleads, "do something about this."

First off, I disclaim authorship of the unusual No Trump, but I have included it in recent books because I believe that, properly handled, it can be of great value.

For example, here is a hand in which my associate Leland Ferer and I used the device to great advantage in a recent tournament in Haiti.

North's bid of 2 No Trump was "unusual," and met all the requirements for that call. First, it was quite evident that the bid did not indicate any real desire to play the hand at No Trump, for if North had held a No Trump hand he would have doubled West's call. Second, to justify asking partner to choose between Diamonds and Clubs at the 3 level, North's hand was such that he might have bid either of the minor suits himself.

One can generally discern when partner's No Trump bid is unusual. When you get into trouble it is because partner has abused the bid in hopes of finding you with strength and length in one or the other of the minors. Good support for a minor is not enough; the unusual No Trump bidder really says, "Partner, I bid 3 Clubs or 3 Diamonds, whichever you prefer." Of course, a bid in those words would be illegal; the unusual No Trump is a legal way to bid both suits at once.

So, getting back to the hand we are discussing—after East bid 3 Spades, my bid (South) of 4 Diamonds on a three-card suit was not startling. All I was doing was raising my partner's implied 3-Diamond bid.

East won the first trick with the Ace of Hearts and led a Spade to dummy's Ace. Dummy led a low Diamond which East ducked, permitting my Queen to win. The King of Hearts, followed by a Heart ruff, cleared the entire suit. A trump lead brought the Ace from East, who then forced dummy by playing the King of Spades.

A Diamond to the King cleared all hands of trumps. As I ran the established Heart suit, East found himself increasingly hard put to find discards. When the last Heart was played, dummy kept the A-Q of Clubs; South's remaining cards were the Jack of Spades and a Club; East held the Queen of Spades and the guarded King of Clubs with one discard yet to be made. At this point he threw in his cards and conceded the last two tricks. East, to be sure, might have fought it out by discarding a Club and compelling me to make the final guess. He chose to pay me the compliment of recognizing that I had his hand "pegged." Making 5 Diamonds produced a top score that helped us to win the pair event.

EXTRA TRICK   Remember that an unusual No Trump is the equivalent of a bid in both minor suits. Remember also that as partner of the unusual No-Trump bidder, when you first mention a minor suit you are really only raising a suit your partner has in effect already bid.

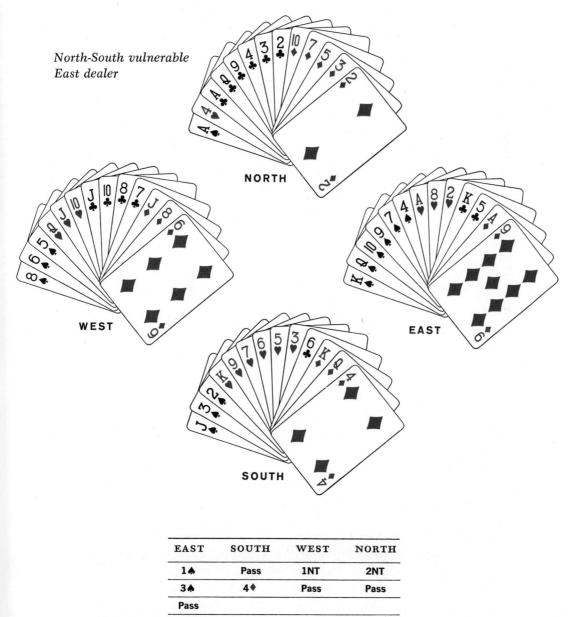

North-South vulnerable
East dealer

NORTH

WEST

EAST

SOUTH

EAST	SOUTH	WEST	NORTH
1♠	Pass	1NT	2NT
3♠	4♦	Pass	Pass
Pass			

Opening lead: Heart Queen

A Greek to beware of

BRIDGE is an international language. I was never more sure of this than when I played in Athens recently with Markos Nomikos, head of the Greek shipping company that bears his name. Although we were many thousands of miles from the Regency Club in New York, the game we played had the flavor of the best hands played at the club.

The opening lead in the game described was unusual. It was made against my partner, Constantin Platsis, who played South and who, with Nomikos, is a member of the Regency. The lead, I am now convinced, did not succeed for the single reason that bridge is international. Because Platsis correctly guessed what was behind the lead, he was able to bring home a touch-and-go slam.

Costa, as Platsis is called, was a high-ranking officer in the Greek Air Force in World War II and a daring flyer. When the Nazis overran Greece, he joined the R.A.F. At the bridge table, as in the air, he is a bold tactician.

In this deal, it was necessary for him as declarer to defy mathematical probabilities in order to reach the right conclusion. Because good players rarely lead an Ace against a slam, South concluded that West expected to win a trump trick to set the contract. So South, crediting West with the missing Spade Queen, took precautions against finding it triply guarded.

After West won the Heart Ace, he shifted to a Diamond, taken by dummy's King. Costa came to his hand with the Ace of Clubs and led the Jack of Spades, letting it ride for a first-round finesse. When it held, he led another Spade to dummy's 9, cashed the King and came back to his hand with the Queen of Clubs to draw West's Queen of trumps, bringing home the slam.

Had West's too-revealing lead of the Ace of Hearts cost him the chance to set the hand? I doubt it. Suppose West fails to cash his Heart trick and leads a Club or Diamond. Instead of guessing the Spade finesse, Costa would try to drop the Spade Queen, hoping that even if the Queen did not fall he could avoid a Heart loser.

Assuming a Club lead, South wins, cashes the Spade Ace and another Club, then leads to dummy's Spade King. If the Spades are three-two, the slam is assured unless the player with the Queen has fewer than three Clubs. Even with the four-one trump break, South makes the hand. He discards his Hearts on the King and Jack of Clubs, cashes dummy's King of Diamonds and comes to his hand by ruffing a Heart. The Ace and Queen of Diamonds are cashed. After that, South leads his fourth Diamond to be taken care of by dummy's 9 of trumps. West can win only his Queen of Spades.

EXTRA TRICK   An Ace is seldom the best lead against a slam contract—unless you have at least one other Ace in reserve. But when there is danger that you will lose your only Ace unless you take it immediately, then lead it fast and hope that another trick will materialize somewhere.

Neither side vulnerable
North dealer

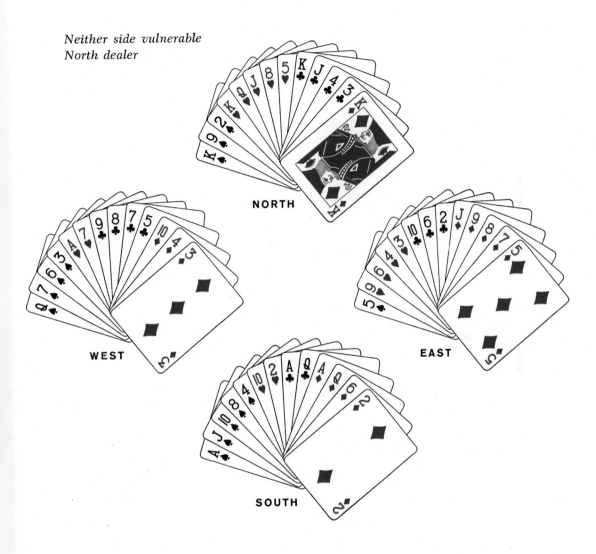

NORTH	EAST	SOUTH	WEST
1♥	Pass	1♠	Pass
2♠	Pass	6♠	Pass
Pass	Pass		

Opening lead: Heart Ace

Hedging your losses

HOW much should you trust your partner? A classic example of two who didn't trust one another at all is the deal in which both partners rescued each other from doubled contracts, beginning at 3 No Trump and ending at 5 Spades. The final bid was set exactly one trick. Not one of the previous contracts that the balky partners so obligingly took each other out of could have been defeated. The hand has become the standard illustration for teaching, rightfully, that you should trust your partner a lot.

Still, there are times in bidding when it is obvious that one partner has gone so far off in the wrong direction that only a quick move to a new suit will hold down losses. When this happens it is worth the risk of going down 200 or 300 points just to get into the right suit. You might even end up a winner, as did the partners in the following hand.

Obviously, both North and South's early bids were made with the hope of finding a profitable sacrifice against the vulnerable opponents. Little can be said for North's free bid of 3 Clubs on a weak hand that included the glaring defect of a void in the suit partner had bid. Such a hand can only promise defensive strength, especially if partner opens the suit he has bid.

South's 4-Spade bid was also rather desperate, but he hoped that North's Club bid included at least neutral Spade support.

However, even though their earlier bids were wrongly reasoned, both North and South were justified in trying to leap from a sure frying pan into what might not be so hot a fire. North would fare better at 5 Clubs than South would at 4 Spades. And South's 5-Diamond bid, if it failed to find backing in North's hand, couldn't cost more than an extra 200 points even if North had to go on to 6 Clubs. Unless North had an eight-card suit, South could expect to find at least distributional support for Diamonds.

South won the first trick with the Heart Ace, ruffed a Spade in dummy, returned by trumping a Club and ruffed another Spade with the Jack of Diamonds. A second Club ruff let South lead a third Spade. He could have played for a one-trick set by trumping this low and leading dummy's King of Clubs, but he decided to go all out.

The third Spade was ruffed with dummy's Diamond Queen and a low Diamond led. South finessed his 10, cashed the Ace to drop East's King and led a fourth Spade, conceding a trick to East's Ace. The defenders collected a Heart trick, but South remained with the last trump and two good Spades, and so brought home his doubled contract. This was worth 550 points, whereas North would have gone down at least 300 at 5 Clubs. South's decision to go all out in the play was based on shrewd visualization of the opposing distribution. He placed East with four Spades, five Hearts (since he had bid that suit rather than Spades), two Clubs (proved by the fall of the Ace on the second lead of that suit), and consequently two Diamonds, which, considering West's failure to double, probably included the King.

EXTRA TRICK I don't mean to imply that bidding duels between partners are usually profitable. The opposite is more apt to be true. But there are no "nevers" in bridge.

East-West vulnerable
North dealer

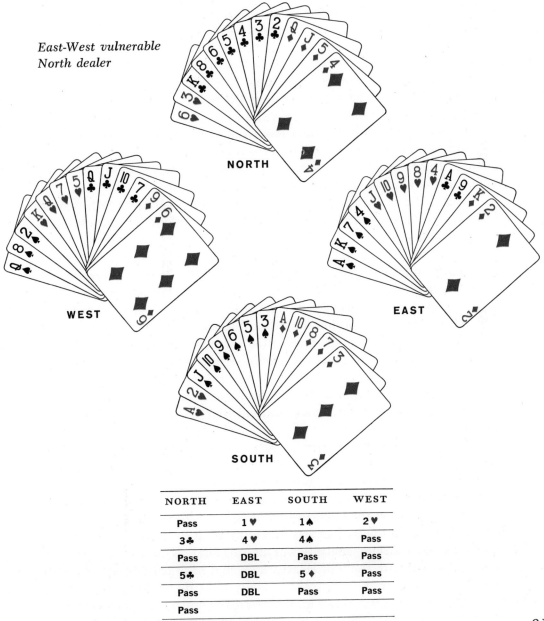

NORTH	EAST	SOUTH	WEST
Pass	1 ♥	1 ♠	2 ♥
3 ♣	4 ♥	4 ♠	Pass
Pass	DBL	Pass	Pass
5 ♣	DBL	5 ♦	Pass
Pass	DBL	Pass	Pass
Pass			

Opening lead: Heart King

The deuce or the dickens

FROM Noah Webster's point of view, it doesn't matter whether your partner gives you the deuce or the dickens. Either way, you get the devil. But a bridge player's view is apt to be different from a lexicographer's, as you will see by the story that stems from the following deal.

Back in the early thirties a series of par contests, called the World Bridge Olympics, was presented to bridge players the world over. Participants in various segments of the globe simultaneously played the same deals against pre-established par results. Recently, under the supervision of the World Bridge Federation, the par Olympics were revived.

Hands for the contest were prepared by a group of Australian bridge experts, chosen because they had had wide experience with such events. The vast distances between Australia's bridge centers make par bridge popular, if not necessary, "down under." This deal, played in the U. S., is typical of the kind the experts usually select.

South had a classic minimum No-Trump opening, and North, whose 9 points are buttressed by a five-card suit and an abundance of intermediate cards—10s and 9s—was justified in jumping to game. It is no sound objection that the partnership count was as little as 25 points. Even with South's minimum holding, the game would have been a laydown if South had held the Jack of Hearts instead of the Jack of Diamonds.

East played the deuce of Spades on the first trick. South took it with his Ace and tried to establish dummy's Clubs, leading the King. West ducked and also let the Queen hold. Notice that on this first lead of Clubs East played the deuce, one of several eloquent signals. On the third Club lead, which West won with the Ace, East dropped the deuce of Diamonds.

West persisted with Spades and declarer gladly accepted the trick, winning two Spades, three Diamonds and four Clubs to bring home the game.

When East pointed the finger of scorn at his partner, he was justified. "I'd have taken five Heart tricks, for down two. It seems to me I made it clear I didn't want you to lead Spades or Diamonds."

West retorted mildly, "Why did you discard the deuce of Diamonds? We didn't have to set the hand two tricks to get a good result. You should have signaled with the 8 of Hearts to tell me what to lead."

West's post-mortem analysis was as unsound as his play. Had East chosen to signal with the 8 of Hearts, he would have parted not only with one of the setting tricks; he would actually have tossed away both. With the 8-spot used as a lavish signal, West's Heart return would allow East to win three Heart tricks. But South's 7 would then control the fourth round.

The defenders would win only three Hearts and one Club, and declarer would still make his nine tricks.

The only chance East had was by telling his partner what suits not to lead. So he was right in giving his partner the deuces as well as the dickens for ignoring them.

EXTRA TRICK   A five-card suit is usually worth an extra trick in the play of a No-Trump contract, so with 9 points and a fair five-carder, raise all the way from 1 No Trump to 3.

Neither side vulnerable
South dealer

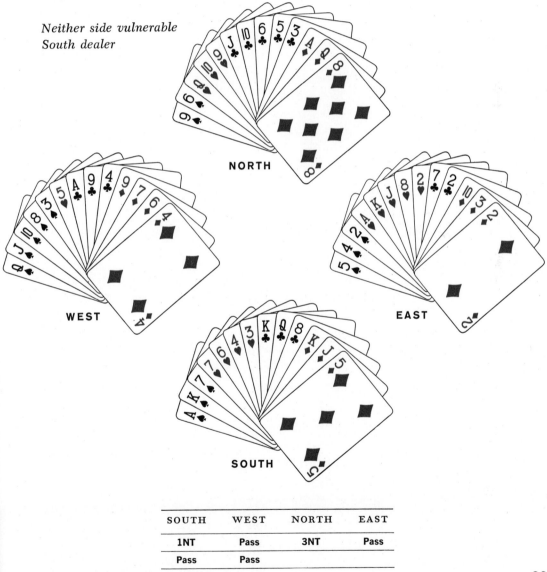

SOUTH	WEST	NORTH	EAST
1NT	Pass	3NT	Pass
Pass	Pass		

Opening lead: Spade Queen

Chic, charming and cool

THE FRENCH make dangerous bridge opponents. Any international competitor who has been chastened by defeat knows that behind the Frenchman's disarming politeness is an intense desire to beat one's brains out. This is particularly hard to remember when competing against French women. Their charm and chic often disguise a solid ability as players.

One such lady is Mme. Gérard Bourchtoff, wife of a member of the French team that won the first World Bridge Team Olympiad in Turin in 1960. As quiet and small as her more famous husband is stentorian and burly, Mme. Bourchtoff (West) demonstrated a practical approach to the problem she encountered in the deal shown at right. It was her job to find an entry to her partner's hand—which required some cool calculation.

The hand was played in a match-point pair game. In this kind of competition a score of minus 200 points is usually the kiss of death, because it is more than the opponents could probably earn from any part-score contract of their own.

Mme. Bourchtoff made her first bright move when she led the singleton Jack of Diamonds, declining the more obvious King of Clubs lead. This decision must have been inspired by feminine intuition; if she had chosen the "safe" lead of the King of Clubs, the contract could not have been defeated.

Declarer won the first trick with the Diamond King and returned a low Club, setting up the threat of a Club ruff by dummy. Now, when Mme. Bourchtoff won the Queen of Clubs, if she knocked out dummy's trumps by cashing her Ace and leading another Spade, declarer could draw the defenders' remaining trumps, go to dummy with a Diamond, discard a Club loser on the third Diamond and take a successful Heart finesse, making 3-odd. But West did not make that mistake.

Instead, she led a low trump. East's Jack forced declarer's King. Another Club lead was won by the Club King, and West cashed the Ace of Spades, removing dummy's remaining trump. Next came the daring but essential play of the 3 of Clubs.

Mme. Bourchtoff recognized that South must hold the Ace of Hearts as part of the required strength for his opening bid. Hence, the only hope of getting partner on lead was to find him with the Club 9.

She led her small Club, and East was somewhat surprised when his 9 won the trick, but he was in no doubt about what to return. His Diamond lead was ruffed by West, the Ace of Clubs was cashed for the setting trick, and then West threw declarer back into his own hand by leading her last trump.

Thus deprived of ever making a lead from dummy (once he had failed to win the first trick with dummy's Diamond Queen), declarer now had to surrender a trick to the Heart King, and went down the critical number — two tricks, for a loss of 200 points.

EXTRA TRICK Don't be a blind hoper. Give your opponents credit for holding the high cards their bidding indicates. Then, if you believe there is a chance your partner could have the card that will lead to the setting trick, play him for it. Though your play may seem daring, it is worthwhile.

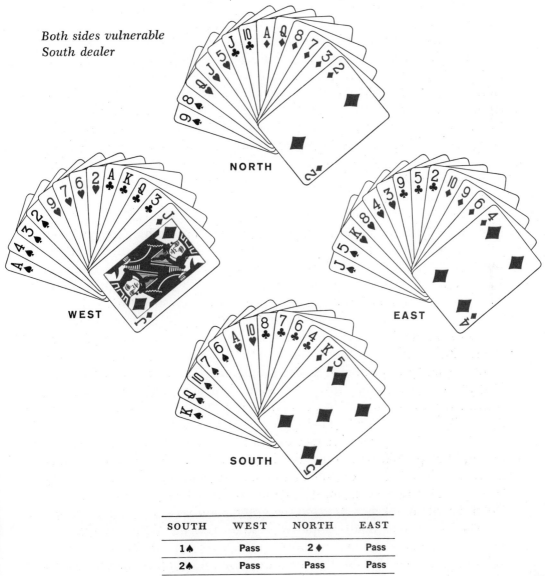

Both sides vulnerable
South dealer

SOUTH	WEST	NORTH	EAST
1♠	Pass	2♦	Pass
2♠	Pass	Pass	Pass

Opening lead: Diamond Jack

Double danger

IN an early book on the subject of contract bridge Ely Culbertson wrote, "The purpose of a penalty double is to defeat the opponents' contract and collect the maximum number of points in undertrick penalties." That definition places the twin aims of a penalty double in the proper order of importance. Somehow, that order has become reversed in the lexicon of the average modern player. Often he is so intent on making a killing that he overlooks the prime target: to defeat the contract.

The moral of the following hand might be: "It does not pay to be greedy." This is not the moral, because both sides were guilty of greed, although only one of them got penalized for it. The "justice," if any, is that victory went to the side best able to exploit the avarice of the other. South's bidding was outrageously greedy. Granted, he knew from North's rebid of Clubs that his partner had a long suit and a better-than-minimum hand (else North would have rebid 2 No Trump in response to South's jump take-out.) South also knew, from North's Blackwood responses, that North held one Ace and two Kings. But that still left two Kings missing, and thus thirteen cold tricks were not in sight.

As for West, he could assume that at least one of his Kings must be safe, since North had only one Ace behind him. But nothing except greed (or unrestrained enthusiasm) can explain West's double of the grand-slam contract. In essence, this double told declarer that both of the missing Kings were off-side. True, there are few players astute enough to profit from such information, but South happened to be one of them.

Normally, South might well have run off his four Diamonds and six Clubs, planning to guess which finesse to take at the end, Spades or Hearts. But with the near certainty that both Kings were wrong, South made a shrewd adjustment. After cashing the four Diamond tricks and discarding a Heart from the table, South laid down the Spade Ace. He then cashed the Club Ace, overtook the Club Jack and ran the rest of the Clubs, discarding his own 5 and Queen of Spades and two Hearts.

West, finally having to reduce to two cards, was over a barrel. He had to keep the Spade King against dummy's Jack, hence was forced to blank his Heart King. Thereupon, sticking to his original sound assumption that West would not have doubled without the two kings, declarer led the Heart directly to his own Ace and the grand slam became a *fait accompli*.

The line of play South employed is known as the Vienna Coup. This involves the deliberate setting up of a trick for an opponent and then squeezing him out of it. Note that South cannot bring off a squeeze against West *without* cashing the Spade Ace before running the long Club suit.

Otherwise, South himself cannot discard profitably on the Club suit; whichever suit he kept, Spades or Hearts, West would keep over him.

EXTRA TRICK Before you double the opponents, think of the odds. In this case, West lost 2,490 points by an action that could not gain more than 100 — not a sound investment.

Both sides vulnerable
North dealer

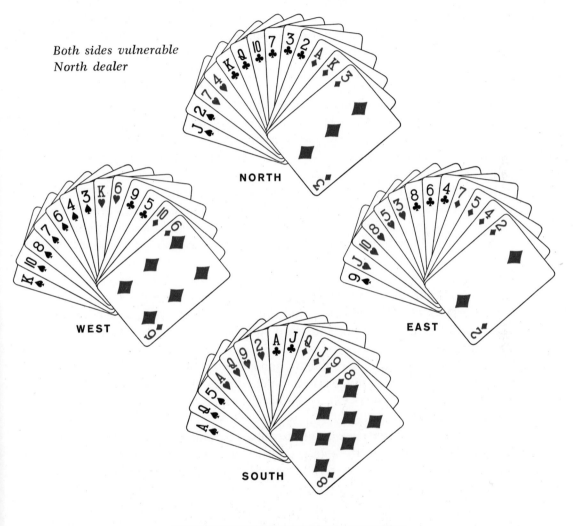

NORTH	EAST	SOUTH	WEST
1♣	Pass	2♥	Pass
3♣	Pass	4NT	Pass
5♦	Pass	5NT	Pass
6♥	Pass	7NT	DBL
Pass	Pass	Pass	

Opening lead: Diamond 10

Finessing the finesse

LEE HAZEN, a New York lawyer, has been one of this country's most respected players for more than twenty years. He also is a talented raconteur. One of his favorite stories is about a player who finessed against both of the defenders for a missing Queen and won both finesses. His first finesse was through Hazen up to dummy's Ace-10-small. Since Hazen had the Queen, this finesse succeeded. Several tricks and many minutes later, declarer led a low card from the board up to his own King-Jack. He played the Jack, and Hazen immediately and erringly followed with a small card rather than his Queen. As Hazen put it, "The only question about this hand was which was worse, declarer's memory or my eyesight."

Recently Hazen came up with a new twist to the two-way finesse. He called it "the two-way non-finesse." The way the bidding went, as shown in the diagram at right, will require a little explanation.

Hazen was South, and let him explain his 3-Diamond bid himself. "I can only tell you that my partner plays what you might term a flexible 2 No Trump. That bid could have meant that he just did not like either of my suits, or that if we were going to play the hand at No Trump he would like to have had the fun of being declarer. Anyway, we got to within one trick of our best contract when North bid 5 Clubs. We could have made 6 in that suit." I cannot say that this is a perfectly satisfactory justification of South's rebid of his four-card suit, but that action did lead to an interesting contract.

At first glance Hazen's problem—namely, how to win eleven tricks at Diamonds—appeared to hinge on guessing which opponent held the Queen of Diamonds, but declarer made the hand by playing both opponents for that card.

South won the first trick with the King of Spades, cashed the Ace of Clubs and the Ace-King of Hearts, then led a Spade to dummy's Ace. He ruffed a low Club with the 8 of Diamonds and trumped his remaining Spade with dummy's Diamond 7 when West showed out, discarding a Club.

A third round of Clubs was trumped with the Diamond 9, dropping West's King. The stage was now set for the double non-finesse. South led a low Heart and trumped it with dummy's Ace of Diamonds. Then he led another Club and trumped that one with his Diamond King.

South now had ten tricks home, and a Heart lead, trumped with dummy's 10 of Diamonds, was bound to produce the eleventh. Either it would win that trick or it would establish South's Jack when, as was the case, East overruffed.

By maneuvering as he did, declarer insured the contract no matter where the Diamond Queen lay. As you will observe, if he had risked an overruff with the Diamond Queen by either defender, a trump return would have beaten him. His line of play precluded this defense.

EXTRA TRICK The next time you are faced with a two-way finesse for a missing Queen, stop and think. The solution of your problem may be the two-way non-finesse. Simply by counting the tricks, you most likely will win without finessing at all.

Neither side vulnerable
South dealer

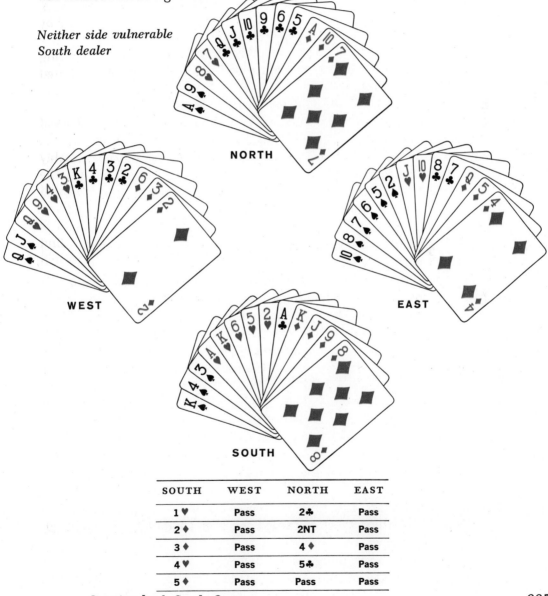

SOUTH	WEST	NORTH	EAST
1 ♥	Pass	2 ♣	Pass
2 ♦	Pass	2NT	Pass
3 ♦	Pass	4 ♦	Pass
4 ♥	Pass	5 ♣	Pass
5 ♦	Pass	Pass	Pass

Opening lead: Spade Queen

One against the book

THE well-known Card School located in New York's Beekman Hotel is soundly staffed with international talent. Included on the faculty is my teammate and friend, Boris Koytchou, a young man born in Russia who has played on the national teams of both France and the U. S. and who, like all good players, will gladly ignore the rules taught to beginners if by doing so he can win a trick.

Koytchou has won the Sally Fishbein Memorial Trophy for outstanding tournament performance, and as a member of my team-of-four contributed substantially to our victory in the Master's Team championships for the Spingold Trophy in 1960.

In the following deal he and his partner, Harold Ogust, had several opportunities to break a "book" rule and took them all.

This was a deal that violated all of the cliché "rules" that presumably guide the beginner toward expert play. First to fall by the wayside was the classic "Lead the fourth highest of the longest and strongest suit." Instead West, Harold Ogust, chose the 9 of Hearts as his opening lead. Leading your long suit when your hand doesn't promise any certain re-entries is usually a futile procedure. It is far better, in such straits, to try to find partner's best suit and hope that he will have the equipment with which the contract may be defeated.

To Ogust, that suit seemed to be Hearts. Dummy's low Heart was played and now East, Koytchou, took his turn at tearing up the rule book. "Third hand high," runs the precept. And, with the Ace in dummy, Koytchou was sure to be able to win the first trick with his Heart King. But West's 9 was marked as a top-of-nothing lead—which meant that South must have Q J 10. That left only two Hearts for Ogust. Suppose East took the first trick and continued the suit. West, if he were able to regain the lead, would not have another Heart to return. So, instead of winning the trick with the King, Koytchou played the 7 to encourage partner to continue the suit, and allowed South to win the trick with the 10-spot.

Declarer's best chance to win nine tricks or more was to establish some Diamonds, so when he won the first trick he led the Diamond 9. Ogust ignored another rule—"second hand low." He rose with the Diamond King to lead a second Heart. This time the finesse lost to Koytchou's King, and a third Heart (on which West discarded the 2 of Diamonds) knocked out declarer's last stopper.

Before staking everything on finding West with the Diamond Ace, declarer took the Queen and Ace of Spades, in hopes that the Jack-10 might fall. When no honor appeared, South fell back on the Diamonds.

But his hope was forlorn. Koytchou had the Ace to gain the lead and cash his two Hearts to put the contract down one trick.

EXTRA TRICK Broad rules of play are reasonably good guides. They will help an inexperienced player to cope with players of greater skill. But rules were not meant to take the place of reason. So, when inspiration points in the direction of the latter, it is well to scrap the rules and let the plus on your score be the answer to your critics.

East-West vulnerable
North dealer

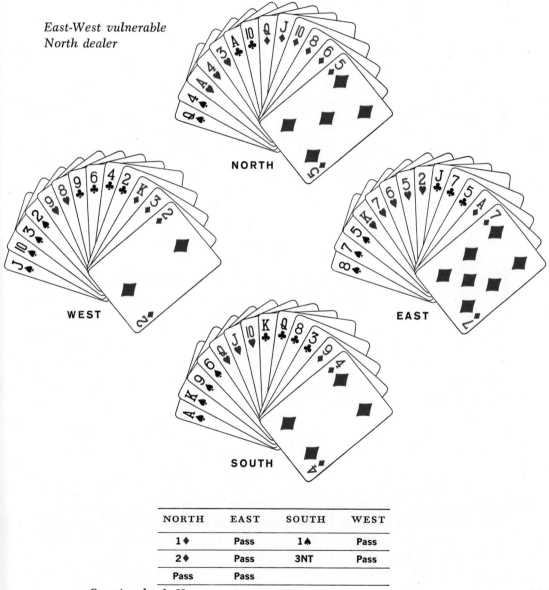

NORTH	EAST	SOUTH	WEST
1♦	Pass	1♠	Pass
2♦	Pass	3NT	Pass
Pass	Pass		

Opening lead: Heart 9

Larceny at the table

BECAUSE there is a bit of larceny in each of us, the favorite hand of the expert player is often one involving a successful swindle.

One of the most delightful swindles I ever encountered was perpetrated by John H. Moran, who played for the U. S. against England in the World Championship Match in 1955. The following hand, however, was played by him in a recent Canadian championship. Moran's partner was Victor Mitchell of New York; his opponents were two of Canada's finest players—Douglas Drury and Eric Murray.

Moran admits that the contract was not precisely ironclad and puts the blame for this on his own leap to 4 Spades. Since Mitchell had all four Aces, one can hardly be critical of his guiding the bidding to a slam. Indeed, he could have believed a grand slam was not out of the question.

Moran saw immediately that his only chance to make the contract was to concoct a scheme that would seem credible to the opponents. Like many another successful swindler, Moran put himself in his adversaries' place, imagined what they did not expect, and played accordingly.

Dummy's Jack of Hearts was covered by East's Queen and trumped by South. This meant that even with a winning Diamond finesse, declarer would be able to get rid of not more than three of his Clubs. With a minimum of one sure loser in the trump suit, South had to find a way to avoid a Club loser. This required forcing a Club lead by the opposition.

Of course, Moran could have led the Ace and another Spade and finessed against East for the Jack. When the 10 forced West's King, the matter of the single trump loser would have been arranged. But West then would have been able to exit with a third trump, negating any chance for an end-play in the Club suit. So Moran visualized the cards exactly as they had to be—and as they were.

His first play after trumping the initial Heart was the Queen of Spades. Of course, West could have foiled the plot by covering. But put yourself in Drury's place. Would *you* cover when, by ducking, you assured yourself of winning a trick with the King later on? Neither would I.

After that maneuver, the rest was a matter of timing and luck. South cashed the King of Diamonds and successfully finessed dummy's Diamond Jack. Next came the Ace of Hearts, on which South threw a Diamond; the Ace of Diamonds on which he threw a Club; then the Ace of Spades; then the King of Hearts, on which declarer discarded a second Club.

Now dummy's remaining Heart was ruffed, and South led his last trump, discarding a Club from dummy. West was in with the Spade King and could lead nothing but a Club. That gave declarer the two Club tricks he needed, and dummy's last Diamond furnished the twelfth trick.

EXTRA TRICK When swindle is your only hope, boldness is the essence of the operation. You must act swiftly before the opponents become suspicious. So, if the swindle is inevitable, relax and employ it.

Neither side vulnerable
East dealer

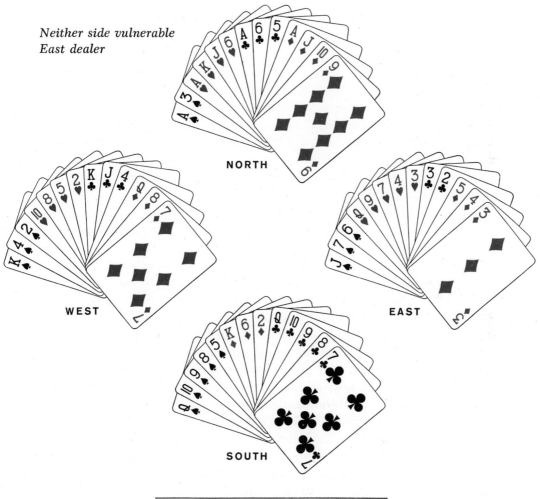

EAST	SOUTH	WEST	NORTH
(*Murray*)	(*Moran*)	(*Drury*)	(*Mitchell*)
Pass	Pass	1♣	DBL
Pass	4♠	Pass	5♣
Pass	5♦	Pass	5♥
Pass	5♠	Pass	6♠
Pass	Pass	Pass	

Opening lead: Heart 2

Sometimes it pays to be bad

IN the early days of my career I became indignant with bids that I felt were bad. But I soon mellowed. It dawned on me that bad bids (*i.e.*, bids *I* wouldn't have made) frequently made good drama. Without them, a bridge script could be dull, like errorless baseball, which can become distressingly mechanical. Not infrequently the team that wins in baseball is one that uses tactics which are so daring that at first they appear suicidal. Similarly in bridge, seemingly unsound procedures may succeed because they also surprise. What lent the following hand its interest was the necessity for a good play imposed by a bad bid.

The hand, which was played in a tournament, was subject to a wide variety of treatment both in the bidding and in the play, but the sequence of bidding that had the greatest number of adherents stopped at 4 Hearts. In most cases, only ten tricks were made; in one, even the 4-Heart contract was defeated.

At the one table where South found himself in the precarious position of having to fulfill a slam contract, North was so pleased with partner's 3-Heart response to his cue bid in Spades that he leaped to 5 Hearts. Since South had been brought upon the scene perhaps unwillingly, North should have been more chary of assuming this risk. If fortune had imposed a bust hand on South, eleven tricks would have been out of reach. Yet South contracted for slam without any qualms. This made sense. His partner having offered to produce eleven tricks singlehanded, South could consider the Ace of Hearts as the surprise card that could bring in the twelfth trick.

When the King of Spades was opened, South would have been willing to call the whole thing off. Indeed, one declarer, who simply didn't know what to do next after trumping the opening Spade lead with dummy's Heart 4, managed to get set at his game contract. Most players brought home ten tricks by ruffing the Spade, cashing the Heart King, overtaking the Queen with the Ace and leading a Club. In addition to losing one Club, they had to concede a Spade to East's Ace and a trick to East's 10 of trumps, but they did manage to make the game.

Playing for a slam, however, our South had to find a plan that offered some hope of twelve tricks. He did it by trusting in good breaks and in East's holding one crucial card—the 10 of Hearts.

The opening Spade was ruffed with dummy's Jack of Hearts. The King of Hearts was cashed, then a low Heart was led, and when East did not play the 10, declarer finessed the 9, which held. A Club was led toward dummy. West ducked, and the King held. A low Club was returned, and West won with the Queen. He followed with a Spade, forcing dummy's

Queen of trumps. A low Club from dummy, ruffed in the closed hand, established the suit. The last trump was drawn, the Jack of Diamonds was discarded, and the rest of the dummy was high.

Needless to say, this was a top score on the deal. However, I fear that it cost North a great many points in future play by failing to punish him for his optimism.

EXTRA TRICK If you are looking for experience in playing difficult contracts, get yourself an optimist for a partner.

Both sides vulnerable
West dealer

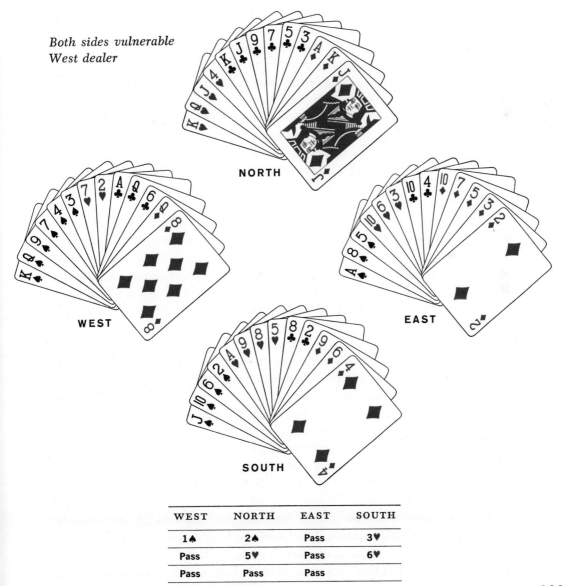

WEST	NORTH	EAST	SOUTH
1♠	2♠	Pass	3♥
Pass	5♥	Pass	6♥
Pass	Pass	Pass	

Opening lead: Spade King

A good habit to kick

LEARNING to play bridge is very often a matter of learning good habits. But habits, like drugs, tend to lull the user into a state of euphoria. Unless treated with respect, they can be dangerous. The declarer in the following hand, for example, kicked away a very good grand-slam contract because he could not shed what in any other circumstance would have been considered a good habit. The contract was the result of an unusual bid. Its loss was the result of lazily following a common principle of play.

West's pre-emptive bid of 4 Clubs robbed the opponents of space in which to exchange information, but North-South were using a convention called the grand slam force. South's opening bid was unlikely to include much in Clubs, North knew, and his only real concern was whether partner held the missing tops in his Spade suit. North's 5 No-Trump bid was intended to resolve that doubt. The burst to 5 No Trump asked partner to bid 7 if he held two of the three top honors in his bid suit, or to sign off at six if he lacked one of the two missing top cards. With a bare minimum bid, South wasn't keen on bidding 7, but since that minimum included the Ace-Queen of spades he had no choice in the matter.

Dummy's Ace won the Club opening and declarer thought he saw thirteen tricks—two top Diamonds, two Diamond ruffs in the North hand, four high trumps in his own hand and four Heart tricks in addition to the Ace of Clubs already won. He played accordingly. After one round of trumps, he cashed the Ace and King of Diamonds, trumped a third Diamond with the Jack of Spades, came back to his hand with a second trump lead and ruffed the fourth Diamond with dummy's Spade King. A Club ruff put South in to draw East's last trump, but, alas, the Hearts were stacked and there was no way for declarer to avoid a losing Heart trick.

South failed when he used dummy's trumps for ruffing. Generally, trumps are shorter in dummy and so as a rule it is worth one or two tricks to trump from the shorter hand. But in this instance trumps were evenly divided. South, to his misfortune, was mesmerized by the prospect of ruffing in dummy and never realized that with an equal number of trumps in each hand the rule governing short-trump hands would not apply. See for yourself what would have happened if South had recognized the need for breaking a habit.

After winning the Club Ace in dummy, declarer should immediately lead another Club and trump it. He cashes the Spade Ace and leads a Spade to dummy's Jack. Next he leads dummy's last Club and ruffs it with his Spade Queen. And on this very trick, unless East gets rid of his trump, he must leave one of the red suits unprotected.

234

Dummy gets in again with the Ace of Diamonds to lead a third trump, on which South discards a Heart. Next comes a lead to South's Diamond King and a Diamond ruff in dummy. Now, no matter how he has played earlier, East will have to unguard Diamonds, making South's last Diamond good, or give up Heart protection, letting South cash in all four Hearts.

EXTRA TRICK Be forewarned by your opponents' bidding. What they say may amount to good evidence that the time has come for you to break old, ordinary rules.

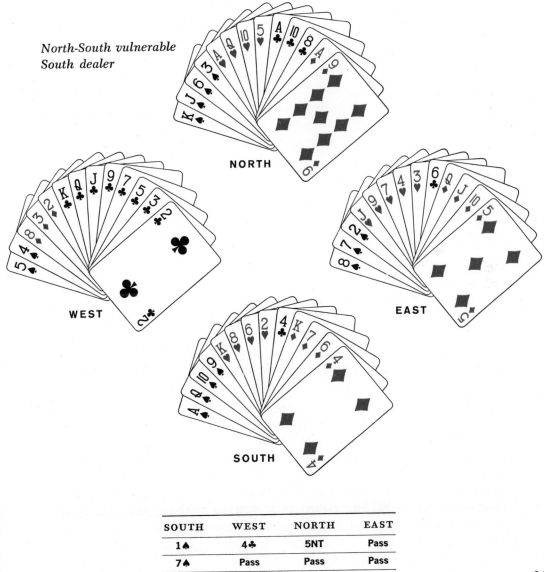

North-South vulnerable
South dealer

NORTH

WEST

EAST

SOUTH

SOUTH	WEST	NORTH	EAST
1♠	4♣	5NT	Pass
7♠	Pass	Pass	Pass

Opening lead: Club King

A fast 500

A FEW days before the Indianapolis 500-mile auto race in 1961 Roger Ward, winner in 1959 and second in 1960, was visibly nervous. His trouble, however, was not that he was scheduled to race again. He was on television playing bridge. Ward had far better reason to be frightened by the 500 than by his bridge, which is excellent.

The program was Easley Blackwood's Bridge Hour, a locally produced show starring the inventor of the 4 No-Trump convention who, when he isn't thinking about bridge, is an Indianapolis insurance executive. Ward and I were playing against Blackwood and one of his favorite partners, Stanley McComas. Bidding as boldly as he drives, Ward had forced the contract to eleven tricks on a hand that appeared to include three losers. The contract, patently, was impossible. Or was it? The deal is at right.

The average player is rarely so disciplined that he will stay out of the bidding with an eight-card suit, but an immediate overcall with the South hand is not sound tactics. Ward correctly stayed off the pace until he could see how the bidding would shape up. When I found the strength for a take-out double with the North cards, however, he skipped immediately to 3 Clubs. Had I then bid 3 No Trump, we would have had an easy game—but no story. When, instead, I bid the five-card Spade suit, Ward went on to 4 Clubs. We were not beyond the point of no return, but in television bridge one is less conservative than he might be in a tournament and I carried on to put Ward in game at Clubs.

After the opening lead of the Diamond deuce, when I put down the dummy it was apparent that declarer had one sure loser in Diamonds and potential losers in Spades and Hearts as well. But Ward made excellent use of the fact that his singleton Diamond happened to be the 8-spot.

He played low from dummy and East took home the Diamond Queen. A Heart return by East would have been best, but, as it turned out, this actually had little effect on the hand. In fact, East returned the Jack of trumps, and declarer let it ride to dummy's Ace.

Ward knew that East must have the Diamond Ace, so he led dummy's Diamond King. East covered and Ward trumped. He returned to dummy with the 10 of Clubs and led the 10 of Diamonds, discarding a Heart from his hand when East played low. West won the trick with the Jack, but the Diamond 9 was now established as a winning parking place for South's second Spade. By giving up two Diamonds instead of the one he was sure to lose, South established a fourth-round Diamond winner, and that card furnished declarer's eleventh trick.

"Where do you think you'll finish in the 500?" Roger was asked. "I can't answer that," the racing star replied. (He finished third.) "But I know where I want the 500 to finish now. Right above the line in our score—where you will kindly chalk up the 500 bonus for game and rubber."

EXTRA TRICK Sometimes the only way to avoid more losers than you can afford is by throwing one loser on another, meanwhile building up a trick that will take care of still a third.

Both sides vulnerable
East dealer

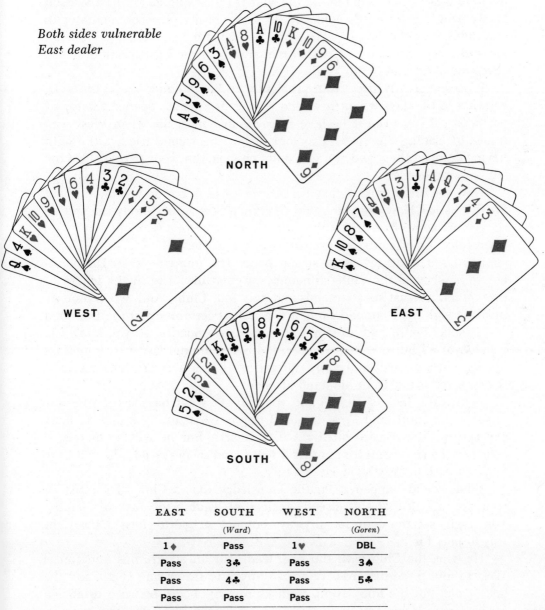

NORTH

WEST

EAST

SOUTH

EAST	SOUTH	WEST	NORTH
	(Ward)		(Goren)
1♦	Pass	1♥	DBL
Pass	3♣	Pass	3♠
Pass	4♣	Pass	5♣
Pass	Pass	Pass	

Opening lead: Diamond 2

Not so elementary

RARELY is a hand dealt in bridge that does not offer a chance to use the powers of deduction for which Sherlock Holmes was remarkable. He could have made a formidable reputation at the card table, even without the ubiquitous Dr. Watson to remind the world of his exploits. Minus a Watson of my own, I am forced, modestly, to serve as my own commentator in describing the following hand, which I defended many years ago. You can share the mystery that confronted me, sitting in the East position, if you cover the West and South cards.

It doesn't greatly affect your problem with East's hand, but let me warn you that in the days when this hand was dealt a player opened the top of partner's bid suit even if he held three to an honor. So, when West continued by leading the Spade 3 to your Ace at the second trick, with South having dropped the 5 and 7, it was quite possible that your partner held the still-missing deuce.

Now you are invited to take over the defense. What do you know about South's hand? How are you going to play to beat him? Surely the setting trick must come from the Club suit. "Correct," Holmes might have said cryptically, "so of course you return the Jack of Hearts!"

South's bidding reveals a strong hand. His jump rebid in Diamonds before he showed the Clubs announces a great disparity in the length of these suits: at least six Diamonds and only four Clubs. And, when dummy turns up with the Diamond King, it is a virtual certainty that the Diamond suit is solid. South had already followed to two Spades, so you know the location of all but one of his cards. If his remaining card is the missing Spade, no return will make any difference. If it is a Heart, it is essential that you remove it from his hand at once.

Return the Jack of Hearts and you will see what happens if you now uncover the South and West hands. Dummy wins the trick and declarer can take a Club discard on the Ace of Hearts. But he will be unable to establish the Heart suit for another discard, and sooner or later he will have to lose a trick to West's Queen of Clubs.

What would happen if, in the knowledge that a Club trick must be won, you attack that suit directly instead of leading the Jack of Hearts? You might set the contract anyway—but not if South guesses the right way to play for it.

He wins the Club with the Ace, leads out all six trumps and forces West to find three discards. West can afford to throw one Heart and the last Spade. But the final trump compels him to choose between establishing dummy's Heart suit or unguarding his Queen of Clubs. The latter is the better choice, since it forces declarer at least to a guess. But the chances are that declarer, if he is a seasoned operator, will guess correctly—if only because he prefers to win by a squeeze rather than by a simple finesse.

EXTRA TRICK Even when the source of the setting trick becomes obvious, attacking that suit may not be the best way to insure cashing in. Stop and count declarer's hand. The solution is often found right there.

Neither side vulnerable
South dealer

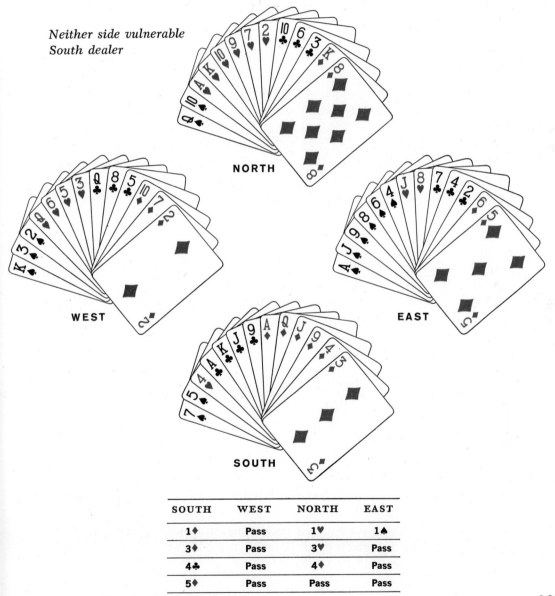

SOUTH	WEST	NORTH	EAST
1♦	Pass	1♥	1♠
3♦	Pass	3♥	Pass
4♣	Pass	4♦	Pass
5♦	Pass	Pass	Pass

Opening lead: Spade King

A star is born

WHEN Italy won the World Championship bridge title for the fifth time in Buenos Aires in 1961, there was double bad news for the other teams in international competition. The key figure in the Italian triumph—Benito Garrozzo—was new to his team. A 32-year-old Neapolitan road builder, he should be around for years to come.

The year before, Italy's "Blue Team," weakened by the absence of Guglielmo Siniscalco and Massimo D'Alelio, could finish no better than sixth. Siniscalco again was absent at Buenos Aires, but with Garrozzo the Italians looked stronger than ever. Proving that he belonged at the top, Garrozzo entered two post-championship matches, gaining a first in one and, playing with Peter Leventritt, a second in the other. This was one of the well-played hands in his partnership with Leventritt.

North's 2-Club response asked South to show a four-card major if he held one. East's double of the artificial bid showed Club strength and was not meant as a take-out. This is the logical method employed by experts for coping with artificial bids. South duly showed his four-card Heart suit and North, with 10 points in high cards and an extra point for his double-ton Club, promptly carried on to game.

West's opening lead was low, from his holding of three to an honor in partner's suit. East took his two top Clubs and shifted to the Spade 10. Garrozzo won with the King and led a trump to dummy's Jack and East's Ace. The deuce of Spades was won by South's Queen, and two more Heart leads cleaned up the trumps. Now, making the contract hinged on finding the Queen of Diamonds.

A simple finesse is a fifty-fifty proposition, but not when the finesse can be taken either way and an expert is playing the hand. Some players be-lieve that the missing Queen will most often be found behind the Jack. There is no mathematical rule, of course, that will back them up, and whatever advantage they feel they get from their theory is not nearly as good as the percentage Garrozzo followed in deciding his play.

He led a third round of Spades, completing his count of the distribu-tion in that suit. Now, East was known to have begun with only two Spades and two Hearts. West's lead had marked him with at least three Clubs. Therefore, East must have started with three and possibly four Diamonds. Mathematically, the player with the most cards in a suit will have the best chance of holding any given card. So, with the odds at least three to two in his favor, Garrozzo played for East to have the Queen of Diamonds. He led low to dummy's King and finessed the 10 on the return lead, thus bringing home his contract.

EXTRA TRICK If your guessing average is only fifty per cent or worse on finesses, the chances are that you are not counting out the unseen hands of your opponents. Whenever you can afford to do so, postpone your guess until you have played out enough cards in other suits to give you an idea which opponent has the most cards in the suit you need to finesse.

Both sides vulnerable
South dealer

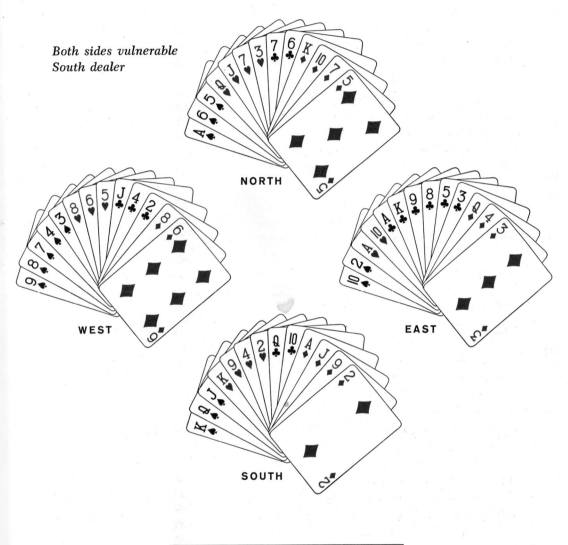

SOUTH	WEST	NORTH	EAST
(Garrozzo)		*(Leventritt)*	
1NT	Pass	2♣	DBL
2♥	Pass	4♥	Pass
Pass	Pass		

Opening Lead: Club 2

Not even a fast shuffle

COMMUTER trains may or may not be fast, but commuter bridge always is. The game has as many versions as there are railroads, and every one of them involves the goulash—a dealing method designed to speed up play, increase scores and make every hand a potential disaster.

The only time the cards are ever shuffled is before the first deal. After that, the unshuffled tricks from the hand just played are gathered together, cut and distributed—not dealt—in packets of five, five and three.

The weird distributions and the ghoulish results that are almost guaranteed by this method of dealing soon suggested the name "ghoulie" for the version of train bridge that I like best. It is the only train bridge game I have heard of that has its own set of written rules and bidding techniques, which are included in the book about the game (*Ghoulie*) written by Philip M. Wertheimer.

One of the principal rules is this: Play out all tricks to the bitter end to make certain that nothing interferes with the freakishness of the next deal. Another rule is that part-score contracts—unless they are doubled or are large enough to complete a full game because of a previous score—are never played at all. The high bidder is conceded a score below the line of one less than he bid. That is, 2 No Trump scores 40; 3 Spades gets 60, and so forth. But a one bid gets its full value. All the other scoring is the same as in regular rubber bridge and, with this method of dealing, slams are frequent. Unless you are wary, so are huge penalties. All this considerably alters basic bidding strategy, as will be seen by this deal from Wertheimer's book.

In ghoulie, it is almost impossible to predict how the bidding will go, but it is possible to show how it should go. Voids are so important that they should be shown whenever a good fit with partner's bid makes it safe to do so. North's hand wouldn't be strong enough for a cue bid in an ordinary game, but it is important for North to tell his partner about his spade void as quickly as possible in the train game. It is even more important for South to bid his void in Diamonds as a prepared defensive measure should the opponents decide to sacrifice.

With a Diamond opening and a Club return putting North in to give South another Diamond ruff, West would go down three tricks at 7 Spades. But with a Heart opening West could make all 13 tricks.

Nevertheless, 7 Spades is a good sacrifice, down 500 points to save a grand slam worth about 1,500 to the opponents. In train bridge, even more than in regular rubber bridge, insurance principles are applicable. It is good policy to take a small set rather than risk having a substantial score made against you.

EXTRA TRICK   Opportunities for tricky strategy abound in train bridge. For example, if East were void in Clubs he would not waste an opportunity to show it and pass the double of 5 Diamonds. Instead, he would cue-bid 6 Clubs to insure getting the right lead if South became declarer. Indeed, even though he held a singleton Club, a 6-Club cue bid might have been made in hopes of inducing the opponents to stop at 6 because they feared a Club ruff. One warning: Train bridge can be the ruination of your regular game.

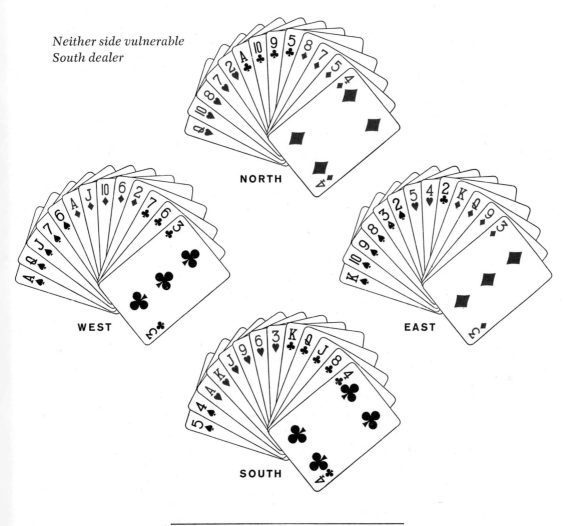

Neither side vulnerable
South dealer

NORTH

WEST

EAST

SOUTH

SOUTH	WEST	NORTH	EAST
1 ♥	1 ♠	2 ♠	4 ♠
5 ♦	DBL	Pass	Pass
6 ♥	Pass	Pass	6 ♠
Pass	Pass	7 ♥	Pass
Pass	Pass	DBL	Pass
Pass	Pass		

Opening lead: Diamond 4

The case for apartness

SINCE I am a lifelong bachelor, let me make it plain that this is not a commentary on what matrimony does for or to a bridge partnership. It is merely a chronicle of what happened at a recent mixed-pair championship. As the name suggests, entry in such events is restricted to pairs composed of one male and one female. Since this same requirement governs issuance of a marriage license, it is not surprising that about half the mixed-pair entries are husband-and-wife duos; as often as not, victory goes to such a pair.

In the Eastern States Championships, however, some kind of record was set in 1961 when the mixed-pair title was taken, not by a married pair or an unmarried pair, but by a de-married pair, the charming Edith Kemp and her former husband, Erwin Seligman. Here is a deal in which their mutual trust contributed substantially to success.

The victory of this team was no overwhelming surprise, by the way. Mrs. Kemp has long been recognized as one of the country's top performers among women bridge players. Seligman, though lately absent from the tournament scene, was a familiar competitor in early contract-bridge tournaments. Yet the fact is that, though they played together frequently in former years, they were never a championship-winning pair while married to one another.

This time it was different. In the deal shown here they managed to get to the only makable game on a combined seven-card trump suit, choosing that unusual contract deliberately.

The first two bids by each of the partners require little explanation. Mrs. Kemp bid her long Club suit first; Seligman showed his biddable Heart suit; Mrs. Kemp then showed her shorter but powerful Spade suit and Seligman naturally returned to Clubs, the suit for which he had better support. Then came East's belated entry into the auction with a powerful Diamond suit. This provided Mrs. Kemp with the opportunity for a brilliant bid. She wanted to be sure of getting to game, but she wasn't certain where. If her partner held a Diamond stopper, the best North-South contract would almost certainly be 3 No Trump. So, in spite of two losing Diamonds in her hand, she cue-bid the opponents' suit.

It was obvious to her partner that this bid could not be showing strength in Diamonds, for if South had a Diamond stopper in her own hand she would surely have bid No Trump herself. Hence, the "asking" character of the Diamond bid was apparent. Not having a Diamond stopper, North showed the next important feature of his own hand, three-card Spade support. That bid, when viewed in terms of his earlier bids, gave a strong indication of North's complete distribution. Concluding that there were only two Diamonds in North's hand, South saw that her own trump length could not be shortened by a third Diamond lead, so she bid 4 Spades.

When dummy was put down, it showed exactly what North had promised. After winning two Diamond tricks, the defenders could not make the South hand ruff by continuing the suit. Consequently, declarer lost only two Diamonds and one Heart trick, making 4 Spades. These same losers, however, would have defeated a 5-Club contract.

EXTRA TRICK   A combined seven-card trump suit will frequently offer a satisfactory vehicle to game, especially when the partnership's weak suit can be ruffed by the short-trump hand.

Both sides vulnerable
North dealer

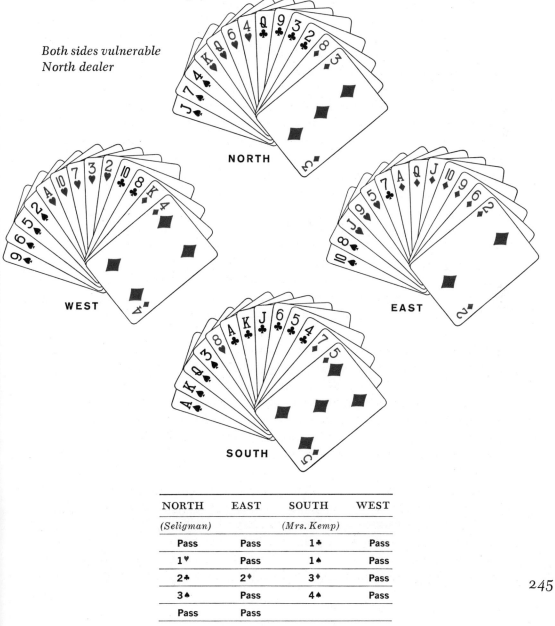

NORTH	EAST	SOUTH	WEST
(Seligman)		*(Mrs. Kemp)*	
Pass	Pass	1♣	Pass
1♥	Pass	1♠	Pass
2♣	2♦	3♦	Pass
3♠	Pass	4♠	Pass
Pass	Pass		

Opening lead: Diamond King

245

A tiger by the tail

A STOUT sea breeze is a stimulating thing that sharpens the appetite and stiffens the spine. But it also seems to destroy all instinctive caution. Those who should be wary suddenly have the boldness of a Blackbeard, it would seem, especially if the breeze happens to be blowing across that Shangri-La of migrated New York bridge fanatics, Miami.

Given a whiff of the sea, these transplanted Northerners evince all of the hardihood and daring of earlier and more westerly pioneers. Witness, for example, the bidding pyrotechnics of one of the first of the Miami migrants, Bill Dunlop. Floridians still talk about this deal, one of many which earned for Bill the affectionate and exceedingly apt nickname of "Tiger."

In a sense, the story is told in the bidding. But some understanding of Tiger's character is also needed. Bill, whose bristly gray mustache and black poodle were landmarks of the beach on any morning, was inevitably to be found in a chair at a surfside bridge game every afternoon. On this occasion he found himself in possession of a part score of 90—a rarity in itself in Miami rubber-bridge circles. At any rate, since 1 Heart was enough to give his side game, Tiger, holding the West hand, entered the auction with rare conservatism.

Neither North nor East found it desirable to contest the matter, but South, with no defense against what was now an opposing game contract, decided to compete with a bid of 1 Spade. I must admit that it would have required some clairvoyance for South to have made no second bid. Against Tiger, however, that would have been far the best course.

Dunlop's next utterance, in a tone just as mild as his 1-Heart bid, was "6 Diamonds." Now, deeply regretting that he had stirred up the animals, South decided to take his beating manfully and sacrifice at 7 Clubs. Tiger then further manifested his ferocity by a quiet but *forcing* pass. (By failing to double after his strong bid, he obligated his partner to take direct action.)

The effect of Tiger's deadly style was immediate, even on so conservative a citizen as his partner, Bill Root. Hesitating only long enough to hear North's bid, Root heeded Tiger's firm but unspoken suggestion by bidding the grand slam. North, too, showed his implicit faith in Tiger by bidding 7 Spades as a sacrifice.

North had not misjudged. 7 Diamonds would have been cold. Winning the bid was a Pyrrhic victory, however, for the cost was 1,100 points.

South trumped the second Heart and led a high Spade. West ducked and won the Spade continuation with the Ace; then he forced South to ruff a third Heart with his last trump. The best that declarer could do was allow the defenders to win three Diamond tricks. Eventually, dummy was able to trump a red card with the Spade 10, draw East's last trump with the Jack, and win a Club finesse for a total of seven tricks.

EXTRA TRICK   When you have already bid very strongly, the next available strong bid may be—as in this case—a forcing pass.

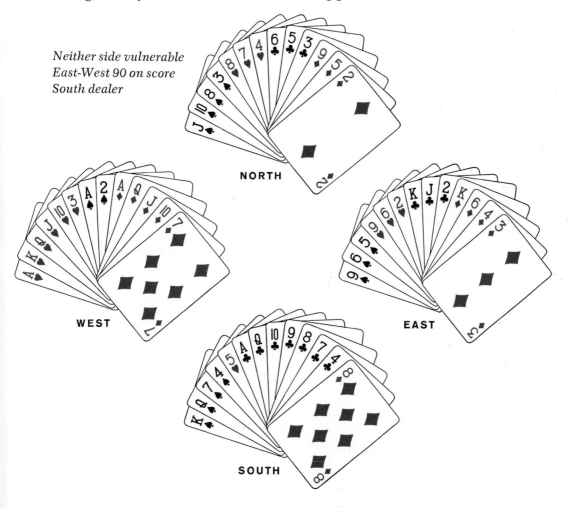

Neither side vulnerable
East-West 90 on score
South dealer

NORTH

WEST   **EAST**

SOUTH

SOUTH	WEST	NORTH	EAST
	("Tiger")		(W. West)
1♣	1♥	Pass	Pass
1♠	6♦	Pass	Pass
7♣	Pass	Pass	7♦
Pass	Pass	7♠	DBL
Pass	Pass	Pass	

Opening lead: Heart King

247

A BRIDGE MASTER'S
PERSONAL ALBUM

WHEN THE NOTED French poster artist, Cassandre, was commissioned by the Hermes store in Paris to design an entirely new deck of cards in 1945, he spent two years at research into the ancient origins of card playing before ever beginning to paint. A sample of his results may be seen in the set of Spade honors on the opposite page. Cassandre's elegant pasteboards are a recent acquisition of the Bielefeld Playing Card Museum, in the city of Bielefeld, West Germany, an institution which boasts one of the world's finest collections of cards. Some of the rarest and most beautiful of these are among the historic cards shown in color on the following pages. Each card is reproduced in exactly the size of the original.

Playing cards began in China, where the companion arts of printing and paper-making flourished long before they were known to the Western world. Chinese paper money was produced as early as the 8th Century, and served for betting as well as commerce. Evidently gamblers worked out ways of playing with and for the actual bank notes, and the pictorial signs on these notes furnished the suit marks for the Chinese playing cards which evolved. By the 14th Century cards had made their way to Europe from the Near East, brought by itinerant merchants or fortune-telling Gypsies or returning Crusaders; nobody really knows. The Europeans promptly Westernized the cards, adopting as honors a group of familiar medieval court figures. Often these royal creatures were based on well-known models; Charlemagne was one of the early kings personified, and Sir Lancelot an early jack. For suit signs, the European card-makers selected a number of prosaic objects from everyday Western life.

In 14th Century Italy a *tarot* deck came into existence which had 78 cards divided into four suits of four face cards and ten numeral cards each, plus 22 special trumps representing the primal forces of the universe. The face cards depicted the king, queen, cavalier or mounted knight, and valet, the young nobleman who served as a knight's page. The suits were swords, cups,

248

Text continued on page 261

A modern deck by the French artist Cassandre blends
a romantic Ace and a gallery of dry, semi-cubist
court figures, firmly based on medieval tradition.

This doll-like Queen of Swords, painted against a rich
gold background, is from an Italian tarot set dated
about 1450 and attributed to the artist Bonifacio Bembo.

A King of Clubs appears on another card of the tarot set, commissioned for the noble Visconti family of Milan and now owned by the Pierpont Morgan Library in New York.

15th C: This German Jack of Bells, from an early woodblock design, wear's a knight's dashing cape.

THE JACK, THROUGH SIX CENTURIES

The French called him valet, the English called him knave, and both words originally meant son. But the Jack was more than just somebody's boy. While he began his career as a gallant figure—the noble youth who served as a knight's attendant—his name in time became a synonym for scoundrel. It was in 17th Century England that he acquired the nickname of the common man: Jack, a helper at any trade. The duality of Jack's nature has been reflected by card designers from the beginning. Seeing in him strength, but also a silly and sometimes deceitful quality, artists in every age have made of him the most interesting personality in the deck.

18th C: In a French comic deck, the Jack appears in the corner of a card depicting a rogue caught stealing.

16th C: On a Florentine card of an artful era the Jack of Swords is a handsome, almost idealized youth.

17th C: A Spanish Jack of Clubs carries the knobby weapon which in his country was the suit emblem.

19th C: A spirited French deck of Napoleonic times shows the Jack on the battle flag of a German soldier.

20th C: This contemporary Jack by the Swedish ceramist, Stig Lindberg, has a jaunty if adolescent look.

Typical of the primitive woodcuts first appearing in the 15th Century is this Italian Jack of Coins.

In contrast, a 5 of Clubs made in 15th Century Spain shows the detail lavished on painted cards of the era.

The history of the graphic arts in the Western world begins with playing cards. German engravers of the early 1400's printed the first European pictures by pressing inked wooden blocks to paper. And among their earliest works were the simple cuts for card figures such as the Jack at left, above. Often colors were applied to

SOME
LANDMARKS
IN DESIGN

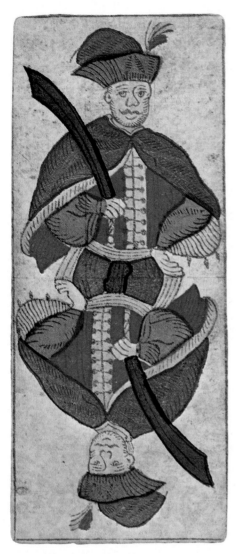

An early example of the double image is a Knight of Swords made in 1803 for the Italian game of trappola.

Transformation cards, such as this one from Germany, were a popular 19th Century novelty in many countries.

these prints by stencil. For a time printed cards and costlier, hand-painted cards circulated together. Then, as printing methods improved everywhere in Europe, the craft of the card painter disappeared. Since the 1500's our standard 52-card deck has changed little in appearance except for adoption, in the 19th Century, of the double image.

CARDS OF MANY KINDS TO LEARN BY

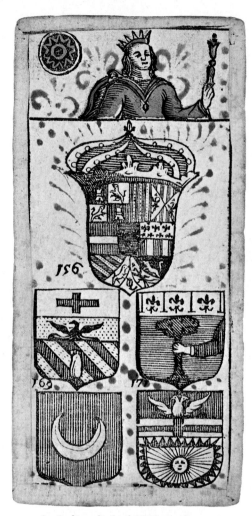

An Italian deck of 1725 taught
card-playing youths to identify the
coats of arms of European courts.

A similar card bears a lesson in
geography, dividing the world into
continents and islands, new and old.

From the 16th Century on, playing cards have appeared
which were designed not only for card games but
to amuse and instruct in other areas of interest as well.
Directed mostly at children—but admired too, in an
age before photography, by a general population starved
for pictures—these educational cards have covered a wide
range of subjects. The method of teaching survives today,
as in the aircraft identification cards of World War II.

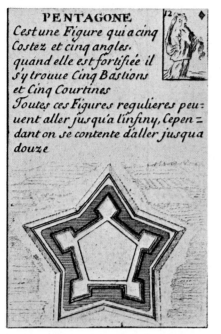

PENTAGONE
Cest une Figure qui a cinq
Costez et cinq angles.
quand elle est fortifiée il
s'y trouve Cinq Bastions
et Cinq Courtines
Toutes ces Figures regulieres peu-
uent aller jusqu'a l'infiny, Cepen-
dant on se contente d'aller jusqua
douze

*Cards designed for young military
students of Louis XIV's reign
gave instruction in fortifications.*

Sol

Sol-dat

*An 1850 French deck taught the
musical scale. Here is sol, and a
visual association with* soldat.

Afrique

Femme de Benin

*The vanished African kingdom of
Benin is included in an 1856 French
deck showing peoples of the world.*

MAJ.-G. ULYSSES S. GRANT.

*During the U.S. Civil War a set
of cards admired in the North bore
the likenesses of Union generals.*

Tiny circular cards of 18th Century India, like the larger contemporary card on the opposite page, have suit marks which represent the ten incarnations of Vishnu.

Chinese "domino" cards, of a type derived from paper money of the Tang Dynasty (618-908 AD), include the bat symbol of luck, evidence of their use by fortunetellers.

Modern Japanese cards for playing the national Flower Game have as suits the traditional flowers which marked successive months in the calendar of Old Japan.

GEMLIKE
MINIATURES
FROM THE ORIENT

The diminutive and odd-shaped playing cards of the East reflect the rich diversity of cultures which spawned them. To the worldly Chinese, cards from the first have provided a practical means for gambling or divining one's fate. In the cards of India, religion and play are found intermixed. The exquisite miniatures of Persia depict the ordered aspects of Near East life, while those of Japan give expression to that nation's tidy belief in the essential orderliness of nature.

Cards of 17th Century Persia, showing men and women in a variety of civilized pursuits, are lacquered on canvas. Here, as in India, the early cards often were painted on ivory.

*This rare deuce of Spades comes
from the tiny state of Sikkim, on
the border between India and Tibet.
Made about 1870, the lacquered disc
merges the Western suit device with
the Oriental symbol of Ananta, the
thousand-headed serpent of Hindu
mythology who supports the world
while the great god Vishnu sleeps.*

coins and clubs—emblems which some scholars believe represented the four estates of medieval life: that is, the noble's sword, the clergyman's chalice, the merchant's money and the peasant's stave.

A simplified deck of 52 cards descended from this. In northern Europe the cavalier and his valet were merged to become the somewhat enigmatic figure that we now call the jack. There were other variations by individual country. In Germany, for example, the earliest suit signs were heart, acorn, bell and leaf—symbols that may have been chosen simply because they were quickly recognizable and easy to draw.

It was the French who introduced order into card-making by dividing the pack into two red and two black suits and standardizing the suit emblems. They adopted the German heart and the German leaf, the latter becoming a *trèfle* or trefoil. (Later this clover emblem became known in English, confusingly, as a club.) The sword used in Italian and Spanish decks was taken over and simplified. By showing just the point of the weapon, it was changed into the device which today we call a spade (from the Spanish *espada* for sword). The fourth suit sign of the French deck, and one that seems to have had no counterpart in other countries, was the simple shape which we identify as a diamond. This deck was introduced into England in the 15th Century, and ultimately became standard throughout the world.

The earliest European cards were exclusively for the nobility; painted by hand, they were necessarily expensive and hard to come by. An Italian court document of 1415 records that the painter Marziano da Tartona was paid 1,500 pieces of gold for executing a set of cards for the Duke of Milan. But a great change came about with the development of woodblock printing in mid-15th Century Germany. Soon the work of the German *Kartenmachers* was being exported by the hogshead from cities such as Nürnberg and Ulm. Mass-production methods caught on in other European countries as well, and now playing cards belonged to the common man. Before long the Church was inveighing against the evils of cards and gaming that kept men from mass. And in England cards proved such a distraction to workmen that an edict of Henry VII in 1495 forbade the use of playing cards to servants and apprentices except during the Christmas holidays.

The deck of cards as we know it today has remained unchanged in its essentials of number and suit for the past 400 years. Playing card design, however, like other forms of art, has gone through frequent departures in the course of history to reflect·the changing humors of mankind. Many of the forgotten customs and interests and aspirations of bygone epochs can be found mirrored in these playthings which have endured.

Andrew Crichton
ASSOCIATE EDITOR
SPORTS ILLUSTRATED

SOME TESTS OF SKILL

EVERY BRIDGE PLAYER *has a high opinion of his own ability at the card table. When bids go down, the loss nearly always can be chalked up to bad luck or to the shortcomings of an obtuse partner. For the player who wants to find out just how good he really is, Mr. Goren has devised a series of revealing tests. On the following pages are eight quizzes, each an all-round examination in bridge comprehension and skill. Answers should be written down, then checked against Mr. Goren's scoring allowances which appear on the pages immediately following each quiz. On the last page, the reader who dares to add up his score will find a key to his actual rating as a bridge player.*

Write your answers to the 18 problems on a sheet of paper, then turn to page 268 to find your score. Neither side is vulnerable unless shown.

1 As *Dealer* you hold:  *What is your opening bid?*

2 As *South* you hold:

SOUTH	WEST	NORTH	EAST
Pass	Pass	1♦	Pass
?			

What do you bid now?

3 As *South* you hold:

EAST	SOUTH	WEST	NORTH
2NT	Pass	4NT	Pass
6NT	Pass	Pass	Pass

What is your opening lead?

4 As *Dealer* you hold:  *What is your opening bid?*

5 As *South* you hold:

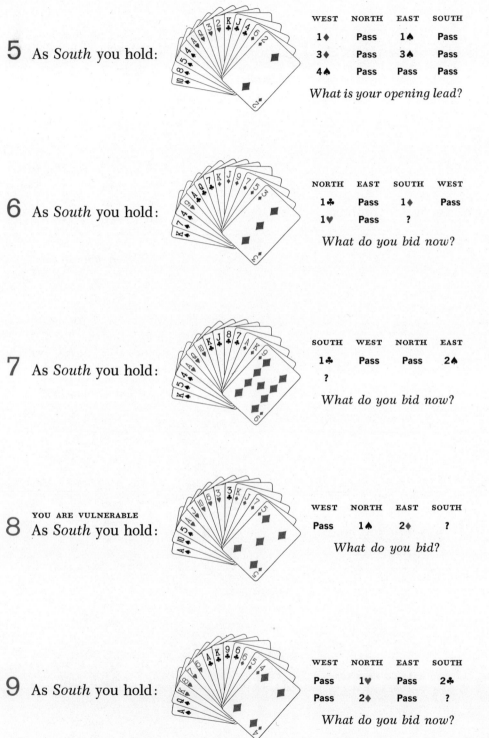

WEST	NORTH	EAST	SOUTH
1♦	Pass	1♠	Pass
3♦	Pass	3♠	Pass
4♠	Pass	Pass	Pass

What is your opening lead?

6 As *South* you hold:

NORTH	EAST	SOUTH	WEST
1♣	Pass	1♦	Pass
1♥	Pass	?	

What do you bid now?

7 As *South* you hold:

SOUTH	WEST	NORTH	EAST
1♣	Pass	Pass	2♠
?			

What do you bid now?

8 YOU ARE VULNERABLE
As *South* you hold:

WEST	NORTH	EAST	SOUTH
Pass	1♠	2♦	?

What do you bid?

9 As *South* you hold:

WEST	NORTH	EAST	SOUTH
Pass	1♥	Pass	2♣
Pass	2♦	Pass	?

What do you bid now?

265

10 As *South* you hold:

Your right-hand opponent opens with a bid of 1 Spade.

What do you bid?

11 As *South* you hold:

SOUTH	WEST	NORTH	EAST
1♣	Pass	1♦	Pass
1♠	Pass	2♥	Pass
2NT	Pass	3♦	Pass
?			

What do you bid now?

12 As *South* you hold:

NORTH	EAST	SOUTH	WEST
1♦	Pass	?	

What do you bid?

13 As *South* you hold:

NORTH	EAST	SOUTH	WEST
1♣	Pass	1♥	Pass
1♠	Pass	?	

What do you bid now?

14 YOU HAVE 60 PART SCORE

As *South* you hold:

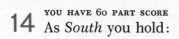

SOUTH	WEST	NORTH	EAST
2♠	Pass	2NT	4♣
?			

What do you bid now?

15 As *South* you hold:

Your right-hand opponent opens with a bid of 1 Diamond.

What do you bid?

16 As *South* you hold:

NORTH	EAST	SOUTH	WEST
1♣	Pass	1♥	Pass
2♥	Pass	?	

What do you bid now?

17 As *South* you hold:

WEST	NORTH	EAST	SOUTH
Pass	Pass	1♠	?

What do you bid?

18 YOU HAVE 90 PART SCORE
As *South* you hold:

NORTH	EAST	SOUTH	WEST
1♠	Pass	?	

What do you bid?

1

| One Spade | 5 POINTS |
| One Diamond | 2 POINTS |

This combination of cards should be handled very delicately. An opening bid of 1 Diamond would prove awkward if partner responded with a bid of 2 Clubs, for you would have no suitable rebid. The recommended bid of 1 Spade allows for a convenient rebid over any action your partner may take. If he bids 2 Hearts, you are in position to raise to 3 Hearts; and if his response is 2 Clubs, you have an easy rebid of 2 Diamonds.

To approach the problem from another angle, you treat the weak five-card Diamond suit as though it were a four-card suit. With two four-card suits we bid first the suit below the singleton, which for the purposes of this rule would be Spades.

2

Three Clubs	5 POINTS
Five Diamonds	3 POINTS
Three Diamonds	1 POINT

Your hand offers distinct slam possibilities, dependent on partner's holding in Spades. The jump shift, therefore, is clearly indicated. In view of your previous pass, this is the strongest hand partner could expect you to hold, and surely you will settle for no less than game in Diamonds.

A jump raise in Diamonds deserves little credit because this call is not forcing when made by a player who has previously passed.

3

| A Heart | 5 POINTS |
| Nine of Spades | 2 POINTS |
| Four of |
| Diamonds | 1 POINT |

On this particular sequence of bidding, your partner can hardly have any great strength. Nevertheless, against the slam contract you have a fairly good chance, particularly if declarer misguesses the location of the Queen of Diamonds. Don't make any lead that might sacrifice a trick or facilitate declarer's work. Aggressive action is usually not advisable against No-Trump slams. Thus, under no circumstances should a Club be led. The passive lead of a Heart is calculated to protect your holdings.

4

One Heart	5 POINTS
Two Hearts or	
four Hearts	3 POINTS

Though you have game in hand, I do not recommend an opening bid of 2 Hearts, because of the danger that duplication of values may cause an unmakable slam to be reached. Remember that one of the requirements of the opening demand bid is that the hand contain four defensive or quick tricks. The fear that your 1-Heart bid will be passed out is more fanciful than real.

5

Four of Clubs	5 POINTS
Ace of Hearts	2 POINTS
Four of Spades	1 POINT

The Club lead is suggested because dummy has shown a very good Diamond suit, which will no doubt provide discards for declarer unless you collect your tricks in a hurry. Waiting leads are not indicated where dummy is known to have a good suit. You should place your hopes on partner's holding of the Ace or Queen of Clubs. If that does not work out, then in all probability there is no chance of defeating the contract.

6

Three Clubs	5 POINTS
Two No Trump	3 POINTS
Three Diamonds	2 POINTS

A jump of some kind is in order, but there is no completely satisfactory call available. A jump to 2 No Trump might turn out well, but we try to avoid that bid on unbalanced hands. Perhaps the least of several evils is a jump to 3 Clubs, although such a bid is usually to be avoided with only three trumps. The 3-Diamond call seems a bit more confining.

7

Pass	5 POINTS
Double	1 POINT

False pride in the possession of 20 points should not induce you to assume any risk at the level of 3 on a hand which does not present the remotest hope for game. Let me remind you that nothing could be deader than the hand of a partner who is unable to keep open a bid of 1 Club.

8

Two Hearts 5 POINTS
Double 3 POINTS

While it is tempting to double and exact from the enemy a suitable toll for what may have been an intemperate act, such a step should be taken with caution when you hold good support for partner's suit. Vulnerability in this case militates against an early double. The chances for game are too bright to accept what might be an inadequate penalty. Were your Clubs and Spades interchanged, we would favor the double.

9

Two Spades 5 POINTS
Four Hearts 3 POINTS
Three Hearts 2 POINTS
Three No Trump 1 POINT

This hand was microscopically short of an immediate jump shift response, and merits very strong treatment. On hands of such potency the proper procedure is to bid new suits twice and then raise partner. There is only a slight risk that partner will take your 2-Spade call as a legitimate suit bid—and if he does, you will correct the impression anyway on the next round when you raise Hearts.

As between the other calls, a rebid of 4 Hearts is stronger than a mere preference-signaling jump to 3 Hearts. A 3 No-Trump bid barely rates a token award.

10

Pass 5 POINTS
Double 0

My Mid-Victorian friends would be horrified at the prospect of staying out of the auction with more than three honor tricks, but hands of this type do not lend themselves to the technique of the takeout double. If you size up your hand as a dummy, it will be clear that your contribution to partner's trick-taking would be very limited. To approach the problem from another standpoint: If you were the dealer, you would not look upon this holding as a sound opening bid, for it contains only 12 points and not even a rebiddable suit. Finally, consider that if you make a takeout double, you will be forcing partner to bid at the level of 2, and this might prove irksome to him.

11

Three Hearts	5 POINTS
Four Diamonds	3 POINTS
Five Diamonds	2 POINTS
Three No Trump	1 POINT

The preferred bid is 3 Hearts. It would be pointless for you to persist with No Trump, since partner is marked with a highly unbalanced hand. Furthermore, he might get the impression that you have very little strength in his suits, which is far from being the case. Partner should realize that you have only three Hearts, inasmuch as you failed to raise that suit immediately. You may be in position to raise Diamonds on the next round.

12

Two Diamonds	5 POINTS
One Heart	2 POINTS
One No Trump	1 POINT

The good old-fashioned single raise provides perhaps the most accurate description of your holding. The response of 1 Heart, which many players would make in a situation like this, is not favored here. If the hand figures to play in Hearts, it will be because partner is in position to bid 2 Hearts over your bid of 2 Diamonds.

13

Three Spades	5 POINTS
Two Spades	3 POINTS
Three Clubs	2 POINTS
Two Clubs	1 POINT

Your hand, which started out as distinctly mediocre, has blossomed into a thing of beauty. Though you have a marked paucity of high cards, the fit in both of partner's suits converts this hand into a powerful holding. Any call less than 3 Spades would be a clear underbid. But at either the 2 or the 3 level, it is preferable to raise Spades rather than Clubs as the shorter road to game.

14

Pass	5 POINTS
Four Diamonds	
* or four Spades*	1 POINT

The pass is clearly indicated. Partner may be in a position to inflict a severe sting, and he should be given the courtesy of the decision. If he does not choose to double, he is obliged to proceed with the bidding, since your original bid was forcing to game.

15

Double	5 POINTS
One Spade	3 POINTS
Two Spades	1 POINT

This hand clearly calls for the take-out double. If partner should respond with 2 Clubs, you would not be in difficulty, for your hand is strong enough to justify a rebid of 2 Spades without involving any great risk. If your answer to the problem was 1 Spade, I take it that your attachment to 100 honors has dimmed the clarity of your view. A bid of 2 Spades might have been justified a generation ago in a case like this to describe a strong hand, but currently the jump overcall is regarded as pre-emptive and is therefore ruled out.

16

Three Clubs	5 POINTS
Three No Trump	3 POINTS
Four Hearts	1 POINT

This is a very powerful holding and might well produce a slam if partner produces just the right hand. In order to learn more about his values, you should make a temporizing bid of 3 Clubs. There is no real danger that this bid will be passed, because when a major suit has been supported the subsequent mention of any other suit must be treated as a force for at least one **round.**

17

Double	5 POINTS
One No Trump	2 POINTS
Two No Trump	1 POINT
Pass	0

Your hand contains 20 points in high cards and is therefore too strong for an overcall of 1 No Trump. The suggested procedure is to double, and if partner responds with 2 of a suit, you can go on to 2 No Trump. This should just about describe the strength of your holding. The 1 No-Trump overcall is given some credit, for it demonstrates the direction you desire to proceed. The hand is 2 points short of the requirements for a 2 No-Trump overcall. But your position over the opening bidder increases the value of your holding, and therefore I would not view this bid as an atrocity.

No credit is given for a pass, because in my view this hand is too strong to permit trapping tactics. It is not to be expected that either of the opponents will make any hazardous commitment.

18

Two Spades 5 POINTS
Two Diamonds 2 POINTS
Three Spades 1 POINT

With the advanced part score, you are not in position to make a temporizing response, for a 2-Diamond bid under the circumstances would not be forcing. Inasmuch as it completes the game, partner would be at liberty to pass. The bid least likely to complicate matters is a simple raise. Because it is a bid over score, partner will recognize that you probably have somewhat more than a normal raise; if his hand contains any excess values, he will be in sound position to take one more step for the purpose of ferreting out a slam.

A single point is awarded for the bid of 3 Spades, simply because it acquaints partner with your desire to investigate slam possibilities. The jump in a minor suit is not to be encouraged with only three trumps.

HOW DO YOU RATE?

78—90: Expert   50—64: Good
65—77: Top Rank   36—49: Average

Under 36: In need of a few lessons

Write your answers to the 18 problems on a sheet of paper, then turn to page 278 to find your score. Neither side is vulnerable unless shown.

1 As *South* you hold:

WEST	NORTH	EAST	SOUTH
1♥	Pass	Pass	DBL
Pass	2♣	Pass	?

What do you bid now?

2 As *Dealer* you hold:

What is your opening bid?

3 EAST-WEST VULNERABLE
As *South* you hold:

WEST	NORTH	EAST	SOUTH
1♠	2♦	2♥	?

What do you bid?

4 YOU ARE VULNERABLE
As *South* you hold:

WEST	NORTH	EAST	SOUTH
1♦	Pass	1♥	?

What do you bid?

5 As *South* you hold:

SOUTH	WEST	NORTH	EAST
Pass	Pass	1♣	Pass

What do you bid now?

6 As *South* you hold:

NORTH	EAST	SOUTH	WEST
1♥	Pass	1♠	Pass
2♣	Pass	2♦	Pass
2♥	Pass	?	

What do you bid now?

7 As *South* you hold:

NORTH	EAST	SOUTH	WEST
3NT	Pass	?	

What do you bid?

8 As *Dealer* you hold:

What is your opening bid?

9 BOTH SIDES VULNERABLE
As *South* you hold:

SOUTH	WEST	NORTH	EAST
1♠	Pass	Pass	2♣
?			

What do you bid now?

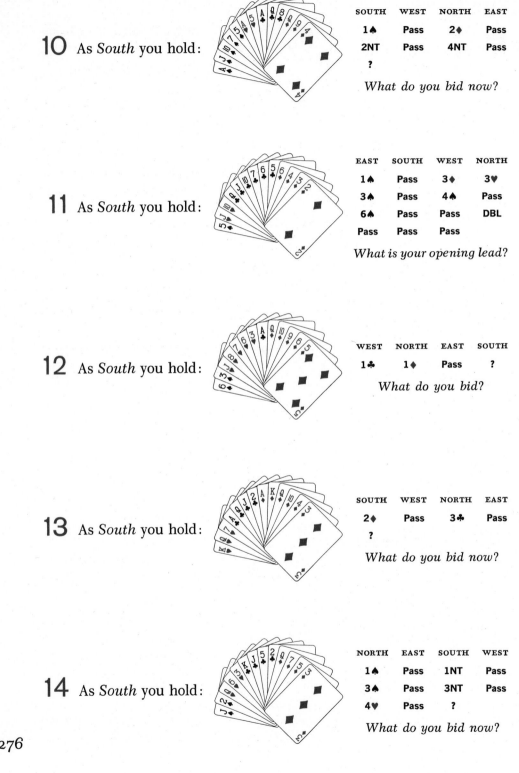

10 As *South* you hold:

SOUTH	WEST	NORTH	EAST
1♠	Pass	2♦	Pass
2NT	Pass	4NT	Pass
?			

What do you bid now?

11 As *South* you hold:

EAST	SOUTH	WEST	NORTH
1♠	Pass	3♦	3♥
3♠	Pass	4♠	Pass
6♠	Pass	Pass	DBL
Pass	Pass	Pass	

What is your opening lead?

12 As *South* you hold:

WEST	NORTH	EAST	SOUTH
1♣	1♦	Pass	?

What do you bid?

13 As *South* you hold:

SOUTH	WEST	NORTH	EAST
2♦	Pass	3♣	Pass
?			

What do you bid now?

14 As *South* you hold:

NORTH	EAST	SOUTH	WEST
1♠	Pass	1NT	Pass
3♠	Pass	3NT	Pass
4♥	Pass	?	

What do you bid now?

15 As *South* you hold: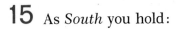

Your right-hand opponent opens with a bid of 1 Heart.

What do you bid?

16 As *South* you hold:

SOUTH	WEST	NORTH	EAST
1♠	Pass	3♣	Pass
3♠	Pass	4♠	Pass
?			

What do you bid now?

17 As *South* you hold:

EAST	SOUTH	WEST	NORTH
1♠	Pass	1NT	2NT
Pass	?		

What do you bid now?

18 As *South* you hold:

NORTH	EAST	SOUTH	WEST
1NT	Pass	?	

What do you bid?

Correct answers begin on the following page

1

Three Clubs	5 POINTS
Four Clubs	2 POINTS

Caution is indicated. Partner may have little or nothing. Any raise beyond 3 Clubs is not justified. After your raise to 3 Clubs, if partner has Hearts stopped he should take a chance on 3 No Trump.

2

One Club	5 POINTS
One Spade	2 POINTS

This hand contains 20 points and is, therefore, short of a 2 No-Trump opening. On the other hand, it is too strong for a 1 No-Trump bid. It must be opened with 1 of a suit, and our choice is 1 Club. Try to avoid opening with a Spade bid, whenever plausible, on hands worth 20 or more points. It is much easier for partner to respond if you open with 1 Club.

3

Five Diamonds	5 POINTS
Three Hearts	4 POINTS
Four Diamonds	3 POINTS
Pass	2 POINTS
Three Diamonds	1 POINT

The direct leap to 5 Diamonds puts the guess right up to the opposition. There may be merit to a cue bid in Hearts, in anticipation of the opponents getting to a high Spade contract, in which case the Heart lead would be called for. A bid of 4 Diamonds deprives the opponents of some bidding room. A pass, with the intention of bidding 5 Diamonds if the enemy gets to game, is better than the unstrategic raise to only 3 Diamonds.

4

Double	5 POINTS
Two Diamonds	3 POINTS
One Spade	0

The double for a takeout gives partner a choice between Clubs and Spades. A sizable demerit should be chalked up against the bid of only 1 Spade. 2 Diamonds has some merit. Your hand is worth 21 points in support of Spades; 20 in support of Clubs.

5

One No Trump	5 POINTS
One Diamond	3 POINTS
Two Clubs	2 POINTS

This hand is a little too good for a simple raise in Clubs. Some mild effort must be made to urge partner to go on, and the best choice is 1 No Trump. This, over a Club bid, indicates from 9 to 11 points. 1 Diamond is an alternative call, but is not as apt to be effective.

6

Pass	5 POINTS
Two No Trump	2 POINTS
Two Spades or three Diamonds	1 POINT

Quit while the quitting is good. This is obviously a misfit, and the best place to play such hands is at as low a level as convenient. One more bid by you may start a barrage of doubles from the enemy. Remember, four suits do not necessarily spell 3 No Trump.

7

Six Hearts	5 POINTS
Six No Trump	4 POINTS
Five Hearts	2 POINTS

The best bid is 6 Hearts. Opposite a hand containing 25 points, you could hardly miss making a slam. If partner happens to have a substantial 3 No-Trump bid with all four Aces, he would be in a position to contract for a grand slam.

A bid of 6 No Trump on your part might work out well, and has the merit of making sure a slam is bid—which a jump to 5 Hearts does not do. 4 Hearts is woefully inadequate.

8

Six Clubs	5 POINTS
Two Clubs	3 POINTS

Our preference is for a bid of 6 Clubs. On holdings of this type, scientific exploration is almost impossible. This hand might be spread for thirteen tricks and might not make more than eleven, but you should be willing to gamble on developing a trick in Spades. Partner might have the Queen. He might have three or four small ones, and in any event the opponents will have a difficult discarding problem. Because of your unusual opening bid, partner is warned against bidding 7 with what may be a useless Ace.

9

Pass	5 POINTS
Double	2 POINTS
Two Spades	1 POINT

Discretion calls for a pass. With a partner who has announced possession of practically nothing, it is futile to carry on the fight when the most you can hope to gain is a part score. You cannot expect to win more than six tricks in your own hand, and since partner may hold a complete blank it is foolish to contract for eight tricks. There is always the danger that West may be lying in ambush waiting for you to come out in the open again. If you cannot resist the urge to act, the double offers far greater safety than a bid of 2 Spades, which could be crippled if trumps happen to be massed in West's hand.

10

Six No Trump	5 POINTS
Five Diamonds	3 POINTS
Five Spades	2 POINTS

It may come as a rude shock to some of the Old Guard that the bid of 4 No Trump in this sequence is not looked upon by the elite as a Blackwood bid. It is just a good, old-fashioned measurement bid, and tends to elicit from partner the information as to how good was South's 2 No-Trump call. Your hand is worth 17 points, contains a good five-card suit and generally attractive features. You should therefore accept partner's invitation by proceeding to slam.

11

A Diamond 5 POINTS
Anything else 0

The lead of partner's suit is ruled out by the double. Nor should you select the unbid suit. The double of the slam calls for an abnormal lead, and in this particular case it appears that the abnormal lead is the dummy's first suit. You may wager a tidy sum that partner can ruff the opening lead of the Diamond deuce.

12

Four Diamonds 5 POINTS
Two Diamonds 3 POINTS
One Heart 1 POINT

The jump to 4 Diamonds is made in the expectation that the opposition will be crowded out of the bidding. It is conceivable that they have the cards to score decisively in one of the black suits, and your jump should have the effect of suppressing any exploratory action on their part.

13

Four Clubs 5 POINTS
Three Diamonds 3 POINTS
Six Clubs 2 POINTS

A raise in Clubs will fix the trump suit. Partner is expected to show an Ace if he has one. If, over your 4-Club bid, he should bid 4 Hearts, a grand slam in Clubs ought to be a cinch. If partner does not have the Ace of Hearts, you will have to settle for a small slam. Blackwood would not be helpful, for if partner should show an Ace, it would be impossible for you to tell which one it was. The Blackwood 4 No-Trump bid should be bypassed when you hold a void.

14

Four Spades 5 POINTS
Pass 1 POINT

Partner has described a hand containing six Spades and only four Hearts. This is clear from the fact that he made a jump rebid in his first suit before showing the other major. The partnership is known, therefore, to possess eight Spades as against only seven Hearts, and your proper call is 4 Spades.

15

Two Diamonds 5 POINTS
One Spade 3 POINTS
Two Spades 1 POINT

Our preferred call of 2 Diamonds is rather unorthodox, but anticipates the fact that the opponents might get up to 4 Hearts before it is next your turn to bid—in which case you could reasonably try a bid of 4 Spades. If you elect to overcall with 1 Spade, you may not feel inclined to try 5 Diamonds on the next round over an adverse 4-Heart bid.

The one-point award to 2 Spades is rendered merely to give acknowledgment to those who recognize the pre-emptive jump overcall as part of the system. However, the bid is not recommended in this particular instance.

16

Six Spades	5 POINTS
Five Clubs	4 POINTS
Four No Trump	
or five Hearts	3 POINTS

Opposite partner's jump shift, you hold a very impressive hand. Though its value at the outset was 14 points, now that Spades have been supported your hand may be revalued at 17 points—1 for the fifth Spade and 2 for the sixth. You may conclude that you have sufficient values for a slam, since partner's jump shift promised at least 19 points. We suggest a direct bid of 6 Spades, but if you wish to enjoy the fun you may prolong the bidding by showing one of your Aces.

17

Four Diamonds	5 POINTS
Three Diamonds	2 POINTS

In this situation it is obvious that partner is employing the unusual No-Trump overcall to ask for your best minor suit. You should jump in Diamonds to designate a good holding. Your distribution enhances prospects for game, and partner should be offered an inducement to proceed.

18

Three No Trump	5 POINTS
Five Diamonds	3 POINTS
Two No Trump	2 POINTS
Two Diamonds	1 POINT

3 No Trump is your best bid. The eight-card Diamond suit will produce seven tricks for partner; if he lacks the Ace, he must have three small Diamonds, since No-Trump openings are not sanctioned with a worthless doubleton. Remember that hands containing eight-card suits do not come within the provisions of the ordinary rules.

HOW DO YOU RATE?

78—90:	Expert	50—64:	Good
65—77:	Top Rank	36—49:	Average

Under 36: Don't play for money

Write your answers to the 18 problems on a sheet of paper, then turn to page 286 to find your score. Neither side is vulnerable unless shown.

1 As *South* you hold:

NORTH	EAST	SOUTH	WEST
1♣	Pass	1♥	Pass
2NT	Pass	?	

What do you bid now?

2 As *South* you hold:

SOUTH	WEST	NORTH	EAST
1♦	Pass	1♥	Pass
?			

What do you bid now?

3 YOU HAVE 70 PART SCORE
As *South* you hold:

NORTH	EAST	SOUTH	WEST
1♦	Pass	?	

What do you bid?

4 As *South* you hold:

SOUTH	WEST	NORTH	EAST
3♦	3♥	DBL	Pass
?			

What do you bid now?

5 As *South* you hold:

SOUTH	WEST	NORTH	EAST
1♠	Pass	2♦	Pass
2♥	Pass	3♣	Pass
?			

What do you bid now?

BOTH SIDES VULNERABLE

6 As *South* you hold:

NORTH	EAST	SOUTH	WEST
1♣	DBL	REDBL	1♥
Pass	Pass	1♠	2♥
DBL	2NT	?	

What do you bid now?

7 As *South* you hold:

EAST	SOUTH	WEST	NORTH
1♦	DBL	2♦	Pass
Pass	DBL	Pass	2♥
Pass	?		

What do you bid now?

8 As *South* you hold:

NORTH	EAST	SOUTH	WEST
1♠	Pass	2♦	Pass
4♦	Pass	?	

What do you bid now?

YOU HAVE 60 PART SCORE

9 As *South* you hold:

EAST	SOUTH	WEST	NORTH
1♣	DBL	1NT	Pass
Pass	DBL	Pass	2♥
Pass	Pass	2♠	Pass
Pass	?		

What do you bid now?

10 As *South* you hold:

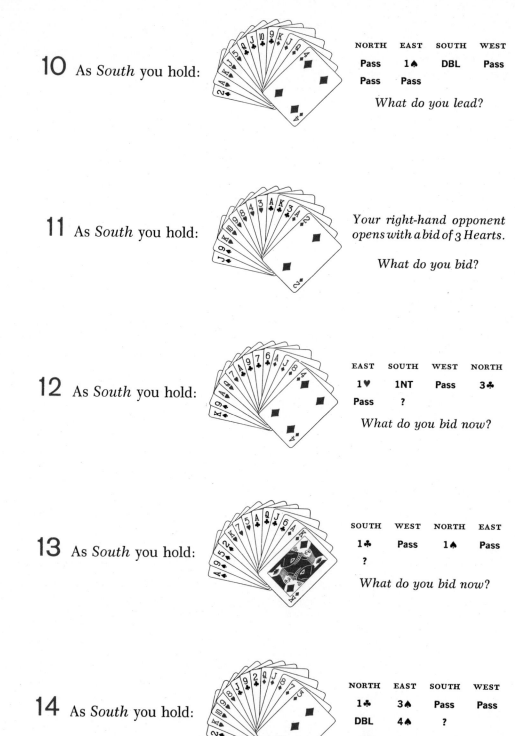

NORTH	EAST	SOUTH	WEST
Pass	1♠	DBL	Pass
Pass	Pass		

What do you lead?

11 As *South* you hold:

Your right-hand opponent opens with a bid of 3 Hearts.

What do you bid?

12 As *South* you hold:

EAST	SOUTH	WEST	NORTH
1♥	1NT	Pass	3♣
Pass	?		

What do you bid now?

13 As *South* you hold:

SOUTH	WEST	NORTH	EAST
1♣	Pass	1♠	Pass
?			

What do you bid now?

14 As *South* you hold:

NORTH	EAST	SOUTH	WEST
1♣	3♠	Pass	Pass
DBL	4♠	?	

What do you bid now?

15 both sides vulnerable
As *South* you hold:

Your right-hand opponent opens with a bid of 1 Spade.

What do you bid?

16 As *South* you hold:

SOUTH	WEST	NORTH	EAST
2♠	Pass	4♠	Pass
?			

What do you bid now?

17 As *South* you hold:

EAST	SOUTH	WEST	NORTH
Pass	1♣	Pass	1♦
Pass	1♠	Pass	2NT
Pass	?		

What do you bid now?

18 As *South* you hold:

EAST	SOUTH	WEST	NORTH
1♦	Pass	2♣	2♥
2NT	Pass	3NT	DBL
Pass	Pass	Pass	

What do you lead?

Correct answers begin on the following page

1

Six No Trump	5 POINTS
Three Clubs	2 POINTS
Five No Trump	1 POINT
Four No Trump	0

You have a good opening bid, plus a shade to spare. Since partner has opened and jumped, there should be a slam. That is all you need to know. A No-Trump contract suits your hand, so there is nothing further to do than to utter the words "6 No Trump." As a check, refer to the point count. You have 15 points. Partner has at least 19, with some sort of fit. The total of 34 is convincing enough for slam. Other calls merit little credit, and a bid of 4 No Trump receives none at all; on this sequence of bidding it would be a No-Trump raise, not the Blackwood Convention.

2

One Spade	5 POINTS
Two No Trump	
or two Spades	1 POINT
Two Diamonds	0

There is no reason for excitement; if partner's hand is predominantly Hearts, you will have nothing to cheer about. Take it easy with a simple rebid of 1 Spade. It is true that such a bid is not absolutely forcing, but if your partner elects to pass, you may be quite sure that you have reached the correct final contract. It should be noted that a 2 No-Trump rebid shows 19 high-card points and is not recommended with a singleton in partner's suit.

3

Two Hearts	5 POINTS
Six No Trump or	
six Diamonds	4 POINTS
Four No Trump	4 POINTS
One Heart	0

To some degree, the form of action you choose depends upon the faith you have in partner. Assuming reliability—a practice which we encourage in these tests—the clear-cut response is 2 Hearts, intending to bid at least a small slam in very short order but testing for 7. If you have some misgivings as to North's reaction to part-score situations or if, by the same line of reasoning, you feel that he may not have sufficient reliance upon you, you had better straightway contract for 6 No Trump or 6 Diamonds.

A response of 1 Heart is useless because, since that call completes the game, it is not forcing under the advanced part score.

286

4		
Pass	5 POINTS	
Three No		
Trump	2 POINTS	
Four Diamonds	1 POINT	
Five Diamonds	0	

There is no occasion for you to assume any further authority. You have told your story by your pre-emptive bid. In fact, you have better defensive values than partner might expect. He has undertaken to defeat the 3-Heart contract under his own steam, and it would ill become you to get in the way. Among the other calls, 3 No Trump has the slight merit of at least reaching for game. A contract of 5 Diamonds, however, is apt to end in disaster.

5		
Three Diamonds	5 POINTS	
Three Spades	3 POINTS	
Three No		
Trump	2 POINTS	
Pass	0	

Many players tend to drift into 3 No Trump as soon as all suits have been named—a step that would be ill advised on this hand. A mere indication of preference for Diamonds over Clubs is sufficient to express your holding. Partner should then be in position to select the best final contract. A rebid of 3 Spades might elicit a raise if partner has a doubleton honor.

6		
Double	5 POINTS	
Four Spades	2 POINTS	
Three Clubs	1 POINT	
Three Spades	0	

Be sure not to block traffic for partner. It is evident the opponents are floundering. By his penalty double of 2 Hearts, partner has indicated that he is anxious to set the enemy, and if you bid any number of Spades it will let them off the hook. Better strategy is to double 2 No Trump. If they run to 3 Diamonds, you can leave it to partner to act.

3 Spades receives no credit, since it is not forcing.

7		
Three Clubs	5 POINTS	
Three Hearts	2 POINTS	
Pass	2 POINTS	
Three Diamonds	1 POINT	
Four Hearts	0	

Our choice of the 3-Club bid may savor a bit of road hog. On the surface, it seems strange to duck out of a suit in which we hold the three top trump honors, but it must be recalled that partner was forced to speak and may have nothing more than four small Hearts in his hand. He might find it most inconvenient to have to ruff Diamonds with the top trumps.

8

Five Clubs	5 POINTS
Five Diamonds	3 POINTS
Four No Trump	2 POINTS
Six Diamonds	1 POINT

You hold the playing strength equivalent of an opening bid, facing a partner who has opened the bidding and jumped. It is appropriate that your fancy should lightly turn to thoughts of slam. A bid of 5 Clubs is a mild step in that direction; if partner does not contract for slam, you may relax, knowing you have done your duty. A bid of only 5 Diamonds will probably end the auction. A leap directly to 6 is an unsound gamble.

9

Pass	5 POINTS
Three Hearts	2 POINTS
Two No Trump	1 POINT
Double	0

You hold a hand of considerable merit, to be sure. Do not, on that account, subject yourself to a deliberate loss. Holdings like this are apt to induce a false pride. Pause to consider your chances of making nine tricks with a poverty-stricken partner, and you will see that discretion calls for a pass.

10

Spade deuce	5 POINTS
Diamond King	
or Club Queen	2 POINTS
Heart King	0

Lets say the opposition hands look like this:

WEST	EAST
♠ J 6 3	♠ A 8 7 6 5
♥ 6	♥ 8 7 5 4 3
♦ 10 7 6 5 3	♦ A
♣ 8 6 4 2	♣ A K

If you open the King of Hearts, a trump shift is too late. Declarer wins with the Ace, ruffs a second Heart in dummy, gets back with a Club, ruffs another Heart and comes back with another Club. He gives South a high Heart, but on the Club return he ruffs and leads his fifth Heart, insuring that he will make contract with an overtrick.

Open the trump, however, and before East can ruff any Hearts, North will get in and draw West's remaining trumps, insuring a two-trick set. Whenever partner has left in a takeout double of a low contract he is asking for a trump lead.

11

Pass 5 POINTS
Three No Trump 2 POINTS
Double 0

One might be tempted under the circumstances to give out with some such outburst as "I double, and how!" But since such practice does not conform with the best standards of propriety, this call isn't available. In our book, a double of an opening 3 bid is a highly cooperative bid, tending rather toward a take-out. It is a virtual certainty that your partner has no more than one Heart, and probably none. He will, therefore, hold the kind of hand on which he will surely bid if you double. So why not pass and take a sure profit? Remember, there is always the chance that partner may have sufficient strength to make a take-out double when the bid gets around to him, in which event you will be delighted to pass.

12

Three Hearts 5 POINTS
Five Clubs 3 POINTS
Four Clubs 2 POINTS
Three Diamonds or three No Trump 2 POINTS
Four No Trump 1 POINT

The fact that East has dragged a red herring across the scene has just become apparent. If East were not stretching the truth, where did North find sufficient high-card strength to justify a jump response? In an effort to expose the deceiver, a cue bid of 3 Hearts is recommended, with the intention of supporting Clubs vigorously on the next round. You have more than you needed for your 1 No-Trump bid, and the quality of your points is first-rate.

Of the other calls, only the immediate jump raise represents an adequate description of your values.

13

Three Diamonds 5 POINTS
Four Spades 4 POINTS
Three No Trump 2 POINTS
Three Spades 0

As the scale of awards indicates, there is a close choice here between a jump raise to 4 Spades and a jump shift to 3 Diamonds—the latter being to our mind the best rebid. It will have the merit of ferreting out a possible slam on certain holdings. While 3 No Trump rates some credit, the 3-Spade rebid deserves nothing because it is not forcing.

14

Five Diamonds	5 POINTS
Four No Trump	4 POINTS
Double	3 POINTS
Five Hearts or	
five Clubs	2 POINTS
Pass	1 POINT

In view of partner's display of strength, you should regard your holding with a bullish eye. Remember, partner has asked you to bid at the level of 4, fully aware that you might have nothing. Your favorable distribution and high cards in the red suits should induce some action at this point to circumvent East's hijacking attempt to silence you.

With an advanced partner, 4 No Trump is an enlightened call, asking him to select the suit. It should be quite clear that your bid is not Blackwood, since you were unable to make a free bid the first time. Nor could it express a desire to play the hand at No Trump, for with adequate Spades you would have doubled East.

A penalty double will at least yield a greater profit than a pass, which shows complete timidity—a charge which can hardly be leveled at anyone who selected a bid of 5 Clubs or 5 Hearts.

15

Pass	5 POINTS
Two Diamonds	2 POINTS
Double	0

Don't crowd a fellow who might be working for you, even when he's an opponent. Give him plenty of elbow room. Any action by you that tends to impede the opposition is bound to prove to your detriment.

16

Pass	5 POINTS
Five Spades	1 POINT
Six Spades	0

Before you decide that your inquisitor is suffering from a fear neurosis, consider the significance of partner's 4-Spade response. The jump raise of an opening bid of 2 in a suit is a specialized bid, describing a hand which contains very good trump support but no Ace, King or singleton. Therefore, it is clear that your side lacks the Club Ace, has a Heart loser to dispose of, and requires a bit of good fortune in the location of the King of Diamonds. Any slam possibility should be regarded as far too remote to consider.

17

Three Diamonds 5 POINTS
Three Clubs or
   three Spades 3 POINTS
Three No Trump 1 POINT

If partner's Heart holding is inadequate, a suit·contract will be mandatory, and the Diamond raise allows for all possibilities. Should partner have good Diamonds, the hand may play best there. If he should have three Spades to an honor, he could still show a belated preference by bidding 3 Spades. If, on the other hand, his Heart stoppers are adequate, he may decide to return to 3 No Trump, but he will do so forewarned of our extreme shortness in the suit.

The opening bid may appear a bit irregular, but bidding a five-card Club suit before a five-card Spade suit is not at all uncommon, particularly where the Spade suit is not very robust. Observe that if the bidding is opened with 1 Spade and partner responds 2 Hearts, opener is in a somewhat untenable position.

18

Heart deuce 5 POINTS
Spade Queen or
   Club Queen 1 POINT

Partner's double is a clear call for you to lead the suit he has bid. The fact that you hold a singleton should not dissuade you. In a normal auction the Queen of Spades or even the Queen of Clubs would be the preferred lead, but here the Heart lead is mandatory.

HOW DO YOU RATE?

78—90:	Expert	50—64:	Good
65—77:	Top Rank	36—49:	Average

Under 36: Better left unsaid

Write your answers to the 18 problems on a sheet
of paper, then turn to page 296 to find your
score. Neither side is vulnerable unless shown.

1 As *South* you hold:

SOUTH	WEST	NORTH	EAST
1♠	2♣	Pass	Pass
?			

What do you bid now?

2 As *South* you hold:

WEST	NORTH	EAST	SOUTH
1♦	Pass	1NT	Pass
Pass	2♥	Pass	?

What do you bid now?

3 As *South* you hold:

NORTH	EAST	SOUTH	WEST
1♣	Pass	1♦	1♠
3♦	Pass	?	

What do you bid now?

4 As *South* you hold:

NORTH	EAST	SOUTH	WEST
1♣	Pass	1♥	Pass
1♠	Pass	?	

What do you bid now?

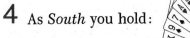

5

BOTH SIDES VULNERABLE

As *South* you hold:

WEST	NORTH	EAST	SOUTH
3♥	3♠	DBL	?

What do you bid?

6 As *South* you hold:

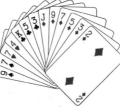

EAST	SOUTH	WEST	NORTH
1♥	2♦	Pass	2NT
Pass	?		

What do you bid now?

7 As *South* you hold:

NORTH	EAST	SOUTH	WEST
1♠	2♦	?	

What do you bid?

8 As *South* you hold:

NORTH	EAST	SOUTH	WEST
1♠	Pass	3♠	Pass
4♣	Pass	5♣	Pass
5♥	Pass	?	

What do you bid now?

9 As *South* you hold:

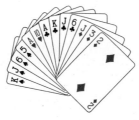

NORTH	EAST	SOUTH	WEST
Pass	1♥	DBL	Pass
2♦	Pass	?	

What do you bid now?

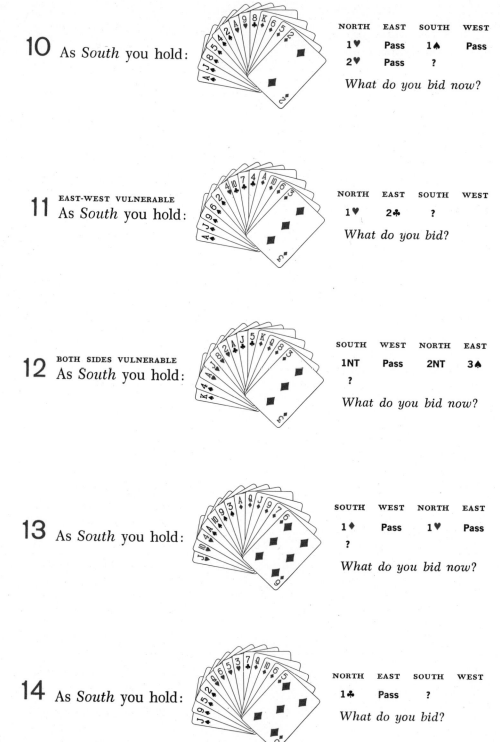

10 As *South* you hold:

NORTH	EAST	SOUTH	WEST
1♥	Pass	1♠	Pass
2♥	Pass	?	

What do you bid now?

11 EAST-WEST VULNERABLE
As *South* you hold:

NORTH	EAST	SOUTH	WEST
1♥	2♣	?	

What do you bid?

12 BOTH SIDES VULNERABLE
As *South* you hold:

SOUTH	WEST	NORTH	EAST
1NT	Pass	2NT	3♠
?			

What do you bid now?

13 As *South* you hold:

SOUTH	WEST	NORTH	EAST
1♦	Pass	1♥	Pass
?			

What do you bid now?

14 As *South* you hold:

NORTH	EAST	SOUTH	WEST
1♣	Pass	?	

What do you bid?

15 As *South* you hold:

SOUTH	WEST	NORTH	EAST
1♠	Pass	2♣	Pass
2♥	Pass	3♣	Pass
?			

What do you bid now?

16 As *South* you hold:

NORTH	EAST	SOUTH	WEST
1♣	Pass	?	

What do you bid?

17 As *South* you hold:

EAST	SOUTH	WEST	NORTH
1♥	?		

What do you bid?

18 As *South* you hold:

SOUTH	WEST	NORTH	EAST
1♥	Pass	1♠	Pass
3♦	Pass	3NT	Pass
?			

What do you bid now?

Correct answers begin on the following page

1

Three Clubs	5 POINTS
Three Spades	4 POINTS
Four Spades	3 POINTS
Double	2 POINTS

This hand possesses enormous offensive possibilities despite partner's failure to take action on the first round. It is true that a cue bid is always very drastic, but partner should recall that in the first instance you did not open with a demand bid of 2 Spades. A jump rebid in Spades is acceptable, but the cue bid is preferred because of your tolerance for a red-suit contract, should partner have some length in either of those suits. A reopening double is not recommended—first, because of its slight inadequacy and, second, because you are not prepared for a penalty pass.

2

Pass	5 POINTS
Two Spades	2 POINTS
Three Hearts	1 POINT

Partner is not attempting to go places. He is merely trying to prevent the adversaries from running off with a cheap part score. If he had even the mildest ambitions he would have entered the auction immediately over the opening bid of 1 Diamond, at which point it would have been easy for him to compete. Therefore, refrain from bidding 2 Spades, a contract which partner may not be prepared to play.

3

Three Spades	5 POINTS
Five Diamonds	3 POINTS
Three No Trump	2 POINTS
Four Diamonds	1 POINT

The 3-Spade call is a cue bid and serves a dual purpose. It may enable partner to contract for 3 No Trump, if that happens to be the best contract, or it may permit him to think in terms of a slam if his hand is suited for the purpose. Your partner has opened the bidding and jumped. Your hand is not far from the equivalent of an opening bid in strength. Your Queen in partner's long Club suit may be enormously valuable. So, slam possibilities are not remote.

4

Two Spades	5 POINTS
Two No Trump	3 POINTS
Two Hearts	2 POINTS
One No Trump	1 POINT

While it is tempting to make the next bid in No Trump, there is, unfortunately, no convenient No-Trump bid available. The hand is a shade too good for the rebid of 1 No Trump, and yet it is not quite strong enough for a jump to 2 No Trump, which is forcing to game. We suggest a raise to 2 Spades, though normally we avoid doing this with only three trumps when partner presumably has a four-card suit. If partner rebids, you can then try 3 No Trump on the next round.

5

Redouble 5 POINTS
Pass 3 POINTS
Three No Trump 1 POINT

This will be an adequate dummy for a vulnerable player who was willing to undertake a nine-trick commitment. East has evidently overestimated the strength of his partner's hand, and even though Spades break badly I would feel confident of fulfilling the contract. There is the added advantage that the redouble may induce West, who has admitted that he has not a strong hand, to run to 4 Hearts. Playing against that contract should provide a delightful afternoon.

6

Three No Trump 5 POINTS
Four Diamonds 1 POINT

Your partner is behaving in a most praiseworthy manner and your appreciation of his efforts should be manifested by a raise to 3 No Trump. You can contribute seven tricks to the cause, and it would be strange indeed if partner could not help along with two, in view of the fact that he acted without your solicitation. If your answer was 3 Diamonds or, for that matter, any number of Diamonds, you may hide your blushes in the nearest corner.

7

Pass 5 POINTS
Anything else 0

Discretion calls for a pass. If there were any assurance that 2 Diamonds would be the final contract, a resounding double would be in order. But it is reasonable to expect that if you doubled there would be a rescue bid, and that your partner, looking to you for certain high-card values, would take some step distasteful to you, such as doubling the rescue.

8

Seven Spades 5 POINTS
Six Diamonds 3 POINTS
Six Hearts 2 POINTS
Six Spades 1 POINT

On the basis of your partner's strong bidding there can be little doubt that the trump suit is solid. It will be observed that North bypassed an easy chance to show the Ace of Diamonds, so it may be assumed that he hasn't got that card. This makes it all the more convincing that you are not faced with a trump loser. So a grand-slam bid in Spades is quite in order.

9

Pass 5 POINTS
Three Diamonds 1 POINT

There is no reason to foresee game possibilities, and there is no action you can take at this point that is not fraught with danger. Partner has been brought into the auction, perhaps much against his will, and he may have little or nothing.

10

Three Diamonds	5 POINTS
Three Hearts	3 POINTS
Four Hearts	2 POINTS
Three Spades	1 POINT

Three Diamonds is a one-round force, and since the picture is not quite clear at the present stage, this temporizing bid is in order. If partner again rebids his suit, you can raise it with assurance. The best alternative call for you is a raise in Hearts. The ragged nature of your Spade suit virtually precludes a jump rebid in that suit.

11

Double	5 POINTS
Pass	2 POINTS

We are almost ready to assess a special demerit for bidding 2 Spades. This bid would be forcing for one round and would probably result in a rebid of 3 Hearts by partner. If you are able to extricate yourself from that predicament, you have greater resourcefulness than I have. It seems safe to assume that you can win three or four tricks against the Club declaration, which, added to the three the opening bidder is expected to win, should produce a sizable profit. This is a clear-cut occasion for the penalty double.

12

Double	5 POINTS
Pass	2 POINTS
Three No Trump	1 POINT

Strike while the iron is hot. This is one double that East should long remember! Do not aim for anything so trivial as a game when a possible 1,100-point plum is there for the picking. The general high-card strength of your hand is enough to insure a four-trick set.

13

One Spade	5 POINTS
Two Hearts	3 POINTS
Two Diamonds *or three* *Diamonds*	1 POINT

The several possible choices include rebidding Diamonds and supporting Hearts. But the hand is too strong for a mere 2-Diamond rebid, and not quite strong enough for a jump to 3 Diamonds. While the suggested bid of 1 Spade is not forcing, in these circumstances partner will exert every effort to speak again, and a better idea of the nature of his hand may be obtained from his next move.

14

One Diamond	5 POINTS
One Heart	3 POINTS
Pass	1 POINT

We are disinclined to pass partner out in a bid of 1 Club where there is any reasonable excuse for bidding. Partner may have Hearts or Spades as his second suit, and a better result will be obtained if he is given the chance to show it. A 1-Diamond response allows for this contingency. The worst possible bid by you would be 1 No Trump.

15

Four Clubs	5 POINTS
Three Hearts	3 POINTS
Three Spades	2 POINTS
Five Clubs	1 POINT

Partner must have a very substantial Club suit to insist upon it in the face of your showing a major two-suiter. A rebid of 3 Hearts might tend to make partner lose interest, since it would merely sound like an effort on your part to force him to show a preference—which he has already refused to do. A bid of 4 Clubs will surely identify your singleton Diamond and have the effect of urging partner on to bigger things.

16

Four No Trump	5 POINTS
Two Spades	3 POINTS
One Spade	1 POINT

This is the ideal type of hand for the Blackwood Convention, since the only losers are Aces. If partner happens to have four Aces, the grand slam is easy. If he has three, you contract for a small slam. If he has two, you stop at 5 Spades and should be safe. If he has only one, it is high time you drew him aside for an intimate little chat.

17

Two Hearts	5 POINTS
Five Spades	3 POINTS
Four No Trump	3 POINTS
Double	3 POINTS

Your first duty is to make a bid which is forcing to game. The only one available is a cue bid in the opponents' suit. Regardless of partner's response, you will then embark on a Blackwood bid to determine the number of Aces he holds. A direct overcall of 5 Spades or 4 No Trump might not be interpreted clearly by partner. The recommended method is surer.

18

Pass	5 POINTS
Four No Trump	1 POINT

Any further conversation by you would be mere filibustering. On the basis of the 1-over-1 response, you have insisted upon a game and partner has shown no enthusiasm. Let us point out that North may have as little as 6 points while you have but 22, and no fit has been established. You are not in slam territory.

HOW DO YOU RATE?

78—90:	Expert	50—64:	Good
65—77:	Top Rank	36—49:	Average

Under 36: Go to the foot of the class

*Write your answers to the 18 problems on a sheet
of paper, then turn to page 304 to find your
score. Neither side is vulnerable unless shown.*

1 As *South* you hold: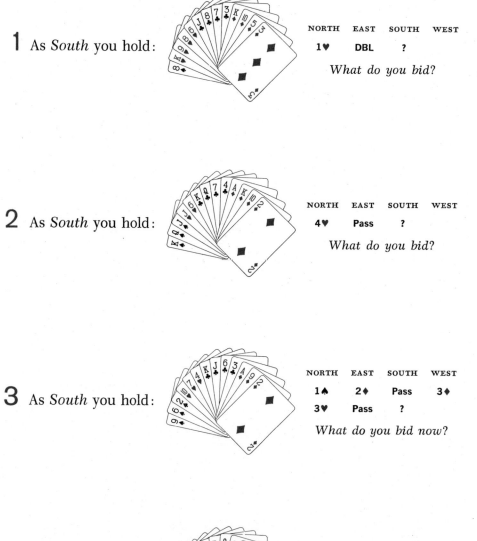

NORTH	EAST	SOUTH	WEST
1♥	DBL	?	

What do you bid?

2 As *South* you hold:

NORTH	EAST	SOUTH	WEST
4♥	Pass	?	

What do you bid?

3 As *South* you hold:

NORTH	EAST	SOUTH	WEST
1♠	2♦	Pass	3♦
3♥	Pass	?	

What do you bid now?

4 As *South* you hold:

SOUTH	WEST	NORTH	EAST
Pass	Pass	1♥	1♠
?			

What do you bid now?

5 BOTH SIDES VULNERABLE
As *South* you hold:

SOUTH	WEST	NORTH	EAST
1♠	DBL	2♣	Pass
?			

What do you bid now?

6 As *South* you hold:

SOUTH	WEST	NORTH	EAST
2♠	Pass	3NT	Pass
?			

What do you bid now?

7 YOU ARE VULNERABLE
As *South* you hold:

WEST	NORTH	EAST	SOUTH
3♠	DBL	Pass	?

What do you bid?

8 YOU HAVE 60 PART SCORE
As *South* you hold:

SOUTH	WEST	NORTH	EAST
1♣	1♦	1♥	1♠
?			

What do you bid now?

9 As *South* you hold:

EAST	SOUTH	WEST	NORTH
1♠	Pass	2♠	3NT
DBL	?		

What do you bid now?

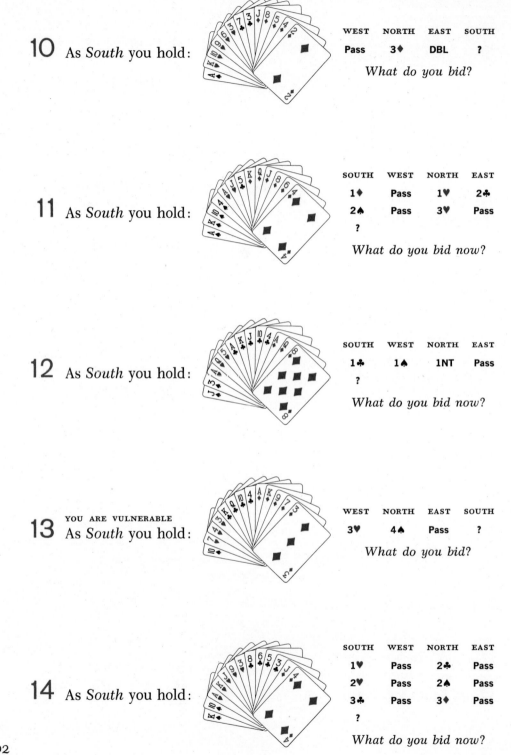

10 As *South* you hold:

WEST	NORTH	EAST	SOUTH
Pass	3♦	DBL	?

What do you bid?

11 As *South* you hold:

SOUTH	WEST	NORTH	EAST
1♦	Pass	1♥	2♣
2♠	Pass	3♥	Pass
?			

What do you bid now?

12 As *South* you hold:

SOUTH	WEST	NORTH	EAST
1♣	1♠	1NT	Pass
?			

What do you bid now?

13 YOU ARE VULNERABLE
As *South* you hold:

WEST	NORTH	EAST	SOUTH
3♥	4♠	Pass	?

What do you bid?

14 As *South* you hold:

SOUTH	WEST	NORTH	EAST
1♥	Pass	2♣	Pass
2♥	Pass	2♠	Pass
3♣	Pass	3♦	Pass
?			

What do you bid now?

15
As *South* you hold:

WEST	NORTH	EAST	SOUTH
4♥	Pass	Pass	?

What do you bid?

16 As *South* you hold:

WEST	NORTH	EAST	SOUTH
1♥	2♦	Pass	?

What do you bid?

17 As *South* you hold:

WEST	NORTH	EAST	SOUTH
1♣	Pass	2♦	?

What do you bid?

18 As *South* you hold:

NORTH	EAST	SOUTH	WEST
1NT	Pass	3♠	Pass
3NT	Pass	?	

What do you bid now?

Correct answers begin on the following page   303

1

Three Hearts	5 POINTS
Four Hearts	3 POINTS
Redouble	2 POINTS

On hands of only moderate strength, when a takeout double has been made and you have a good fit with partner's opening, best results are usually obtained by offering an immediate jump raise. Do not redouble simply because you are satisfied with Hearts.

2

Pass	5 POINTS
Four No Trump	0

A slam is entirely out of the question. Partner could not have a solid Heart suit and a side Ace, or else he would not have pre-empted. You should be satisfied with a game.

3

Four Diamonds	5 POINTS
Four Spades or four Hearts	4 POINTS
Three No Trump	3 POINTS

Since partner contracted for nine tricks on his own, a return to 3 Spades would be highly inadequate. The suggested cue bid of 4 Diamonds is not as drastic as it may appear to be, for partner must recall that you failed to act on the first round. Contracting for game in either major is also acceptable.

4

Two Hearts	5 POINTS
Three Hearts	2 POINTS
Four Hearts	1 POINT

Any desire to take drastic action could only be induced by possession of the fifth trump, which may look good but has little practical value. This hand is not rich in playing strength and adds up to just about a good single raise, which is the recommended bid.

5

Four Clubs	5 POINTS
Five Clubs	4 POINTS
Three Diamonds	2 POINTS
Three Clubs	1 POINT

Four Clubs gets our nod, but we would not look askance at a direct leap to game. Although partner's bid over the double does not show strength, it should be based on a long Club suit, which is just about all he requires. Don't be intimidated by the circumstance that your partner "bid over the double."

6

Four Clubs	5 POINTS
Four Spades	3 POINTS
Six Spades	1 POINT

It is well to control the blood pressure at this point. You opened with a minimum demand bid (you yourself have just nine tricks) and are by no means assured of a slam. Partner could have King-Queen of Diamonds and another King. An attempt must be made to ascertain whether partner's values are in the Club suit. If he has King-Queen of Clubs you will wish to attempt the slam. The suggested call is therefore 4 Clubs. If North supports that suit, big things are in order.

7

Three No Trump 5 POINTS
Pass 3 POINTS
Five Clubs 2 POINTS

Partner has shown a very good hand. It is evident that he is not doubling on Spades but on strength in the red suits. While a profit will accrue if the double is left in, it is doubtful that it will be adequate to compensate you for missing out on a game.

8

Three Hearts 5 POINTS
Four Hearts 4 POINTS
Two Spades 2 POINTS
Three Clubs 1 POINT

Some effort should be made here to reach slam. The suggested call is 3 Hearts, overbidding the score. If partner bids 3 Spades to show the control, you may jump to 5 Hearts. This should make it clear that if partner has second-round control of Diamonds he may then contract for slam. If in response to your 3-Heart bid partner bids 4 Diamonds, you may safely contract for 6 Hearts yourself.

9

Pass 5 POINTS
Four Hearts 0

A bid of 4 Hearts as a rescue would be entirely unjustified. Partner is obviously not interested in hearing about your Hearts. If he were, he would have made a takeout double of the 2-Spade bid. His jump to 3 No Trump was doubtless based on a long minor suit. In any event you should permit him to work out his own destiny.

10

Three Hearts 5 POINTS
Five Diamonds 4 POINTS
Six Diamonds 3 POINTS
Pass 2 POINTS
Four Diamonds 1 POINT

We favor an unorthodox call of 3 Hearts for purely strategic purposes. In view of your mediocre holding with its great length in partner's pre-emptive bid, there is a strong likelihood that the opponents will bid a slam in Spades. If they do, a Heart lead from partner, through the strong hand, may be of vital importance. So you must get in the "lead director" now. You, of course, plan to sacrifice in Diamonds, the opponents permitting.

11

Four Hearts 5 POINTS
Five Diamonds 3 POINTS
Four Diamonds 1 POINT

Partner may not have much high-card strength, but he ought to have great length in Hearts—which is enough for your purposes. Little is to be gained by rebidding the Diamonds, as partner is well aware that you have a preponderance of Diamonds and Spades.

305

12

Five No Trump	5 POINTS
Six No Trump	4 POINTS
Four No Trump	2 POINTS
Three Clubs	1 POINT

The 5 No-Trump bid is not conventional but rather a direct raise inviting partner to bid a slam. Your 21 high-card points, when added to the 10 partner is known to have, give you at least 31, which puts you in the slam zone. Furthermore, you have the advantage of knowing that your strength is well placed with relationship to the enemy assets. With a partner who is known to be conservative, we would incline toward a direct slam bid.

13

Six Spades	5 POINTS
Five Spades	4 POINTS

The lack of trump support should not deter you from acting. Partner has made it clear that his Spade suit is self-sustaining. He should be able to win nine of the ten tricks for which he has contracted, and you can win at least three. The opposition has made scientific investigation impossible, and we are in favor of a bid of 6 Spades, or at least 5.

14

Three Spades	5 POINTS
Three Hearts	3 POINTS
Four Clubs	2 POINTS
Three No Trump	1 POINT

Partner is obviously fishing around for big things, and he is doing so in the face of our minimum pronouncements. Because we have been careful to show no enthusiasm, and because the mild Spade fit can be conveniently shown below the game level, one forward move is in order.

15

Five Hearts	5 POINTS
Double	3 POINTS
Four Spades	1 POINT

This hand is worth 25 points in support of any suit partner can bid. Because as little as a King or a long suit in his hand will probably produce a slam, a mere double on your part would be placing too much pressure on him. You must take matters in your own hands and force him to speak, even at the 6-level.

16

Pass	5 POINTS
Two Spades	2 POINTS

You have an exactly average hand in high cards (10 points), which will normally not produce game opposite a partner who was only able to overcall. It would be extremely bad tactics to try 2 No Trump merely because you have Hearts stopped and a smattering of high cards.

17

Three Diamonds 5 POINTS
Double 2 POINTS

Something, you can be sure, is rotten here. There is scarcely enough outstanding strength to piece together an opposing opening bid, and to combine that with a jump shift suggests sheer fantasy. Surely you will not wish to retire at less than the 5-level in one of your major suits, and in order to be sure that the bidding does not suddenly subside, a game-forcing cue bid of 3 Diamonds is recommended.

18

Four Diamonds 5 POINTS
Six No Trump 4 POINTS

A temporizing bid of 4 Diamonds is suggested. If partner supports that suit on the next round, contract for slam in the minor. However, with this holding it is not a bad move to go directly to 6 No Trump.

HOW DO YOU RATE?

78—90: Expert   50—64: Good

65—77: Top Rank   36—49: Average

Under 36: Never marry a bridge player

Write your answers to the 18 problems on a sheet of paper, then turn to page 312 to find your score. Neither side is vulnerable unless shown.

1 As *South* you hold:

NORTH	EAST	SOUTH	WEST
1♣	Pass	?	

What do you bid?

2 As *South* you hold:

Your right-hand opponent opens with a bid of 1 Spade. What do you bid?

3 As *South* you hold:

NORTH	EAST	SOUTH	WEST
Pass	Pass	1♦	Pass
1♠	Pass	1NT	Pass
2♥	Pass	?	

What do you bid now?

4 As *South* you hold:

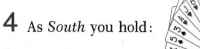

SOUTH	WEST	NORTH	EAST
1NT	Pass	Pass	2♣
Pass	Pass	2♦	Pass
?			

What do you bid now?

5 As *South* you hold:

NORTH	EAST	SOUTH	WEST
1♦	Pass	1♠	Pass
3♦	Pass	?	

What do you bid now?

6 As *South* you hold:

SOUTH	WEST	NORTH	EAST
1♠	Pass	2♣	Pass
2♠	Pass	3♦	Pass
3♥	Pass	3♠	Pass
?			

What do you bid now?

7 YOU ARE VULNERABLE
As *South* you hold:

NORTH	EAST	SOUTH	WEST
1♣	1♥	?	

What do you bid?

8 As *South* you hold:

NORTH	EAST	SOUTH	WEST
1♦	Pass	1♠	Pass
3♥	Pass	?	

What do you bid now?

9 YOU HAVE 60 PART SCORE
As *South* you hold:

SOUTH	WEST	NORTH	EAST
1♥	Pass	1♠	2♦
?			

What do you bid now?

10 As *South* you hold:

SOUTH	WEST	NORTH	EAST
1♠	2♥	DBL	Pass
?			

What do you bid now?

11 As *South* you hold:

SOUTH	WEST	NORTH	EAST
1♦	1♠	2♥	Pass
?			

What do you bid now?

12 EAST-WEST VULNERABLE
As *South* you hold:

EAST	SOUTH	WEST	NORTH
1♦	Pass	Pass	1♥
DBL	?		

What do you bid now?

13 As *South* you hold:

SOUTH	WEST	NORTH	EAST
1♥	Pass	1♠	Pass
2♣	Pass	4♠	Pass
?			

What do you bid now?

14 As *South* you hold:

SOUTH	WEST	NORTH	EAST
1♦	2♣	2♥	Pass
?			

What do you bid now?

15 BOTH SIDES VULNERABLE
As *South* you hold:

NORTH	EAST	SOUTH	WEST
1♣	1♥	2♦	Pass
3♣	3♥	?	

What do you bid now?

16 As *South* you hold:

SOUTH	WEST	NORTH	EAST
Pass	Pass	1♣	1♦
Pass	2♦	DBL	Pass
?			

What do you bid now?

17 As *South* you hold:

SOUTH	WEST	NORTH	EAST
1♠	Pass	2♥	Pass
?			

What do you bid now?

18 As *South* you hold:

NORTH	EAST	SOUTH	WEST
1♣	Pass	1♥	Pass
2♦	Pass	?	

What do you bid now?

1

Two Diamonds	5 POINTS
One Diamond	3 POINTS
Three Clubs	1 POINT

The jump shift to 2 Diamonds suggests slam possibilities. Your good trump fit and controls fully justify such optimism. We look with little favor on a bid of 3 Clubs, because if partner should rebid 3 No Trump it would leave you in something of a dilemma.

2

One No Trump	5 POINTS
Double	3 POINTS
Two Clubs	2 POINTS

You have the high-card requirements for an initial bid of 1 No Trump, with protection in three suits. A mere overcall of 2 Clubs would not do justice to your holding. Though the hand possesses the high-card essentials of a takeout double, we are not inclined to favor this bid, for if partner were to make the more or less probable response of 2 Hearts you would find yourself in an awkward position. An effort to extricate yourself by bidding 2 No Trump would be an exaggeration of your values and attended with some danger. If partner happens to be weak, you might just as well play the hand at 1 No Trump.

3

Three Spades	5 POINTS
Two Spades	3 POINTS
Three Hearts or two No Trump	1 POINT

Up until now you have sounded like a person with a very minimum opening bid, yet this is not the case. Your points are of the gilt-edged variety and include an excellent fit for both of partner's suits. Game is quite probable, even opposite a rather weak hand, and a jump bid is necessary to convey this message to partner.

An immediate Heart raise is not recommended with only three trumps, and a rebid of 2 No Trump is a wasted move since partner has clearly indicated that he does not care for No Trump.

4

Pass	5 POINTS
Three Diamonds	2 POINTS
Two No Trump	0

When partner passed your 1 No-Trump bid he made it clear that there was no hope of going places. He is now merely competing for a part score with some very weak hand that contains perhaps five Diamonds. Actually we ought to assess a demerit for a rebid of any number of No Trump.

5

Three Hearts	5 POINTS
Five Diamonds	3 POINTS
Four No Trump	2 POINTS
Four Diamonds	1 POINT

You have the equivalent of an opening bid, and partner has opened and jumped. This suggests a slam. Among ways of communicating the idea to partner, one of the most common is a cue bid. Your 3-Heart bid will be recognized as Ace-showing when later you vigorously support partner's Diamonds.

6

Four Clubs	5 POINTS
Four No Trump	3 POINTS
Six Spades	2 POINTS
Five Spades	1 POINT

Up to this point you have given no indication of additional values. By force of circumstance your bidding has had a somewhat doleful tone, whereas your partner has put on a display of power. He has named both minor suits in the reverse order and has supported Spades. A slam becomes highly likely, and this is an appropriate time to show the Ace of Clubs.

7

Pass	5 POINTS
Double	3 POINTS
One Spade	1 POINT
Two Diamonds	0

With a void in partner's suit, a free bid at this point would be an extremely hazardous undertaking. No consideration should be given to a bid of 2 Diamonds; this might force partner to the level of 3 with a hand that does not look very helpful. The penalty double is a conceivable bid, but we regard it as premature in the present instance.

8

Three Spades	5 POINTS
Five Hearts	3 POINTS

The 3-Spade bid is a temporizing measure, for there are obvious slam possibilities on this hand. The best way of describing your holding is to show a good five-card suit and to follow up with a strong Heart raise. If over 3 Spades partner bids 3 No Trump, you will bid 5 Hearts. If he raises Spades or rebids Diamonds, you will still show strong Heart support.

9

Three Clubs	5 POINTS
Two Spades	3 POINTS
Two Hearts	1 POINT

On the surface it would appear that a single raise to 2 Spades, which completes the game, is the proper call. The reason for preferring a 3-Club bid is to be found in the principle of anticipation. In view of the score, you may expect a further competitive bid of 3 Diamonds. If partner is unable to go further and the bid reverts to you, you will be in considerable doubt as to the best procedure. If, however, you have bid 3 Clubs over the 2-Diamond bid, then when the opponents bid 3 Diamonds you will be in a strategic position to bid 3 Spades. In this way, you will have exhausted the possibilities of all three suits instead of restricting your chances to Hearts and Spades.

10

Pass	5 POINTS
Three Hearts	3 POINTS
Three Clubs	2 POINTS
Three Spades	1 POINT

Ordinarily the possession of a six-card major suit, combined with a void in the suit doubled, is sufficient ground for overriding partner's penalty double. However, in this particular case you should stand for the double because you have such defensive strength that the proceeds of the penalty could be highly gratifying. Furthermore, it is likely that partner is short in Spades, so that you may find it difficult to reach a convenient spot for game.

11

Three Clubs	5 POINTS
Four Hearts	3 POINTS
Three Hearts	2 POINTS

While you have adequate Heart support, a further temporizing bid of 3 Clubs is recommended. When you raise partner's suit on the next round, he will then have a complete picture of your distribution and may be in position to proceed.

12

Redouble	5 POINTS
Pass	3 POINTS
Two No Trump	1 POINT

The fact that you have but a singleton Heart should not deter you from making the redouble. You have sufficient high-card values to render partner's contract safe. The important consideration is to have yourself designated temporary captain of this team, which the redouble will do. Such action beseeches partner to let you have the next bid; if the adversaries, in an effort to extricate themselves from the redouble, bid into your hand, you can inflict a punishing double.

13

Five Diamonds	5 POINTS
Four No Trump	4 POINTS
Six Spades	3 POINTS

You have not yet begun to describe the strength of your hand. In view of partner's vigorous action despite the fact that there might be, for all he knows, a near minimum in your hand, the conclusion is now inescapable that the combined holding will produce a slam.

14

Two Spades	5 POINTS
Two No Trump	2 POINTS
Three Diamonds	1 POINT

The opportunity to probe for a possible Spade fit should not be neglected. Partner's free bid of 2 Hearts has placed you in an awkward position, and 2 Spades is a cheaper bid at this point than 2 No Trump. Had partner's bid been 2 Diamonds, we would recommend a pass because of the minimum nature of your holding. But he has actually indicated possession of a strong hand, and you should proceed on that basis.

15

Double	5 POINTS
Pass	3 POINTS
Three No Trump	2 POINTS
Four Diamonds	1 POINT

Game for your side is by no means certain, especially since a satisfactory fit has not been found. The wisest procedure therefore is to take the sure profit of a double. Your hand should produce at least three tricks which, along with the expected three from partner, adds up to a 500-point sting. It could be more.

16

Three Diamonds	5 POINTS
Four Clubs	3 POINTS
Two Spades or two Hearts	1 POINT

The 3-Diamond bid is forcing to game and suggests that partner bid any four-card major he may hold. In view of partner's persistance despite your previous passes, you should be confident that the partnership assets equal at least 26 points. Put it up to him to choose between Spades and Hearts.

17

Three Hearts	5 POINTS
Three Spades	2 POINTS
Two Spades	1 POINT

The showing of a six-card major suit should be subordinated to the more important consideration of showing that you have a good hand. The proper rebid is therefore 3 Hearts. A mere rebid of 2 Spades, while it would describe the texture of your Spade suit, would announce that you had opened on only moderate strength—which is not an accurate description of matters now that partner has responded with Hearts. A jump to 3 Spades would be a mild overbid and might result in complete suppression of the Heart support.

18

Three No Trump	5 POINTS
Two Spades	3 POINTS
Three Clubs	2 POINTS
Two No Trump	1 POINT

Partner has reversed (a non-jump rebid in a higher ranking suit) at the 2 level—showing a hand of around 19 points, which with your hand puts you in the slam neighborhood. It is always wise to make your display of strength below the game level, and the jump in No Trump should provide partner with an accurate picture of your hand.

HOW DO YOU RATE?

78—90:	Expert	50—64:	Good
65—77:	Top Rank	36—49:	Average

Under 36: Don't let anyone kibitz

Write your answers to the 18 problems on a sheet of paper, then turn to page 320 to find your score. Neither side is vulnerable unless shown.

1 As *Dealer* you hold:

What is your opening bid?

2 As *South* you hold:

NORTH	EAST	SOUTH	WEST
1♠	DBL	?	

What do you bid?

3 As *South* you hold:

NORTH	EAST	SOUTH	WEST
2NT	Pass	?	

What do you bid?

4 As *South* you hold:

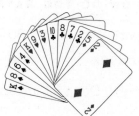

NORTH	EAST	SOUTH	WEST
1♣	1♠	Pass	2♠
3♦	Pass	?	

What do you bid now?

5 As *South* you hold:

NORTH	EAST	SOUTH	WEST
1♠	2♣	DBL	Pass
2♠	Pass	?	

What do you bid now?

6 As *South* you hold:

EAST	SOUTH	WEST	NORTH
1♥	Pass	Pass	1NT
Pass	?		

What do you bid now?

7 As *South* you hold:

WEST	NORTH	EAST	SOUTH
1♥	DBL	Pass	?

What do you bid?

8 As *South* you hold:

NORTH	EAST	SOUTH	WEST
1♣	1♥	?	

What do you bid?

9 As *South* you hold:

NORTH	EAST	SOUTH	WEST
1NT	Pass	?	

What do you bid?

10 As *South* you hold:

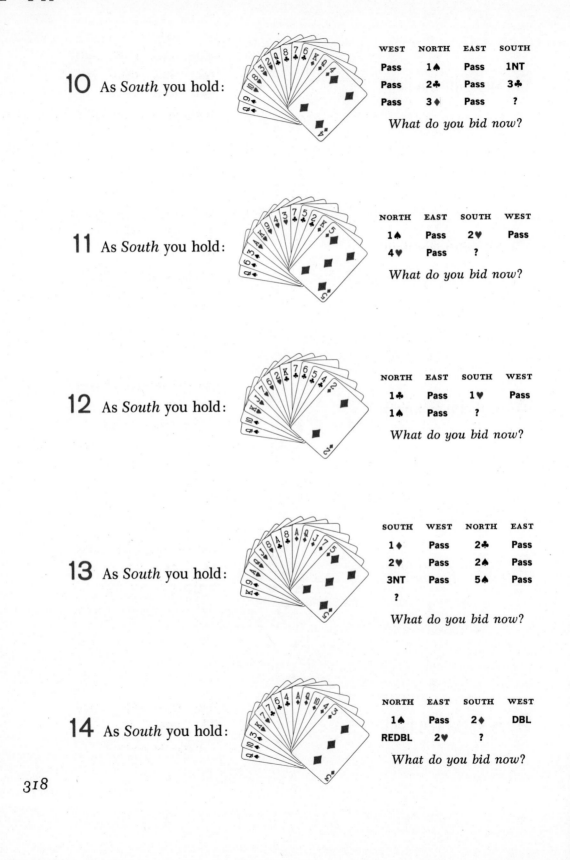

WEST	NORTH	EAST	SOUTH
Pass	1♠	Pass	1NT
Pass	2♣	Pass	3♣
Pass	3♦	Pass	?

What do you bid now?

11 As *South* you hold:

NORTH	EAST	SOUTH	WEST
1♠	Pass	2♥	Pass
4♥	Pass	?	

What do you bid now?

12 As *South* you hold:

NORTH	EAST	SOUTH	WEST
1♣	Pass	1♥	Pass
1♠	Pass	?	

What do you bid now?

13 As *South* you hold:

SOUTH	WEST	NORTH	EAST
1♦	Pass	2♣	Pass
2♥	Pass	2♠	Pass
3NT	Pass	5♠	Pass
?			

What do you bid now?

14 As *South* you hold:

NORTH	EAST	SOUTH	WEST
1♠	Pass	2♦	DBL
REDBL	2♥	?	

What do you bid now?

15 As *South* you hold:

NORTH	EAST	SOUTH	WEST
1♣	Pass	1♠	Pass
1NT	Pass	?	

What do you bid now?

16 As *South* you hold:

WEST	NORTH	EAST	SOUTH
1♠	Pass	2♠	?

What do you bid now?

17 As *South* you hold:

NORTH	EAST	SOUTH	WEST
1♥	Pass	3♥	Pass
5♥	Pass	?	

What do you bid now?

18 As *South* you hold:

EAST	SOUTH	WEST	NORTH
1♠	2♣	Pass	3♣
Pass	?		

What do you bid now?

Correct answers begin on the following page

1

One Spade	5 POINTS
One Heart	3 POINTS

On opening bids of moderate strength, where you have touching suits in which the lower-ranking suit is longer than the higher-ranking, you pretend that you do not possess the fifth card in the longer suit and treat both as if they were four-card suits. This is done for the convenience it affords in rebidding. After opening with 1 Spade, you then have a natural rebid in your Heart suit. Through this tactic, partner is permitted to show a preference at one level lower if he prefers your first-bid suit.

2

One No Trump	5 POINTS
Pass	2 POINTS
Two Clubs	1 POINT

You lack the strength for a redouble, yet if you pass it may prove difficult to enter the auction later. The best strategy is to advise partner of your moderate values by bidding 1 No Trump. This will place him in position to contest further, should that be expedient.

3

Four Clubs	5 POINTS
Three Spades	2 POINTS
Six Spades	1 POINT

An immediate response of 4 Clubs to an opening bid of 1, 2 or 3 No Trump must be construed as the Gerber convention asking for Aces. If partner responds with 4 Diamonds, showing all four Aces, you will be able to count thirteen tricks and will bid a grand slam. (Remember, the 4 Diamond response can show either four Aces or none.) If he shows three Aces, you will settle for a small slam. If he shows only two Aces, it is recommended that he reread the rules on the requirements for an opening 2 No-Trump bid.

4

Three No Trump	5 POINTS
Five Clubs	4 POINTS
Four Clubs	2 POINTS

Partner has announced a hand of outstanding strength by his 3-Diamond call, risking the possibility that you might be compelled to return to 4 Clubs with a complete "bust." A mere bid of 4 Clubs at this point would designate something like that, and would almost surely elicit a pass from North. If No Trump has a tendency to frighten you, then you should bid 5 Clubs.

5

Three Spades	5 POINTS
Two No Trump	2 POINTS
Pass	1 POINT

Though partner has indicated by taking you out of the penalty double that his hand is not suitable for defense against Clubs, it may be strong enough offensively to justify a try for game. A single raise, therefore, is indicated.

320

6

Pass	5 POINTS
Two Spades	2 POINTS
Two No Trump	1 POINT

A game is not even remotely in view. In this sequence the 1 No-Trump call is not a strength-showing bid, but merely a refusal to sell out. You must bear in mind that partner failed to double, which is the indicated re-opening procedure with a good hand.

There would be little point in mentioning Spades, since you have no reason to believe that would be a superior contract.

7

One Spade	5 POINTS
One No Trump	3 POINTS
Pass	0

A pass is not to be considered. You are in no position to prevent West from making all his Heart tricks, and he is liable to wind up with an overtrick. A bid of 1 Spade is easily the safest strategy, and strongly preferred to a bid of 1 No Trump, which might indicate to partner a mild desire to go places.

8

Two Spades	5 POINTS
Two Hearts	2 POINTS
One Spade	1 POINT

A jump shift declares your interest in slam. Later you will cue-bid in Hearts, announcing control of that suit. Then support for Clubs may be shown, depending upon how the bidding develops.

On the first round you are faced with the choice of an immediate cue bid in Hearts or the jump shift in Spades. I prefer the latter, because if the cue bid is made first you may find it difficult to portray the quality of your splendid Spade suit. The Spade bid, followed by a rebid of Spades, should convince partner of the excellence of your trump suit.

9

Two Clubs	5 POINTS
Two No Trump	4 POINTS
Two Spades	1 POINT

Here you have a nearly even choice. A raise to 2 No Trump is entirely acceptable. However, it might be more advantageous to respond with the artificial bid of 2 Clubs, because it is quite possible that the hand would play better at Spades—and you should not miss an opportunity to show that suit at the proper time. If over your 2-Club bid partner's rebid is 2 Diamonds, denying a four-card major suit, you will show your Spade suit; similarly, if he rebids 2 Hearts you will bid 2 Spades. It should be pointed out that your bid of 2 Spades in this sequence is not forcing. If partner has a rock-bottom minimum he may exercise the option to pass. But he may, on the other hand, raise Spades or even go on with No Trump.

10

Three Spades	5 POINTS
Four Clubs	3 POINTS
Four Diamonds	2 POINTS
Three No Trump	1 POINT

Your previous raise in Clubs limited the extent to which you could fit Spades, and partner should not expect more than what you hold. Since ten tricks may easily be the limit of the hand, some suggestion of a possible major-suit game should be offered.

A bid of 3 No Trump is not recommended, since you have no true Heart stopper and partner's mention of the other three suits clearly indicates that he is short in Hearts.

11

Five Hearts	5 POINTS
Four Spades	4 POINTS
Four No Trump	2 POINTS

Possession of an opening bid facing a partner who has opened and jumped spells a probable slam. The overbid of game will convey your interest and ask partner to go on if he has adequate controls on the side. A possible alternative call is 4 Spades. Since it is a bid made after game has been reached, it is mildly suggestive of an ambitious attitude.

A Blackwood inquiry is less advisable, because the mere knowledge of how many Aces partner has would not necessarily reveal whether or not slam is a sound undertaking.

12

Two Clubs	5 POINTS
Three Clubs	3 POINTS
Two Hearts	1 POINT

Two Clubs is a distinct underbid, but a jump at this stage could catapult your side into a game contract for which there might be no play. Despite the excellent fit, unless partner can be coaxed into bidding once more you are not apt to miss bigger things. The rebid of 2 Hearts is given a very low rating because, in the face of a two-suiter in partner's hand, this suit is not of the texture to justify a rebid.

13

Seven No Trump	5 POINTS
Seven Clubs	2 POINTS
Six No Trump	1 POINT

Partner has described a holding of six Clubs and five Spades. From his leap to 5 it is quite apparent that he has at least the Ace, Queen and Jack of Spades, and his Clubs, bolstered by your Ace, should be solid. It is easy to count thirteen tricks, and you should accordingly contract for a grand slam at No Trump.

14

Pass	5 POINTS
Two Spades	2 POINTS
Two No Trump	1 POINT

In this type of situation it is proper to give partner the courtesy of the road. You are not in a position to determine what will be the best course of action. Partner's redouble announces not only that he has a good holding, but that the situation is well in hand.

15

Three Diamonds 5 POINTS
Three No Trump 3 POINTS
Two No Trump 2 POINTS

This hand requires special treatment. We would insist upon game, but make allowances for the hand to be played at either Spades or No Trump. The suggested call is 3 Diamonds. (2 Diamonds would not be forcing after a 1 No-Trump rebid.) If partner prefers Spades, we would be inclined to play for game in the major suit.

16

Four Hearts 5 POINTS
Three Hearts 3 POINTS
Double 1 POINT

With this hand you should be unwilling to play for less than game, and we recommend a bid of 4 Hearts.

As between the other possible calls, the 3-Heart bid is distinctly preferred, since the bidding has already reached an advanced level and it is desirable to mention a suit before further crowding takes place.

17

Pass 5 POINTS
Six Hearts 1 POINT

Although you have an absolute maximum raise, North's slam invitation must be declined, for it is clear that the partnership is off two Aces. North had a reasonable opportunity to show the Ace of Spades or the Ace of Clubs, and his failure to do so is indication that he has neither.

18

Three Spades 5 POINTS
Four Clubs 3 POINTS
Five Clubs 2 POINTS
Three No Trump 1 POINT

The temptation, if any, to try 3 No Trump at this juncture should be resisted. Without protection in either red suit you may meet with a surprise attack. After you show the Spade control, you may rely on partner to reach for 3 No Trump if he is well prepared to cope with Hearts and Diamonds.

HOW DO YOU RATE?

78—90: Expert   50—64: Good
65—77: Top Rank   36—49: Average

Under 36: Pray for lots of luck

Write your answers to the 18 problems on a sheet
of paper, then turn to page 328 to find your
score. Neither side is vulnerable unless shown.

1 As *South* you hold:

NORTH	EAST	SOUTH	WEST
1♠	Pass	2♣	Pass
2♠	Pass	?	

What do you bid now?

2 As *South* you hold:

NORTH	EAST	SOUTH	WEST
1♣	Pass	?	

What do you bid?

3 As *South* you hold:

SOUTH	WEST	NORTH	EAST
1♠	2♥	Pass	Pass
?			

What do you bid now?

4 As *South* you hold:

EAST	SOUTH	WEST	NORTH
Pass	1♠	Pass	3♠
Pass	?		

What do you bid now?

5　YOU ARE VULNERABLE
As *South* you hold:

WEST	NORTH	EAST	SOUTH
1♣	1♥	Pass	?

What do you bid?

6　As *South* you hold:

NORTH	EAST	SOUTH	WEST
1♠	DBL	?	

What do you bid?

7　As *South* you hold:

NORTH	EAST	SOUTH	WEST
1♥	Pass	2♦	Pass
2♥	Pass	?	

What do you bid now?

8　As *South* you hold:

NORTH	EAST	SOUTH	WEST
1♣	DBL	REDBL	Pass
Pass	1♠	?	

What do you bid now?

9　As *South* you hold:

SOUTH	WEST	NORTH	EAST
1♥	Pass	1♠	Pass
?			

What do you bid now?

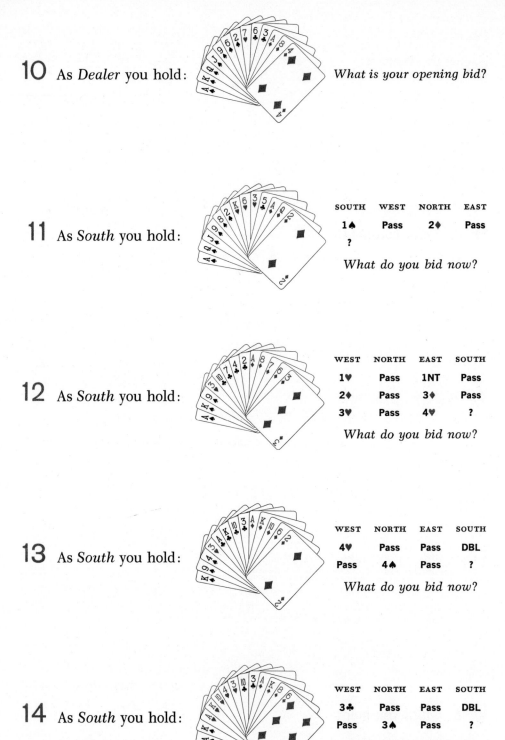

10 As *Dealer* you hold: *What is your opening bid?*

11 As *South* you hold:

SOUTH	WEST	NORTH	EAST
1♠	Pass	2♦	Pass
?			

What do you bid now?

12 As *South* you hold:

WEST	NORTH	EAST	SOUTH
1♥	Pass	1NT	Pass
2♦	Pass	3♦	Pass
3♥	Pass	4♥	?

What do you bid now?

13 As *South* you hold:

WEST	NORTH	EAST	SOUTH
4♥	Pass	Pass	DBL
Pass	4♠	Pass	?

What do you bid now?

14 As *South* you hold:

WEST	NORTH	EAST	SOUTH
3♣	Pass	Pass	DBL
Pass	3♠	Pass	?

What do you bid now?

15 As *South* you hold:

EAST	SOUTH	WEST	NORTH
Pass	1♥	1♠	Pass
2♣	?		

What do you bid now?

16
EAST-WEST VULNERABLE
As *South* you hold:

SOUTH	WEST	NORTH	EAST
1♦	1NT	Pass	Pass
?			

What do you bid now?

17 As *South* you hold:

NORTH	EAST	SOUTH	WEST
1♦	Pass	1♥	Pass
1♠	Pass	2♥	Pass
2♠	Pass	?	

What do you bid now?

18 As *South* you hold:

NORTH	EAST	SOUTH	WEST
1♣	Pass	Pass	1♦
2♦	Pass	?	

What do you bid now?

Correct answers begin on the following page 327

1

Three Diamonds	5 POINTS
Four Spades	2 POINTS

3 Diamonds is a temporizing bid that should be made with the intention of giving partner a strong Spade raise on the next round. A jump to 4 Spades would be quite inadequate. It is hardly necessary to stress the point that the 3-Diamond bid, a new suit by responder, is absolutely forcing for one round.

2

One Heart	5 POINTS
One Diamond	4 POINTS
Two No Trump	1 POINT

This hand contains only 12 points and is therefore fractionally short of the high-card requirement for a 2 No-Trump response. It is preferable to show the major suit first and then try No Trump later. A bid of 1 Diamond would also be acceptable.

3

Double	5 POINTS
Three Spades	3 POINTS
Three Diamonds	2 POINTS
Two Spades	1 POINT

The double is the bid best calculated to portray the real strength of your hand. It says, "Partner, in spite of the opponents' bidding, I believe this is our hand and I am prepared for any action you may take." An immediate jump to 3 Spades does not quite do justice to this hand, and more or less rules out the possibility of either playing a Diamond contract or defending in the event that partner's values are concentrated in the other suits.

4

Four Hearts	5 POINTS
Four No Trump	1 POINT
Five Spades	1 POINT

Prospects for slam are good (your hand on revaluation is worth 19 points), and you should show your interest at this point by cue bidding your side Ace. A Blackwood call would not be highly sound because you hold a worthless doubleton in Clubs; if partner showed one Ace, you would have no idea what further action to take. Furthermore, if a Blackwood bid is necessary on this hand, it should come from your partner's side of the table.

5

Two Hearts	5 POINTS
Two Diamonds	2 POINTS
One Spade	1 POINT

While you have less than normal trump support for the Heart raise, partner's vulnerable overcall marks him with a good enough suit to withstand your lack of a third Heart. If you had one more trump, a jump raise should be seriously considered.

A 1-Spade bid would be quite pointless, since North's failure to double tends to indicate a lack of interest in the unbid suits. Furthermore, you do not wish to invite a Spade lead should West become the declarer.

6

Pass   5 POINTS
Redouble   2 POINTS
Two Spades   1 POINT

This holding falls just short of the requirements for a redouble. An immediate raise should be offered only on a hand with less high-card strength and more distributional values. You are forced to compromise by passing for the time being, with every intention of offering competition on the next round.

7

Three Hearts   5 POINTS
Four Diamonds   3 POINTS
Three Diamonds   1 POINT

There is no completely satisfactory call to be made on this hand. 3 Hearts is something of an underbid, but we dislike raising all the way to 4 with just two trumps. The alternative bid of 4 Diamonds may land you in an unmakable Diamond game with a holding that could produce 4 Hearts with little effort. The simple Heart raise leaves open to partner the possibility of trying for game at No Trump.

8

Two Spades   5 POINTS
Three Clubs   3 POINTS
Five Clubs   1 POINT

An immediate cue bid in Spades will greatly facilitate your later bidding. You can content yourself with raising Clubs on the next round and leave any further aggressive action to partner. A direct leap to game would be a strictly take-charge action.

9

Three Diamonds   5 POINTS
Six Hearts   4 POINTS
Four Hearts   2 POINTS

This hand might seem to qualify for a simple game rebid in Hearts, but such a call could easily result in the loss of a laydown slam. Note that if partner holds five Spades to the Ace, King and nothing else, you can win all thirteen tricks. An immediate jump shift followed by a Heart rebid is best calculated to show partner your slam ambitions. And a direct leap to 6 Hearts would not be looked on as completely out of order.

10

One Spade   5 POINTS
Four Spades   2 POINTS

Although you have eight tricks in hand at Spades, the possession of a side Ace, which adds to your defensive strength and promotes the possibilities of a slam, makes this holding too strong for a pre-emptive bid. It is better to open 1 Spade.

11

Three Spades   5 POINTS
Three Diamonds   3 POINTS
Four Diamonds   2 POINTS

After partner has shown a reasonably good hand, you should insist upon game; and a jump rebid, even in the same suit, is forcing after a response at the 2 level. If the bidding develops constructively, you may show the Diamond support later.

329

12

Double	5 POINTS
Pass	2 POINTS

The double is not as speculative as it may seem. The bidding very strongly indicates that your partner is void of Diamonds and has at least four Hearts. An opening Spade lead will likely give you a choice of defenses, depending upon the appearance of the dummy. You may decide to give partner two Diamond ruffs or continue leading Spades in an effort to force declarer. Such an attack may well result in declarer's loss of control by reason of depletion of his trumps.

13

Pass	5 POINTS
Five Spades	2 POINTS
Four No Trump	1 POINT

Partner's 4-Spade bid may be based upon a long, weak suit, in a situation where he feels sure that there is not adequate defense against 4 Hearts. A slam effort should not be made, for a contract of 5 Spades is by no means safe. You must count on losing a Heart, and even though partner's Spades may be solid, there is no assurance that you can bring in the minor suits without the loss of a trick.

14

Four Clubs	5 POINTS
Four Hearts	3 POINTS
Four Spades	1 POINT

If you consider the 4-Club bid rather odd, my sympathies are all with you; but we are in an awkward position here. The bidding has been crowded by West's pre-empt, and although you have a tremendous hand, no fit has yet been established. While the cue bid is technically a falsehood (you do not have first-round control of Clubs), it may serve to clarify the situation. If partner has a secondary suit he will now be induced to show it, and if he rebids Spades you can accept that contract as the best available. All things considered, it seems best to resort to a white lie.

15

Two No Trump	5 POINTS
Double	3 POINTS
Three Hearts	2 POINTS
Two Hearts	1 POINT

Prospects for game have not been entirely dimmed by partner's pass, but the shorter, No-Trump route to game looks like the best shot at this point—since all partner needs to contribute is a couple of face cards strategically placed.

A takeout double has some merit, though the bid is less direct in nature. A jump to 3 Hearts will work out well in certain instances and is certainly to be preferred over a mere 2-Heart rebid.

16

Pass	5 POINTS
Double	3 POINTS
Two Hearts	2 POINTS
Two Diamonds	1 POINT

Your best chance of showing a profit is to pass and permit West to work for you. If he is honest, you can make nothing. If he is fooling, vulnerability will take care of him. The trouble with doubling is that your partner may not be in position to stand for the double. If he should bid, a black suit response would be quite distasteful to you.

17

Three Clubs	5 POINTS
Three Diamonds	4 POINTS
Three Hearts	2 POINTS
Two No Trump	0

North's sequence of bids indicates a six-five distribution. On the surface, therefore, it seems that a return to 3 Diamonds, the suit in which the partnership is known to have eight trumps, is clearly indicated. However, it is our belief that South gives himself an extra chance at this point by bidding 3 Clubs. North has only two cards between Hearts and Clubs. If he has one of each, he will naturally return to 3 Diamonds, which South will pass; likewise if he has two Clubs. But if he happens to have two Hearts and no Clubs, he might be induced to give a delayed Heart preference—in which event South can decide whether to gamble for game.

18

Three Diamonds	5 POINTS
Two Hearts	3 POINTS
Two Spades	1 POINT

The choice of 3 Diamonds may appear to be a bit eccentric, but actually the bid has great merit. There is nothing quite so dead as a hand that will not respond to a 1-Club opening. Since you have already marked yourself as a corpse, no amount of activity on your part will appear violent thereafter. If partner can do business with a bust hand—which he apparently can do—you have that hand. Ask him to choose the major suit.

HOW DO YOU RATE?

78—90:	Expert	50—64:	Good
65—77:	Top Rank	36—49:	Average

Under 36: Why not take up golf?

A BRIDGE MASTER'S ALBUM

IN THIRTY YEARS *of traveling the world as a competitor, teacher and all-round ambassador of bridge, Charles Goren has logged more miles than many an airline pilot and shaken more hands than many a career Congressman. Bridge is a superb leveler—of nationalities and professions and social classes. And the Bridge Master has found himself at one time or another sitting happily at the card table with individuals of every category. In the international language of bridge, he speaks on equal terms with princes and philosophers and big-league ball players alike. On the following pages appear some of the notable men and women who have shared his enthusiasm for the game, with comments by Mr. Goren.*

NOVELIST SOMERSET MAUGHAM

"Willie Maugham characterizes himself as a 'reasonably good bridge player of the second class.' On the basis of games we have had in New York, Paris and Cap Ferrat, I would rate him a lot higher than that. But then I enjoy being with him so much that my judgment may be colored a bit. I must say he's the finest octogenarian player you could ever hope to meet."

COLUMNIST ELSA MAXWELL

"I seldom pass through Paris without giving Elsa Maxwell a call at her headquarters in the Ritz Hotel. Once I checked in by phone and told her I was on my way to Nice. 'No, you are not,' came the stern reply. 'I need you for bridge tomorrow night. The Duchess of Windsor is coming to dinner.' I knew there was no way in the world to oppose this charming autocrat—but I had to be in Nice the next morning to make the draw for an important tournament, and there was no flight back to Paris the same day. A bridge-playing friend who is an airline executive came to my rescue. He got me rerouted from Nice to Paris via Geneva, and— luckily for me—I made it to Elsa's all right for dinner."

ACTOR HUMPHREY BOGART

"Of the stage and screen stars I have known, few have intrigued me as much as Humphrey Bogart. Given a situation demanding hard lines, whether on camera or in real life, he delivered them with a convincingly tough air—yet he was capable of the most extraordinary gentleness too. I found out that he was also capable of some excellent bridge."

GOLF CHAMPION BOBBY JONES

*"Among a variety of professional men in the field of
tournament bridge, the most successful, it seems, have been
those with legal training. This is an awkward thing for
me to say because I once practiced law myself, a fact which
I hope has not prejudiced my thinking in the matter.
I suppose the reason why so many lawyers turn out to be
excellent bridge players is that logic is the basis of their
practice and, also, they are in close contact with people
and are good judges of what behavior to expect. Bobby Jones
is an attorney in point. He took up the game of bridge in
his middle years after illness had barred him from
the golf course, and his talents very soon became apparent."*

THE DUKE OF MARLBOROUGH

"*I am indebted to the Duke for one of my proudest journalistic feats. It was through his good offices that I was able to get a photographer into the Portland Club in London for the first pictures ever to be taken in those august precincts (see page 36). A nephew of Harold S. Vanderbilt, the inventor of contract bridge, Marlborough is a fine player in his own right.*"

THE BASEBALL DODGERS

*"It wasn't so many years back that the professional athlete
would have sneered at bridge as sissy stuff. If any baseball
player got out a deck of cards, it would have been for poker,
or perhaps twenty-one. But times have changed. When I dropped
in to the Dodger dressing room one day at Ebbets Field, just
before the team left Brooklyn for Los Angeles, a spirited
game of contract was going on around a big trunk for a card
table. Involved as players and kibitzers were PeeWee Reese,
Gino Cimoli, Ed Roebuck, Gil Hodges, Duke Snider, Billy
Herman and Manager Walt Alston. As a long-time baseball buff,
I took delight in sitting in for a few hands in this company
and got trounced on one deal by Billy Herman."*

CHIEF JUSTICE FRED VINSON

*"Early in 1953 I was the Chief Justice's partner in one of
the last bridge games he ever played. It was at the
country home of Harry Watkins, a judge of the U. S. District
Court in Fairmont, W. Va., and we were meeting a team of
West Virginia bar members in a marathon bridge game. We were
far out in front, when suddenly I took an 1100-point set
on what I can only describe as an injudicious bid. Justice
Vinson was furious. I had never suspected such wrath
could reside within that placid exterior. We were playing
for nothing a point, which made his ire the more noteworthy.
I regret that I do not recall the hand today. No doubt
under the strain of embarrassment I promptly forgot it."*

THE DUCHESS OF WINDSOR

"It took me eight years to break down her resistance to playing with an 'expert.' Often at parties we were placed at the same table, and each time the Duchess would shy away before the cards could be dealt. Finally, one day at the Charles Munns' house in Palm Beach, the Duchess conquered her fears and sat down with me. Then she played with great assurance."

COMEDIAN CHICO MARX

*"Chico, who plays a rugged Hollywood brand of bridge,
was a star performer on my very first television bridge show.
On the opening deal he made a brazen free bid on a hand
which contained only two high-card points, causing my eyebrows
to rise a bit (although, in mitigation, I am constrained to
point out that he did have a six-card suit headed by
the 10). He promptly took a shellacking. In the post-mortem
discussion on camera, Chico, undaunted by the defeat,
remarked: 'Well, it was a close match until the first hand.'"*

BRIDGE CHAMPION HELEN SOBEL

*"My most frequent and most favorite partner. Helen and I
think alike. We run interference for each other.
Sometimes she's carrying the ball and I do the blocking;
when I carry the ball she runs interference. We don't
get in each other's way. Helen is just about the most
aggressive player I know, but her judgment is splendid in
the taking of calculated risks. She and I never play
scared bridge. Of course, most of my success depends on
Helen. If I didn't play with her I wouldn't have a chance."*

PRINCE ALY KHAN

"The Prince was an intense competitor in whatever field he tried. I knew him best, of course, at the bridge table, where he showed the same degree of enterprise that was characteristic of him on the racing turf and in his speedy cars. As most of my friends know, I have long made it a practice to avoid high-stake games, but in Aly's house you had to play for big money. He usually insisted on 40 francs a point, which amounted to 9¢ at the time I played with him. Quite a little above the level of our domestic games!"

343

GENERAL DWIGHT EISENHOWER

*"I had the fun of adjudicating a small dispute for General
Eisenhower one time when Mrs. Rogers Denkla approached
me at the Sulgrave Club in Washington and told me about this
hand which he had held at her house the previous evening:
♠ 5; ♡ 9 6 4 2; ◇ A 7 4; ♣ Q J 10 8 3. His left-hand opponent
had opened 1 Spade and his partner had made a take-out
double. What should the General have bid? I wrote down this
order of preference: 2 Clubs; 2 Hearts; 3 Clubs. 'That's
divine,' cried Mrs. Denckla. 'Your first choice is what General
Eisenhower bid, your second choice is General Gruenther's
preference, and your third choice is mine.' When Ike got the
news, he was so delighted he sent me a letter of thanks."*

344

DDE

14 November 1947

Dear Mr. Goren:

Thank you very much for your memorandum to me sent
by Mrs. Denckla. I am compelled so often to bow
my head to Al Gruenther's superior wisdom in the
business of bridge that it is a relief to find
that on this occasion at least my laborious mental
processes are supported by the preeminent authority. I still confess, however, that had I been
a little surer of the reliability of my partner
I might have put in a feeble jump response on
the off-chance that my partner might have held
a freak, and been highly delighted with my bid.
I see from your comment that even this would be
wrong and I am glad I rejected it.

I anticipate with a great deal of pleasure reading your answer slowly and with great emphasis,
to my friend Al (you will probably hear from him).

Again, many thanks.

                    Cordially,

                    Dwight D Eisenhower

Mr. Charles H. Goren
Cooper Hall
Southampton
New York

THE GOREN SYSTEM

NO BRIDGE PLAYER *today needs introduction to the main elements of card-table strategy advocated by Charles Goren. In the amiable warfare of bridge, he dominates the modern game like a drawing-room Clausewitz. But the rules of point-count bidding and the correct play in each of thousands of subtly differing situations are not easy to hold in mind. All but the most expert players need occasionally to check back for authoritative answers to problems that arise. The next 133 pages of this book are given over to the Goren System of rules for bidding and play, updated by Mr. Goren to incorporate a number of recent improvements in technique. It can serve as a text for the beginner and as a convenient reference section for the more advanced player.*

1 Opening suit bids of 1

THE OPENING BID is the start of a bidding campaign carried on by the partnership to arrive at the best final contract. This campaign may entail a considerable exchange of information regarding both the strength and distribution of the two hands. To make the exchange effectively, a player must plan ahead beyond each bid and know what his next call will be. If he makes an opening bid with no consideration for the future, he may find himself in an embarrassing position when next it is his turn to speak.

The first step is to decide the value of your hand.

Valuing a hand

The basis for deciding the relative strength of any bridge hand is this:

THE STANDARD POINT-COUNT TABLE

Ace = 4 points

King = 3 points

Queen = 2 points

Jack = 1 point

In valuing a hand, deduct 1 point if you have no Ace.

Add 1 point if you have all four Aces.

An unprotected honor loses some of its value unless your partner has bid the suit. When opening the bidding, therefore, a singleton King should be reduced from 3 points to 2. A Queen alone or accompanied by one small card should be reduced from 2 to 1. A Jack alone should be reduced from 1 to 0. (J x x, however, receives its normal value of 1.)

For making a No-Trump bid, you need only to consider the foregoing high-card values. But where a hand is being sized up for bidding a suit, distributional values must also be taken into account. To figure the value of a hand at a suit bid, count your high-card points, then add:

> 3 points if your hand contains a void;
> 2 points for each singleton it contains;
> 1 point for each doubleton.

Remember that a partnership holding of 26 points will normally produce game in a major suit.

29 points will normally produce game in a minor suit.

Biddable suits

If an opening bid is to be made with a major suit of only four cards, the suit must contain at least four high-card points. If the opening bid is made in a minor suit, greater liberties can be taken. Under special circumstances, will be shown in a later section, the player may open with 1 Club (and sometimes with 1 Diamond) with only a three-card suit, if that three-card suit contains one of the high honors. Any five-card suit is considered biddable, even if it contains no high-card strength.

A rebiddable suit is one which the player may bid a second time without having received support in that suit from his partner. To qualify as rebiddable, a five-card suit should contain at least two of the high honors. For example, the following suits are rebiddable:

$$K \; Q \; 10 \; x \; x$$
$$A \; J \; x \; x \; x$$

Any six-card suit is rebiddable, regardless of honor strength.

Requirements for the opening bid of 1 in a suit

To properly launch the bidding, a player must have a better than average hand. The minimum requirements are 13 points, counting both high cards and distribution.

If your hand contains 13 points, it is considered an optional opening.* You may open if you find it convenient to do so; that is, if your next bid will not prove embarrassing to you.

If your hand contains 14 points, you *must* open.

There is one further requirement when opening with minimum values. Make sure that you have at least two quick tricks. A quick trick is a trick that you could reasonably expect to take even if the opponents wound up playing the hand. The table of quick (or defensive) tricks is as follows:

$$A\ K = 2 \text{ quick tricks}$$
$$A\ Q = 1\tfrac{1}{2} \text{ quick tricks}$$
$$A \text{ or } K\ Q = 1 \text{ quick trick}$$
$$K\ x = \tfrac{1}{2} \text{ quick trick}$$

(Note that for defensive purposes only the first two rounds of a suit are considered, since it is very likely that one of the opponents will not follow to the third lead.)

The new-suit forcing principle

Perhaps the most important convention in contract bridge is this: *When opener bids 1 of a suit and responder names any new suit, opener must bid again if responder has not previously passed.*

This new-suit forcing rule permits a free and relaxed exchange of information at a relatively low level. As far as the opening bidder is concerned, he should always be prepared to make a second bid, for if his partner responds in a new suit he is obliged to speak once more.

Where the opening bidder has a single long suit there is no problem, but where he has two or three suits he must plan his bidding campaign well in advance.

Let us consider various possibilities.

---

* The experienced player will occasionally open with 12 points on a hand containing a good five-card major suit. For example:

♠ A K 10 x x ♥ A x x ♦ x x x ♣ x x

A great many players would decline to pass this hand. The quality of the suit makes it relatively simple to offer the forced rebid of 2 Spades if partner should take out to 2 Clubs or 2 Diamonds.

Which suit to bid first?

If you have two five-card suits, you should bid first the suit which is higher-ranking, even though the other may be a stronger suit. For example, you hold:

♠ Q J 10 x x   ♥ A K J x x   ♦ x   ♣ x x

You open the bidding with 1 Spade. If partner responds with 2 Clubs or 2 Diamonds, you will then rebid 2 Hearts. If partner wishes to return to your first suit, he may do so by bidding 2 Spades without increasing the contract.

If you had bid the Hearts first and then shown the Spades, partner would have been obliged to bid one level higher in order to show a preference for Hearts.

With suits of unequal length, bid first the longer one.

If you have two biddable suits, one of five cards and the other of four, bid the five-card suit first. Here length takes precedence over strength. For example:

♠ A K Q J   ♥ A J x x x   ♦ K x x   ♣ x

Bid 1 Heart. When you mention Spades on the next round, partner will recognize that you have more Hearts than you have Spades.

BY WAY OF EXCEPTION: *On hands of moderate strength, where the opening bidder has a five-card suit and four-card suit which are adjacent in rank (Spades and Hearts, Hearts and Diamonds, Diamonds and Clubs), if the higher-ranking suit is the four-carder but is reasonably strong, better results are obtained by treating the suits as though they were of the same length. The higher-ranking suit is bid first, even though it is only four cards long. For example, you hold:*

♠ A K J x   ♥ Q J 9 x x   ♦ J x   ♣ K x

Bid 1 Spade, intending to rebid 2 Hearts if partner responds with 2 of a minor suit.

Or, if you hold:

♠ x x x ♥ x ♦ A K J x ♣ A J x x x

Bid 1 Diamond, intending to make a rebid of 2 Clubs over partner's response at the level of 1.

If you have two biddable suits, one of six cards and one of five cards, bid the six-card suit first and then the five-card suit twice.
You hold:

♠ x ♥ x ♦ A Q J x x ♣ A K x x x

With this hand your correct opening is 1 Club. Suppose responder bids 1 Spade. You bid 2 Diamonds. At this point, partner is under the impression that you have five Clubs and four Diamonds. But that impression will soon be corrected. Over your 2 Diamond bid, let us suppose responder bids 2 No Trump. Now you should bid 3 Diamonds. This is the only way to show your partner that you have five Diamonds, because four-card suits are not rebid unless supported by partner. When your partner finds that you have five Diamonds, he will know that you have six Clubs, because you bid them first. If you had rebid 3 Clubs over partner's 2 No Trump he might still be under the impression that you had five Clubs and four Diamonds.

Opening with four-card suits

The hands that may appear to present the greatest difficulty are those which contain no long suit. In such situations the rule is this: If you have two or more biddable four-card suits to choose from, look first for the shortest suit in your hand (singleton or doubleton) and bid the suit that ranks next below it. If the suit which ranks immediately below is not biddable, bid the next suit below that. For the purpose of this rule you should consider that Spades rank next below Clubs. For example, you hold:

♠ x x ♥ A Q x x ♦ A K Q x ♣ x x x

Your doubleton is Spades, so you bid 1 Heart, the suit below the doubleton. If partner responds with 2 Clubs, your rebid is 2 Diamonds.

You hold:

♠ x x   ♥ J x x x   ♦ A K 10 x   ♣ A Q x

Bid 1 Diamond. The doubleton is Spades; the suit immediately below is Hearts, but the Heart suit is not biddable. Therefore, proceed to the next lowest suit, Diamonds, which is biddable.

You hold:

♠ K Q J x   ♥ x   ♦ K J 10 x   ♣ A x x x

Bid 1 Diamond, the first biddable suit below the singleton.

You hold:

♠ A Q J x   ♥ J x x   ♦ A K J x   ♣ x x

Bid 1 Spade. The doubleton is Clubs, and the suit below Clubs for the purpose of this rule is Spades.

THERE IS ONE EXCEPTION TO THIS RULE. *Whenever you hold biddable suits of four Clubs and four Hearts, it is suggested that you open the bidding with 1 Club. To see why let us take an example:*

♠ x x   ♥ A K J x   ♦ x x x   ♣ A J 10 x

If you open the bidding with 1 Heart and partner responds with 1 Spade you can conveniently rebid 1 No Trump, which designates a minimum hand with balanced distribution. However, if partner bids 2 Diamonds over 1 Heart you will find yourself in an awkward position. The Hearts are not rebiddable and you would be obliged to enter the 3 level to show the Clubs—which is somewhat drastic with a minimum opening bid.

If you open the bidding with 1 Club you will have a convenient rebid available at the 1 level. If partner responds with 1 Diamond, you may now bid 1 Heart. If he bids 1 Spade you can say 1 No Trump.

The Short-Club bid

Where you have no biddable suit or where the normal opening bid may lead to an embarrassing rebid situation, you may find it more convenient to open with 1 Club on a three-card suit. This is not part of any convention, but rather an optional choice on the part of the opening bidder to take care of awkward hands. (I do not recommend a general discussion of this bidding tactic with your partner, or else he is apt to doubt that you have the suit whenever you open the bidding with 1 Club. So if anyone asks if you play the short Club, respond with a firm no.)

Suppose you hold:

♠ J 10 x x   ♥ Q x x x   ♦ A x   ♣ A K x

This hand containing 14 points is a mandatory opening, and the only convenient way to get the bidding started is with 1 Club. Note that neither of your four-card major suits is biddable since they lack the required 4 high-card points. If partner bids either suit, however, you have a natural raise.

You hold:

♠ A K Q x   ♥ x x x   ♦ x x x   ♣ K Q x

Here again you have 14 points and must open, but a 1 Spade bid may readily lead to rebid complications. What will you do, for example, if partner responds with 2 Diamonds? Therefore, open the bidding with 1 Club and rebid 1 Spade if partner responds with a red suit.

Third-hand bidding

When partner has passed originally the situation is somewhat altered. If he bids a new suit over your opening bid it is no longer forcing, since his original pass limits the strength of his hand. In third position, therefore, an opening bid may be made with less than the normal requirements. With a good suit, you may open in third seat with as little as 11 points. You are not obliged to bid again and your call will serve a useful strategic

OPENING BIDS OF 1 IN A SUIT

To value your hand, compute the total of high-card points and add:

> 3 points for a void
> 2 points for each singleton
> 1 point for each doubleton

With 14 points you must open the bidding

With 13 points and two quick tricks you should open if convenient

In third-hand position, you may open with 11 points and a good suit

BIDDABLE SUITS

Any five-card suit is biddable

A four-card major suit must contain 4 high-card points to be biddable

WHICH SUIT TO BID

Bid your longest suit first

With two five-card suits, bid the higher-ranking suit first

With two or more four-card suits, bid the suit which ranks next below the singleton or doubleton in your hand purpose on defense if the opponents should buy the contract. For example:

♠ K Q J x x   ♥ A x x   ♦ x x x   ♣ x x

This is a sound 1-Spade bid in third position. You may be able to make a part score, and in the event you are outbid it is surely desirable to suggest a Spade lead to partner.

It is not advisable to shade the requirements for an opening bid in fourth-hand position.

2 Opening No-Trump bids

$$\begin{array}{ll}
\text{ACE} & = 4\ \textit{points} \\
\text{KING} & = 3\ \textit{points} \\
\text{QUEEN} & = 2\ \textit{points} \\
\text{JACK} & = 1\ \textit{point}
\end{array}$$

IN SUIT bidding, we have seen that distribution as well as high cards are taken into consideration in valuing a hand. At No Trump only high-card points are counted. The pack contains 40 points (10 points in each suit). A partnership will normally be able to make game (3 No Trump) with a combined holding of 26 points. However, if one of the partners holds a long suit, the game may be won with a little less than 26 points.

To qualify as an opening No-Trump bid, a hand must have not only the right point count, but the right shape in suits. There are only three acceptable shapes, and here they are:

4 3 3 3

4 4 3 2

5 3 3 2

A No-Trump opening should not be made with a hand containing a worthless doubleton. The doubleton should be headed by one of the high honors (A, K or Q).

An opening bid of 1 No Trump shows a count of 16 to 18 points.

If a hand counts 19, 20 or 21 points, it is too big for 1 No Trump. This does not mean that it should be opened with 2 No Trump, for in a moment we shall see that an opening 2 No-Trump bid requires 22 points. These 19, 20 and 21 point hands should be opened with a bid of 1 of a suit. Opener will show the excess values of his hand on the next round by jumping the bid in No Trump.

Examples of opening bids of 1 No Trump:

♠ A x x ♥ K Q J x ♦ A Q J ♣ x x x

♠ A x ♥ Q J x x ♦ A K x x ♣ K x x

Each of these hands has 17 high-card points and should be opened with 1 No Trump. But not the following hands:

♠ A x x x ♥ K x x x ♦ K x ♣ A J x

This hand has protection in all four suits but lacks by 1 point the high-card requirements for a standard 1 No-Trump opening. (It has only 15 points, and while there are some players who have reduced their requirements to 15 points, I have not seen fit to change my views and adhere rigidly to the 16-point opening.)

♠ A K J ♥ Q J x ♦ A J 10 x ♣ A x x

This hand contains 20 points and is above the limit of a 1 No-Trump bid. It should therefore be opened with 1 Diamond, with the intention of jumping in No Trump over partner's response.

Opening bid of 2 No Trump

This bid describes a hand of the No-Trump family—with all four suits protected—and point count of 22, 23, or 24:

♠ K J 10 ♥ A Q ♦ A Q J ♣ K Q x x x (22)

♠ A K ♥ A Q x ♦ A J x x ♣ K Q 10 x (23)

Opening bid of 3 No Trump

This bid describes a hand of the No-Trump family—with all four suits protected—and a point count of 25, 26 or 27:

♠ A x x ♥ A K 10 ♦ K Q J x ♣ A K J (25)

3 Responses to No-Trump bids

THE NATURE of No-Trump reponses varies with the type of hand held by responder. *It normally requires about 26 points to produce a game at No Trump.* But the requirements may be shaded by a point if one of the partners holds a workable five-card suit.

Where the responding player is considering a raise, he merely adds his own points to the number of points the opening No-Trump bidder has announced in order to determine the parnership potential.

Raise 1 No Trump to 2 No Trump with 8 or 9 points. With less than this, pass.

Raise 1 No Trump to 3 No Trump with 10 to 14 points.

In looking ahead to your ultimate contract, keep in mind the following:

A partnership holding of 33 points will usually produce a small slam.

A partnership holding of 37 points will usually produce a grand slam.

In all the following examples your partner opens with 1 No Trump. You hold:

♠ J x   ♥ x x x   ♦ Q x x   ♣ K x x x x

Pass. You have only 6 points.

♠ J x   ♥ K Q x   ♦ K x x   ♣ x x x x x

Raise to 2 No Trump. You have a balanced hand with 9 points.

♠ x x x   ♥ Q x   ♦ K Q x x   ♣ A Q x x

You have 13 points and should bid 3 No Trump. No thought should be given to a possible slam, for even if partner has 18 points the partnership together cannot have more than 31.

♠ x x x ♥ x x ♦ Q x x x x ♣ A K J

Raise to 3 No Trump. You have a count of 10. The partnership is assured of at least 26 points.

♠ K Q x ♥ J x x ♦ K J x x ♣ A J 10

Raise to 4 No Trump. The count is 15. This is not a conventional bid and does not request partner to show his Aces. If his opening No-Trump hand is of minimum proportions, he should certainly pass. If his hand is approximately maximum, there should be a good chance for slam.

♠ A Q x ♥ A x x x ♦ K x x ♣ A 10 x

Raise to 6 No Trump. Your 17 points, plus partner's announced minimum of 16, brings the total to at least 33. But it is clear that the partnership cannot have more than 35 points. Thought of a grand slam should not be entertained.

With a high-card holding sufficient for a raise to 2 No Trump, responder should not show a minor suit but should bid the No Trump even if he has a six-card suit. A singleton in his hand is no bar to such action.

The 2-Club Convention

If responder bids 2 Clubs over an opening No Trump, it is an artificial call which shows 8 high-card points or more, and at least four cards in one of the major suits. The bid asks partner to show a biddable four-card major (Q x x x or better) if he has one. If the No-Trump bidder lacks a major, he is required to bid 2 Diamonds. This is an artificial call and has nothing to do with the Diamonds in his hand.

After opener's rebid, the responding hand should take charge of the proceedings. With 10 points or more he must see to it that the partnership reaches a game contract. If a major suit fit has been uncovered, responder may raise directly to 4 of the suit. If no fit has been established, he should usually jump to 3 No Trump.

With 8 or 9 points, responder either raises his partner's major or else returns to 2 No Trump.

For example:

$$
\begin{array}{cc}
\textit{Opener} & \textit{Responder} \\
\text{1 NT} & ?
\end{array}
$$

A] ♠ K Q x x ♥ A J x x ♦ x ♣ x x x x

B] ♠ K x x x ♥ x x ♦ K Q x x ♣ x x x

The correct response is 2 Clubs in either case. With (A), responder is prepared to bid a game. If partner shows a major suit, responder will raise to 4; if the opener bids 2 Diamonds, he will jump to 3 No Trump. With (B), responder will raise a 2-Spade rebid to 3; if the opener bids either 2 Diamonds or 2 Hearts, responder will return to 2 No Trump.

Rebids by opening No-Trump bidder

If the response has been 2 Clubs, the opening bidder should proceed as follows:

With four Spades (Q x x x or better)	— Bid 2 Spades
With four Hearts	— Bid 2 Hearts
With both majors	— Bid 2 Spades
With no four-card major	— Bid 2 Diamonds

Takeout to 2 Diamonds, 2 Hearts or 2 Spades

This is a weakness response showing a five-card suit or longer with less than 8 high-card points. The opening No Trumper is requested to pass. If, however, he has a maximum No Trump with a good trump fit, he may offer a single raise to 3 of the responder's suit. Under no circumstances should he rebid 2 No Trump.

Takeout to 4 of a major

A leap to 4 Hearts or 4 Spades over a 1 No-Trump opening indicates a hand with a long suit, at least six cards, and less than 10 points in high cards. Responder should be able to develop slightly more than five tricks in his own hand with that suit as trump. For example, partner opens with 1 No Trump. You hold:

♠ x x   ♥ A 9 x x x x   ♦ x   ♣ Q 10 9 x

Bid 4 Hearts. Opposite a No-Trump opening, your hand will develop more than five tricks between the long Hearts and the Club suit. Opener is required to pass, since your leap to 4 in a major denies the high-card values necessary for a slam.

Takeout to 3 of a suit

The jump-shift is made on a hand that possesses the high-card values for a raise to 3 No Trump (that is, at least 10 points) but is unbalanced, causing responder to feel that a suit contract will be preferable.

Partner opens with 1 No Trump. You hold:

A]   ♠ K Q J x x   ♥ A J 10   ♦ x   ♣ x x x x

B]   ♠ x   ♥ K Q J x x   ♦ A 10 x x x   ♣ K x

With (A), respond 3 Spades. You have the ingredients of a raise to 3 No Trump (11 points in high cards), but your hand is unbalanced and you prefer to suggest a suit contract first. With (B), bid 3 Hearts. Your hand is unbalanced and, moreover, you will make an effort to reach a slam by trying 4 Diamonds on the next round if partner rebids 3 No Trump.

Responses to opening bids of 2 No Trump
WITH BALANCED HANDS

Always add your points to those shown by partner's opening bid (in this instance, 22) to determine the potential for slam.

With 4 to 8 points, raise to 3 No Trump. You know there is no slam, since the most partner can have is 24 points (24 plus 8 equals 32).

With 9 points, raise to 4 No Trump. There may be a slam if partner has the maximum of 24 points (24 plus 9 equals 33).

OPENING NO-TRUMP BIDS

Count high-card values only. No points are given for distribution

Open 1 No Trump with 16 to 18 points

Open 2 No Trump with 22 to 24 points

Open 3 No Trump with 25 to 27 points

RESPONSES

Raise to 2 No Trump with 8 to 9 points

Raise to 3 No Trump with 10 to 14 points

Raise to 4 No Trump with 15 to 16 points

Raise to 6 No Trump with 17 to 18 points

Bid 2 Diamonds, 2 Hearts, or 2 Spades with a five-card suit and less than 8 points

Bid 3 of a suit with a five-card suit and 10 points

Bid 4 Hearts or 4 Spades with a six-card suit and less than 10 points

THE 2-CLUB CONVENTION

Bid 2 Clubs over partner's 1 No-Trump opening if you have 8 points and a four-card major

Opening No-Trump bidder should then respond:

2 Spades with a four-card Spade suit

2 Hearts with a four-card Heart suit

2 Spades with both major suits

2 Diamonds with neither major suit

With 10 points, there will be a slam unless partner has a minimum (22 points). Therefore, first bid a suit and then raise to 4 No Trump. Bidding a suit and then raising to 4 No Trump is stronger than just bidding 4 No Trump.

With 11 or 12 points, bid 6 No Trump.

With 13 or 14 points, first bid a suit and then bid 6 No Trump. This is stronger than just bidding 6 No Trump directly. It asks partner to bid 7 if he has a maximum.

With 15 points, you may bid 7 No Trump (22 plus 15 equals 37).

Responses to opening bids of 2 No Trump

WITH UNBALANCED HANDS

After a 2 No-Trump opening by partner, you should bid any six-card major suit regardless of the high-card content of your hand.

Bid any five-card major suit if your hand contains at least 4 points in high cards.

Jump to 4 in a major with a six-card suit and a hand containing about 8 points in high cards.

With 4 high-card points and a four-card major, bid 3 Clubs. This requests partner to show a four-card major suit. With no biddable major, opener rebids 3 Diamonds.

Responses to opening bids of 3 No Trump

The same principles are applicable here as in the responses to 2 No-Trump openings. However, in this case partner is known to have 25 to 27 points. Add your points to his, keeping an eye on the figure 33 for a small slam and 37 for a grand slam. Remember that with a very long suit you may make the grade with somewhat less in point count.

There is no such thing as a "rescue" bid when partner opens with 3 No Trump. Therefore, any response is construed as a mild slam attempt. With a five-card biddable suit and a point count of 5, bid that suit. Any reasonably good six-card suit should be shown at the 4 level. With a balanced hand and a point count of 7, raise to 4 No Trump, which partner will pass if he has only 25 points.

Partner opens with 3 No Trump. You hold:

♠ x x x x   ♥ A x x   ♦ J x x   ♣ Q x x

Raise to 4 No Trump (point count of 7).

♠ A x   ♥ K J x   ♦ K Q x x   ♣ x x x x

Bid 7 No Trump. You have 13 points and are assured of a combined holding of 38.

Rebids by opening No-Trump bidder

If you have opened with 1 No Trump, you should pass in several instances:

1] When partner raises to 3 No Trump.

2] When partner jumps to 4 Hearts or 4 Spades.

3] When partner raises to 2 No Trump, if you have only 16 points.

4] When partner takes out to 2 Diamonds, 2 Hearts or 2 Spades, if you have only 16 or 17 points and no good trump fit.

4 Opening 2 bids in a suit

A PLAYER occasionally has the good fortune to pick up a hand that contains the essentials of a game contract regardless of partner's holding. In fact, if the responder happens to have a few key values a slam may be in the offing. To allow for a full exploration of the possibilities, an opening bid of 2 in a suit is made. *This is an absolute demand for game and is unconditionally forcing on both partners, not just for one round, but until game is reached.* The only exception occurs when the opposition enters the auction and the bidder's side elects to double for penalties.

Whenever a player contemplates a demand opening bid he must consider that his partner may have little or nothing. The opener should therefore have virtually a game in his own hand. The hand must contain at least nine winners in a major suit or ten winners with a minor suit as trump. The defensive requirements for such a bid are at least four quick tricks. Remember, it takes about 26 points to produce game. If you open with a 2 demand bid, you should have at least 25 of them in your own hand, unless you have a very long suit. On a point-count basis, the following table of requirements will serve as a well-nigh foolproof guide:

1] With a good five-card suit —   25 points.
2] With a good six-card suit —   23 points
3] With a good seven-card suit —   21 points.
4] With a second good five-card suit — 1 point less than above.

You hold:

♠ x ♥ A K x x ♦ A K x x ♣ A K x x

This hand is worth 23 points, 21 in high cards and 2 for distribution. Bid 1 Club. Don't consider a demand bid despite what the previous generation might have referred to as six honor tricks. If partner has nothing, you will have no game. (Observe that the normal procedure of bidding the suit below the singleton is bypassed in the present case to facilitate partner's response. He will find it much easier to show his suit at the 1 level, particularly if his values are primarily distributional.)

♠ A K Q J x x x   ♥ A x x   ♦ A x   ♣ x

Bid 2 Spades. This hand contains 21 points and a good seven-card suit and fulfills the other requirements; namely, nine winners in a major suit and four or more quick tricks.

Responses to opening 2 bids in a suit

Whenever partner opens the bidding with 2 of a suit, this is a demand on the responder to bid and continue bidding until a game contract is reached, unless the opponents in the meantime have been doubled in a contract of their own.

Since the opening bidder has virtually a game in his own hand, he is not expecting much assistance from partner. The conventional response with a weak hand is 2 No Trump. This bid has no reference to responder's distribution but merely describes a lack of the point count required for a positive bid. For example, suppose that partner has opened with 2 Diamonds, and you hold:

♠ K 10 9 x x x   ♥ x x x x   ♦ x   ♣ x x

You should bid 2 No Trump, the negative response. On the next round you can show the Spade suit, and partner will understand that while you have length in Spades you do not have much in the way of high cards.

If you have 7 points and the equivalent of one quick trick you may make a positive response. The natural response may take the following forms:

1] A raise in partner's suit

2] An ordinary suit takeout

3] A response of 3 No Trump

The minimum requirement in each case is 7 points if the hand contains one quick trick, or 8 points if the hand contains only one half a quick trick.

As responder you may have trump support, or a good suit of your own, or Aces and Kings. All three are of prime importance, and perhaps the most important is the trump support. Remember, when partner opens with

GOREN HIGHLIGHT

OPENING DEMAND BIDS OF 2 IN A SUIT

Requirements are:

With a good five-card suit— 25 points

With a good six-card suit— 23 points

With a good seven-card suit— 21 points

With a second five-card suit— 1 point less than above

The bidder must have four defensive tricks

The bidder must have nine winners if he bids a major suit, or ten winners if he bids a minor suit

RESPONSES

With less than 7 points, bid 2 No Trump

With 7 points and one quick trick, or 8 points and ½ quick trick, make a natural response as follows:

Raise partner (x x x or better in trumps)

Bid a suit (Q J x x x or better)

Bid 3 No Trump (8 points and a balanced hand)

Responder is required to keep the bidding open until game is reached.

a demand bid he normally has a pretty good suit. If you have a fit it is essential to tell him about it immediately so that the full limits of the hand may be explored.

Partner opens with 2 Hearts. You hold:

♠ x x　♥ J 10 x　♦ x x x x　♣ K Q J x

Bid 3 Hearts. Your hand is worth about 8 points in support of Hearts and the trump support is adequate. A direct raise may be offered with three small trumps and occasionally with a doubleton, provided it is headed by a high honor.

The single raise may also be given with stronger hands, when responder expects to do considerable bidding on subsequent rounds. The purpose is immediately to establish the trump and encourage descriptive bidding. Such descriptive bidding will be outlined in the chapter on slams.

Where responder has 7 or 8 points and a biddable suit, the suit should be shown as a natural response. (I advise against responding with very weak suits and suggest that a five-card suit be headed by at least Q-J.) Lacking both trump support and a biddable suit, but with a hand containing at least 8 high-card points, respond with 3 No Trump. Such hands will usually produce a slam; the opener presumably has 25 points, which, added to your 8, amounts to 33.

Partner opens with 2 Hearts. You hold:

♠ Q x x　♥ x x　♦ x x x　♣ K Q x x x

Respond 3 Clubs, a natural bid showing a Club suit and a little over 7 points.

♠ J 10 x　♥ x x　♦ Q x x x x　♣ A J x

Respond 3 No Trump, a natural bid showing a balanced hand containing about 8 or 9 high-card points. The Diamond suit is too weak to bother with.

♠ Q x x　♥ x x　♦ A K J x　♣ Q x x

Bid 3 Diamonds, a natural response showing a Diamond suit. On this particular hand you will surely reach a slam and you are merely awaiting developments. You have 12 points in high cards alone, and partner's hand is presumably worth at least 25 points, so the total is at least 37.

5 Pre-emptive bids

AN OPENING bid at the level of 3, 4, or 5 in a suit is made for the purpose of disrupting the opponents' line of communications. It describes a hand containing a good long suit—usually at least seven cards—but having little or no defensive value. If you have more than 10 high-card points, you should not pre-empt, for you may shut partner out of the conversation as well as the opponents. With a good hand you are anxious to hear from partner, and it may be very difficult for him to speak at such a high level.

Whenever a player risks a pre-emptive bid, he should expect to be doubled. If he can limit his losses to a maximum of 500 points, the bid is justified. The bidder must not count on any support from his partner; his calculations must be made solely on the basis of his own hand. Therefore, if vulnerable he may overbid by two tricks; if not vulnerable, by three tricks. For example:

A] ♠ K Q J x x x x x ♥ x x x ♦ x ♣ x

B] ♠ Q 9 x x x x x ♥ x x ♦ A J x ♣ x

C] ♠ K Q J x x x x ♥ K Q x ♦ x x ♣ x

(A) is worth a 4-Spade opening if not vulnerable, an overbid of three tricks. If vulnerable, a bid of 3 Spades is called for. Neither (B) nor (C) is a sound pre-emptive bid. The suit is too weak in (B); if you are doubled the loss may be very severe. Example (C) is too strong to pre-empt. This hand should be opened with 1 Spade.

In responding to a pre-emptive bid, the player should remember that his partner has announced a strictly one-suited hand. The only values that are apt to be helpful to him are top controls and trump support. In deciding whether or not to raise, the responder should add the tricks he can reasonably expect to win to those the pre-emptor has announced by his bid. For example, partner has opened with 3 Hearts and your side is not vulnerable.

You hold:

♠ x   ♥ J x   ♦ A K x x x   ♣ K Q x x x

Your hand figures to produce about four tricks, and since partner has announced six winners, you have enough to raise to 4 Hearts. Observe that there is nothing to be gained by showing one of your suits. Since the pre-emptive bidder guarantees a very good suit, a raise may be made with two small trumps or a singleton honor.

6 Responses to bids of 1 in a suit

WHEN partner opens the bidding with 1 of a suit, a certain degree of responsibility devolves on you to keep the bidding alive, in case he has a very good hand and wants to rebid. To give partner another chance to speak, the bidding should be kept open for one round if the responder has as much as 6 points, counting distribution values plus high cards.

Responding with weak hands

With a weak hand, you may respond in any one of the following ways:

    1] Bid 1 of a new suit.
    2] Bid 1 No Trump.
    3] Give partner a single raise in his suit.

The response of 1 of a suit

This bid may be made with as little as 6 points, including points allowed for distribution. As will be seen shortly, the response in a new suit at the 1 level is ambiguous; the same bid may be made on a very good hand where responder wants to reach game but first needs to probe for the best contract. That is why the bid of a new suit by responder is forcing on the opening bidder for one round. However, for the moment we are concerned with the 1-over-1 response as a means of keeping the bidding open with a weak holding.

Suppose partner opens the bidding with 1 Diamond and you hold:

    A]   ♠ K x x x   ♥ Q x x   ♦ x x   ♣ x x x x

    B]   ♠ x x x x x   ♥ K J x   ♦ x   ♣ x x x x

With either of these hands the proper response is 1 Spade. You have a biddable suit and 6 points, as follows:

A] 5 points in high cards and 1 for the doubleton;
B] 4 points in high cards and 2 for the singleton.

Of course, your response is in the nature of a "courtesy bid," but if partner happens to a have very powerful hand, game is not altogether beyond the realm of possibility.

The response of 1 No Trump

Bear in mind that in making any No-Trump response, only high-card values are counted. No points are assigned for doubletons or singletons.

When you have at least 6 points in high cards, it is your duty to keep the bidding alive. Bid 1 No Trump if that happens to be the cheapest available bid, providing you do not have more than 10 points in your hand. With more than 10 points, some other response should be chosen.

Partner opens with 1 Spade and you hold:

♠ x x   ♥ K x x x x   ♦ Q x x   ♣ x x x

Pass. You have only 5 points in high cards. Observe that if partner's opening bid had been 1 Diamond, you would have had enough for a 1 Heart response (6 points counting 1 for the doubleton). But over 1 Spade you are not nearly strong enough to increase the level of bidding by saying 2 Hearts.

♠ x x x   ♥ A K x   ♦ x x x x   ♣ K x x

Respond 1 No Trump. You have 10 points. If you held any more points, you should make a decided effort to get partner to speak again. Remember, when you respond with 1 No Trump, partner may pass—and frequently does.

♠ x   ♥ K x x   ♦ x x x x   ♣ A J x x x

Respond 1 No Trump. You have 8 high-card points. The hand is not strong enough to justify increasing the contract to 2 Clubs. Note that possession of a singleton is not a deterrent to the 1 No-Trump response. While No-Trump bids normally indicate balanced distribution, the responder may find in a case like this that he has no other call available, and to keep the bidding open he must bid 1 No Trump.

With a weak hand, the cheapest response is the best response. One of a suit is cheaper than 1 No Trump. Therefore, do not respond with 1 No Trump when able to respond with 1 in a suit. You hold:

♠ x x x x   ♥ K J x x   ♦ x x   ♣ K x x

If partner opens with 1 Diamond, you should respond with 1 Heart. This is a cheaper response than 1 No Trump. For the purpose of bidding Hearts, your hand is worth 8 points (7 in high cards and 1 for the doubleton).

♠ Q x x   ♥ 10 x x x   ♦ K J x x   ♣ x x

Partner opens with 1 Club. Respond 1 Diamond, not 1 No Trump. With a point count of 6, it is obligatory for you to make a response. With this weak hand, 1 Diamond is the cheapest bid available. It has the merit of permitting partner to bid again at the level of 1. But if partner opens with 1 Spade, your proper response is 1 No Trump. Your hand is not strong enough to justify a 2-Diamond response, which would require at least 10 points.

The single raise

The raise from 1 to 2 of partner's suit may be made with a holding of 7 to 10 points. The bid describes a hand that is "fair to middling," not a strong hand. To give a single raise, responder must have normal trump support; that is: x x x x, or Q x x, or J 10 x. Unless it is otherwise proven, you must assume that partner holds a four-card suit.

If partner rebids his suit, you are to assume that it is a five-card suit, and normal trump support becomes x x x, or Q x. If partner bids a suit for the third time without your having supported it, you may assume he holds six, and you may raise with only two small trumps or the singleton Queen. Generally speaking, the partnership should hold at least eight trumps to make the suit an adequate vehicle.

"Dummy points"

When raising partner's suit bid, special values are allowed for short suits in responder's hand. Thus:

> Add 1 point for each doubleton.
>
> Add 3 points for each singleton.
>
> Add 5 points for a void.

(Note the difference in valuation of short suits between the opening bidder's hand and the responder's hand. Short suits assume greater significance whenever you are contemplating a raise of partner's suit, because they represent potential ruffing opportunities in the dummy hand. Where you have trump support, a void can kill the power of an opponent's Ace and a singleton can render ineffective his King.)

There is another refinement in valuing a hand for raising partner's suit that has to do with the extra potency of trump honors. In counting points, the Jack of partner's suit is promoted to a Queen, the Queen is promoted to a King, and the King is promoted to an Ace. The Ace receives no promotion, and any trump holding that is already worth 4 or more high-card points receives no promotion.

A deduction of 1 point is made when holding a hand, potentially the dummy, which contains a flaw. The following are flaws when raising partner's suit:

1] Possession of only three trumps

2] A four-three-three-three distribution

Partner opens with 1 Heart. You hold:

♠ A x x x   ♥ A x x x   ♦ x x   ♣ J x x

Raise to 2. You have normal trump support and 10 points in support of a Heart bid—9 in high cards and 1 for the doubleton.

♠ x x   ♥ A x x x   ♦ Q x x x   ♣ x x x

Raise to 2 Hearts. Your hand is worth 7 points in support of a Heart bid—6 in high cards and 1 for the doubleton.

375

♠ Q J x x x ♥ K Q x ♦ x x ♣ x x x

With this hand you are faced with a choice of responses. You can bid 1 Spade or raise partner to 2 Hearts. Preference goes to the raise. If your hand were somewhat stronger and merited two forward-going bids, an initial response of 1 Spade would be proper with the intention of support-ing Hearts on a later round. But with hands that fall within the 7 to 10-point range, an immediate raise of partner's suit is recommended, as it may be vital to show the trump fit directly. With such limited strength, responder does not contemplate taking any further action unless the open-ing bidder does something drastic on the next round.

Free bids at the level of 1

When partner opens the bidding and the next hand overcalls, you are no longer burdened with the responsibility of keeping the bidding alive. Your partner is automatically assured of another opportunity to speak. Therefore, any action taken by you is in the nature of a voluntary or "free" bid and should be based on more than the requirements for a mere courtesy response.

For example, you are South and the bidding has proceeded:

NORTH	EAST	SOUTH	WEST
1 ♣	1 ♦	?	

A] ♠ Q x x x ♥ K J 10 x ♦ x x x ♣ x x

B] ♠ K x x ♥ A Q x x x ♦ x x ♣ x x x

With (A) you should pass. If East had not overcalled, you would have kept the bidding open with 1 Heart, since you have 7 points. But in the present circumstances a bid of 1 Heart would show better values than you actually possess.

Example (B), a hand which contains 10 points, qualifies for a free bid of 1 Heart. With less than 9 points, voluntary action at the 1 level by the responder is not recommended. Unless the opening bidder is able to compete further on his own initiative, there need be no fear that the part-nership is being talked out of anything.

RESPONDING TO SUIT BIDS OF 1—WITH WEAK HANDS

Bid 1 of a new suit with 6 points in high cards and distribution

Bid 1 No Trump with 6 to 10 points in high cards alone

Raise partner's suit with trump support (x x x x, J 10 x or better) and 7 to 10 points. In adding up your points for this bid:

A] Count high cards at normal values

B] Promote honors in partner's suit

C] Add 1 point for each doubleton
  3 points for each singleton
  5 points for each void

D] Deduct 1 point if your hand contains only three trumps

E] Deduct 1 point if your hand is distributed 4–3–3–3

A free bid of 1 in a suit shows not less than 9 points in high cards and distribution values

A free bid of 1 No Trump normally shows 10 to 12 points in high cards and a stopper in opponent's suit.

Free bids of 1 No Trump

When partner opens the bidding and next hand overcalls, a bid of 1 No Trump indicates strength. In addition to guaranteeing protection in the adversely bid suit, it shows a high-card value ranging from 10 to 12 points. (The bid may sometimes be made with 9 points, provided a double stopper is held in the adverse suit.)

For example, partner opens with 1 Diamond; next hand bids 1 Heart. You hold:

♠ J x x   ♥ A x x   ♦ x x x   ♣ K x x x

Pass. You have a count of only 8, and a free bid of 1 No Trump is not in order. Had second hand passed, you would have kept the bidding open with 1 No Trump.

♠ K x x   ♥ A J x   ♦ x x x   ♣ K x x x

Bid 1 No Trump over the adverse Heart bid. You have a count of 11.

Responding with good hands

Keeping the bidding open is not always a burden. Sometimes you pick up a good hand and then partner provides pleasant news by opening the bidding. There are a number of ways to apprise him of the situation, depending upon your distribution and over-all strength:

1] Jump-raise in partner's suit (1 Spade to 3 Spades)

2] Jump-takeout in No Trump (1 Spade to 2 No Trump)

3] Jump in a new suit (1 Heart to 2 Spades)

4] Takeout into 2 of a new suit (1 Heart to 2 Diamonds)

5] Takeout into 1 of a suit (1 Club to 1 Heart)

We shall take up the alternatives in order.

Jump raise from 1 to 3

This is a demand for game (unless responder has previously passed, in which case opener may use his own judgment). Responder must have at least four trumps, preferably headed by the Jack. Three good trumps will not do. We have seen previously that to be an adequate vehicle the combined partnership trump holding should normally be eight cards long. Since the opening bidder may have only a four-card suit, the responder should have four himself to insist on that suit as trump.

His hand must contain 13 to 16 points, counting high-card points and distributional values as a dummy hand (dummy points). In other words, responder's hand must be the equivalent of an opening bid. *An opening bid facing an opening bid will usually produce game.*

Partner opens with 1 Spade. You hold:

♠ K J x x ♥ x x x x ♦ A x ♣ A J x

Bid 3 Spades, forcing to game. Your hand contains 13 points in high cards and 1 distributional point for the doubleton. You have the required trump support, and with 14 points your hand is the equivalent of an opening bid.

Partner opens with 1 Heart. You hold:

♠ x ♥ A 10 x x ♦ A x x x ♣ K Q x x

You have the required trump support. Bid 3 Hearts. You have 13 points in high cards and 3 for the singleton—a total of 16 points, the equivalent of a strong opening bid.

Partner bids 1 Spade. You hold:

♠ A x x x ♥ x ♦ x x x x ♣ K Q x x

You have 12 points in support of Spades (9 in high cards and 3 for the singleton). This is not quite enough for a jump raise, but it is much too strong for a single raise. You should temporize with a bid of 2 Clubs, intending to raise Spades on the next round. Partner will then know that you have a good hand, for with a mediocre holding you would have raised Spades directly rather than taking time to show a suit of your own first.

Raising from 1 to 4 in a major suit

While the jump raise from 1 to 3 of a suit shows the equivalent of an opening bid, the raise from 1 to 4 of a major suit is a pre-emptive measure. You must have exceedingly ample trump support (usually five trumps) and good distribution (a singleton or void) but not more than 9 points in high cards. With greater strength, some other response should be made.

Partner opens with 1 Spade. You hold:

♠ A x x x x ♥ x ♦ x x ♣ K x x x x

Bid 4 Spades. This hand contains only 7 points in high cards, has the required singleton and more than ample trump support.

♠ A 10 x x x ♥ x x ♦ x ♣ A Q 10 x x

This hand is too strong for a 4-Spade response. Bid either 3 Spades or a temporizing bid of 2 Clubs.

Jump takeout to 2 No Trump

This response is forcing to game and shows a hand with all unnamed suits protected, at least two cards in partner's suit, and a point count of 13 to 15. For example:

Partner opens with 1 Spade. You hold:

♠ x x x ♥ K 10 x ♦ K Q x x ♣ A J x

Respond 2 No Trump (13 points, all unbid suits protected).

♠ 10 x ♥ A K x ♦ K x x x x ♣ K J x

Respond 2 No Trump (14 points, all unbid suits protected).

♠ Q x x ♥ x x x ♦ A K x ♣ K Q x x

Do not respond 2 No Trump. You have 14 points but no protection in Hearts. Bid 2 Clubs and await developments.

Jump takeout to 3 No Trump

This is a specialized bid that should be reserved for hands of four-three-three-three distribution, with protection in all three unbid suits and a point count of 16 to 18.

Partner opens with 1 Spade. You hold:

♠ J x x   ♥ K J 10   ♦ K Q x x   ♣ A Q J

You have the right type of distribution and 17 points, with all suits protected. Bid 3 No Trump.

Jump takeout in a new suit

This bid is absolutely forcing to game and strongly suggests slam possibilities. It should be made only where responder has a strong suit of his own or good support for partner's suit. Responder's point count should be at least 19.

The reason for such a high requirement is this: the jump shift announces that responder suspects there is a slam within reach. The number of partnership points needed for a small slam is 33. Responder must be able to see 32 points before he talks of slam. Assuming partner has a normal minimum opening of 13 points, his 13 plus 19 equals 32.

Partner opens with 1 Spade. You hold:

♠ A 10 x x   ♥ A Q J x x   ♦ K Q x   ♣ x

Bid 3 Hearts. Since Spades are the contemplated trumps, you should value your hand as a dummy. Your hand is worth 19 points, 16 in high cards and 3 for the singleton. It looks very much like a slam. Even if partner has only 13 points, you will have a combined holding of 32.

Partner opens with 1 Spade. You hold:

♠ x   ♥ x x   ♦ A K Q 10 9 x   ♣ A K x x

Bid 3 Diamonds, a slam signal. Although you have no fit for partner, you have a virtually solid suit of your own and 19 points (16 in high cards and 3 in distribution). Remember, when you contemplate being the declarer you should value your hand as if you were the opening bidder.

Partner opens with 1 Heart. You hold:

♠ A Q x x x   ♥ x   ♦ K x x   ♣ A Q J x

Respond 1 Spade. Do not make a jump shift despite the high-card holding. No fit has been established, and you cannot as yet visualize a slam. The hand is worth only 18 points, valued at your own suit.

1-over-1 response

It has been pointed out earlier that a response of 1 in a suit is ambiguous. The bid may show the weakest holding, a hand containing as little as 6 points. Or it may show a very powerful hand, perhaps 18 points, one on which responder is just short of the requirement for a jump shift. How can the opener tell which it is? He can't on the first round, and that's why he is forced to bid again. On the second round of the auction, responder can be expected to clarify the situation. If his hand is a weak one, he will take no further action on his own initiative and may pass unless the opening bidder forces him to bid again. On the other hand, if responder has a strong holding, his second bid will show it.

Partner opens with 1 Club. You hold:

♠ Q 10 x x x   ♥ x x x x   ♦ K x x   ♣ x

Respond with 1 Spade. You do not intend to bid any more, unless partner jumps in a new suit.* Your hand is worth 7 points, 5 in high cards and 2 for distribution.

---

* While any change of suit by responder is forcing on the opening bidder, the opening bidder must make a jump-shift rebid in order to force his partner to bid again. If the bidding proceeds:

Opener	Responder
1 ♥	1 ♠
2 ♦	

—the responding hand may pass. He is not forced to bid again by a mere change of suits. However, if the bidding proceeds:

Opener	Responder
1 ♥	1 ♠
3 ♦	

—the responding hand may not pass. The 3-Diamond rebid is absolutely forcing. The opening bidder has made a jump shift and responder must keep the bidding open until game is reached.

♠ A J 10 x x ♥ K Q x x ♦ x x ♣ K x

Respond 1 Spade. You intend ultimately to contract for at least game, but your 1 Spade bid is forcing, and when partner rebids, you will make another force on the next round. Opener will then learn that you have a good hand. Valued at Spades, your hand is worth only 15 points, 13 in high cards and 2 for distribution. It does not, therefore, approach the 19 points required for an immediate jump shift. Until you have a clear idea of where you are going, there is no occasion to crowd the bidding.

The response of 2 in a suit

While a response in a new suit at the level of 1 does not necessarily show a good hand, a response at the level of 2 does. Both bids are forcing for one round. You should not increase a contract by bidding 2 of a new suit unless your hand contains 10 or more points. For example:

♠ x x ♥ K x x ♦ A Q x x x ♣ x x x

If partner opens with 1 Club, you may respond 1 Diamond, since that bid promises only 6 points. But if partner opens with 1 Spade, your hand is not good enough to increase the contract to 2 Diamonds. You do not have 10 points in high cards, and you should therefore respond 1 No Trump.

You may feel freer to respond at the level of 2 if you have a six- or seven-card suit. For example:

♠ x ♥ x x ♦ A K J x x x x ♣ x x x

With this hand, it would be acceptable to bid 2 Diamonds over partner's 1-Spade opening.

Choice between raising partner and bidding your own suit

Whether to raise partner or bid your own suit depends first upon the strength of your hand. If your hand is valued within the minimum range

—that is, 6 to 10 points—you cannot afford to make two constructive bids. You should try to bid only once. In this situation it is much better to raise your partner than to bid your own suit. This is especially true if partner's suit happens to be a major.

If, as responder, you hold a hand that is worth 11 points or more, you should arrange to bid twice. Your hand is too good for a single raise. You therefore bid your own suit first and support partner later.

Partner opens with 1 Heart. You hold:

♠ x x   ♥ K Q x   ♦ A 10 x x x   ♣ x x x

This hand is worth 9 points in support of Hearts. At first glance it appears to be worth 10 points—9 in high cards and 1 for the doubleton. But it possesses the flaw of having only three trumps, so we deduct a point. Now, a 9-point hand does not justify two forward bids, so a single raise to 2 Hearts is clearly indicated.

♠ x   ♥ A x x   ♦ K Q x x x   ♣ 10 x x x

This hand is worth 11 points in support of Hearts—9 in high cards and 3 for the singleton, less 1 point deducted for having only three trumps. It is too strong for a simple raise to 2 Hearts, the upper limit for which is 10 points. It is necessary to bid 2 Diamonds first, with the intention of supporting Hearts on the next round.

Similarly, if you hold:

♠ x   ♥ A x x x   ♦ K Q x x   ♣ K Q x x

This hand is worth 17 points in support of Hearts—14 in high cards and 3 for the singleton. You have too much to give partner a jump raise to 3 Hearts, a bid for which the range is 13 to 16 dummy points. However, the hand is not quite strong enough for a jump shift, which promises 19 points. You must therefore make a series of temporizing bids, showing first the Diamonds, then the Clubs, to be followed by a Heart raise. By showing each feature of your hand in turn, you can readily convey to partner a picture of your full strength.

Responding with two suits

When responder has two suits, he must decide whether his hand is strong enough to justify showing both. If his hand contains 11 or 12 points, he should show both suits. If his hand contains from 6 to 10 points, it is sounder to bid only once, unless partner does something sensational on the next round.

When, as a responder, you have a hand strong enough to bid both suits, show them in the logical order. That is, bid a five-card suit ahead of a four-card suit, and when both suits are of equal length, bid the higher-ranking first.

♠ x x   ♥ A K 10 x   ♦ x x   ♣ K Q x x x

Partner opens with 1 Diamond. Your hand contains 12 points in high cards, and both suits should be named. Respond 2 Clubs, the longer suit. Do not make the mistake of bidding 1 Heart first because it is cheap. It is not necessary to keep the bidding low with hands of this strength. If you bid Hearts first, partner will never ascertain your exact distribution.

♠ x x   ♥ Q J x x   ♦ x x   ♣ A x x x x

With this weaker hand, the proper response to an opening Diamond bid is 1 Heart. You have only 7 points in high cards, and you cannot afford to show both suits on your own initiative. Furthermore your hand is not good enough to take out to the level of 2. Rather than bid 1 No Trump, you respond with 1 Heart, not intending to take further action unless partner makes a very aggressive rebid.

Responding when you have previously passed

The usual forcing principles do not apply strictly when a player has previously passed. If, after passing, responder bids a new suit, he could not be expected to have as many as 14 points. If the opening bidder has opened a little light in third or fourth position to try for a part score, he may choose to pass the response.

Bear in mind, therefore, that when you have previously passed, any bid you make may be the final call (unless it is a jump in a new suit or a cue bid of the opponent's suit).

A jump in the same suit (1 Spade to 3 Spades) or a jump in No Trump (1 Spade to 2 No Trump) now becomes strongly invitational but not forcing. However, a jump in a new suit (1 Spade to 3 Diamonds) is forcing even when the jump comes from a passing partner.

When partner opens the bidding after you have passed, and you feel confident you can make game in his suit, it is recommended that you go right ahead and bid the game.

Let us consider a few cases where the bidding has proceeded:

You	*Partner*
Pass	1 ♥
?	

♠ x ♥ A x x x ♦ K Q x x ♣ x x x x

This hand is worth 12 points in support of Hearts and would normally have called for a temporizing response of 2 Diamonds with the intention of raising Hearts later. But in light of your original pass, there may be no later. If you bid 2 Diamonds partner may leave you there, since the mere naming of a new suit by a passed hand is not forcing. A direct bid is therefore indicated, and the recommended call is a jump raise to 3 Hearts. The customary range for this bid is 13 to 16 dummy points, but after passing you may shade the requirement to 11 or 12 points. Partner is not required to go on, but if he has values approaching a sound opening bid he will be encouraged to carry on to game.

♠ A ♥ J x x x ♦ Q x x x x x ♣ K x

This hand adds up to about 15 points in support of Hearts—10 points in high cards, 4 in distribution, and 1 extra point for the promoted value of the Jack of Hearts. A raise to 3 Hearts would not do justice to the hand, since a jump raise is not forcing, and you want to try for game even if partner's opening bid was a bit light. A direct jump to 4 Hearts is recommended.

♠ K x x ♥ x x ♦ Q 10 x x ♣ A Q 10 x

Normally a jump response to 2 No Trump indicates a hand containing between 13 and 15 points and is forcing to game. After you have passed,

GOREN HIGHLIGHT_____

RESPONDING TO SUIT BIDS OF 1
—WITH STRONG HANDS

Jump-raise with 13 to 16 dummy points and four trumps

Jump to 2 No Trump with 13 to 15 points in high cards and all unbid suits stopped

Jump to 3 No Trump with 16 to 18 points in high cards and all unbid suits stopped

Jump in a new suit with 19 points and a self-sustaining suit or good support for partner's suit

A 1-over-1 bid can be made with a holding anywhere between 6 and 18 points

A 2-over-1 bid can be made with a holding anywhere between 10 and 18 points however, you may jump to 2 No Trump with 11 or 12 points. Such a jump is not forcing, and partner may decide whether or not to continue the bidding on the basis of your combined assets. He will know, of course, that you do not have 13 to 15 points, else you would have opened the bidding. Therefore, with the above hand, over partner's 1-Heart bid respond 2 No Trump (11 points). Partner should pass if he opened with a minimum holding.

Once again, *a jump in a new suit, after a previous pass, is forcing.*

Partner in third position opens with 1 Club. You hold:

♠ K Q J x x x   ♥ x x   ♦ x   ♣ Q J 10 x

Respond 2 Spades. Game seems reasonably well assured even if partner's opening bid is shaded. The jump in a new suit will give you time to explore for the best contract. If partner has a sound hand and developments proceed favorably, there might even be a slam in prospect. For example, if he raises Spades, you would be justified in showing your Club support on the next round.

7 Rebids by the opening bidder

ON HIS second turn to bid, the opening bidder should try to describe his hand both as to precise strength and type of distribution. It should be noted that unless his opening was in No Trump, responder has only a vague idea of what he holds; the hand may be light, moderate, or very strong. Opener's point count may range anywhere from 13 to as many as 22 or 23 points. The second bid serves to classify the hand.

Suppose, for example, that you hold:

♠ A K Q x x ♥ J x ♦ K 10 x ♣ Q J x

You open with 1 Spade; partner responds 2 Hearts. Your rebid should be 2 No Trump to show the strength of your hand. A rebid of 2 Spades to show a good suit would be improper, since such a rebid describes a rebiddable suit with only a mediocre hand, ranging between 13 and 16 points. You have 16 high-card points with plus values in the form of a very good five-card suit and an honor in partner's suit.

On the other hand, suppose that, on the same bidding sequence, you hold:

♠ A Q x x x ♥ x x ♦ A x x ♣ K x x

Now a rebid of 2 No Trump would be improper, even though you have a balanced hand with stoppers in the side suits. This is a minimum opening bid—only 13 points in high cards—and the way to explain the situation to partner is to simply rebid your original suit. Bid 2 Spades.

The following table shows the type of rebid to make in accordance with the strength of your opening bid.

With 13 to 16 points

Your hand is in the minimum range. You may or may not elect to bid again, unless partner's response to your opening bid is forcing.

With 16 to 19 points

You have a good hand and you are in a position to make a constructive rebid. Avoid making any rebid which your partner might construe as discouraging.

With 19 to 21 points

You have a very good hand. This is in the jump rebid range. You may jump in No Trump, jump in your own suit, or jump in partner's suit.

With 21 and up

This is a powerful hand. Of course you are going to game. You must see to it by making a jump shift, which is forcing to game. Remember, *unless the opponents enter the auction there is only one way in which the opening bidder can force his partner to bid again, and that is by jumping in a new suit.*

The reader may note that the upper limit of each category in the foregoing table coincides with the lower limit of the next higher category. These are "judgment points." The decision as to which category your hand belongs in should be made on the basis of any extra values or flaws there are in the hand. In most cases the appropriate action will be clear.

Rebid when partner has given you a single raise

The easiest rebids to make are when partner's response has limited the strength of his hand. When he raises your opening suit bid from 1 to 2, he is saying that he has from 7 to 10 points and a trump fit. All you have to do is add your points to the number shown by partner to determine whether or not game is in sight.

At this stage we have one final table of distributional values to present. When your partner raises your suit, any cards you have beyond four in that suit become enhanced in value. An additional point should be added, therefore, for the fifth trump and two additional points for the sixth and each subsequent trump in your hand.

For example, you open with 1 Heart; partner raises to 2. You hold:

♠ K x ♥ K Q J x x ♦ A x x ♣ x x x

Your hand was originally worth 14 points. Now that partner has raised your suit, you add 1 point for the fifth Heart, giving you an adjusted valuation of 15 points. You see that there is no hope for game, because even if partner has the upper limit of 10 points, together you will not have the necessary 26. You should therefore pass and be content to try for a part score.

♠ x ♥ K Q 10 x x x ♦ x x x ♣ A Q J

This hand also had an original valuation of 14 points, but when partner raises Hearts you add 1 point for the fifth trump and 2 for the sixth trump. This gives you an adjusted value of 17 points, which means that game is a possibility. If partner has 9 or 10 points, together you will have the required 26. Since his raise may be light, however, caution is indicated. You should bid 3 Hearts, which invites him to carry on to game if his raise was a near maximum.

♠ A x x ♥ A Q J x x ♦ K Q x x ♣ x

With this hand you should bid 4 Hearts. Your hand had an original valuation of 18 points. Since partner has supported Hearts, you add 1 point for the fifth card of that suit, giving your hand an adjusted valuation of 19 points. Even if partner has raised with only 7 points, you will certainly have enough for game. A bid of 3 Hearts would be improper, because partner would be under no obligation to carry on, and you might not arrive at game.

♠ A ♥ K Q J x ♦ A Q 10 x ♣ x x x x

Bid 3 Diamonds. You have 18 points, and if partner's raise was a sound one there should be a good possibility of game. Therefore, you should encourage him to bid again.

Rebid when partner responds 1 No Trump

Like a single raise, a 1 No-Trump response is a limited bid. The opening bidder can therefore make a reasonable approximation of the partnership high-card total and take appropriate action.

When your partner responds with 1 No Trump and you have a balanced hand yourself—that is, one distributed:

4 3 3 3

4 4 3 2

5 3 3 2

—you should stick to No Trump. Raise if you think there is a chance for game, or pass if you are unable to raise. The best place to play an indifferent hand is at 1 No Trump.

Partner has told you that he has between 6 and 10 points. If your hand is suitable for No Trump and you know that the partnership has 26 points, go directly to 3 No Trump. If the partnership assets may or may not reach 26 points, raise to 2 No Trump, which invites partner to go on if he has 8 to 10 points or pass if he has less.

If you know that it is impossible for your partnership to have 26 points, don't bid any more, unless you have an unbalanced hand and want to play at a suit contract. Remember, when No-Trump bids are contemplated you do not count distributional values, just high cards.

Let's consider a few cases where partner has responded to your opening bid with 1 No Trump. You hold:

♠ A x x ♥ x x ♦ A K 10 x x ♣ Q J x

Pass. You have 14 points, and even if partner has 10, you will be far removed from the 26 necessary to make game. Since your hand is balanced, there is no occasion to rebid the Diamond suit.

♠ x x ♥ A K Q x ♦ A Q x x ♣ x x x

Pass. You have 15 points, but there won't be much chance to make a game even if partner happens to have the absolute maximum of 10. You have a balanced hand, so there is no occasion to mention the Diamond suit.

♠ x x ♥ A K 10 x ♦ K Q x x ♣ A Q x

With this holding, a raise to 2 No Trump is clearly indicated. You have 18 points. If partner has 6 or 7, he will pass. If he has 8, 9 or 10, you will have the combined values for a game contract and he should bid it.

♠ A J x   ♥ A K 10 x   ♦ A x x x   ♣ K J

Bid 3 No Trump. You are assured of having the required 26 high-card points. You have 20 points and partner is known to have at least 6. When you are sure where you are going and how far to go, there is no need to dilly-dally.

♠ x x x   ♥ A Q x x x x   ♦ x   ♣ A x x

Bid 2 Hearts. Although you have a minimum hand and are not looking for game, this distribution is not suitable for No Trump. The six-card major should be rebid.

♠ K x x   ♥ A K 10 9 x x   ♦ x   ♣ A Q x

Your hand had an original value of 18 points. A try for game is definitely in order, but with a strong six-card major suit and a singleton, a suit contract is to be preferred. Bid 3 Hearts, which is not forcing but begs the responder to carry on if he has the slightest bit more than a minimum response.

♠ K x x   ♥ A K Q x x x   ♦ x   ♣ A Q x

Here you have 20 points, enough for game when partner says he has at least 6 points. Therefore bid 4 Hearts.

♠ K Q 10 x x   ♥ A Q 10 x x   ♦ x   ♣ A Q

You have opened with 1 Spade; partner has responded 1 No Trump. You have 20 points. With this fine hand you should not play for less than game, and partner would very likely pass a rebid of 2 Hearts. Bid 3 Hearts, a jump shift, which is forcing to game.

Rebid when responder bids 1 of a suit

When responder makes a 1-over-1 takeout, his bid is ambiguous. It may be a mere courtesy response based on as little as 6 points, counting high cards and distribution; or he may have a very powerful holding, just short of the requirements for a jump shift. Opener should indicate on his rebid the approximate nature of his hand. If he has a minimum holding he can show it in one of three ways:

1] By a rebid of 1 No Trump.
2] By a rebid of his own suit.
3] By naming a new suit at the level of 1.

Opener, holding a minimum hand, may also rebid a new suit at the level of 2, if it is the cheapest way to show his two-suiter. Here are some examples:

You open with 1 Heart; partner responds with 1 Spade.

♠ x x ♥ A Q 10 x x ♦ A x x ♣ K x x

Rebid 1 No Trump, showing a minimum hand of the balanced type. Observe that there is no occasion to rebid 2 Hearts merely to show a good suit. The 1 No-Trump bid gives a better picture of your entire holding.

♠ x ♥ A J 10 x x x ♦ K x x ♣ K x x

Rebid 2 Hearts, showing a minimum hand of the suit type

♠ x x ♥ A K J x x ♦ x ♣ A x x x x

Rebid 2 Clubs. The hand is a two-suiter, and this is the lowest level at which you can show your second suit. If partner prefers Hearts, he can return to that suit himself without increasing the level of the contract.

You open with 1 Club; partner responds with 1 Diamond.

♠ J x x ♥ A K x x ♦ x x ♣ A J 10 x

Rebid 1 Heart. To show a new suit at the level of 1 requires no additional values.

Raising responder from 1 to 2

To raise responder's suit bid from 1 to 2 normally shows a little more than a bare minimum opening bid. Opener revalues his hand as though it were a dummy for his partner; if he has a little more than 13 but not more than 16 points, he may give a single raise, provided he has normal trump support.

♠ K x x x   ♥ A K J x x   ♦ x x x   ♣ x

You open with 1 Heart; partner responds 1 Spade. Raise to 2 Spades. Valued as a dummy, your hand contains 15 points—12 in high cards, counting a point for the promoted value of the King of Spades, plus 3 for the singleton.

♠ A J x   ♥ A K 10 x x   ♦ x x x   ♣ x x

You bid 1 Heart and partner responds with 1 Spade. Although you have adequate trump support, an immediate raise in Spades is not recommended. Your hand had an original value of 13 points, but revalued as a dummy for partner it is worth only 12 points (1 point must be deducted for having only three trumps when you contemplate raising partner's suit). The suggested rebid, therefore, is 2 Hearts.

♠ A Q   ♥ Q x x   ♦ A 10 x x x   ♣ J x x

You open with 1 Diamond; partner bids 1 Heart. Rebid 1 No Trump. You have a minimum hand with balanced distribution.

♠ A 10 x   ♥ x   ♦ A K J x x   ♣ x x x x

You open with 1 Diamond; partner responds 1 Spade. A raise to 2 Spades is justified. You have 14 points in support of Spades, which is a little more than a bare minimum.

Raising responder from 1 to 3

The jump raise of responder's bid is the equivalent of saying: "Partner, I have a good hand in support of your suit, but not quite enough to insist on game if you were just barely able to keep the bidding open for me. If you have the least bit extra, please carry on to game."

395

To raise responder from 1 to 3, opener should have 17 to 19 points, and his holding must include at least four trumps.

♠ A x x x   ♥ x   ♦ A K x x   ♣ K J 10 x

You open with 1 Club; partner responds 1 Spade. Rebid 3 Spades. Your hand has a value of 18 points in support of Spades, 15 in high cards and 3 for the singleton.

This jump to 3 Spades is not forcing. If partner's 1-Spade bid was made with only 6 points, he may exercise his option to pass. If he has more than that, he should bid 4 Spades.

♠ A J x x   ♥ x x   ♦ A K x x   ♣ K J x

You open with 1 Club; partner responds 1 Spade. Rebid 3 Spades. Your hand is worth 17 points in support of Spades, and your trump support is more than adequate.

♠ A x x   ♥ x   ♦ A K x x x   ♣ A J x x

You open with 1 Diamond and partner responds 1 Spade. This hand is worth 18 points in support of Spades, but you have only three trumps, so an immediate jump raise is not in order. The recommended procedure is to temporize with a rebid of 2 Clubs, hoping to coax another bid from partner. A delayed Spade raise may then be given to complete the description of your hand.

Raising responder from 1 to 4

The raise of responder's bid from 1 to 4 shows a hand which contains 20 or 21 points, and therefore is good enough to make game even if partner's response was a rock-bottom minimum. This is by no means a "shut-out" bid, and if responder has a reasonably good hand he is expected to go further.

♠ x   ♥ A Q x x   ♦ A K x x x   ♣ A x x

You open with 1 Diamond; partner responds 1 Heart. Bid 4 Hearts. Your hand has a valuation of 20 points in support of Hearts, and you should not risk the possibility that partner will pass a raise to 3 Hearts. After all, he may have been sporting enough to bid 1 Heart with a holding something like this:

♠ x x x   ♥ K x x x x   ♦ x x   ♣ Q x x

Jump rebid to 2 No Trump

Keep your eye on the figure 26 for the combined partnership assets necessary to produce game. If you are sure you have them, contract for game. If there is some slight doubt, invite your partner to undertake a game contract.

The jump rebid to 2 No Trump describes a balanced hand containing 19 or 20 high-card points, with protection in all unbid suits. In other words, it shows somewhat greater strength than is required to open the bidding with 1 No Trump.

The jump rebid to 2 No Trump is not forcing; responder may quit if his initial response was based on only 6 points.

♠ x x   ♥ A K x   ♦ A Q 10 x   ♣ K Q J x

You open with 1 Diamond; partner responds 1 Spade. Bid 2 No Trump. You have 19 points in high cards. All you know for certain about partner's hand at this stage is that he has 6 points, some of which may be distributional. It will take about 7 high-card points in his hand to give you a reasonable play for game. Since it is not yet known if he has the required number, you are not in position to contract for game. However, by jumping to 2 No Trump you announce to partner that you are on the verge of a game at No Trump, and he should contract for it if he has anything more than 6 points.

It is a common error for opener to jump to 2 No Trump on the second round simply because he has more than an opening bid. Try to avoid it.

♠ x x   ♥ K J 10   ♦ K Q x x   ♣ A Q x x

If over your Diamond opening partner responds with 1 Spade, be content to bid 1 No Trump. If he takes no further action, you need have no fear of missing a game.

Jump rebid to 3 No Trump

The jump rebid to 3 No Trump is made on a hand which is some-what stronger than required for a rebid of 2 No Trump. In other words, you should hold about 21 or 22 points. Even if partner has a shaded re-sponse—that is, 5 or 6 points—you may expect to make game.

♠ J x   ♥ A Q J   ♦ A K 10 x x   ♣ K Q J

You open with 1 Diamond; partner responds 1 Spade. Rebid 3 No Trump. You have 21 points, which should provide a good play for game even if partner has less than 6.

(Observe how No-Trump bids fall within prescribed limits. Balanced hands containing 13 to 15 high-card points are opened with 1 of a suit and followed by a rebid of 1 No Trump; 16 to 18-point hands are opened with 1 No Trump; 19 to 21-point hands are opened with 1 of a suit and followed by a jump rebid in No Trump; and so on. No-Trump contracts are simple to determine, since it is just a matter of adding your points to the number shown by partner.)

Jump Rebid in opener's suit

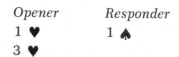

Opener	Responder
1 ♥	1 ♠
3 ♥	

When the bidding proceeds as above, the jump rebid shows a very fine trump suit which requires little trump support from partner (two small trumps or a singleton Queen are adequate). Since the suit is self-sustain-ing, opener revalues it for his rebid just as though partner had supported that suit.

Such a jump rebid in the same suit by the opening bidder is not forcing. It announces 19 to 21 points in rebid valuation. It strongly urges responder to bid again, but responder may pass if he has a minimum count and feels that his holding presents no particular distributional advantages.

$$\spadesuit \ A \ x \quad \heartsuit \ A \ K \ Q \ 9 \ x \ x \quad \diamondsuit \ x \ x \quad \clubsuit \ K \ 10 \ x$$

You open with 1 Heart; partner responds 1 Spade. Rebid 3 Hearts. Your hand had an original valuation of 18 points. But your Heart suit is self-sustaining, so you revalue it. Adding 1 point for the fifth trump and 2 points for the sixth trump gives your hand a rebid valuation of 21 points, justifying the jump.

$$\spadesuit \ x \quad \heartsuit \ A \ K \ Q \ J \ x \ x \quad \diamondsuit \ K \ x \ x \quad \clubsuit \ x \ x \ x$$

You open with 1 Heart; partner responds 1 Spade. You should not jump to 3 Hearts, despite the very fine trump suit. Your hand had an original valuation of 15 points, to which 3 points are added for the long trumps—bringing it up to 18, a little short of the requirement. Rebid 2 Hearts; then if partner takes any further constructive action, your next bid should be 4 Hearts.

Jump rebid to 4 of opener's suit

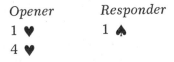

Opener	Responder
1 ♥	1 ♠
4 ♥	

The jump bid to 4 of opener's suit is made with 22 or 23 points in rebid valuation. It describes a hand that can win between eight and nine tricks by itself.

$$\spadesuit \ K \ x \quad \heartsuit \ A \ K \ Q \ x \ x \ x \ x \quad \diamondsuit \ x \ x \quad \clubsuit \ A \ x$$

You open with 1 Heart; partner responds 1 Spade. Rebid 4 Hearts. You can win about nine tricks yourself and should not incur the risk of having partner pass short of game. This is by no means a "shut-out" bid. If you had held nothing but a long string of trumps, you might have opened the bidding with 4 Hearts.

Jump shift by opening bidder

Opener	Responder
1 ♥	1 ♠
3 ♦	

Unless the opponents intervene, the only way in which opener can force responder to bid again is to jump in a new suit. This bid, made with 21 points and up, is forcing to game; responder may not pass, even if he regrets ever having responded at all.

♠ J x   ♥ A Q J 10 x   ♦ A K 10 x x   ♣ A

You open with 1 Heart; partner responds 1 Spade. Regardless of how weak his response may be, you want to insist upon a game contract, so you must rebid 3 Diamonds. A rebid of only 2 Diamonds could be dropped by responder.

Sometimes the opening bidder has a powerful hand containing an excellent fit for responder's suit, and a jump raise to game does not do full justice to his holding. Thus:

♠ K x x x   ♥ x   ♦ A K Q x x   ♣ A K x

You open with 1 Diamond; partner responds 1 Spade. This hand revalues to 23 points in support of Spades. Game is assured, of course, and there is a good chance for slam if partner has a few key cards. A jump to 4 Spades, while it is a strong bid, may not induce partner to go on. The proper rebid is a jump in a new suit, forcing to game. You have no new suit, to be sure, but for the purpose of executing a jump shift you may improvise one. Your best rebid is 3 Clubs, with the intention of supporting Spades on the next round.

Rebid by opener when responder bids 2 of a new suit

When partner responds at the 2 level in a new suit, he is showing a reasonably good hand—at least 10 points. If the opener has distinctly more than a minimum he should think in terms of game, provided a reasonable contract is in sight.

OPENER'S REBID AFTER A SINGLE RAISE

Pass with 13 to 16 points
Bid 3 of a suit with 17 or 18 points
Bid 4 of a suit (game) with 19 points

OPENER'S REBID AFTER A 1 NO-TRUMP RESPONSE

Pass with 13 to 16 points
Bid 2 No Trump with 17 to 19 points
Bid 3 No Trump with 20 points

OPENER'S REBID AFTER A 1-OVER-1 RESPONSE

Bid 1 No Trump with 13 to 15 high-card points and a balanced hand

Bid 2 No Trump with 19 or 20 high-card points and a balanced hand

Bid 3 No Trump with 21 high-card points and a balanced hand

Raise responder's suit (from 1 to 2) with 13 to 16 points and normal trump support

Make a jump raise (from 1 to 3) with 17 to 19 points and at least four trumps

Make a double jump (from 1 to 4) with 20 points and at least four trumps

Make a simple rebid of your opening suit with 13 to 16 points and a good five-card suit

Make a jump rebid of your opening suit with 17 to 19 points (19–21 rebid points) and a good six-card suit

Make a jump rebid to game with 20 points (22 rebid points) and a good six-card suit

Rebid in a new suit at the 1 level (or a lower ranking suit at the 2 level) with 13 to 18 points

Make a jump rebid in a new suit with 20 points or more, when you want to force the bidding to game

With a minimum, however, the opening bidder should not take aggressive action. He should not make any rebid that takes him past the level of 2 in his own suit. He may rebid that suit, or show a second suit of lower rank.

For the opening bidder to make a second bid at the level of 3, he should have a very strong hand. For example:

Opener	Responder
1 ♥	2 ♦
3 ♣	

Opener advertises a hand of considerable strength—at least 17 points.

When opener's rebid is 2 No Trump, even though this is not a jump he promises a good hand, for he has gone beyond a simple rebid in his own suit. For example:

Opener	Responder
1 ♥	2 ♦
2 NT	

Opener promises that he has at least 15 points in high cards.

♠ A Q x   ♥ A K J x x   ♦ K J x   ♣ x x

You open with 1 Heart; partner responds 2 Clubs. Rebid 2 No Trump. You have a point count of 18 in high cards. Don't make the mistake of rebidding 2 Hearts, which would describe a hand in the minimum range (13 to 16).

♠ K x   ♥ A J 10 x x   ♦ Q x x   ♣ K x x

You open with 1 Heart; partner responds 2 Clubs. You have trump support but no additional values to justify a raise to 3 Clubs. You have a balanced hand with protection in all suits, but only 13 high-card points, so a rebid of 2 No Trump is out of the question. You must content yourself with a rebid of 2 Hearts.

Whenever you ask yourself: *Shall I raise partner or rebid my suit?* —the answer is: *Raise partner if you wish to take the aggressive step; rebid your suit if you do not wish to sound too encouraging.*

8 Rebids by responder

BY THE time the bidding gets back to the responder for his second call, he will usually have a pretty good idea of the best contract to shoot for. The opener's rebid will have clarified his holding as to over-all strength and distribution, and if responder's first bid was indefinite in nature, it is now up to him to clarify matters in turn.

For example, when responder has made a takeout to 1 of a suit, it usually devolves upon him, on the second round of bidding, to show whether he has a weak, moderate, or strong hand. The following table may serve as a general guide in deciding your appropriate rebid as responder.

With 6 to 10 points

Your hand is minimum and you should make a mild response. With 6 or 7 points, do not bid again unless forced to. With 8 to 10 points, bid once more if partner coaxes you to.

With 10 to 13 points

You have a good hand. It is worth two bids.

With 13 to 16 points

You have a very good hand and must see to it that you reach game. (Remember, an opening bid facing an opening bid generally produces a game.) Either bid game directly or continue to make forcing responses until you reach a satisfactory game contract.

With 16 to 19 points

You have a very powerful hand. You must show that you have more than an opening bid. You may do this by jumping to 3 No Trump, or by bidding a suit and then making a big jump on the next round.

With 19 and up

This hand will produce a slam unless partner has a minimum. You may give the immediate slam signal by jumping in a new suit.

Examples of rebids by responder

♠ A K J x x　♥ J x x　♦ A x　♣ x x x

Partner opens with 1 Heart; you respond 1 Spade. He now bids 2 Hearts. You have learned from partner's rebid that he has a good Heart suit, for which you now have adequate support. Your hand is equal to an opening bid (14 points), and it faces an opening bid, so there should be game. Since you have a convenient contract, you should bid a game in Hearts without further ado.

♠ A K x x x　♥ J x x　♦ K x　♣ x x x

Suppose the bidding has proceeded as in the previous example. Once more you are certain that Hearts will make a good contract, but you are not quite sure how far to go. Your hand is worth 12 points, almost enough for game facing an opening bid. You should raise to 3 Hearts, inviting partner to carry on if he has anything in excess of a bare minimum.

♠ x x　♥ A J 10 x x　♦ K Q x　♣ K J x

Partner opens with 1 Spade; you respond 2 Hearts; partner rebids 2 Spades. You have 14 points in high cards, with balanced distribution and adequate protection in all unbid suits. Even though partner has announced near minimum values by rebidding his own suit, you have enough for a game and should bid 3 No Trump directly. Remember, partner might pass if you bid only 2 No Trump, since that call would not be forcing.

♠ K x　♥ K Q J x x　♦ A x x　♣ 10 x x

Partner opens with 1 Club; you respond 1 Heart. Partner's rebid is 1 No Trump, showing a balanced hand of moderate strength. You have 13 points; your partner, to open on a balanced hand, must have at least 13 — so the required 26 points are there. Bid 3 No Trump.

♠ A x x ♥ K Q J x x x ♦ Q x x ♣ x

Again the bidding has gone: 1 Club by partner; 1 Heart by you; 1 No Trump by him. You have 14 points, enough to bid game in No Trump. But with a singleton Club and a fine six-card suit, Hearts may be a superior contract. You should jump to 3 Hearts, which is forcing to game. If partner rebids 3 No Trump you will of course pass. But he may elect to carry on to 4 Hearts.

♠ J x x ♥ K Q x x x ♦ J x x ♣ A x

Partner opens with 1 Diamond; you respond 1 Heart. Partner rebids 1 No Trump. You have 11 high-card points, not enough to produce game if partner has a minimum. But there is still hope; if partner has 15 points, the necessary 26 will be there. You raise to 2 No Trump, which partner will pass if he has a minimum.

♠ x ♥ Q J x x x ♦ K 10 x x ♣ x x x

Partner opens with 1 Diamond; you respond 1 Heart; he rebids 1 No Trump. You have only 6 high-card points and, since the opening bidder has shown a maximum of 15 by virtue of his rebid, there is no prospect for game. However, your hand is unbalanced and a suit contract offers greater safety than No Trump. You should return to 2 Diamonds. This bid, although it increases the contract, is not a show of strength. If you had held any real offensive ambitions you would have jumped in Diamonds.

Rebids by responder who has previously given a single raise

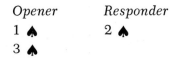

	Opener	*Responder*
	1 ♠	2 ♠
	3 ♠	

Here responder has given a single raise and opener has made another bid. What message is opener attempting to get across? Something like this: "Partner, at this time I do not know whether you have a weak raise or a good one. If you have a good one, I'd like to go to game. If not, pass. It's up to you." If you have raised on 7 or 8 points, pass. If you have raised on 9 or 10 points, bid game.

Suppose the bidding has proceeded:

Opener	Responder
1 ♥	2 ♥
3 ♥	

As responder you hold:

♠ K x   ♥ J x x x   ♦ A x x   ♣ x x x x

Bid 4 Hearts. You have a good raise—10 points in support of Hearts.

♠ x x   ♥ K x x x   ♦ Q x x x   ♣ x x x

Pass. This is a weak raise, with a bare 7 points in support of Hearts.

Now let's suppose the bidding has gone:

Opener	Responder
1 ♥	2 ♥
3 ♦	

The 3-Diamond bid is testing the quality of responder's raise. It is forcing for one round. Hearts are the agreed trump suit, and responder either bids 3 Hearts with a minimum raise or goes to game if he is near the maximum. Some examples:

A] ♠ K x   ♥ Q x x   ♦ J x x   ♣ J x x x x
B] ♠ x x x   ♥ J x x x   ♦ A x   ♣ Q x x x
c] ♠ Q J x   ♥ K x x   ♦ x x x   ♣ A 10 9 x

Bid 3 Hearts with (A). This hand is worth barely 8 points in support of Hearts, and a minimum preference should be shown.

Bid 4 Hearts with (B). You have 9 points, a solid raise.

Bid 3 No Trump with (c). You have 10 points in high cards, enough to accept the invitation. But with evenly balanced distribution, No Trump appears more inviting than Hearts. Partner is at liberty to return to the suit contract if he is so inclined.

Rebid when opener raises responder's suit

Opener   Responder
1 ♦   1 ♠
2 ♠

When his suit is directly raised by the opener, responder doesn't need quite the equivalent of an opening bid in order to proceed to game. The opener, by his raise, has shown that he has a little more than a minimum. In other words, he may be counted on for about 14 points.

For example, you hold:

♠ K J x x x   ♥ A J 10   ♦ x x   ♣ x x x

Partner opens with 1 Club; you bid 1 Spade, and he raises to 2 Spades. Your hand had an original valuation of 10 points—9 in high cards and 1 for the doubleton. Since Spades have been supported, you may add an additional point for the fifth Spade, which brings your hand to 11 points. Partner is known to have at least 14, since he has opened the bidding and raised you. Bid 3 Spades. If partner has any additional value at all, he should go to game.

♠ K x x x x   ♥ A x x   ♦ K Q x   ♣ x x

In the same bidding sequence, with this hand you should go to 4 Spades. You have the equal of an opening bid yourself, facing an opening bid, and a good fit has been found. There is nothing more to it.

Rebids by responder after he has responded 1 No Trump

Opener   Responder
1 ♥   1 NT
2 NT

What is the opener trying to convey by his 2 No-Trump bid? He knows that responder, because he has bid 1 No Trump, has from 6 to 10 points. Opener is now saying: "There may or may not be game here. If your 1

No Trump is in the lower bracket—6 or 7 points—we probably have no game; but if it is in the upper bracket—9 or 10 points—game is very likely. Please act accordingly."

Suppose the bidding has proceeded as above. As responder you hold:

A] ♠ x x x ♥ x x ♦ K x x x ♣ A x x x

B] ♠ Q x x ♥ J x ♦ x x x x ♣ A Q x x

With (A) you should pass. You have only 7 points, almost a minimum No-Trump response. With (B) you should bid 3 No Trump, since you have 9 points. Partner is asking you to continue if your hand is in the upper bracket.

Now the bidding has gone:

Opener	Responder
1 ♥	1 NT
2 ♦	

As responder you hold:

A] ♠ x x x x ♥ J x ♦ Q x x ♣ A x x x

B] ♠ x x x ♥ K x ♦ Q x x x ♣ A x x x

With (A) you should pass. You have only 7 high-card points and prefer Diamonds to Hearts. If partner had been strongly interested in reaching game, he would have jumped on the second round.

With (B) you should bid 3 Diamonds. You have 9 high-card points and a good fit for the opener's second suit. The raise at this point is not a drastic act, since you have already limited the strength of your hand. It simply gives partner another opportunity to go on, if he is interested in doing so.

Choosing between suits as responder

When the opening bidder has shown two suits, responder should select the trump which will best serve the partnership interest, not the one he personally prefers. In making a choice, numerical superiority is the deciding factor; three small trumps are superior to A-K alone. It should be realized that the doubleton A-K will take tricks even though another suit is selected as trump.

When responder has the same length in each of partner's suits, he generally returns to the first suit, since it will more often than not represent the longer combined trump holding. For example, you hold:

♠ A x x x x   ♥ 10 x x   ♦ K x x   ♣ x x

Partner opens with 1 Heart and you respond 1 Spade. He now bids 2 Diamonds. You should return to 2 Hearts even though you have the same number of Diamonds plus a high honor in that suit. Partner may have something like:

♠ x   ♥ K Q J x x   ♦ A Q J x   ♣ A x x

Repeated Spade leads might make a Diamond contract unmanageable, whereas the force could be accepted more gracefully in Hearts. (Observe too, that by showing a Heart preference in the present instance, a potential game contract will be uncovered, for the opening bidder is sure to carry on.)

Sometimes it is necessary for responder to increase the contract with a mediocre hand in order to arrive at the best trump. For example, you hold:

♠ Q x   ♥ x x x   ♦ K x x x   ♣ J 10 x x

Opener bids 1 Heart; you respond 1 No Trump; opener bids 2 Spades. You should return to 3 Hearts. The partnership has eight Hearts as against only six Spades. Partner has shown five Hearts and four Spades.

When responder is forced to speak again

The showing of a new suit by the responder is forcing on the player who has opened the bidding. But the reverse does not hold true. Responder may check out any time it suits him if the opening bidder merely bids a new suit.

When the opener *jumps* in a new suit, responder must speak again,   *409*

GOREN HIGHLIGHT_____

ASSESSING YOUR HAND FOR A REBID

—AS OPENER

13 to 16 points (*minimum hand*)	You may or may not bid again, unless partner's response is forcing.
(*good hand*) 16 to 19 points	Encourage partner by making a constructive rebid.
19 to 21 points (*very good hand*)	Make a jump rebid in your own suit, in partner's suit, or in No Trump.
21 points and up (*powerhouse*)	Make a jump shift rebid, forcing the partnership to game.

—AS RESPONDER

6 to 10 points (*minimum hand*)	With 6 or 7 points, do not bid again unless forced; with 8 to 10, bid if partner coaxes.
10 to 13 points (*good hand*)	Your hand is definitely worth a second bid.
13 to 16 points (*very good hand*)	Bid game directly, or make forcing responses until you reach game.
16 to 19 points (*powerhouse*)	Jump to 3 No Trump, or bid a suit and make a big jump on the next round.
19 points and up (*rock crusher*)	Jump in a new suit to signal for slam.

and continue to bid until game is reached. Also, if an opponent enters the bidding and partner cue-bids the opponent's suit, that cue bid is forcing to game.

However, as responder you need not bid again when the opener jumps in the same suit (that is, a suit previously mentioned by either of you), or if he jumps in No Trump.

Suppose you hold:

♠ x x x   ♥ Q x x x   ♦ K 10 x x x   ♣ x

Partner opens with 1 Club; you respond 1 Diamond.

1] If partner's rebid is 1 Spade you should pass. Spades suit you better than Clubs, and the new suit does not force you because you are not the opener.

2] If partner's rebid is 2 No Trump, you should pass. If 5 points are all that partner needs, he should jump to 3 No Trump himself, for he knows you have at least that count.

3] If partner's rebid is 3 Clubs or 3 Diamonds, you should pass. He is jumping in a suit previously bid by the partnership.

4] If partner's rebid is 2 Hearts, a jump in a new suit, you are not permitted to pass. You should bid 3 Hearts.

5] If partner's rebid is 2 Spades, you do not raise that suit with three trumps, since opener is presumed to have only four Spades. But you must speak. Your best bet is to bid 2 No Trump and hope for the best.

9 Partnership language

WHAT bids are forcing?

What bids are encouraging?

What bids are discouraging?

Bids that suggest a willingness to quit are sometimes called "sign-offs." The original bidder may sign off:

1] By rebidding his own suit or another suit at the lowest possible level.

2] By rebidding 1 No Trump.

When the original bidder signs off, he does not imply that he wants his partner to retire from the scene. He merely announces that his hand is in the minimum range—that is, 13 to 16 points. Responder should not abandon hope for game if it is still possible that the partnership has a total of 26 points.

Repeated bids in the same suit at minimum levels denote length of suit but no additional high-card values. For example, opener holds:

♠ x ♥ A Q 10 9 x x ♦ x x ♣ A x x x

Opener	Responder
1 ♥	1 ♠
2 ♥	2 NT
3 ♥	

The 3-Heart bid announces a six-card suit, but shows a hand with minimum high-card content and an unwillingness to play No Trump. With greater strength, the opener would have contracted for game on the third round.

If opener had held:

♠ x   ♥ A K J 10 x x   ♦ x x   ♣ A x x x

—the bidding would have proceeded in the same way on the first two rounds, but after the 2 No-Trump bid, opener would have gone on to 4 Hearts, not 3.

When the opener signs off by rebidding 1 No Trump, it should be noted that the new suit forcing principle no longer applies. Since opener has strictly limited his hand, it takes a jump by responder to force another bid from him. You hold:

♠ K x x x x   ♥ x   ♦ A x x x x   ♣ x x

Partner	You
1 ♣	1 ♠
1 NT	?

You may bid 2 Diamonds at this point as a safer haven, and partner is at liberty to pass if he prefers your second suit. However, if your hand is:

♠ A J 10 x x   ♥ x   ♦ A K x x x   ♣ x x

—your rebid should be a jump to 3 Diamonds, forcing to game.

A simple show of preference by responder when he has not previously increased the contract is not encouraging.

Opener	Responder
1 ♦	1 ♥
2 ♣	2 ♦

Responder has merely indicated that he prefers Diamonds to Clubs, and his response did not increase the contract. He may have as little as 6 points, in a hand like this:

♠ Q x x   ♥ K J x x x   ♦ 10 x x   ♣ x x

In the same manner:

Opener	Responder
1 ♦	1 ♠
1 NT	2 ♦

Responder may have a weak hand that is too unbalanced to play No   413

Trump. All his second bid promises is good trump support for Diamonds.

A preference shown by responder after he has previously increased the contract is encouraging.

Opener	Responder
1 ♠	2 ♦
2 ♥	2 ♠

The 2-Spade bid is constructive even though it is made only as a preference. The bid indicates that responder has support for Spades. Why, then, did he take time to show his Diamond suit on the first round instead of raising immediately to 2 Spades? The answer is that his hand must be too good for a single raise. It is fair to assume that he has more than 10 points. His hand might be something like this:

♠ A x x   ♥ x x   ♦ A Q J x x   ♣ x x x

Similarly:

Opener	Responder
1 ♠	2 ♣
2 NT	3 ♠

The 3-Spade bid is definitely forward-going, for responder's sequence of bids clearly indicates that he has a good hand. He has twice increased the contract. If he had a mediocre hand he would have given an immediate raise to 2 Spades. He probably holds something like:

♠ A J x   ♥ x x   ♦ x x x   ♣ K Q J x x

—and is asking opener to choose between 4 Spades and 3 No Trump.

Rebids by responder when opener makes a jump rebid

When opener jumps in the same suit (either his own or partner's), responder need not bid again if his original response was below normal in strength. If responder does make another bid, then the partnership becomes committed to game.

Opener	Responder
1 ♥	1 ♠
3 ♥	?

As responder you hold:

A] ♠ K x x x x ♥ x ♦ Q x x ♣ x x x x

B] ♠ K x x x ♥ x x ♦ Q 10 x ♣ K x x x

c] ♠ K Q 10 x x ♥ x ♦ K x x x ♣ x x x

With (A), you should pass. You have the barest sort of courtesy response. If that was all partner needed, he would have bid game himself.

With (B), you should bid 3 No Trump. You have 8 high-card points, which is a little more than was required for your 1-Spade response, and a game commitment is a reasonable speculation.

With (c), bid 3 Spades. You have enough strength to accept partner's invitation, but the best contract is not yet apparent. Your Spade rebid shows a good suit and is 100 per cent forcing; with a very weak hand you would have passed 3 Hearts.

Opener	Responder
1 ♥	1 NT
3 ♥	?

As responder you hold:

A] ♠ K J x ♥ x x ♦ Q x x x ♣ x x x x

B] ♠ Q x x ♥ J x x ♦ K x ♣ x x x x x

With (A), you should pass. You have a minimum No-Trump response of 6 points.

With (B), you might choose to raise to 4 Hearts. While your response was based on only 6 points, there are other factors to consider, such as the three-card trump support and the doubleton Diamond. However, don't be surprised if partner goes down a trick at the 4-Heart contract.

Opener	Responder
1 ♣	1 ♠
2 NT	?

As responder you hold:

♠ K J x x ♥ x x ♦ J x x ♣ x x x

With this hand, you should pass. You have only 5 points for purposes of No Trump, which is below normal expectancy. It would be a mistake to rebid the Spades; partner would surely go on to game, which you should be persuaded is unattainable.

Interpretation of various bids

The significance of the final bid is indicated in the following chart:

1]
Opener	Responder
1 ♠	3 ♠ ?

Game force

2]
Opener	Responder
1 ♠	2 NT?

Game force

3]
Opener	Responder
1 ♠	2 ♣ ?

One-round force

4]
Opener	Responder
1 ♦	1 ♥ ?

One-round force

5]
Opener	Responder
Pass	1 ♠
3 ♠ ?	

Not forcing, strongly invitational

6]
Opener	Responder
Pass	1 ♥
2 ♠ ?	

One-round force

7]
Opener	Responder
Pass	1 ♠
2 ♥ ?	

Not forcing

8]
Opener	Responder
1 ♣	1 ♦
1 ♥ ?	

Not forcing

9] *Opener*   *Responder*
1 ♥   1 ♠
3 ♠ ?
Strongly invitational

10] *Opener*   *Responder*
1 ♥   1 NT ?
Limit bid (6 to 10 high-card points)

11] *Opener*   *Responder*
1 ♥   1 ♠
2 NT ?
Strongly invitational

12] *Opener*   *Responder*
1 ♠   2 ♠
3 ♠ ?
Invitational

13] *Opener*   *Responder*
1 ♠   2 ♠
3 ♦ ?
One-round force

14] *Opener*   *Responder*
1 ♥   1 ♠
3 ♥   3 ♠ ?
Game force

15] *Opener*   *Responder*
1 ♥   1 ♠
2 ♣ ?
Not forcing

16] *Opener*   *Responder*
1 ♠   2 ♦
2 ♠   3 ♣ ?
One-round force

17] *Opener*   *Responder*
1 ♠   1 ♦
2 ♠   3 ♠ ?
Strongly invitational

18] *Opener*   *Responder*
1 ♥   1 ♠
1 NT   2 ♣ ?
Not forcing

19] *Opener*   *Responder*
1 NT   2 ♣ ?
Forcing. Requests opener to show a major suit

20] *Opener*   *Responder*
1 NT   2 ♠ ?
Sign-off

21] *Opener*   *Responder*
2 NT   3 ♠ ?

Game force

22] *Opener*   *Responder*
1 ♥   1 NT
2 ♠ ?
Showing great strength

23] *Opener*   *Responder*
1 ♥   2 ♦
3 ♣ ?
Showing great strength

24] *Opener*   *Responder*
1 ♠   2 ♠
2 NT   3 ♠ ?
Sign-off

25] Opener   Responder
   1 ♦   1 ♠
   2 ♣   2 ♦ ?
Not encouraging

26] Opener   Responder
   1 ♦   1 ♠
   2 ♣   3 ♦ ?
Game force

27] Opener   Responder
   1 ♠   2 ♥
   2 ♠ ?
Not encouraging

28] Opener   Responder
   1 ♥   1 ♠
   1 NT ?
Not encouraging

29] Opener   Responder
   1 ♠   2 ♣
   2 NT ?
Strength-showing

30] Opener   Responder
   1 ♠   2 ♦
   2 ♠   3 ♦ ?
Mildly encouraging

31] Opener   Responder
   1 ♠   2 ♦
   2 NT   3 ♠ ?
Game force

32] Opener   Responder
   1 ♥   2 ♦
   3 ♠ ?
Game force

33] Opener   Responder
   1 ♥   1 ♠
   4 ♥ ?
Showing great strength

34] Opener   Responder
   1 ♦   1 ♠
   4 ♠ ?
Showing great strength

35] Opener   Responder
   1 ♥   1 ♠
   3 ♣ ?
Game force

36] Opener   Responder
   1 ♦   1 ♥
   1 NT   2 ♠ ?
One-round force

37] Opener   Responder
   1 ♦   1 ♥
   1 NT   3 ♦ ?
Game force

38] Opener   Responder
   1 ♦   1 ♥
   1 NT   3 ♥ ?
Game force

10 Slam bidding

DIAGNOSING a slam is quite similar to diagnosing a game. If your partner opens the bidding and you have the equivalent of an opening bid yourself, you know at once that a game is in prospect ($13 + 13 = 26$ points), providing an acceptable contract can be found.

To make a small slam, the partnership must be able to win two more tricks, which requires about 7 additional points, ($26 + 7 = 33$ points) and must have the same assurance of a suitable contract. Once the bidding has reached the point where you can see a combined total of 33 points and a satisfactory fit, you know that slam is a possibility.

Where No-Trump bids are involved, the calculation is relatively simple. Since only high-card points are counted, the total in the pack always equals 40. If your side has 33 points, a small slam should be attempted. It is not necessary to check up on Aces, because it is impossible for the opponents to have two Aces when you have 33 points in high cards; they can have at most only 7. Similarly, when your side has 37 points, you know that a grand slam may be attempted because it is impossible for the opponents to have an Ace; they can have at most only 3 points.

How do we determine that there are 33 or 34 points in the combined hands? By simple addition. For example, you hold:

♠ A x ♥ K Q x ♦ A x x x ♣ K J 10 x

Your partner opens the bidding with 1 No Trump, showing a balanced hand ranging from 16 to 18 high-card points. You have a balanced hand with 17 high-card points. The partnership has a combined total ranging between 33 and 35 points. This is ample for a small slam but not enough for a grand slam. Since No Trump is a highly acceptable contract, you should just rise up and bid 6 No Trump.

419

♠ K J x ♥ K Q 10 x x ♦ A x ♣ A x x

Partner opens with 1 Diamond; you respond 1 Heart; partner raises to 2 Hearts. You should sense a slam. Your hand had an original valuation of 18 points. Now that partner has supported Hearts, you add 1 point for the fifth Heart, giving you a total of 19. Your partner, by opening the bidding and then giving you an immediate raise, has shown slightly more than a minimum. Therefore you may count on him for at least 14 points and 14 plus 19 equals 33.

With this hand, I suggest that you go right ahead and bid 6 Hearts without asking any questions. (At a suit contract it is sometimes advisable, however, to check for controls, since some of the partnership points will be of the distributional variety; even if you have a total of 33, it is conceivable for the opponents to hold two fast tricks. This subject is dealt with in a following section on the Blackwood Convention.)

♠ K x x ♥ A J x x x ♦ x x ♣ K Q x

Partner opens with 1 Diamond; you respond 1 Heart; partner jumps to 3 No Trump. You have 13 high-card points and you know from partner's rebid that he has 21, which gives you a combined total of at least 34. The recommended bid is 6 No Trump.

Looking at matters another way, let us assume the bidding has proceeded:

Opener	Responder
1 ♥	2 ♣
2 NT	?

Opener, by rebidding 2 No Trump, has shown a hand that is worth at least 15 points. If your own hand totals 18 or more points in high cards, you should go all out to reach a slam.

Slam diagnosis by the opener

The opening bidder may become aware of slam possibilities the moment he hears partner's response. If you open and your partner responds in No Trump, you can tell what he holds within 2 points, and can determine immediately whether or not there is a chance for slam. For example:

♠ Q J 10 x x　♥ A K Q　♦ K Q x　♣ x x

You open with 1 Spade; partner responds 3 No Trump. You have 17 points; partner has at least 16; 33 points with a five-card suit is all you need. Bid 6 No Trump.

♠ x x x　♥ A Q J　♦ A K x x　♣ x x x

You open with 1 Diamond and partner responds 3 No Trump. You have 14 points and partner has between 16 and 18. Even if he has a maximum 3 No-Trump bid, you will have only 32 points. You should pass.

♠ J x　♥ K Q x x x　♦ A K x　♣ K Q x

You open with 1 Heart; partner responds 2 No Trump. You have 18 points; partner has between 13 and 15. If he has a maximum 2 No-Trump holding of 15, there will be enough to attempt a slam (33, with a five-card suit). But since he may have only 13 points, you are not in position to bid a slam yourself. You should inquire as to the quality of partner's 2 No-Trump response by overbidding the game to 4 No Trump. This is not a Blackwood bid. It is a raise of the No-Trump bid and invites partner to bid a slam if he has a maximum count.

Whenever you open the bidding with 1 of a suit and partner gives a jump raise (such as 1 Spade to 3 Spades), you know that his hand ranges from 13 to 16 points in support. If you have a minimum opening bid, there will be no slam, since the partnership assets will fall somewhat short of the required 33.

But if you have 17, 18, or 19, there may well be a slam, depending on either the quality of partner's raise or the location of his assets. With 20 or more points slam is virtually assured, provided you have sufficient controls. For example:

♠ x x　♥ A Q J x x　♦ A Q x　♣ K x x

You open with 1 Heart; partner responds 3 Hearts. Your hand was originally worth 17 points (16 in high cards and 1 for the doubleton), to which must be added 1 point for the fifth Heart, now that the suit has been supported. Partner is known to have between 13 and 16 points. If he has a minimum, slam will be improbable. If he has a near maximum, there will be a good chance for slam. Bid 4 Diamonds and await his reaction. If he merely returns to 4 Hearts you must quit, for a contract of 5 might not be safe. (It will be noted that the 4-Diamond call is a cue bid denoting first-round control rather than a playable suit. Since Hearts are agreed on as trump, there would not be much point in branching out into another suit.)

♠ x   ♥ A K J x x   ♦ A K x x x   ♣ x x

Your opening 1-Heart bid receives an immediate jump raise to 3. This hand is worth 19 points and prospects for slam are extremely bright, since the partnership is assured of a minimum of 32 points (19 + 13). So you bid 4 Diamonds. Now if partner returns to 4 Hearts, he is signing off, but you should not abandon all hope. You have attractive distribution, and an eleven-trick contract should be safe. Since you have no further controls to show, bid 5 Hearts. If partner has adequate controls in the black suits, he should go on to slam. (Observe that the Blackwood Convention will not solve your problems on this hand if partner has only one Ace, for you won't know which one it is. He may have a very fine raise with no top control in Clubs. It is appropriate, therefore, to find out where his "stuff" is rather than how much he has.)

While for all general purposes a singleton in the opener's hand carries no special weight, when a slam is in contemplation the singleton is a decided asset, for it affords secondary control of the suit; that is, it prevents the opponents from cashing two tricks in that suit and gives declarer a chance to get on with his development of the hand. Thus:

♠ A J 10   ♥ A Q J x x   ♦ x   ♣ K Q x x

You open with 1 Heart; partner jumps to 3 Hearts. Your hand revalues to 20 points and partner guarantees at least 13. You have a control in every suit, so that slam is a virtual certainty, and a contract of 6 Hearts is recommended. Just to make sure that partner has not made a jump without an Ace, you might check up with a Blackwood bid.

♠ A K x   ♥ A K J x x   ♦ x   ♣ K Q 10 x

Here your hand revalues to 23 points, and serious consideration should be given to a grand slam. A Blackwood bid is in order; if partner shows two Aces and a King, the grand slam should be a laydown.

When responder makes a jump shift, the opener may diagnose a slam with very few excess values. Since the jump shift shows at least 19 points, 32 points in the combined hands are immediately assured.

The bidding has proceeded:

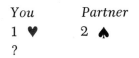

You	Partner
1 ♥	2 ♠
?	

You hold:

♠ K x x   ♥ A 10 x x x   ♦ K x x   ♣ K x

A raise to 3 Spades is clearly indicated, even though you have a minimum opening bid of 14 points. Partner's jump shift shows that you have an assured total of 33 points. He should be apprised of your good trump fit, and he can then determine how far to go.

Cue-bidding

When either player bids a suit which an opponent has previously mentioned, it indicates an ability to win the first trick of that suit, either with the Ace or by trumping. This device, known as a cue bid, is forcing to game and is used to suggest an interest in slam. It usually implies very good support for partner's suit.

♠ none   ♥ A 10 x x x   ♦ A K x x   ♣ K x x x

Partner opens with 1 Heart; opponent bids 1 Spade. Your hand is worth 19 points in support of Hearts, and prospects for slam are very bright. You may so indicate by bidding 2 Spades. Heart support will be shown on the next round. Naturally the cue bid should be made only with ample trump support and sufficient high-card values to justify the suggestion that there is a slam in prospect. Don't use this bid just to get to game.

♠ K Q J x   ♥ A K J x x x   ♦ none   ♣ Q J x

You open with 1 Heart and partner responds 1 Spade. The next player bids 2 Diamonds. You may bid 3 Diamonds. All that partner needs to produce a slam is the Ace of Spades and the King of Clubs. Of course, if part of his valuation rests on the Ace of Diamonds, that card will be worthless, and your cue bid will serve to acquaint him with the fact.

Developing the slam

Let us explore some typical avenues to slam. Suppose you hold:

♠ Q 10 x   ♥ A K x x x   ♦ A Q 10 x   ♣ x

Partner opens with 1 Spade and you respond 2 Hearts. He rebids 2 Spades, showing a minimum opening (13 to 16 points). Your hand is worth about 18 points in support of Spades, and prospects for slam are definitely present. You should bid 3 Diamonds, which is another one-round force. When you raise Spades on the next round, partner will know that you have a very good hand. If you had merely been interested in reaching game, you would not have taken time out to bid Diamonds, but would have raised Spades directly when the opener rebid his suit.

♠ A Q x   ♥ K 10 9 x x   ♦ x x   ♣ A x x

Partner opens with 1 Club; you respond 1 Heart; he raises to 3 Hearts. You have 15 points, facing a partner who by his opening bid and jump raise has shown at least 17 points. This suggests a slam. Bid 4 Clubs. This shows the Ace rather than Club support, for Hearts are the agreed trump suit. If partner now cue bids the Ace of Diamonds, you can take a chance of bidding a slam yourself. If he simply returns to 4 Hearts over 4 Clubs, you may make one more try by bidding 4 Spades. The rest will be up to him.

♠ Q x x   ♥ A K x x x x   ♦ K x   ♣ x x

Partner opens with 1 Spade; you respond 2 Hearts; partner bids 3

Spades, a game force. You have 12 points in high cards plus a good fit for partner, who has opened and jumped. A slam is therefore probable. The usual way to suggest this is by showing a side Ace; but since you have none to show, you must invite slam by overbidding the game with a jump to 5 Spades. To bid 4 Spades would be grossly inadequate, and partner is apt to pass, since by merely carrying on to game you do not indicate any extra values.

♠ x x   ♥ J x   ♦ A K x x x x   ♣ A x x

Partner opens with 1 Heart; you respond 2 Diamonds; partner raises to 3 Diamonds. This looks like a slam. Partner has more than an opening bid, and you have more than an opening bid. Bid 4 Clubs, showing the Ace. If partner shows the Ace of Spades, you should bid a slam.

The Blackwood Convention

Blackwood is probably the most abused convention in bridge. Properly employed, it is a valuable tool, but experience has shown that it serves a useful purpose in only about 25 per cent of the cases involving slam bidding. Its main function—contrary to general thinking and practice—is to stay out of slams that cannot be made.

Slam prospects are dependent on many different factors. Sometimes the problem centers on control of a particular suit; what may be required is a specific Ace, or perhaps the King-Queen, or even a singleton. But this is not always the case. Some slams require refined treatment; others resist the scientific approach, so that blasting may be the best technique.

In any event, there is no royal road to success in slam bidding. The relative ease with which Blackwood can be learned should not encourage anyone to employ the convention as a substitute for thinking. Perhaps the best suggestion I can offer is to ask yourself this question every time you are considering the use of Blackwood: "Are the number of Aces and Kings in partner's hand the only problem with which I am concerned?" Unless the answer is an unqualified yes, then perhaps you should use some other approach.

When the preliminary rounds of bidding have indicated that a slam is probable, and a suit has been agreed upon directly or by inference, either player may institute the Blackwood Convention by calling 4 No Trump.

No special holding is required, but the person making the 4 No-Trump bid must be quite convinced that the hand will play safely for eleven tricks.

The responses are:

> With no Aces, bid 5 Clubs.
>
> With one Ace, bid 5 Diamonds.
>
> With two Aces, bid 5 Hearts.
>
> With three Aces, bid 5 Spades.
>
> With four Aces, bid 5 Clubs.

After Aces have been shown, the 4 No-Trump bidder may ask for Kings by bidding 5 No Trump. However, there is a very distinct proviso that the 5 No-Trump bid must never be made unless it has previously been determined that the partnership is in possession of all four Aces. Presumably the purpose in asking for Kings is to look for a grand slam, for if the Blackwooder is content to settle for a small slam there can be no need for any further exploration.

Suppose you hold:

♠ K Q x x x x   ♥ K Q x x   ♦ A x   ♣ A

You open the bidding with 1 Spade and partner gives a jump raise to 3 Spades. Since the number of controls is your sole concern, you bid 4 No Trump, asking for Aces. If partner responds with 5 Hearts, showing two, a small slam is assured. The only question left is whether or not he has a King. If he does, you will have a parking place for the little Diamond, and a grand slam will be a laydown. You should therefore bid 5 No Trump now to ask for Kings.

On the other hand, if partner's response to 4 No Trump had been 5 Diamonds, you would have known immediately that the opponents held an Ace, and you would have been obliged to settle for a small slam.

The responder to the 5 No-Trump bid shows the number of his Kings exactly as he shows the number of his Aces in response to the 4 No-Trump bid, but at one level higher.

Caution must be employed in using the convention where the agreed trump is a minor suit. For example, if the agreed suit is Clubs, the 4 No-Trump bidder must have at least two Aces; otherwise, after a 5-Diamond response, the partnership will find itself in a slam with the opposition holding two Aces.

As a general rule, the player with the stronger of the two hands or the one with the better distributional features should be given the opportunity to start the convention, because he can better judge what the partnership will produce. For example, you hold:

♠ A K x x x   ♥ x x x   ♦ A x   ♣ K x x

It would not be advisable for you to start the Blackwood Convention, for the information about how many Aces and Kings your partner has would not make it possible for you to determine the trick-taking capacity of the hand. With balanced holdings of this type, you should offer partner the chance to use Blackwood. When you tell him that you have two Aces and two Kings, he will be in a much better position to determine the slam potential.

Holdings such as:

♠ A K Q J x x   ♥ K Q J x x   ♦ x   ♣ x
or
♠ A Q J x   ♥ A K   ♦ K x   ♣ K Q J x x

lend themsleves ideally to the employment of Blackwood, for your only concern is the matter of lining up Aces and Kings.

One of the basic provisions of the Blackwood Convention is that the 4 No-Trump bidder becomes the captain of the team. Except where a grand slam is being sought, he alone has the prerogative of deciding on the final contract. This means that if the Blackwood bidder signs off at the 5 level after partner's Ace-showing response, responder must pass. Unless the Blackwooder doesn't know what he is doing, the partnership will be off two Aces.

However, once it has been determined that the partnership has all four Aces, either player may use his own discretion in deciding whether to go all the way or settle for a small slam.

It should be noted that a void in the responding hand is not treated as equivalent to an Ace in responding to a 4 No-Trump bid. While on the subject of voids: a player who holds a void suit is not in strategic position to make a Blackwood bid. If he finds out that his partner has an Ace, he won't know whether or not the Ace is in that suit.

Suppose that you pick up the following hand:

♠ A K Q x x   ♥ K Q J x   ♦ A Q J x   ♣ none

The bidding has proceeded:

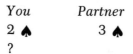

When partner makes a positive response by raising Spades, you surely want to try for slam, but there is little point in using Blackwood as the means. You are concerned with only two cards—the Ace of Hearts and the King of Diamonds. Finding out how many controls partner has is not as important as where they are. Instead of asking for Aces, you should tell about them. Bid 4 Diamonds to show the Ace. If partner now shows the Ace of Hearts by bidding 4 Hearts, you will be well on the way. You can bid 5 Clubs next, giving him a chance to bid 5 Diamonds if he has the King. (Remember that after the trump suit is agreed on, all subsequent bids in other suits show controls.)

When a 4 No-Trump bid is not Blackwood

When your side has not mentioned a suit, the 4 No-Trump bid is not Blackwood. An opening bid of 4 No Trump denotes a hand that is somewhat stronger than an opening 3 No-Trump bid; it shows possession of 28 or 29 points. Suppose you are opener and you hold:

♠ A K x   ♥ K Q J x   ♦ A K Q   ♣ K Q J

Bid 4 No Trump. You have 28 points and a balanced hand, and this is the only way to properly describe your values. However, if you have:

♠ A K Q J 10 x   ♥ A   ♦ x   ♣ K Q J 10 x

—you should open the bidding with 2 Spades. True, your only concern is whether or not partner has an Ace or two, but there will be time to make a Blackwood bid later, after the trump suit has been set.

When an opponent opens with a pre-emptive bid of 4 Spades and your partner bids 4 No Trump, that is not Blackwood. No suit has been mentioned by your side. The 4 No-Trump bid is used in a case of this sort as a means of forcing partner to name his best suit.

A 4 No-Trump bid is not Blackwood when you are raising a No-Trump bid which your partner has previously made. The sudden burst to 4 No Trump when a suit has apparently been agreed upon is the mark of the Blackwood Convention.

Suppose the bidding has proceeded:

SOUTH	WEST	NORTH	EAST
1 ♠	4 ♥	4 ♠	Pass
4 NT			

Since it is apparent that Spades are agreed upon, South's 4 No-Trump bid is Blackwood. It seems highly unlikely that South would prefer No Trump to Spades in the sequence as shown.

Opener	Responder
1 ♠	3 ♦
4 NT	

The jump shift to 3 Diamonds was a slam signal, so the 4 No-Trump bid is obviously to be construed as Blackwood.

Opener	Responder
1 ♥	4 NT

A suit has been mentioned, so the jump to 4 No Trump must be Blackwood.

Opener	Responder
1 ♥	1 ♠
2 NT	4 NT

Here the 4 No-Trump bid is not Blackwood. It is a quantitative raise and invites the opener to bid a slam in No Trump if he has maximum values for his jump rebid.

The Gerber 4-Club Convention

A sudden burst to 4 Clubs in response to an opening bid of 1, 2 or 3 No Trump is an artificial bid asking for Aces in the Blackwood manner. The responses are:

> With no Aces, bid 4 Diamonds
> With one Ace, bid 4 Hearts
> With two Aces, bid 4 Spades
> With three Aces, bid 4 No Trump
> With four Aces, bid 4 Diamonds

If the 4-Club bidder wishes to ask for Kings next, he rebids 5 Clubs. The response is made in the same fashion as above, one level higher. Any rebid other than 5 Clubs is a natural call and places the final contract.

For example, partner opens with 1 No Trump, and you hold:

♠ K Q x   ♥ K Q 10 x x x   ♦ A x   ♣ x

The fate of this hand rests entirely on the number of controls partner has. You therefore bid 4 Clubs. If his response is 4 No Trump, showing three Aces, you will ask for Kings next by bidding 5 Clubs. If he shows a King by bidding 5 Hearts, you can go all the way.

If partner shows two Aces, you will bid 6 Hearts. If he shows only one Ace, you can safely sign off at 4 Hearts.

11 Defensive bidding

Overcalls

AN OVERCALL is a bid made after an opponent has opened the bidding, but before your partner has entered the auction. The bid should be made only with a definite purpose in mind. Since the opponent announces he has a fairly good hand by virtue of his opening, the prospects of a game for your side are considerably diminished.

In making overcalls, do not place too much reliance on point count. The consideration of paramount importance is the texture of your trump suit. When you overcall at the level of 2, you guarantee to partner that you will not lose more than two tricks in the suit named. Beware of over-calling with suits like this, particularly at the level of 2:

A Q x x x

K J x x x

Q J x x x

Holdings with the same high-card content but more body will provide considerably better protection if you run into a bad break:

A Q 10 9 8

K J 10 9 8

Q J 10 9 8

Bidding a suit of this texture provides a good lead director to partner if the opponents should buy the contract.

Suppose an opponent has opened 1 Heart and you hold:

A] ♠ x x ♥ x x x ♦ A J x x x ♣ A K x

B] ♠ x x ♥ x x ♦ K Q 10 9 x x ♣ A x x

Hand (A) represents a very unsound 2-Diamond overcall. Although you have 13 points, enough for an opening bid, a commitment at the 2 level with a hand that may produce only four tricks if Diamonds break badly is dangerous. Among reasons for passing is the further consideration that you have excellent defense against the opponents.

Hand (B), though it contains only 11 points, is a reasonable 2-Diamond overcall. You should be able to take at least five or six tricks on your own hook. On defense, your bid may suggest the killing lead to partner should the opponents get to 3 No Trump.

Overcalls in suits in which you cannot stand the lead are frowned upon. Thus:

♠ K x   ♥ x x x   ♦ J x x x x   ♣ A K x

If opponent opens with 1 Club, with this hand it is not advisable to overcall 1 Diamond.

Action by partner of overcaller

When your partner overcalls an opponent's opening bid, particularly at the 2 level, he can be counted on to have a good suit and a certain number of playing tricks—that is, he will be able to come within two or three tricks of fulfilling his bid, depending on vulnerability. You will now have a fairly good idea of the partnership's offensive potentialities and can act accordingly.

There is no need to keep the bidding open for an overcaller, so don't bid unless your motives are constructive. If partner has overcalled in a major suit, strive to raise him wherever possible. For example, as South you hold:

♠ x x x   ♥ K J 9 x x   ♦ A   ♣ x x x x

With both sides vulnerable, the bidding has proceeded:

WEST	NORTH	EAST	SOUTH
1 ♦	1 ♠	Pass	?

You should bid 2 Spades. Partner can be counted on to have a good five-card suit by virtue of his vulnerable overcall. Since you have adequate trump support for him, there is nothing to be gained by showing the Hearts.

When your hand is a little bit stronger, with adequate trump support, you can raise partner to 3 of his suit. This call is not forcing.

♠ A Q x ♥ A x x x x ♦ x ♣ x x x x

Bid 3 Spades. Your hand figures to take about four tricks. Partner should have five winners for the vulnerable overcall. If he has a little more, he will be encouraged to proceed to game.

The jump overcall

The jump overcall, once used only on very strong hands, is now employed to describe a good suit with little or no side strength. It is a pre-emptive measure that either lays the groundwork for a sacrifice bid or else indicates to partner the best lead.

The requirements are: (1) a good six-card suit; (2) a maximum of 9 high-card points, concentrated mostly in the overcaller's suit; (3) assurance that the bidder will be able to limit his losses to 500 points if doubled. In other words, the jump overcaller should be able to take within three tricks of his bid in his own hand, not vulnerable, and within two tricks of his bid if vulnerable.

For example:

	EAST	SOUTH
	1 ♦	?

A] ♠ x ♥ K Q J 10 x x ♦ x x x ♣ x x x

B] ♠ K Q J 9 x x ♥ A 10 x x ♦ x x ♣ x

c] ♠ A Q J 9 x x ♥ x x x ♦ A K ♣ K x

Hand (A) is an excellent 2-Heart bid if not vulnerable, for you can expect to win five tricks in your own hand. Hand (B) is too strong for a pre-emptive bid and an overcall of 1 Spade is indicated. Hand (c) is too strong for any type of overcall. Your proper strategy is to double first and then bid an appropriate number of Spades on a subsequent round.

433

The 1 No-Trump overcall

To overcall an opening bid with 1 No Trump, a player should have the equal of a normal opening 1 No-Trump bid or a little better (16 to 19 points), and the adverse suit safely stopped.

The unusual No-Trump overcall

When a player overcalls with any number of No Trump, and it is obvious the bid cannot possibly mean what that bid normally does, then the No-Trump overcall should be construed as a takeout double requesting partner to respond in his best minor suit.

For example, as South you hold:

♠ x   ♥ A   ♦ K J x x x   ♣ A Q 10 x x

WEST	NORTH	EAST	SOUTH
1 ♥	Pass	2 ♥	?

If you decide to bid 3 Diamonds and get doubled, you won't know whether to stay there or try 4 Clubs. On the other hand, if you make a takeout double, partner will surely bid Spades. In this dilemma, you bid 2 No Trump, which cannot logically be interpreted as a natural No-Trump call, and partner is expected to show his longest minor suit.

(To avoid misunderstanding: it still remains true that an *immediate* overcall in No Trump, *directly over the opening bid*, retains its normal meaning—i.e., 1 No Trump shows 16 to 18 or 19 points and the adverse suit stopped; 2 No Trump shows 22 to 24 points; 3 No Trump shows about eight or nine winners.)

The takeout double

Sometimes an opponent opens the bidding, and you find yourself with the equivalent of an opening bid or more, with scattered values and no good suit to mention. Or you have a good suit and too much strength to chance a mere overcall, which partner might pass. The best way to indicate such strength is by a takeout double. This is a demand for partner to bid. His only excuse for passing would be a fair certainty on his part of inflicting a penalty on the opponents.

It is important to differentiate between a takeout double and one that is intended for penalties. A double is intended for takeout:

1] When partner has made no bid, double, or penalty pass;

2] When the double is made at the doubler's first opportunity to double that suit;

3] When the double is at the level of 1, 2 or 3 of a suit.

All three conditions must be present.
A double of 2 No Trump is always for penalties.
A double of 1 No Trump is primarily for penalties, but partner may refuse to leave it in if his hand lacks defensive strength.
As an example, the bidding has proceeded:

EAST	SOUTH	WEST	NORTH
1 ♠	Pass	1 NT	Pass
2 ♠	DBL		

This is not a takeout double, as it was not made at the first opportunity to double Spades. On the other hand:

A] WEST	NORTH	EAST	SOUTH
Pass	Pass	1 ♥	DBL

B] WEST	NORTH	EAST	SOUTH
1 ♥	Pass	2 ♥	DBL

C] WEST	NORTH	EAST	SOUTH
Pass	Pass	Pass	1 ♦
1 ♥	Pass	Pass	DBL

These are all examples of takeout doubles. Each of the three necessary conditions is present in the three bidding sequences.

435

Suppose that as South you hold:

♠ A 10 x x   ♥ x   ♦ J 10 x x   ♣ A K x x

EAST	SOUTH
1 ♥	DBL

This is a perfect takeout double. You have a sound opening bid with good support for any suit partner is likely to name. When he bids, you will have found the best vehicle if your side is to play the contract. If he has a smattering of strength, it may be possible to score a game.

A takeout double may be repeated when the opponents have interfered and prevented partner from bidding. For example, as South you hold:

♠ K Q 10 x   ♥ A K x x   ♦ x   ♣ K Q x x

EAST	SOUTH	WEST	NORTH
1 ♦	DBL	2 ♦	Pass
Pass	?		

You should double again to show a very strong hand and insist on a bid from partner, though he is known to have a weak hand. He may be unable to take action on his own, and there is danger that the opponents will steal off with a cheap contract.

With the same holding, suppose the bidding has proceeded:

SOUTH	WEST	NORTH	EAST
1 ♣	1 ♦	Pass	Pass
?			

You should double, insisting that partner take some action. This affords him the opportunity to bid 1 Spade, 1 Heart, or 2 Clubs. Note that a player who has previously opened the bidding may make a takeout double, provided that his partner has not yet bid. Incidentally, a takeout double by the opening bidder to reopen the bidding indicates a holding that is well above the minimum.

Requirements for a takeout double

Normally, a takeout double announces about 13 points and the ability to support any suit partner might bid, or a good suit of your own to fall back on in case of trouble.

Be prepared for partner to respond in your weakest suit. If you are unable to cope with such a response, the double is unsound, even if your hand contains more than 13 points. For example, you hold:

♠ A 10 x x   ♥ x   ♦ A 10 x x   ♣ A Q x x

If your right-hand opponent opens with 1 Spade, it would be unsound to double. Partner will almost surely bid 2 Hearts, leaving you with no safe place to go. Your best chance for a profit is to pass and hope that the opponents bid themselves into trouble. But:

♠ x x   ♥ A Q J x x   ♦ x x   ♣ A K J x

This hand gives you a proper takeout double of a 1-Spade opening bid. If partner responds with 2 Diamonds, you have a reasonably safe haven in 2 Hearts. If he prefers Clubs, you can play the hand in that suit.

Double of 1 No Trump

The double of 1 No Trump is made primarily for penalties, but partner of the doubler may exercise his own judgment on how to proceed.

An immediate double of an opening 1 No-Trump bid should be made only with a hand that is at least the equivalent of an opening 1 No-Trump bid; that is, it should contain 16 points.

If the partner of the doubler has at least 6 points, he should leave the double in. Sixteen plus 6 equals 22, which means the opposition can have no more than 18, and your side should be able to outscore them. There is the further consideration that the opening bidder is going to be confronted with a virtually worthless dummy, and he will find playing the hand anything but a pleasure.

437

Responses to takeout doubles

The following table is recommended as a help in sizing up your hand when responding to a takeout double:

A hand containing 6 points is a fair hand.
A hand containing 9 points is a good hand.
A hand containing 11 points is a probable game hand.

In using this table, count both high-card and distributional points.

The requirement for responding to partner's takeout double is zero points. The less you have, the more urgent it is to respond; if the opponents are permitted to play their doubled contract, they may score a number of overtricks which can prove very costly. Do not pass because you are in distress. If you don't have a four-card suit to bid, respond in a three-card suit as cheaply as possible. For example, you hold:

♠ 10 x x ♥ Q J x x ♦ x x x ♣ x x x

If partner makes a takeout double of 1 Heart, bid 1 Spade. This does not promise anything at all. You are merely fulfilling partner's request to bid.

To make a penalty pass of the takeout double, you must be able to take four tricks defensively, and three of these tricks must be in the trump suit. For example:

A] ♠ x x x x ♥ K J 9 x x ♦ x x ♣ x x

B] ♠ x x x ♥ K Q J 9 x ♦ K x ♣ x x x

If partner makes a takeout double of 1 Heart, you should bid 1 Spade with (A). Your hand will not produce the required four tricks. With (B) you should pass. You will be able to take at least three Hearts and one Diamond, and the doubler may be counted on for a minimum of three tricks.

In responding to partner's takeout double, prefer a four-card major to a five-card minor suit at the level of 1. For example:

♠ A x x x ♥ x x ♦ x x ♣ Q 10 x x x

Partner doubles 1 Heart. Respond 1 Spade rather than 2 Clubs. If partner has a good double, it may be possible to score a game, and Spades are the more likely vehicle.

Your partner doubles 1 Diamond. You hold:

♠ K J x x   ♥ K J x x   ♦ x x   ♣ x x x

You have 9 points, a good hand. You should plan to bid both major suits, showing Spades first.

In responding to a takeout double, prefer a major suit to 1 No Trump, but prefer 1 No Trump to a minor suit if you hold a fairly good hand — that is, 8 or 9 points in high cards. For example, partner doubles 1 Heart and you hold:

♠ A 9 x   ♥ Q J 9 x   ♦ x x   ♣ Q 10 x x

Your best response is 1 No Trump. This hand contains 9 points and has a double Heart stopper. (It should be pointed out here that the 1 No-Trump bid is never used in response to a takeout double as a rescue bid.)

Your partner doubles 1 Heart and you hold:

♠ K 9 x x   ♥ K J x   ♦ x x x   ♣ Q x x

While this hand is strong enough to justify a 1 No-Trump response to partner's double (9 points), a bid of 1 Spade is to be preferred.

Responding with strong hands

When you hold a hand with 11 points — or a little less with a long suit — you should so advise partner by bidding one more than necessary in response to his takeout double, even though your suit is not very impressive. For example:

♠ A Q x   ♥ K x x x   ♦ K x x   ♣ x x x

Partner has doubled 1 Club. Your proper response is 2 Hearts, despite the weakness of the suit. If you bid only 1 Heart, the takeout doubler may pass with sufficient values to score a game. Remember, you would have been justified in bidding 1 Heart without a single face card.

♠ K x x　♥ A x x　♦ K J x　♣ J 10 x x

Partner has doubled 1 Diamond. Respond 2 No Trump. (This bid should rarely be made with a point count of less than 12.)

♠ x x　♥ K x x　♦ K x x　♣ A Q 10 x x

Partner has doubled 1 Spade. Respond 3 Clubs.

Responding after an intervening bid

When partner has doubled the opening bid and your right-hand opponent inserts a bid, you are relieved of your obligation to speak. But if you hold 8 points, counting both high cards and distribution, you should make every effort to bid. For example, as South you hold:

A]　♠ K 10 x x x　♥ J x x　♦ K x x　♣ x x

B]　♠ Q 10 x x x　♥ x x x　♦ K Q x　♣ x x

The bidding has proceeded:

WEST	NORTH	EAST	SOUTH
1 ♣	DBL	1 ♥	?

With either of these holdings you should make a free bid of 1 Spade. You have 8 points—7 in high cards and 1 for distribution—enough for a free bid at the level of 1.

Action by doubler after partner's response

The doubler should be cautious in any subsequent action he takes. His partner was forced to bid and may hold nothing, so the doubler should not embark on a contract that he is not prepared to underwrite in his own hand.

To put it another way, the takeout doubler should subsequently underbid, since he has already advertised a good holding. His partner, on the other hand, should overbid. Unfortunately, in actual play the opposite is too often the case: the doubler waxes more and more eloquent, and his partner creeps further and further into his shell. This means that the best contract is often missed.

As South you hold:

♠ K Q x x　♥ K x x x　♦ x　♣ A Q x x

The bidding has proceeded:

EAST	SOUTH	WEST	NORTH
1 ♦	DBL	Pass	1 ♠
Pass	?		

You should raise only to 2 Spades. Partner may have little or nothing. The mere fact that you bid again shows a desire to go on.

Note that the above hand was valued at 16 points when you doubled, 14 in high cards and 2 for distribution. However, since partner responded in the suit which you can support, you revalue your hand as dummy. The singleton is worth 3 points, and your hand now has a value of 17. If your partner has 9 points, you can expect to hear further from him.

When contemplating a raise of partner's suit, the following is a reasonably accurate guide for the takeout doubler:

> With 16 points, you may go to the 2 level.
> With 19 points, you may go to the 3 level.
> With 22 points, you may go to the 4 level.

Action by doubler's partner when doubler raises

When your partner doubles and then raises your response, you should feel impelled to bid again with any inducement at all. For example:

A]　♠ K x x　♥ J 10 x x　♦ x x　♣ A x x x

B]　♠ K x　♥ 10 x x x x　♦ x x　♣ K J x x

Partner doubles a bid of 1 Diamond, you respond 1 Heart, and partner raises to 2 Hearts. With (A), you should bid 3 Hearts. You have a good hand of 9 points—8 in high cards and 1 for the doubleton. With (B), you should go to game. Your hand is worth 10 points—7 in high cards, 2 for the doubletons, and 1 for the fifth trump when partner raises. Partner, by his double and subsequent raise to 2 Hearts, has indicated that he has at least 16 points, which brings the combined total to the necessary 26.

Once again, remember that as far as your partner is concerned, you might have had nothing in the hand.

Action by opener's partner over a double

When your partner opens the bidding and the next player doubles:

1] With a good hand of 11 or more points, even without trump support for partner, you should redouble.

2] With in-between hands of 6 to 9 points, it is usually better to bid immediately.

Partner opens with 1 Spade, second hand doubles, and you hold:

A] ♠ x   ♥ Q J 10 x   ♦ A J x x   ♣ A Q x x

B] ♠ x x   ♥ K Q x x   ♦ x   ♣ A K x x x x

c] ♠ J 10 x x   x   ♦ Q 10 x x x   ♣ x x x

D] ♠ x x   ♥ x x x   ♦ J 10 x   ♣ A Q J x x

With (A) and (B), redouble, even though you lack support for partner. The redouble announces a good hand and insists that partner pass the opponent's takeout around to you. You intend to double for penalties, with hand (A), no matter where the opposition lights. With (B), you will show your Club suit if the opponents find a haven in Diamonds.

With (c), raise to 2 Spades. It is a weak hand, but your bid will serve as a mildly pre-emptive move. If you don't come in at once, the bidding may reach too high a level on the next round for you to act safely.

With (D), bid 2 Clubs. The hand is neither good nor bad, but this is the only time it will be convenient for you to show your suit.

Overcall in opponent's suit

The immediate cue bid is the most powerful of defensive calls and is the equivalent of an opening 2 demand bid. It is forcing to game. It an-

DEFENSIVE BIDDING

For an overcall you need:

A good five-card suit (not more than two trump losers when bidding at the 2 level)

The assurance that you can hold your losses to 500 points if doubled

For a takeout double you need:

The equivalent of an opening bid, 13 points (16 points if doubling 1 No Trump)

Support for all unbid suits, or a good suit of your own to fall back on

In responding to a takeout double:

Bid your longest suit, regardless of high-card strength

Prefer a four-card major to a five-card minor suit at the 1 level

Bid 1 No Trump with 8 high-card points and a stopper in the adverse suit

Jump in your best suit with 11 points or more

Pass with four defensive winners including three trump tricks

After partner responds to your takeout double:

Raise to the 2 level with 16 points

Raise to the 3 level with 19 points

Raise to the 4 level with 22 points

nounces the ability to win the first trick in the adverse suit. For example, an opponent opens with 1 Diamond. You hold:

♠ A Q x x x   ♥ A K 10 x   ♦ none   ♣ K Q J x

You wish to insist upon a game even if partner has no strength. The proper bid is 2 Diamonds, forcing to game.

The 3 No-Trump call

An overcall of 3 No Trump shows a desire to play at that contract. Partner should not rescue with any five- or six-card suit unless game surely can be made in that suit.

The 3 No-Trump overcall is usually made with a long minor suit that can be run. For example, the opening bid is 3 Hearts. You hold:

♠ x x   ♥ K x   ♦ A x   ♣ A K Q 10 x x x

Overcall with 3 No Trump. With a Heart lead you should be able to run nine tricks, whereas a game in Clubs would depend on your finding several high cards in partner's hand.

12 Penalty doubles

THE business double for penalties represents perhaps the greatest single source of profit at the bridge table. And yet a great deal of potential wealth from this source remains unrealized because the average player fails to diagnose penalty-double situations, particularly at the lower levels. When the opponents have reached a contract of 4 or 5, they have had plenty of opportunity to exchange information and find their best spot. But when one of them makes an overcall at the level of 1 or 2, he has not yet heard from his partner and may very well be indulging in a bit of speculation. If you can strike with a double at this point, you will often score heavily.

A double is for penalties rather than for takeout:

1] Whenever the doubler's partner has previously indicated strength, as by bidding or doubling.

2] Whenever the double is of 4 or more of a suit.

3] Whenever the doubler has had a previous opportunity to make a takeout double of that suit but has failed to do so.

4] Whenever the double is of a No-Trump contract. (Doubles of 1 No Trump are primarily for penalty, but the partner with little or no defensive strength may exercise the option to take them out.)

Penalty doubles should be made on a strictly businesslike basis. Count those tricks which you expect to win, add them to the number that partner is expected to win, and decide if the double is warranted. A tally of points will not serve as a complete guide unless the opponents are playing a No-Trump contract.

Here is the way you can count your probable tricks:

1] Where partner opens with 1 of a suit, count on him for three tricks.

2] Where partner opens with 1 No Trump, count on him for four tricks.

3] Where partner has made a takeout double, count on him for three tricks.

4] Where partner has overcalled or has given you a single raise, count on him for only one trick.

5] Where partner has made a pre-emptive bid, count on him for no tricks.

6] Against a suit contract, do not count on more than two tricks in one suit. Where your suit is long and partner has supported it, do not expect to win more than one trick in that suit.

7] Be slow to double when you have length in partner's suit. Be quick to double when short in partner's suit.

8] Count one defensive trick for a holding of four adverse trumps, even though they are small ones.

Now let us see how these rules apply in some concrete situations.

When partner opens the bidding and your opponent overcalls in the suit which you had wanted to bid, double for penalties. For example, you hold:

♠ K J 9 x   ♥ Q x x x   ♦ A x x x   ♣ x

Partner opens with 1 Club; opponent overcalls 1 Spade. Since you wanted to bid 1 Spade had your opponent passed, you should double for penalties. Without the Ace of Diamonds in the hand you would have a mere courtesy response, and if the opponent makes a 1-Spade overcall you should pass; you could expect to take three trump tricks, which, added to the three tricks expected from partner by virtue of his opening bid, would give you a combined total of only six.

When partner opens, an opponent overcalls, and you find yourself tempted to bid 2 No Trump, you will obtain better results by doubling instead. For example, as South you hold:

♠ x x   ♥ K J 9 x   ♦ A x x x   ♣ Q x x

NORTH	EAST	SOUTH	WEST
1 ♠	2 ♥	?	

Do not bid 2 No Trump. Double. You should be able to win four tricks and partner can be counted on for three. This means at least a two-trick set. If partner has more than a minimum, so that game your way might have been a possibility, the penalty will be all the greater and will provide adequate compensation.

As a safety rule, do not double for penalty unless you expect to beat the contract by at least two tricks. You may, however, double a bid of 2 Clubs or 2 Diamonds with a lesser expectation, since the contract if fulfilled will not produce a game.

Avoid doubling when you have nothing but length in the opponent's suit. Thus:

♠ x x　♥ x x　♦ J x x　♣ Q J 9 x x x

NORTH	EAST	SOUTH (YOU)	WEST
1 ♥	2 ♣	?	

With this hand you should pass, even though you expect to defeat the 2-Club contract. If you double, your left-hand opponent, who is obviously short in Clubs, may run to another spot. And if your partner doubles the rescue bid, he will probably be counting on you for defensive tricks that do not materialize in the play.

Lead-directing doubles

The double of a slam contract by the player who is not on opening lead has a conventional meaning to guide the opening leader. The convention is this:

1] The double demands the lead of the first side suit bid by dummy.
2] If dummy has not bid a side suit, the double demands the lead of the first side suit bid by declarer.
3] If neither opponent has bid a side suit, then the double calls for an unusual lead. Under no conditions may the leader open a suit bid by his own side.
For example, as South you hold:

♠ x x x x　♥ A x x　♦ none　♣ J 10 9 x x x

The bidding has proceeded:

WEST	NORTH	EAST	SOUTH
2 ♥	Pass	3 ♦	Pass
3 ♥	Pass	4 ♥	Pass
6 ♥	Pass	Pass	?

What should you do? Double, to demand the lead of dummy's first-bid side suit, Diamonds. You will ruff the lead, and your Ace of Trumps will then provide the setting trick.

Doubles of 3 No-Trump contracts

The double of a 3 No-Trump contract by the player not on lead also has a special meaning. The convention is this:

1] If the doubler has bid a suit, the double unconditionally demands the lead of that suit.

2] If the opening leader has bid a suit, the double requests the lead of that suit.

3] If neither defender has bid, the double suggests the lead of dummy's suit.

As South you hold:

♠ Q J 10 9 8 x   ♥ x   ♦ x x x x   ♣ x x

The bidding has proceeded:

NORTH	EAST	SOUTH	WEST
1 ♥	1 NT	Pass	3 NT
DBL	Pass	Pass	Pass

What should you lead? The answer is a Heart. Partner's double commands the lead of his suit, and though you have an excellent suit of your own, his instructions should not be disregarded. Partner has guaranteed the defeat of the contract with a Heart lead; a Spade opening might give the opponent time to establish nine tricks.

13 Opening leads

IT HAS been calculated by experts that 50 per cent of all successful contracts could be defeated if the defenders were able to select the perfect opening lead.

There are a number of old wives' tales concerning the opening lead that are believed by inexperienced players, such as: "Never lead away from a King," "Always lead the highest of your partner's suit," "When in doubt, lead trumps," etc. The first lesson to be learned on the subject is to put all these superstitions out of mind. As a general truth, the selection of an opening lead is not an exact science; in a given situation, a number of experts might disagree as to the correct card to lead. There are, however, some fundamental principles which the player should keep in mind.

In selecting opening leads, it is advisable to get into the habit of classifying various hands. A lead may be proper against a No-Trump contract which would be quite improper against a suit contract. You must ask yourself: "Am I leading against a part score, a game, or a slam contract? Has my partner bid? Has my partner suggested a lead? Will the opponents probably make this hand or will they more likely go down?"

Often the opening lead is determined by the manner in which the opponents have reached their contract. If the bidding has gone smoothly and your chances of defeating the contract look to be remote, desperate measures may be justified. On the other hand, if the opponents seemed uncertain in their bidding and you feel there is a good prospect of defeating the contract, then you should play safe and make a conservative opening lead.

Leads against No Trump

First to be considered is the problem of the opening lead against hands where no specific information has been obtained from the bidding.

A case in point would be this sequence:

NORTH	SOUTH
1 NT	2 NT
3 NT	

Against No-Trump contracts it is often possible to develop tricks out of small cards. For example, if you hold A Q 7 4 3, against a suit contract you could hardly expect to take more than the Ace and the Queen. But at No Trump there is a very good chance that the smaller cards will be winners. Therefore, your longest suit should usually be selected as the opening lead.

A common error of the average player is to lead a new suit each time he obtains the lead. An estimate has been made that every time the defense leads a new suit it results in the average loss of a half trick. So, as a matter of general policy, stick to the suit you open unless you have a good reason for shifting.

The most desirable opening lead is from the top of a complete sequence. Suppose you hold:

♠ 9 6 4
♥ 7 3
♦ J 10 9 6
♣ K J 5 2

The Jack of Diamonds is a much more desirable lead than the 2 of Clubs because it is certain not to lose a trick, regardless of the adverse holding; the Club lead might permit declarer to win a trick with the Queen, which otherwise he might not be able to do.

♠ Q 6 3 2
♥ 9 6 3
♦ 8 2
♣ Q 10 8 3

With this hand, I would recommend a Club lead rather than a Spade because the Club holding is more nearly a sequence. Note that if your partner holds only the Jack of Clubs you have not lost a trick; in fact, you are well on your way toward developing two tricks in that suit. If you lead a Spade and find your partner with the Jack, you are still not certain of developing a trick unless partner also has the 10.

Where you have a choice between two suits of exactly the same texture, the auction having given you no information, it is the general practice to lead the major suit rather than the minor—the theory being that the opponents will sometimes conceal a biddable minor suit but they will usually mention a long major suit if they have it.

Sometimes you have a choice between two suits, one of which is longer, the other more solid. Under these circumstances, it is difficult to select the proper lead. Usually, however, quality should take precedence over quantity. For example:

♠ Q J 10 9
♥ 8 3
♦ Q 7 4 3 2
♣ 6 3

The Queen of Spades is the proper lead. This cannot lose a trick, whereas a Diamond lead might permit declarer to win an undeserved trick with the Jack.

It is often heard that "leads from a tenace should be avoided." Like most thumb rules, this is an unsound generalization. The propriety of such a lead against a No-Trump contract depends entirely on how many cards you hold in the suit. The lead from A Q 6 2 is undesirable, but the lead from A Q 6 4 2 is extremely desirable. In the first case, you are almost sure to give up a trick to declarer. In the second case, you are giving up the same trick, but when partner gets in and returns the suit, you have a reasonable expectancy of winning the four remaining tricks. The following hand illustrates the principle:

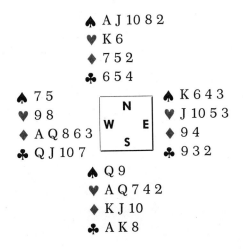

♠ A J 10 8 2
♥ K 6
♦ 7 5 2
♣ 6 5 4

♠ 7 5   ♠ K 6 4 3
♥ 9 8   ♥ J 10 5 3
♦ A Q 8 6 3   ♦ 9 4
♣ Q J 10 7   ♣ 9 3 2

♠ Q 9
♥ A Q 7 4 2
♦ K J 10
♣ A K 8

If West should open the Queen of Clubs, declarer will win and take the Spade finesse, which loses to East. Now a Diamond shift comes too 451 late, and the defense can take only two Diamonds and the King of Spades. But if the 6 of Diamonds is opened, declarer is forced to win with the Jack. Now when he takes the Spade finesse and East gets in, a Diamond return defeats the contract.

When you have several high cards for entries, your longest suit invariably should be selected. For example:

♠ A 8 4 3
♥ 7 5
♦ Q 7 6 4 2
♣ A 5

The proper lead is the 4 of Diamonds, because even though you lose a trick at the opening, you hope to build up several tricks in that suit while you still have two Aces as entry cards.

♠ Q 8
♥ K J 5 3
♦ 10 4
♣ J 8 5 3 2

On this hand you have a choice between a weak five-card minor and a strong four-card major. The best lead is a Club, because it gives you a chance to develop more tricks for your side if the suit breaks well.

Leading from bad hands

It is good policy not to waste efforts on a hopeless hand. If you have no trick-taking possibilities, don't bother to lead your long suit. For example:

♠ 10 9 4
♥ 10 8 5 4 2
♦ 7 3
♣ 5 3 2

This hand, for all practical purposes, is dead. There is no point in leading your fourth best Heart. It would suggest to your partner that you were trying to build up that suit and invite him to continue it. Yet if by chance the Hearts did become established, you have no means of getting in to cash them.

Your side's only trick-taking possibilities are in your partner's hand. The only thing you can do is give him the best start possible in the race to take tricks. Your best bet is to lead the 10 of Spades, hoping that you may strike partner's strong suit. This is known as a short-suit lead. Note that you do not look for the shortest suit in your hand (Diamonds) and lead that; you lead what you think will prove to be the best suit despite the fact that your holding is short.

The short-suit lead

The type of lead described above in connection with hopeless hands is made also on strong hands where you fear to lead anything else because you have great hopes of taking tricks. For example:

♠ K 10 8
♥ J 4 3 2
♦ A Q 10 4
♣ 10 9

This presents no desirable opening lead. I regard the Diamond as the most undesirable. If you adopt waiting tactics, the declarer will probably never be able to win a trick in that suit. If you lead the Diamond, he will almost surely take at least one trick. The next in order of undesirability is the Spade. In the first place, your partner will probably misread the lead of the 8; second, you may very easily sacrifice a trick by that lead. The Heart lead, therefore, appears to be the logical one. However, experience has shown that a lead from the Jack and three small cards is, in the long run, not very profitable. From holdings such as those in Spades, Hearts, and Diamonds, the best results are obtained by waiting. By the process of elimination, therefore, we arrive at the Club lead, and the 10 of Clubs should be selected.

Leading when your partner has bid

Of course you do not always lead the suit your partner has bid, although against a No-Trump declaration it is usually best to do so.

Assuming that you are about to lead your partner's suit, it is important to select the proper card. Experienced players very rarely lead the highest of partner's suit. In fact, the only time it is correct to do so is when you have only two cards of that suit, or three unimportant cards, or a holding which is headed by two honors in sequence. In all other cases the low card is the correct lead.

In the following table the underlined card is the one to lead from partner's suit at No Trump:

A 2	K 2	Q 2	9 2	9 6 2	7 5 4
A 6 2	K 6 2	Q 6 2	J 6 2	10 6 2	A 6 3 2
K 6 3 2	Q 6 3 2	J 6 3 2	9 6 3 2	5 4 3 2	9 6 4 3 2
Q J 6 2	K Q 6 2	J 10 6 2			

It will be seen that, in most cases, where you have four or more of partner's suit, you lead the fourth from the top. Where you have three of partner's suit, headed by an honor, you lead the lowest. Here is an example of why:

```
                    ♠ 6 5
                  ┌─────────┐
                  │    N    │
      ♠ Q 7 2     │ W     E │    ♠ A 10 8 4
                  │    S    │
                  └─────────┘
                    ♠ K J 3
```

East has bid Spades and South No Trump, expecting to take two Spade tricks. If West leads the Queen, South will win two tricks. The lead of the 2 of Spades enables the defense to capture South's Jack.

When you are in doubt whether to lead your partner's suit or your own, give him the benefit of the doubt. There should be greater inducement to lead partner's suit when he has overcalled than when he has opened the bidding with that suit. Opening bids are frequently made on weak suits, but overcalls are nearly always based on strong ones.

There are some situations that provide valid reason for not leading partner's suit. Holding a singleton in the suit is usually a good excuse, provided you have an alternative lead that offers the hope of establishing tricks in your own hand. But even a singleton of partner's suit should be led if your hand is hopeless.

Holding two small cards of partner's suit may be an excuse for not leading it, if you have a five-card suit of your own to be established. But not unless your suit is a good one. Thus:

♠ 6 2
♥ 9 7 3
♦ J 8 6 4 2
♣ 7 5 2

Partner has bid Spades. The Diamond lead is not to be considered with this feeble holding. Lead the 6 of Spades.

Leading the opponent's suit

When your best suit contains a complete sequence, at No Trump it should be led even though the opponents have bid it. For example:

♠ Q J 10 9 4
♥ Q 10 7 3
♦ 8 4
♣ 4 3

You should lead the Queen of Spades even though that suit has been bid by your right-hand opponent.

But suppose your hand looks like this, and your right-hand opponent has bid Spades:

♠ K J 8 3 2
♥ Q J 9 3
♦ 6 4
♣ 7 5

Here you have an entirely different situation. The lead of a Spade will probably be into declarer's A-Q, thus presenting him with a trick. In this case your proper lead is the Queen of Hearts.

In modern bidding a player will very often open 1 Club without really having a biddable Club suit. Therefore, when a Club lead from your hand is indicated, as a general rule you should not refrain from leading it simply because the suit has been bid by the declarer. For example:

♠ K 9 2
♥ 8 6
♦ A 4 3
♣ K J 9 4 3

The bidding has been opened on your right with 1 Club, and declarer is playing at a No-Trump contract. Lead the 4 of Clubs. If your partner has the Queen of that suit, it will be established at once. If he has the 10, there is a good chance to build up the suit while you still have two likely entries.

Leading when partner has doubled No Trump

When a final No-Trump contract is doubled by a player who does not have the opening lead, that double carries a special message to the opening leader, as follows:

1] If the doubler has bid a suit, the leader must absolutely lead that suit even if he has only a singleton in it and might prefer to develop a good suit of his own.

2] If the opening leader has bid a suit, partner's double demands that he lead that suit.

3] If both partners have bid, the opening leader may use his judgment in selecting the suit to lead.

4] If neither partner has bid, the doubler is suggesting the lead of dummy's first-bid suit, unless the leader has a very good opening of his own. The double in this case is a suggestion, not a command.

Leads against suit contracts

Many of the principles outlined in the foregoing sections as applicable to leads against No Trump will not apply when leading against a suit contract. At No Trump, much attention must be given to building up tricks from small cards; therefore the length of a suit is often the most important consideration in selecting your opening lead. Against a suit contract, your eye is fixed on the first two or three rounds of the suit to be led.

Holding K Q 6 4 2, against No Trump the correct lead is the 4-spot. Against a suit contract, you lead the King to be sure that you build up at least one trick.

Holding A K 6 4 2, against No Trump the correct lead is the 4, in hopes that you will take tricks with the remaining cards. Against a suit contract that lead would be absurd; you do not expect to take more than two tricks.

You probably have heard a great deal about never leading away from a King against a suit contract. Forget that word "never." It can only be said that here, as in No Trump, it is unattractive to lead away from any honor —King, Queen or Jack—when that honor is not part of a sequence.

There is one important difference. At No Trump we quite properly lead away from an Ace. At a suit contract, the lead away from an Ace should be avoided. If that suit must be led, lead the Ace, not the small card. The reason, of course, is that at No Trump you cannot lose your Ace; at a suit contract, if you lead away from the Ace it may be trumped on the next round.

When leading your partner's suit, the same principles apply as at No Trump. That is, you lead the highest of partner's suit only when you hold two cards, or three worthless cards, or a sequence. With four small cards of his suit, you lead the lowest, to give partner a count on how many cards are out against him. However, if you hold the Ace, regardless of how many cards are with it, the Ace should be led.

Avoid leading Aces of other suits at random. Aces are best used to capture Kings and Queens. The player who opens with an Ace just to have a look at the dummy is paying a steep price for the privilege.

Singleton leads

A singleton should not be led simply as a matter of course. Sometimes it is the ideal lead; at other times it can be the worst.

These are favorable conditions for the singleton lead:

1] When you have a sure trump trick, enabling you to regain the lead early in the play if the first trick loses.

2] When you have surplus trumps for ruffing, as when you hold A x, A x x, or K x x.

3] When partner has bid, giving you a good chance to reach his hand to obtain the ruff.

These are unfavorable conditions for the singleton lead:

1] When you hold K x, Q x x, or Q J x of trump, so that you are not at all anxious to use a trump for ruffing.

2] Whenever you hold four or more trumps. (In this case, your longest side suit should be led in an effort to force declarer to use up his trumps.)

3] When you hold a singleton King or Queen, which should almost never be led unless partner has bid the suit.

Doubleton and tripleton leads

The favorable and unfavorable conditions for leading from a doubleton are the same as for the singleton lead, above. However, the doubleton lead is made less often with the idea of obtaining a ruff than for the purpose of exiting when no really attractive lead is available.

A holding of A x, K x, Q x, or J x provides an extremely undesirable lead. It should not be considered unless the situation is desperate.

When holding a doubleton A-K and desiring a ruff, the conventional procedure is to lead first the Ace and then the King. This announces to your partner that you have no more of the suit.

When you have a choice of leading from a worthless doubleton or a worthless tripleton, by all means select the doubleton lead, because it does at least provide the outside chance of bringing home a third-round ruff.

Sometimes you will be obliged to lead from a three-card suit. If my choice is between K 6 2 and Q 6 2, I always lead from the King rather than from the Queen. If I lead into an A-Q, my King may still live to take a trick; but if the lead from the Queen loses to a lower honor, I have no hope for the future. In other words, a King is strong enough to survive a bad lead; a Queen probably is not.

Holding A K J, with or without others in a side suit, a good idea is to lead the King first and then shift to partner's suit, so that if the Queen is in the closed hand your partner can lead through and capture it.

The trump lead

The old saw about leading trumps when in doubt is very bad advice. You should lead trumps when that looks like the best defensive move to be made, and particularly if the bidding implies that the dummy has a short suit.

Trump leads are indicated under the following circumstances:

1] When declarer has bid two suits and the dummy has supported only one of them.

2] When the opponents' bidding has proceeded:

NORTH	SOUTH
1 ♠	2 ♠
4 ♠	

3] When the opponents' bidding has proceeded:

NORTH	SOUTH
1 ♠	2 ♠
2 NT	3 ♠
3 NT	4 ♠

Trump openings should be avoided when you suspect from the bidding that the dummy has a good suit which you will be unable to stop. In this case the trump lead is dangerous because, with the trumps extracted, declarer will obtain discards upon dummy's good suit.

A trump opening is almost a "must" when you have made a take-out double of a suit bid of 1 and your partner has left it in. By his action, partner has predicted that he will take more tricks in that suit than the declarer, and your side might as well draw trumps without delay.

Leads against slams

Against slam contracts a very popular lead is an Ace. This is not always a good tactic. It takes two tricks to defeat a small slam, and cashing an Ace will not attain your end unless, of course, you have reason to believe partner has the King. Usually you should attempt to set up another trick first.

459

When a suit has been bid and rebid by the opponents, it is usually futile to lead the Ace of that suit. Leading the Ace of an unbid suit, on the other hand, will usually turn out well.

The following examples will serve to illustrate when an Ace should be led against slam and when it should not. In each case the opening lead is to be made against a contract of 6 Spades:

♠ Q 6 5
♥ A 9 7 4
♦ 5 3 2
♣ 8 6 2

I feel that I have a fair chance to make my Queen of Spades. Therefore I would cash the Ace of Hearts.

♠ 7
♥ A 9 6 4
♦ 8 6 4 2
♣ 7 6 4 3

If Spades have not been vigorously supported by dummy, I would reason that there is a fair chance my partner has a trump trick, and I would cash my Ace.

♠ 8 5 4
♥ A 9 6
♦ 10 9 8 4
♣ 5 3 2

Here the only prospect of a second trick is that my partner may be able to take one in Clubs or Diamonds. I would lead the 10 of Diamonds, hoping that partner has something like the King behind dummy's Ace, so I would build up a trick for him before releasing my Ace. If I were to lead my Ace at the start, it might establish some Heart tricks in dummy upon which declarer could discard a losing Diamond or Club.

♠ 8 6 5
♥ A 7 4 2
♦ 9 7 3
♣ Q 3 2

If the dummy has bid Hearts, I would open a Club, in the hope that partner holds at least the King of that suit. Here it is urgent to build up a trick before my Ace is driven out, so that declarer cannot obtain discards on dummy's Heart suit.

Trump leads against slam are not recommended as a rule, although occasionally they turn out well. For example, if declarer has bid two suits and you have the other one well under control, a trump lead may cut down dummy's ruffing power.

The singleton lead against a slam contract from a completely worth- less hand is very attractive. Partner probably holds a trick; if it happens to be the Ace of that suit, the slam is immediately defeated. Or, if partner happens to hold a quick trump trick he will return the suit in time to defeat the slam.

Aggressive leads are usually not desirable against No-Trump slams. In other words, unless you have a complete sequence do not take a chance to build up tricks. It is better to wait. For example:

♠ 9 8 6
♥ J 6 4 2
♦ Q 6 5 3
♣ J 4

Against 6 No Trump I would lead the 9 of Spades, even though the suit had been bid.

Leads against doubled slams

When partner has doubled a slam contract and you have the opening lead, the accepted convention is that you are not entitled to any choice of suit. The double calls for a specific lead, as outlined below.

This convention is based upon the theory that when the opponents have reached a slam contract they will rarely go down more than a trick; a double should not be made merely for the purpose of scoring an addi- tional 50 or 100 points, but should be utilized to gain special advantage by directing your partner's lead. The doubler of a slam contract says, in effect: "Partner, please do not make the normal opening lead."

Here are the leads required by partner's double of a slam:

461

1] If dummy has bid any suit other than trumps, the doubler demands the lead of that suit. If dummy has bid more than one suit, he demands the lead of the first suit bid by dummy.

2] If dummy has bid no side suit but the declarer has, the doubler demands the lead of the first side suit bid by declarer.

3] If declarer and his partner have bid no side suit, the doubler demands the lead of an unbid suit. (In other words, you absolutely must not lead trumps.)

4] If the doubler or his partner has bid a suit, the double announces: "Partner, please do not lead that suit."

As an example, you are North and hold:

♠ 6 5 2
♥ A 9 7
♦ 7 4 3
♣ 10 9 4 2

The bidding has proceeded:

WEST	NORTH	EAST	SOUTH
1 ♠	Pass	3 ♣	3 ♥
3 ♠	Pass	4 ♠	Pass
6 ♠	Pass	Pass	DBL

A Club lead is demanded of you.

Table of opening leads

The following table shows the proper card to select for the opening lead from various holdings in a suit. (There are some exceptions when leading partner's suit, as outlined in previous sections.)

It will be seen that where you have a complete sequence (K Q J, Q J 10, J 10 9) you always lead the top card. Two adjoining honors are not considered a sequence; holding K Q 3 2, the proper lead is the 2.

However, there are some combinations which, though not forming a complete sequence, are treated as such for the purpose of the opening lead. For example: K Q 10 2; Q J 9 2; J 10 8 2. Each is within a card of being a complete sequence. The proper leads are the King, the Queen, and the Jack, respectively. The rule is that where the third card is only one removed from the perfect sequence it may be promoted—so that K Q 10 equals K Q J; Q J 9 equals Q J 10; and J 10 8 equals J 10 9.

HOLDING	AGAINST NO TRUMP	SUIT BIDS AGAINST
A K Q J	A	K
A K Q x x x	A	K
A K Q x x	K	K
A K Q x	K	K
A K x	K	K
A K J 10 x	J	K
A K J 10	A	K
A K J x	K	K
A K 10 x	K	K
A K J x x	x	K
A K J x x x x	A	K
A K x x x x	x	K
A K 10 9 x	10	K
A K 10 9 x x	10	K
A K x x x	x	K
A Q J x x	Q	A
K Q J x x	K	K
K Q 10 x x	K	K
K Q 7 4 2	4	K
Q J 10 x x	Q	Q
Q J 9 x x	Q	Q
Q J 7 4 2	4	4
J 10 9 x x	J	J
J 10 8 x x	J	J
J 10 7 4 2	4	4
10 9 8	10	10
10 9 7 4	4	10
A Q 10 9 x	10[1]	A
A Q 8 7 4 2	7	A

[1] The Queen is led when you suspect the King is dummy.

HOLDING	AGAINST NO TRUMP	AGAINST SUIT BIDS
A J 10 8 2	J	A
A 10 9 7 2	10	A
K J 10 7 2	J	J
K 10 9 7 2	10	10
Q 10 9 7 2	10	10
A J 4	4	4
A 7 4	4	A
K J 4	4[2]	4
K 7 4	4	4
Q 10 4	4	4
J 7 4	4	4
K 9 8 7	7[3]	7

[2] Unattractive lead, but sometimes made necessary by the bidding.

[3] Do not treat the 9 8 7 as the top of an inferior sequence because partner may improperly read it as the top of nothing.

14 Play by declarer

THE BIDDING has been completed, the opening lead made, and the dummy spread out on the table. Now is the time for the declarer to take stock of his resources and map out a plan of action. A good habit to develop is never to play a card from dummy until some plan has been formulated.

Here is the way to begin:

1] When playing a hand at a suit contract, estimate your probable and possible losers. If these add up to more than you can afford to lose, try to figure out some way to eliminate a loser.

2] When playing a No-Trump contract, count your sure and probable winners. If these are less than you need to fulfill contract, cast about to see which suits may produce an extra winner. Bear in mind that these winners must be obtained before the defenders are given a chance to capture enough tricks to defeat you.

Overtricks are of little consequence, and declarer's efforts should be concentrated on fulfilling the contract.

Leading toward high cards

An elementary principle in play is that most high-card combinations produce better results if you lead toward the high cards than if you lead from the hand in which the high cards are contained. For example:

```
              8 5 3
                 N
   10 9 7 6   W     E   A J 4
                 S
              K Q 2
```

You want to win tricks with both the King and Queen. This can be done only if East holds the Ace and if he is compelled to play before you. The proper procedure is to lead a small card from the North hand. If East plays the Ace, your troubles are over. If he plays small, you win with the Queen and enter the North hand again to repeat the process. Note that if you had led the King out of your hand you could have taken only one trick, with the Queen. By the same token:

8 6 5 3

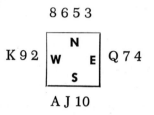

K 9 2   Q 7 4

A J 10

Your object is to win two tricks in the suit. If you lead from the South hand, this is impossible, but if you lead from the North hand and play the 10, West will win a trick with the King. You subsequently enter the North hand and lead the suit again. If East plays small, you win with the Jack. Here again you have obtained the maximum by compelling the opponent to play before you use your high card.

Now consider the following situations:

NORTH
A 9 3

SOUTH
Q J 4

Suppose you need two tricks in a hurry. It now becomes proper to lead the Queen, because if West has the King and covers, your Jack immediately becomes good. If he fails to cover, the Queen will win the trick.

NORTH
A J 5

SOUTH
K 4 2

In this example your problem is to win all three tricks. If you are to accomplish this, West must have the Queen. First play the King from the South hand and then lead a low card toward the A-J in the North hand.

If West plays low, you put on the Jack, which will hold the trick if he has the Queen.

Leads toward tenaces

A tenace is a sequence with either one or two of the middle cards missing (A Q, K J, A Q 10, A J 10, K Q 10, etc.). All suits containing a tenace should be led up to, if possible. Thus:

NORTH

K J x

SOUTH

x x x

Here, if you lead twice toward the K J x, you win two tricks if West has both the Ace and Queen. You win one trick if West has either Ace or Queen. But if you lead from the North hand toward the three small cards in the South hand, you may not win any tricks.

NORTH

A Q x

SOUTH

x x x

In this example, you lead toward the North hand from the three small cards in the South hand. If West has the King, you win two tricks. If you lead from the North hand, you can win only one trick.

Now consider the following:

1	2	3
NORTH	NORTH	NORTH
A Q 10	A J 10	A J 9
SOUTH	SOUTH	SOUTH
x x x	x x x	x x x

In the first example, lead twice toward the honors and finesse first the 10 and then the Queen. This will gain one trick in addition to your Ace   *467* when the King is in one hand and the Jack in the other. If West has both King and Jack, you will succeed in capturing all three tricks.

In the second example, lead twice toward the honors, playing the 10 first and then the Jack. This insures your capturing two tricks whenever West has the Queen or King, or both.

In the third example, lead twice toward the honors. Finesse the 9 first and the Jack next. Whenever West holds Queen and 10, or King and 10, or all three, you will succeed in capturing two tricks. Note that it is unsound to play the Jack on the first lead. This will succeed only where West has exactly King, Queen, and small cards.

As an exercise in leading up to various card combinations, here is a complete hand to play:

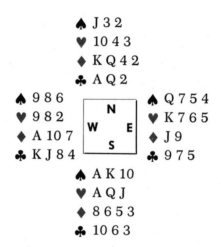

```
                    ♠ J 3 2
                    ♥ 10 4 3
                    ♦ K Q 4 2
                    ♣ A Q 2
      ♠ 9 8 6          N          ♠ Q 7 5 4
      ♥ 9 8 2     W         E     ♥ K 7 6 5
      ♦ A 10 7                    ♦ J 9
      ♣ K J 8 4        S          ♣ 9 7 5
                    ♠ A K 10
                    ♥ A Q J
                    ♦ 8 6 5 3
                    ♣ 10 6 3
```

No Trump is the contract. West leads the 4 of Clubs. We shall provide you with this minor clue: the first correct play from the dummy hand—that is, North—is the 2 of Clubs. You should be able to win twelve tricks with this holding if you play the cards in proper sequence, leading up to your strong-card holdings and taking all necessary finesses.

Entry cards

Even if a player understands the advantage of leading toward certain high-card combinations, he will find himself stymied if the hand from which he wants to lead does not contain a card that can take a trick. In this case he cannot place the lead – that is, gain entry to the weak hand and thereby advantageously lead toward the strong hand.

In formulating your plan as declarer, you must note whether there are sufficient entry cards in the combined hands to let you make the necessary number of leads toward each high-card combination. In a simple case, where one hand holds the Ace and the other the King in the same suit, you obviously have entry into both hands.

There are combinations which contain hidden entries, and a careful player will make good use of them. Here is an example:

NORTH
♠ x x x
♥ x x x
♦ x x x
♣ A K Q 3

SOUTH
♠ A K J
♥ A Q J
♦ K Q x
♣ J 10 9 2

If a Spade is opened, note that it will be advantageous to lead twice toward South's Heart holding and twice toward South's Diamond holding. There are apparently only three cards of entry in the North hand. However, there are five Clubs outstanding, and if these divide three-two, which is normal, they can be picked up in three leads. Therefore, South's first play toward the second trick should be the 9 of Clubs, and North should win with the Queen. The second lead of the Club suit should be the 10 of Clubs which North wins with the King. If both opponents have followed to the two Club leads, there is only one more Club outstanding. Therefore, South can overtake the Jack of Clubs with North's Ace, which will be the third entry card, and now the 3 of Clubs will provide the fourth entry card. This series of plays enables North to lead four times toward the South hand. On the other hand, if North's 3 of Clubs is expended on either Jack, 10, or 9 in the South hand, North will be able to gain the lead only three times.

Similar combinations are the following. If two entry cards are needed in the North hand, how would you play in each case?

1	2
NORTH	NORTH
A 6 4 2	A 5 3 2
SOUTH	SOUTH
K Q 7 3	K 8 6 4

In the first example, whenever the Ace is played from the North hand, the 7 is played from the South hand and not the 3. On the fourth round of the suit, the 6 in the North hand will be an entry card. In the second example, the 4 in the South hand and the 5 in the North hand are carefully conserved for the fourth round of the suit to create a second entry card in the North hand.

When to finesse

The object of finessing is to capture an adverse card which is missing from a tenace held by the declarer. Sometimes the location of that card has become obvious through the bidding or through some accident of the play. In the absence of any clue as to the whereabouts of the missing card, the question of when a finesse should be tried and when it should be passed up is probably best answered as follows:

Assume that the adverse cards in the suit are divided between the opponents as evenly as possible—specifically, that two will be divided one-one; three divided two-one; four, two-two; and five, three-two. Declarer should also assume that in the case of a two-one or three-two division the card to be captured is held by the opponent who is known to have the larger number of cards in the suit, if that information is available.

All of which brings us to this table:

HOLDING	TOTAL CARDS OF SUIT IN DECLARER'S TWO HANDS	PLAY
A Q	Eleven	A
A Q	Ten or less	Q
A K J	Nine or more	K
A K J	Eight or less	J
A Q 10	Nine or ten	Q
A Q 10	Eight or less	10

The double finesse

NORTH

A Q 10 9 2

SOUTH

6 5 3

What is the proper play to realize the maximum number of tricks with this holding?

The correct procedure is for South to play a low card, intending to finesse the 9 in the dummy hand. If this succeeds in driving out the King, your troubles are over. If the 9 loses to the Jack, the declarer's hand is re-entered and the finesse is repeated, hoping that West now holds the King. Note that when West holds either King or Jack declarer will succeed in winning four tricks, and when West holds both honors, declarer will succeed in winning all five tricks.

Some elementary plays

1	2	3
DUMMY	DUMMY	DUMMY
Q 7	Q 10 3	Q 7 3
DECLARER	DECLARER	DECLARER
A 8 2	A 7 2	A 8 2

In the above diagrams you are South, declarer, at No Trump. West leads the 5 of the suit. What card do you play from dummy?

In the first diagram, obviously the Queen must be played. Your only hope is that West is leading from the King and that the Queen will hold. If it does not win this trick, it can never win a later one, for it will now be alone. If you play the 7 from dummy, East will not play the King even if he has it, so that either a 9, 10, or Jack will force your Ace.

In No. 2, the 10 is the proper play, in the hope that it will force the King from East. You will thereupon win with your Ace and the Queen will be high. If the 10 is covered by the Jack, you will win with the Ace and, 471 hoping that West has the King, you will then lead toward the Queen, expecting to win a trick with it.

In No. 3, there is no hurry about playing the Queen, because if West has the King, the Queen will still be protected and can be developed into a winning trick later on.

Ducking

1	2	3
DUMMY	DUMMY	DUMMY
♠ A K 7 6 3	A 9 7 6 3	A Q 2
DECLARER	DECLARER	DECLARER
♠ 5 4	5 4 2	10 6 3

In No. 1, assume that you are playing a No-Trump contract and that the North hand has no other entry cards. You are anxious to take four tricks in dummy's suit. How is this to be done? Since your opponents have six Spades, your only hope is that each of them will have three. If you play the Ace, King, and another, the two remaining Spades will be good, but you will have no means of getting over to dummy to use them. The proper procedure, therefore, is to give the opponents their trick at the beginning rather than at the end. Play a small card from dummy, allowing the opponents to win the first trick. If the suit then does divide three-three, the Ace and King left in dummy will clear the suit and you will be able to take four tricks.

In No. 2, assume that you need three tricks in the suit shown with no other entry cards in the North hand. Since the opponents have five cards between them, including K Q J 10, you will have to lose two tricks in the suit. Permit the opponents to win the first two tricks, saving your Ace. If the suit divides three-two, the Ace, played on the third trick, will pick up the remaining card and you will be able to make three tricks in the suit.

In No. 3, West leads the 4 of the suit. The correct play from dummy is the deuce. This is the one way to make all three tricks in case West has both the King and the Jack. If West is leading from the King and East has the Jack, nothing is lost, because the finesse of the Queen can be taken next time. If West is leading from the Jack and East has the King, the gain is obvious.

The hold-up

The hold-up play consists of refusing to take a trick early in the hand when advantage can be gained by taking the trick later. It is most frequently employed in No-Trump contracts, but can be used occasionally with profit at a suit declaration.

The purpose in holding up is to run one of the opponents out of a particular suit. In a common application, the declarer holds up with an Ace following the opening lead, refusing to take a trick in that suit until the partner of the opening leader will have no more of the suit to return to him.

Perhaps the best way of demonstrating when to hold up is to cite the converse. Here, then, are the conditions under which the declarer should *not* hold up:

1] When it is apparent that the partner of the opening leader cannot be exhausted of the suit. Thus:

NORTH
5 2

SOUTH
A 8

The opening lead is the 3. In this obvious case, both opponents are known to have more cards than you in the suit led. Since you cannot successfully hold up, you may as well win the first lead.

2] When the hand can be so managed that the leader's partner never will obtain the lead.

3] When there is a greater menace in the hand in the form of a shift to some other suit by the leader's partner. For example:

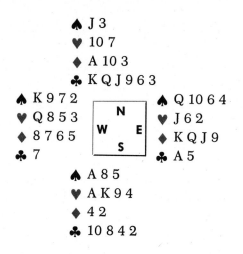

♠ J 3
♥ 10 7
♦ A 10 3
♣ K Q J 9 6 3

♠ K 9 7 2   ♠ Q 10 6 4
♥ Q 8 5 3   ♥ J 6 2
♦ 8 7 6 5   ♦ K Q J 9
♣ 7   ♣ A 5

♠ A 8 5
♥ A K 9 4
♦ 4 2
♣ 10 8 4 2

South is the declarer at a contract of 3 No Trump. West leads the 2 of Spades, the Jack is played from dummy, and East plays the Queen. Unless West is false-carding, he has only four Spades and there is no danger in the hand. If East is permitted to win the trick, he may shift to Diamonds, which would defeat the contract. The first trick, therefore, should be taken.

4] When declarer can see that he is able to insure the contract by taking the trick.

5] When by not holding up declarer can develop an additional trick out of lower cards in the suit. Here are two illustrations:

1	2
DUMMY	DUMMY
♠ J 2	♠ 9 3
DECLARER	DECLARER
♠ A 10 3	♠ A 10 8 2

In example No. 1, West leads the 5 of Spades. Dummy plays the 2, and East plays the Queen. It would be absurd for South to hold up, because he would then be able to take only one trick in the suit, whereas if he takes the Queen with the Ace, he is assured of an additional trick, because the Jack will drive out the King and thus establish the 10.

In example No. 2, West leads the 5 of Spades. Dummy plays the 3; East plays the Queen. It would be unsound to hold up, because by taking the first trick declarer is assured of another trick, inasmuch as the 8 and 9 will drive out the Jack and King, establishing the 10 as a winner.

Now for some cases in which the hold-up is advisable.

DUMMY

4 3 2

DECLARER

A J 5

In this situation, if West leads the King—assuming that there is no other suit that South is worried about—he should permit West to hold the trick, for if the suit is continued, declarer will now win with both the Jack and the Ace.

Here is a full-hand illustration of the most common type of hold-up:

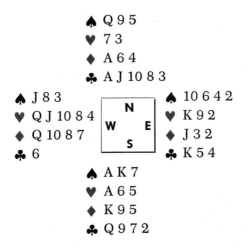

♠ Q 9 5
♥ 7 3
♦ A 6 4
♣ A J 10 8 3

♠ J 8 3
♥ Q J 10 8 4
♦ Q 10 8 7
♣ 6

♠ 10 6 4 2
♥ K 9 2
♦ J 3 2
♣ K 5 4

♠ A K 7
♥ A 6 5
♦ K 9 5
♣ Q 9 7 2

You are South; the contract is 3 No Trump. West leads the Queen of Hearts. This is the suit which you fear may defeat your contract. If you take the first trick and lose the lead, the opponents will cash four Heart tricks and the King of Clubs. You refuse, therefore, to take the Heart trick until the third round, hoping that by this time East will have no more Hearts. Now if the Club finesse loses to East, he will be unable to return his partner's suit. You are able, therefore, to take the rest of the tricks yourself. Note that if you had taken the first or second Heart, East would have had one left to return to his partner when he won with the King of Clubs.

Holding up with a double stopper

As a general rule, when two key cards need to be dislodged, and you hold two stoppers in the suit led and do not fear a shift, it is good policy to refuse the first trick.

Here is an illustration:

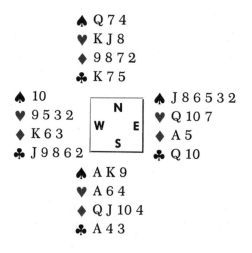

♠ Q 7 4
♥ K J 8
♦ 9 8 7 2
♣ K 7 5

♠ 10
♥ 9 5 3 2
♦ K 6 3
♣ J 9 8 6 2

♠ J 8 6 5 3 2
♥ Q 10 7
♦ A 5
♣ Q 10

♠ A K 9
♥ A 6 4
♦ Q J 10 4
♣ A 4 3

You are South, at a contract of 3 No Trump. West leads the 6 of Clubs; East plays the Queen. You should permit the Queen to hold. The suit will be continued. You win and drive out the Ace of Diamonds, but East has no Clubs to return. If West wins the first Diamond trick, his Club suit will become harmless, because he will have no entry card permitting him to use them. Observe that if you hold up on the second lead of Clubs instead of the first you cannot make the hand.

Safety plays

The safety play is just what the name indicates. It means protection against a bad break, a method of play calculated to hold your losses in a particular suit within certain limits in the event of unforeseen distribution.

Let us assume that to fulfill your contract you need three tricks. It would be extremely unwise for you to attempt, by a risky play, to win more than this if there were a safer way to win the three tricks needed. That is the theory of the safety play. Many times, in a safety play, one trick is sacrificed in order to run the least possible risk of losing two tricks. Here is a simple illustration:

DUMMY

A Q 10 8 2

DECLARER

9 6 5 3

In this situation, if you needed five tricks in the suit, you would hope that West held the King and one other, and you would lead from the South hand and finesse the Queen. But let us suppose that you need only four tricks in this suit to fulfill your contract. Assume that you play in the same manner. If the Queen loses to the King, what do you do next time? If you play the Ace, it may turn out that East is now void and you lose to West's Jack. To guard against such a mischance, the absolute insurance play is the Ace first. If East has either honor alone or both honors alone, your troubles are over. If two small cards fall on the first trick, you re-enter your hand and play toward the Queen. If West follows, it must be with either the Jack or King, and again your troubles are over. If West shows out, you will lose two tricks, but then nothing could ever have been done about it. You would have had to lose two tricks in any event.

Sometimes a safety play costs nothing:

DUMMY

A 9 4 3

DECLARER

K Q 10 7 5

Having nine cards, you can lose a trick in the suit only if one opponent has all four, including the Jack. If, however, you find out which one has the four cards, you can finesse against the Jack either way. Therefore, the safety play is to lead first the King from the South hand. If West shows out, the 10 can subsequently be finessed against East. If East shows out, then the 9 can be finessed in the North hand. Of course, if both follow to the first trick, there will be no problem.

A slight variation of the above is the following:

DUMMY
K 9 6 5

DECLARER
A Q 8 7 4

Can you possibly lose a trick with this combination? The answer is yes, if one of the opponents has all four outstanding cards. Can you do anything about it? If West has them, nothing can be done about it; if East has them, both honors may be captured. Play the King from dummy first, and two subsequent finesses against East will enable you to pick up the entire suit.

Ruffing

As a general principle, it is not profitable for declarer to use up his own trumps for the purpose of ruffing losing cards. The theory of the ruff is to make a trick with a trump which would otherwise be useless. Where the dummy has small trumps, and one or more of dummy's trumps can be used separately before trumps are drawn, they will be tricks in addition to the trump tricks in the declarer's hand. The following will illustrate:

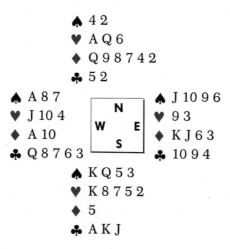

♠ 4 2
♥ A Q 6
♦ Q 9 8 7 4 2
♣ 5 2

♠ A 8 7   ♠ J 10 9 6
♥ J 10 4   ♥ 9 3
♦ A 10   ♦ K J 6 3
♣ Q 8 7 6 3   ♣ 10 9 4

♠ K Q 5 3
♥ K 8 7 5 2
♦ 5
♣ A K J

South is declarer; Hearts are trumps. West opens a Club. It will be seen that South can lead Spades, and after West takes his Ace, South can ruff a third round of Spades with dummy's 6. The 6 of Hearts has no value as a high card but can be used to save this loser.

South could also ruff his last Spade, but it would not save a trick, for he would use dummy's Queen of Hearts to ruff it, and the Heart Queen is needed to draw the opponents' trumps.

Preventing the dangerous lead

There are many cases in which it would be extremely dangerous to have one adversary lead a particular suit through you. You must, if at all possible, play the hand so as to prevent that opponent from getting in to lead. For example:

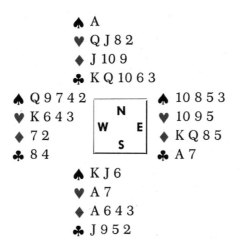

♠ A
♥ Q J 8 2
♦ J 10 9
♣ K Q 10 6 3

♠ Q 9 7 4 2   ♠ 10 8 5 3
♥ K 6 4 3   ♥ 10 9 5
♦ 7 2   ♦ K Q 8 5
♣ 8 4   ♣ A 7

♠ K J 6
♥ A 7
♦ A 6 4 3
♣ J 9 5 2

South is declarer at a contract of 3 No Trump. West leads the 4 of Spades. What is declarer's next play? At first glance it might seem that the Ace of Clubs should be driven out without delay. But this will result in East's obtaining the lead and returning the Spade suit through your K-J.

What you must do is to make sure that East does not obtain the lead too soon. West can be given the lead with safety, since, if he leads Spades, it will be up to declarer's K-J. The proper play is the Queen of Hearts. If the finesse should win, the Ace of Clubs is immediately driven out and nine tricks are assured. If the finesse loses to West, he is unable to continue Spades profitably; declarer has time to drive out the Ace of Clubs and still is assured of nine tricks.

WHEN defending against a contract, communication between partners is extremely important. Even with a completely useless hand, you sometimes can be of great assistance to the defense by giving your partner information that he needs. You give him information by the size of the card you play to the various tricks. These are known as signals. They may be red, meaning "Stop"; they may be green, meaning "Go ahead"; and they may be yellow, meaning "Not quite sure."

Generally speaking, the discard of a 6 or a higher card encourages partner to continue the suit led, and the discard of a lower card discourages continuance of the suit. If you wish to encourage partner, you should signal with the highest card you can spare. For example, assuming that you hold K 8 6 2, if partner leads the Ace and you urgently desire the suit continued, you should signal with the 8 rather than the 6, to make your message more emphatic.

Signaling at No Trump

Here are typical situations calling for a signal at No Trump. In each case your partner, West, leads the Queen. What card should you play?

DUMMY

6   EAST

K 8 4

The answer here is definitely the 8. Your partner is leading from either the Q J 10 or Q J 9, and you must encourage him to continue the suit.

DUMMY

6   EAST

8 7 4

East should play the 4, a discouraging signal. If West's suit is solid, such as Q J 10 9, he will not need encouragement and will go ahead with the suit anyhow.

Signals at suit play

The following hands are at suit play. You are East and your partner leads the King of Hearts.

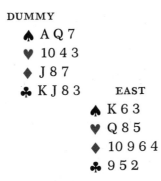

DUMMY
♠ A Q 7
♥ 10 4 3
♦ J 8 7
♣ K J 8 3

EAST
♠ K 6 3
♥ Q 8 5
♦ 10 9 6 4
♣ 9 5 2

You should signal with the 8, because you wish your partner to continue with three rounds of that suit.

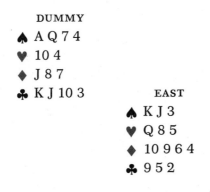

DUMMY
♠ A Q 7 4
♥ 10 4
♦ J 8 7
♣ K J 10 3

EAST
♠ K J 3
♥ Q 8 5
♦ 10 9 6 4
♣ 9 5 2

Here you must not play the 8, because when your partner follows with the Ace you will have to play the 5 and he will think you desire a third round of the suit—which is exactly what you do not want. You desire instead a shift to the Spade suit. Your proper play to the King of Hearts, therefore, is the lowest card you possess, the 5.

481

Discards

Signals may be given when not following suit—that is, when discarding.

The discard of a low card from a suit shows your partner that you are not interested in that suit. But when in discarding you play first a high card and then a low one, you are drawing partner's attention to that suit and calling for its lead. Thus, if you discard the 3 of Spades and then the 5 of Spades, partner will think nothing of it; but if you discard the 5 and then the 3, he will understand that you are asking for a Spade lead.

The trump echo

When a defender follows high-low in trumps, it is a signal to his partner which says: "Partner, I have three trumps and I may be able to ruff something."

If you are defending and you hold only two trumps, you should ruff with the lower. If you hold three or more trumps, the first trick should be ruffed with a card which is not the lowest, and the second should be ruffed with the lowest. This will signal your partner that you have another trump.

Discarding in partner's suit

After having led the highest of partner's suit, it is conventional to discard from the top down. Thus, if you hold 9 6 2 in the suit your partner has bid, and you lead the 9, the 6 should be played next time and finally the 2. At this point your partner will know that you have no more of the suit.

16 Covering honors

AN ANCIENT precept handed down from whist days had it that a player should "always cover an honor with an honor." The rule is today more honored in the breach than the observance.

The question of when to cover and when not to cover an honor is sometimes difficult to decide. The following illustrations may help to clarify the matter:

NORTH

WEST · · · · A J 3

K 10 2

If declarer, South, leads the Queen, it is obvious that West should play the King. If West refuses to cover, declarer will pass the Queen and be able to capture three tricks in the suit. When West covers, the 10 may become promoted to winning rank.

NORTH

Q J 9 · · · · EAST

K 8 3

Declarer leads the Queen from the North hand. As East, should you cover with the King? The answer is no. In covering with the King, you can only hope to produce a trick if your partner, West, holds the 10. But declarer can finesse dummy's 9 against West's 10, and your cover will have been to no avail. When the Jack is led, the King should be played on it, because now if West has the 10 it will be promoted to winning rank.

A good general rule is this: Cover the last honor led from two or more touching honors.

THE LAWS OF BRIDGE

ALONE AMONG CARD *games, bridge is governed
by a world code, formulated and agreed to by
official groups representing the players of many
nations. In the Western Hemisphere, this code
is promulgated by the Laws Commission
established by the American Contract Bridge
League and the Whist Club of New York. Set forth
on the following pages are the International
Laws of Contract Bridge as they apply to rubber
bridge. Duplicate bridge is governed by a
separate international code, identical in so far
as the nature of the game allows. To settle
any question of correct procedure at the card
table, including penalties for improper action
of any kind, these are the authoritative and
unchallengeable regulations of bridge.*

I Definitions

THE PLAYERS

Partner The player with whom one plays as a SIDE against the other two. He occupies the opposite seat at the table.

Opponent A player of the other side.

Declarer The player who for his side first bid the denomination named in the contract.

Dummy Declarer's partner.

Contractor Declarer or dummy.

Defender An opponent of declarer.

HONOR Any Ace, King, Queen, Jack or 10.

HAND The cards originally dealt to a player or the remaining portion thereof.

ROTATION The order of progression applying in the game, which is from player to player clockwise.

DENOMINATION The suit or No-Trump named in a bid.

ODD TRICK A trick won by declarer in excess of six.

CALL A comprehensive term applicable to a bid, a double, a redouble or a pass.

BID An offer to contract to win at least a specified number of odd tricks in a specified denomination.

PASS A call signifying that a player does not, on that occasion, elect to bid, double or redouble.

PLAY   To contribute a card to a trick, including the first card which is the **LEAD**.

TRUMP   Each card of the suit, if any, named in the contract.

FOLLOW SUIT   To play a card of the suit led.

REVOKE   To play a card of another suit when able to follow suit.

OVERTRICK   A trick won by declarer in excess of his contract.

UNDERTRICK   A trick by which declarer falls short of his contract.

SLAMS: *Grand slam*—the winning of thirteen tricks by one side; *little slam*—the winning of twelve tricks by one side.

VULNERABLE   Having won a game toward rubber.

The meaning of the following terms is clarified in the laws: Pack, section 1; Deal, section 8; Contract, section 22-b; Sufficient Bid, Insufficient Bid, section 23; Double and Redouble, sections 24 and 25; Trick, section 47; Penalty Card, sections 67, 68 and 69; Game, section 94; Rubber, section 95.

II The draw, the shuffle, the cut, the deal

The pack—rank of cards and suits

1] Contract Bridge is played by four players with a pack of 52 cards, comprising 13 cards in each of 4 suits. The suits rank downwards in the order—Spades (♠), Hearts (♥), Diamonds (♦), Clubs (♣). The cards of each suit rank downwards in the order—Ace, King, Queen, Jack, 10, 9, 8, 7, 6, 5, 4, 3, 2. When practicable, two packs with distinguishable backs are used.

The draw *

2] Before every rubber, each player draws a card from a shuffled pack spread face downwards on the table. A drawn card should not be exposed until all players have drawn. If a player exposes more than one card, or draws one of the four cards at either end of the pack, or draws a card from the other pack, he must draw again. In drawing, equal cards rank according to suit.

Partnerships

3] The two players who draw the highest cards play as partners against the other two. The player with the highest card deals first and has the right to choose his seat and the pack with which he will deal. He may consult his partner but, having announced his decision, must abide by it. His partner sits opposite him. Thereafter, the opponents may, after consultation, determine their respective occupancy of the two remaining seats.

* If more than four persons desire to play, it is customary to follow the rules for Club Procedure to determine which of them shall have the right to play.

The shuffle

4] The pack for each deal is prepared by the player on the left of its dealer, if practicable while the other pack is being dealt. Preparing a pack consists of collecting the cards, shuffling them, and placing the shuffled pack face downwards on the left of the next dealer. The cards should be shuffled thoroughly and in full view of all players, but without exposing the face of any card.

5] A properly prepared pack should not be disturbed until its dealer picks it up for his deal, at which time he is entitled to the final shuffle. No player may shuffle a pack other than its dealer and the player on his left.

The cut

6] A pack must always be cut immediately before it is dealt. The dealer presents it to the player on his right, who lifts off a portion and places it on the table toward the dealer beside the bottom portion. Each portion must contain at least four cards. The dealer completes the cut by placing the bottom portion uppermost.

New shuffle—new cut

7] Before the first card is dealt, any player may demand a new shuffle or a new cut. There must be a new shuffle and cut if a card is faced in cutting, or if there is a redeal. When there is a new shuffle, only the dealer may shuffle.

The deal

8] The dealer must deal the cards face downwards, one at a time in rotation into four separate hands of 13 cards each, the first card to the player on his left and the last card to himself. If he deals two cards simultaneously or consecutively to the same player, he may rectify the error, provided he does so promptly and to the satisfaction of his opponents.

9] The dealer must not allow the face of any card to be seen while he is dealing. Until the deal is completed, no player may look at the face of any card, and no one but the dealer may touch any card except to correct or preclude an irregularity.

Changing the dealer

10] The turn to deal passes in rotation unless there is a redeal, in which case the same dealer redeals.

Changing the pack

11] The packs should be used alternately unless there is a redeal. The pack originally belonging to a side must be restored if reclaimed, but a deal may not be stopped to restore a pack. A pack containing a distinguishable damaged card must be replaced.

III General laws covering irregularities

Redeal

12] There must be a redeal:

A] If, before the last card is dealt, a redeal is demanded because a player is dealing out of turn or with an uncut pack.

B] If it is ascertained before the last card is dealt that the cards have not been dealt correctly, or that a card is faced in the pack elsewhere.

C] If it is ascertained before the first call is duly made that a player has picked up another player's hand and seen a card in it.

D] If it is ascertained before the cards have been mixed together that one player has picked up too many cards, another too few; or that the pack, when the deal began, did not conform in every respect to the requirements of section 1.

E] If the players have allowed their hands to be mixed together before finding a missing card, or in the belief that a redeal is in order.

There may not be a redeal except as provided above.

Missing card

13] A missing card, when found, is deemed to belong to the deficient hand.

When clause (D) or (E) of section 12 applies, there must be a redeal.

When neither clause applies, the deal stands, and, if the missing card was found in a trick, the defective trick law (section 80 or 81) applies. The missing card may become a penalty card under section 26 or 67, or failure to have played it may constitute a revoke. It must be placed in the deficient hand unless it becomes a penalty card or is found in a trick that stands as played.

Surplus card

14] If a player has too many cards, there must be a redeal unless he has omitted to play to a trick, in which case the defective trick law (section 80 or 81) applies.

Drawing attention to an irregularity

15] When an irregularity is committed, any player (except dummy if he has looked at another player's hand) may draw attention to it and give or obtain information as to the law covering it. The fact that the offending side draws attention to its own irregularity does not in any way affect the rights of the opponents.

Enforcement of a penalty

16] Either opponent individually (but not dummy) may select or enforce a penalty. If the opponents consult as to penalty selection or enforcement, or if either opponent waives the penalty, the right to penalize is canceled; but the rectification provisions (if any) of the applicable section still apply.

17] After attention has been called to an irregularity, no player may call or play until all questions in regard to rectification and penalty enforcement have been determined.

18] The penalty provisions of the laws apply only after agreement on the fact that an irregularity has been committed, and after specific statement of the penalty to be applied.

19] All questions as to what course to follow must be settled by the players before the game continues. A penalty once paid or other action once taken stands, even though at some later time it is discovered to have been incorrect.

Improper remarks and gestures

20] If by a remark or unmistakable gesture a player other than declarer discloses his intentions or desires, or the nature of an unfaced hand, or the presence or absence of a card in an unfaced hand; or improperly suggests a lead, play, or line of play; or improperly directs attention to the cards on a trick to which his partner has yet to play:

A] If the offense occurred before the auction closed (penalty), either opponent may require the offending side to pass whenever it is its turn to call; and if the offending side become defenders, declarer may require or forbid the opening lead of a specified suit.

B] If the offense occurred after the auction closed (penalty), declarer or either defender, as the case may be, may require the offender's partner to withdraw any lead or play which may have been suggested by the improper remark or gesture, and to substitute a card which does not conform to the improper suggestion. This penalty may be exacted on any trick subsequent to the offense but only on one such trick. The offender's partner may not be required to withdraw his card from a trick to which an opponent has played after him. Before this penalty may be enforced, a majority of the players must agree as to what lead, play or line of play has been improperly suggested.

IV The auction

Duration of auction

21] The auction begins when the last card of a correct deal has been placed on the table. The dealer makes the first call, and thereafter each player calls in rotation. After the first call has been made, the auction continues until three players have passed in rotation. This closes the auction.

Procedure after auction is closed

22] After the auction is closed:

A] If no player has bid, the hands are abandoned and the turn to deal passes in rotation.

B] If any player has bid, the last bid becomes the contract and the play begins.

Bids

23] Each bid must name a number of odd tricks, from one to seven, and a denomination, and must supersede any previous bid by naming either a greater number of odd tricks or the same number in a higher denomination. A bid that supersedes the previous bid is sufficient; one that does not is insufficient. The denominations rank downwards in order: No Trump, Spades, Hearts, Diamonds, Clubs.

Doubles and redoubles

24] A player may double only if the last preceding bid was made by an opponent and no call other than a pass has intervened. A player may redouble only if the last preceding call other than a pass was a double by an opponent.

25] All doubles and redoubles are nullified by a proper subsequent bid. If there is no subsequent bid, the scoring value of the contract is increased as provided in section 98.

Card exposed during the auction

26] If during the auction a player faces a card on the table, or sees the face of a card belonging to his partner:

A] If an Ace, King, Queen or Jack, or a lower card prematurely led, or more than one card * (penalty), the owner's partner must pass when next it is his turn to call. Every such card must be left face up on the table until the auction closes; and if its owner is then a defender, it becomes a penalty card.

B] If a single card, lower than a Jack and not prematurely led, there is no penalty.

IMPROPER CALLS †

Improper call prematurely overcalled in rotation

27] If a player calls before the penalty for an improper call by his right-hand opponent has been enforced (see section 17), the auction proceeds as though it had been a proper call; except that if the improper call was a bid of more than 7, or a double or redouble made when only a pass or bid could be a proper call, the auction proceeds as though the improper call had been a pass.

Changing a call

28] If a player changes a call in any way and does so practically in the same breath, his last call stands. There is no penalty unless he has changed

* If two (or more) cards are faced or seen at different times, clause A] applies to both of them even though one has been picked up as provided in clause B].

† All possible improper calls are listed under this heading. Calls not recognized by nor dealt with in these laws are merely improper remarks. The auction proceeds as if an improper remark had not been made, unless the remark is sufficiently informative to warrant the imposition of a penalty under section 20(a).

to an improper call, in which case the appropriate "improper calls" section applies.

29] If a player changes a call in any way, and does not do so practically in the same breath, the change of call is void, and:

A] If the first call was improper, the appropriate "improper calls" section applies.

B] If the first call was a proper call, either the offender must allow his first call to stand, in which case (penalty) his partner must pass when next it is his turn to call; or the offender must substitute any other proper call, in which case (penalty) his partner must pass whenever it is his turn to call.

Insufficient bid

30] If a player makes an insufficient bid, he must substitute either a sufficient bid or a pass.* If he substitutes:

A] The lowest sufficient bid in the same denomination, there is no penalty.

B] Any other bid (penalty), the offender's partner must pass whenever it is his turn to call.

C] A pass (penalty), the offender's partner must pass whenever it is his turn to call; and if the offending side become the defenders, declarer may require or forbid the opening lead of a specified suit.

Call out of rotation

31] A call out of rotation is void. The auction reverts to the player whose turn it is to call, and:

A] If a player has passed out of rotation before any player has bid, or when it was the turn of the opponent on his right to call (penalty), the offender must pass when next it is his turn to call.†

B] If a player has made any call out of rotation other than a pass

---

* As provided in section 18, a player is entitled to select his substituted call after the applicable penalties have been stated. Any call he may have substituted previously is void, unless his left-hand opponent has overcalled it, in which case section 27 applies.

† *Example:* North (dealer) 1 Heart, South pass. The pass is void, and the auction reverts to East. After East has called, South must pass. Thereafter, North and South may in rotation make any proper call.

listed in (A) (penalty), the offender's partner must pass whenever it is his turn to call.*

32] A call is not out of rotation when made without waiting for the right-hand opponent to pass, if he is required to pass because of a law infringement.

33] If a player, whose turn it was to call, calls before attention has been drawn to a call out of rotation by his left-hand opponent, the auction proceeds as though that opponent had not called.

Simultaneous calls

34] A call made simultaneously with another player's proper call is deemed to be a subsequent call.

Naming bid incorrectly in doubling †

35] If a player in doubling or redoubling names an incorrect number of tricks or a wrong denomination, he is deemed to have doubled or redoubled the bid as made.

Doubling when the only proper call is a pass or bid

36] If a player doubles or redoubles a bid which his side has already doubled or redoubled (penalty), he must substitute any proper call, and his partner must pass whenever it is his turn to call. In addition, if the offender elects to pass, either opponent may cancel all previous doubles and redoubles.

37] If a player doubles his partner's bid, redoubles an undoubled bid, or doubles or redoubles when there has been no bid (penalty), the offender must substitute any proper call, and his partner must pass whenever it is his turn to call.

---

* *Example:* North (dealer) 1 Heart, South 1 Spade. The 1-Spade bid is void, and the auction reverts to East. After East has called, South may make any proper call. Thereafter, North must pass whenever it is his turn to call, but South may make any proper call whenever it is his turn to call.

† It is improper to state the number of tricks or the denomination in doubling.

Bid, double or redouble when required to pass; bid of more than 7

38] If a player bids more than 7, or bids, doubles or redoubles when required by law to pass: the offender is deemed to have passed, and (penalty) the offending side must pass whenever it is its turn to call, and if the offender becomes a defender, declarer may require or forbid the opening lead of a specified suit.

Doubly improper call

39] If a player makes a call subject to penalty under two or more "improper calls" sections, either section may be applied but not both.

Call after the auction is closed

40] A call made after the auction is closed is canceled. If it is a pass by a defender, or any call by a contractor, there is no penalty. If it is a bid, double or redouble by a defender (penalty), declarer may require or forbid the other defender to lead a specified suit when first it is the latter's turn to lead.

REVIEWING THE AUCTION

41] A player who does not hear a call distinctly may forthwith require it to be repeated. There is no redress for a call based on a misunderstanding or on misinformation.

42] A player is entitled to have previous calls restated either when it is his turn to call, or after the auction closes but before the opening lead has been duly made. His request should be responded to only by an opponent. Dummy, or a player required by law to pass, should not ask to have calls restated, but may review the auction at an opponent's request and should correct errors in restatement.

43] After the opening lead, calls may not be restated, but declarer or a defender is entitled to be informed what the contract is and whether, but not by whom, it was doubled or redoubled.

V The play

Commencement of play

44] After the auction closes, the defender on declarer's left makes the opening lead. After the opening lead dummy spreads his hand in front of him on the table, face up and grouped in suits with the trumps on his right. Declarer plays both of the contractors' hands.

Dummy's rights

45] Dummy should refrain from all comment and from taking any active part in the play, except that he may:

A] Give or obtain information as to fact or law.

B] Question players regarding revokes as provided in section 71.

C] Draw attention to an irregularity, or try to prevent one apparently about to be committed.*

Dummy forfeits these rights if he looks at a card in another player's hand.

Dummy's limitations

46] Dummy should not exchange hands with declarer, lean over to see a defender's cards, leave his seat to watch declarer play, or, on his own initiative, look at the face of a card in any other player's hand. If dummy, as a result of any such act, sees a card in any other player's hand, and thereafter:

A] Is the first to draw attention to a defender's irregularity, declarer may not enforce any penalty for the offense.

* *Example:* He may warn declarer against leading from the wrong hand, but only when it is apparent that declarer is about to do so.

B] Warns declarer not to lead from the wrong hand (penalty), either defender may choose the hand from which declarer shall lead.

C] Is the first to ask declarer if a play from his hand constitutes a revoke, and the revoke card is consequently withdrawn (penalty), either defender may require declarer to substitute his highest or lowest correct card.

LEADS AND PLAYS

The sequence and procedure of play

47] The leader to a trick may play any card in his hand. After a lead, each other hand in rotation plays a card, and the four cards so played constitute a trick.

48] In playing to a trick, each player must if possible follow suit. This obligation overrides all other requirements of the laws. If unable to follow suit, a player may play any card.

49] A trick containing a trump is won by the hand playing the highest trump. A trick that does not contain a trump is won by the hand playing the highest card of the suit led. The hand winning a trick leads to the next trick.

Played card

50] A card in any hand is played when named as the one a player proposes to play; but a player may change his designation if he does so practically in the same breath.

51] A card in any unfaced hand is played when it touches the table face upwards after being detached from the remaining cards with apparent intent to play; a defender's card so detached is also played as soon as his partner sees its face.

52] A card in dummy or any other faced hand is played when touched, unless for a purpose other than play either manifest or mentioned.

Taking back played card

53] A played card may not be withdrawn except:

A] To comply with a penalty.

B] To correct a revoke.

C] To correct the error of playing more than one card to a trick.

D] To substitute another card after an opponent has corrected either a revoke or a failure to comply with a lead or play penalty.

Premature lead or play by a defender

54] If a defender leads to the next trick before his partner has played to the current trick, or plays out of rotation before his partner has played (penalty), declarer may require the offender's partner to play:

A] His highest card of the suit led; or

B] His lowest card of the suit led; or

C] A card of another specified suit.

If declarer has played from both contractors' hands, a defender is not subject to penalty for playing before his partner.

Lead out of turn

55] A lead out of turn may be treated as a correct lead. It must be so treated if the non-offending side plays a card before attention is drawn to the irregularity.*

56] If either defender requires declarer to retract his lead out of turn, the card wrongly led is replaced without penalty; and if declarer has led from the wrong hand, he must lead from the correct hand and (penalty), if he can, a card of the same suit. A defender's drawing attention to declarer's lead out of turn is equivalent to requiring its retraction.

57] If declarer requires a defender to retract his lead out of turn:

A] If it was a contractor's turn to lead, declarer leads from the correct hand and the card led out of turn becomes a penalty card.

* If, after an opening lead by the wrong defender, declarer exposes his hand, see section 65.

B] If it was the other defender's turn to lead (penalty), declarer may forbid the lead of that suit, in which case the card wrongly led is picked up; or may treat the card led out of turn as a penalty card, in which case any card may be led.

Simultaneous leads or plays

58] A lead or play made simultaneously with another player's proper lead or play is deemed to be subsequent to it. If a defender leads or plays two or more cards simultaneously, he may play either card, and the other card becomes a penalty card.

Inability to lead or play as required

59] If a player is unable to lead or play as required to comply with a penalty, either because he has no card of the required suit or because of his obligation to follow suit, he may play any correct card. The penalty is satisfied, except in the case of a penalty card, which must be played at the first legal opportunity.

Playing before penalty has been enforced

60] If declarer plays from either hand before enforcing a lead or play penalty, he is deemed to waive the penalty.

61] If a defender plays to a contractor's lead out of turn after declarer has been required to retract it, the defender's card becomes a penalty card.

62] A play by a member of the offending side, before a penalty has been enforced, does not affect the right of the non-offending side to enforce a penalty.

EXPOSED CARDS

Declarer exposing cards

63] Declarer is never subject to penalty for exposure of a card, and no card of declarer's ever becomes a penalty card.

64] If declarer plays more than one card he must designate which is his play, and must restore any other card to his hand.

65] If declarer exposes his hand after an opening lead by the wrong defender, and before dummy has spread any part of his hand, dummy becomes declarer.

66] If declarer intentionally exposes his hand otherwise than as provided in the preceding section, it is treated as a claim or concession of tricks and section 88 applies.

Defender exposing cards

67] If a defender faces a card on the table, or sees the face of a card belonging to his partner before he is entitled to see it in the normal course of play or penalty enforcement: any such card becomes a penalty card, except as otherwise provided in these laws.*

Disposition of a penalty card

68] A penalty card must be left face upward on the table until played. A defender should not pick up a penalty card and restore it to his hand; but if he does so, and if declarer plays from his own hand or dummy before requiring that the card be faced on the table again, such card ceases to be a penalty card.

69] A penalty card must be played at the first opportunity, whether in leading, following suit, discarding or trumping. The play of a penalty card is always subject to the obligation to follow suit, or to comply with a lead or play penalty. If a defender can play two or more penalty cards, declarer may designate which one is to be played.

---

* Exceptions to section 67: A card led out of turn may be treated as a correct lead (section 55) or may be picked up (section 57-b). An exposed card may not be treated as a penalty card if dummy improperly (section 46-a) draws attention to it, or to the irregularity that caused its exposure.

Defender improperly exposing his hand

70] If a defender improperly exposes his remaining card or cards, declarer may treat the remaining cards of either defender as penalty cards. The hand of the other defender, if exposed, may be picked up.

THE REVOKE*

Inquiries regarding a revoke

71] Any player, including dummy, may ask a player who has failed to follow suit whether he has a card of the suit led, and may demand that an opponent correct his revoke.

Correcting a revoke

72] A player must correct his revoke—

A] Made in any of the first eleven tricks, if aware of it before it becomes established.

B] Made in the twelfth trick, if aware of it before the cards have been mixed together. There is no penalty for a revoke made in the twelfth trick and it never becomes established.

73] To correct a revoke, the offender withdraws the revoke card and follows suit with any card. A revoke card from a defender's unfaced hand becomes a penalty card; any other revoke card may be replaced without penalty. The non-offending side may withdraw any card it played after the revoke but before attention was drawn to it.

Acts that establish a revoke

74] A revoke in any of the first eleven tricks becomes established when the offender or his partner leads or plays to a subsequent trick or signifies his intention of doing so by naming a card, by claiming or conceding a trick, or by exposing a hand.

---

* The penalty provisions of the revoke law are subject to section 46 if dummy has forfeited his rights. A claim of revoke does not warrant inspection of turned tricks except as permitted in sections 78 and 79.

Procedure when a revoke is established

75] When a revoke is established, the revoke trick stands as played. It counts in transferring tricks as a trick won "after the revoke."

76] If a revoke becomes established, after play ceases two tricks are transferred to the non-offending side if the revoking side has won two or more tricks after the revoke. One trick only is transferred if the revoking side wins but one trick after the revoke. There is no penalty for an established revoke:

A] If the revoking side wins no trick after the revoke.

B] If it is a subsequent revoke in the same suit by the same player.

C] If attention is first drawn to it after the cards have been mixed together.

D] If it is made in failing to play any card faced on the table, including a card from dummy's hand or a penalty card.

TRICKS

Gathering and arranging tricks

77] Each completed trick must be gathered and turned face down on the table by the side winning it. The cards of each turned trick should be kept together so that the trick can be readily identified. All the tricks taken by a side should be arranged together in front of declarer or of one defender in such manner that their number and sequence are apparent.

Inspecting tricks; mixing cards before a claim is settled

78] Declarer or either defender may, until his side has led or played a card to the next trick, inspect a trick and inquire what card each hand has played to it. Except as above provided or to account for a surplus or missing card, turned tricks may be inspected before play ceases only with the other side's consent.

79] After play ceases, the tricks and unplayed cards may be inspected to settle a claim of a revoke or of honors, or the number of tricks won or lost. If, after such claim, an opponent so mixes the cards that the claim cannot be proved, it must be allowed.

Defective trick

80] If a hand has played too many cards to a trick, or has omitted to play to it, and if attention is drawn to the irregularity before a player of each side has played to the next trick, the error must be rectified. A card withdrawn from a defective trick, if played from a defender's unfaced hand, becomes a penalty card.

81] If attention is drawn to a defective trick after a player of each side has played to the next trick, the defective trick stands as played, and:

A] A hand with too few cards plays the hand out with fewer cards than the other hands, does not play to the final trick (or tricks), and if it wins a trick with its last card the lead passes in rotation.

B] A hand with too many cards forthwith faces and adds to the defective trick (but without changing its ownership) a card it could properly have played to it.

Trick appropriated in error

82] A trick appropriated by the wrong side must be restored on demand to the side that played the winning card, and, in any case, its scoring value must be credited to that side, subject to section 93.

FAILURE TO COMPLY WITH A LEAD OR PLAY PENALTY

83] If a player is able to lead or play a penalty card, or a card or suit specified by an opponent in conformity with an agreed penalty, but instead plays an incorrect card:

A] The offender must correct his error if aware of it before he or his partner plays another card. If the incorrect card was played from a defender's unfaced hand, it becomes a penalty card. A card played from the hand on the offender's left may be withdrawn if it was played after the error and before attention was drawn to it.

B] After the offender or his partner has played another card, the incorrect card may not be withdrawn. After play ceases (penalty), there is a transfer of tricks to the non-offending side as though the offense were an established revoke (section 76).

CLAIMS AND CONCESSIONS

Concession of trick which cannot be lost

84] The concession of a trick which cannot be lost by any play of the cards is void if attention is called to the error before the cards have been mixed together.

Concession of trick which has been won

85] If a player concedes a trick he has in fact won (as by claiming nine tricks when his side has already won ten, or conceding defeat of a contract his side has fulfilled), the concession is void. If the score has been entered it may be corrected as provided in section 93.

Defender claiming or conceding tricks

86] A defender may show any or all of his remaining cards to declarer for the purpose of establishing a claim or concession. If a defender makes a claim or concession in any other manner, he may be liable to penalty under section 20.

87] A concession of tricks by a defender is not valid unless his partner accedes. This provision does not preclude the enforcement of a penalty for a defender's irregularity.

Declarer claiming or conceding tricks

88] If declarer intentionally exposes his hand, specifically claims or concedes one or more of the remaining tricks, or suggests that play may be curtailed, it is deemed to be a claim by declarer, and:

507

A] Play should cease; and declarer should place and leave his hand face upwards on the table and forthwith make an adequate statement of his intended line of play.

B] At any time after declarer's claim a defender may face his hand and may suggest a play to his partner. Declarer may not enforce any penalty for an irregularity committed by a defender whose hand is so faced.

C] Declarer's claim must be allowed if both defenders accede to it, or if either defender allows his hand to be mixed with other cards.

D] Either defender may require that play continue, in which case section 89 applies.

89] If either defender requires that play continue after declarer's claim, declarer must play on, leaving his hand face upwards on the table. Declarer may make no play inconsistent with any statement he may have made. Unless declarer has stated his intention to do so at the time of making his claim:

A] He may not lead a trump while either defender has a trump.

B] He may not finesse either in the suit led or in trumping the suit led. If declarer attempts to make a play prohibited by this section, either defender may require him to withdraw it, provided neither defender has played a card after it.

VI The score

Keeping score

90] Each side has a trick score and a premium score. The scores of the respective sides for each rubber should be entered in two adjacent vertical columns, the trick points in descending order below a horizontal line separating the trick and premium scores, the premium points (i.e., all points other than trick points) in ascending order above this line. A scorer should enter scores made by his side in the left-hand column. Whenever a game is scored, a line should be drawn across the trick score of both sides and underneath all trick point entries made in that game, none of which carry over to the next game. Subsequent trick points should be entered only below lines so drawn. Lines drawn prematurely should be forthwith erased.

Recording the score

91] When play ceases, all four players are equally responsible to see that the number of tricks won by each side is correctly determined, and that all scores are promptly and correctly entered in the score or scores, in accordance with the scoring table (section 98).

Scoring transferred tricks

92] A transferred trick ranks for all scoring purposes as a trick won in play by the side receiving it.

Correcting the score

93] A proven or admitted error in any score may be corrected at any time before the rubber score is agreed, except that: If each player keeping

509

score has made an error in entering or failing to enter a part score, or in omitting to score a game or in awarding one; such an error may not be corrected after the last card of the second succeeding correct deal has been dealt, unless a majority of the players consent.

A game—the rubber

94] A game is won by the side which first scores a total of 100 or more trick points for odd tricks bid and won.

95] A rubber ends when a side has won two games, and the winners of the final game add to their score: 500 points if their opponents have won one game, 700 points if their opponents have not won a game. At the end of the rubber the trick and premium points of each side are added. The side with the larger total score wins the rubber, irrespective of the number of games (if any) which it has won. The difference between the two totals represents the number of points won.

Effect of incorrect pack

96] Scores made as a result of hands played with an incorrect pack are not affected by the discovery of the imperfection after the cards have been mixed together.

Scoring an unfinished rubber; player obliged to leave

97] If for any reason a rubber is not finished, the score is computed as follows: If but one game has been completed, the winners of that game score 300 points; if but one side has a part score (or scores) in an unfinished game, that side scores 50 points; the trick and premium points of each side are added, and the side with the larger total score wins the difference between the two totals.

98]

	Odd Tricks Bid and Won in	Undoubled	Doubled
TRICK POINTS FOR CONTRACTORS	Clubs or Diamonds, each	20	40
	Hearts or Spades, each	30	60
	No Trump { first	40	80
	each subsequent	30	60

Redoubling doubles the doubled points for Odd Tricks.
Vulnerability does not affect points for Odd Tricks.
100 Trick Points constitute a game.

		Not Vulnerable	Vulnerable
PREMIUM POINTS FOR CONTRACTORS	Overtricks		
	Undoubled, each	Trick Value	Trick Value
	Doubled, each	100	200
	Making Doubled or Redoubled Contract	50	50
PREMIUM POINTS FOR DEFENDERS	Undertricks		
	Undoubled, each	50	100
	Doubled { first	100	200
	each subsequent	200	300

Redoubling doubles the doubled points for Overtricks and Undertricks, but does not affect the points for making Doubled Contracts.

PREMIUM POINTS FOR CONTRACTORS — HOLDERS	Honors in One Hand	{ 4 Trump Honors	100
		5 Trump Honors or 4 Aces at No-Trump	150
	Slams Bid and Won	{ Little, not vulnerable 500, vulnerable	750
		Grand, not vulnerable 1000, vulnerable	1500
	Rubber Points	{ Two game	700
		Three game	500

Unfinished Rubber—Winners of one game score 300 points. If but one side has a part score in an unfinished game, it scores 50 points.
Doubling and Redoubling do not affect Honor, Slam, or Rubber points.
Vulnerability does not affect points for Honors.

THE PROPRIETIES

1] It is reprehensible to profit by information gained as a result of an irregularity committed by one's own side for which no penalty, or a penalty incommensurate with the information gained, is prescribed.

2] It is improper to infringe a law deliberately, as by making an insufficient bid, whether or not a penalty is prescribed.

3] A player should refrain from:
 a] Varying the formulae used in calling; *
 b] Calling with special emphasis, inflection or intonation;
 c] Passing or doubling with exceptional haste or reluctance;
 d] Making a call with undue delay which may result in conveying improper information to partner;
 e] Indicating in any way approval or disapproval of partner's call or play;
 f] Giving by word, manner or gesture an indication of the nature of the hand held;
 g] Making a remark or gesture or asking a question from which an inference may be drawn;
 h] Giving unauthorized information as to an incident of the auction or play;
 i] Volunteering information which should be given only in response to a question;
 j] Requesting, except for his own benefit, a review of calls or a placing of cards played to a trick;
 k] An unnecessary hesitation, remark or mannerism which may deceive the opponents;
 l] Attracting attention to the score, except when necessary to do so for his own information;
 m] Calling attention to the number of tricks needed to complete or defeat the contract or to the fact that it has already been fulfilled or defeated;

---

* The recommended calling formulae are: "Pass" (avoid "I pass" or "no bid"); "1 Heart (avoid "I bid"); "1 No Trump" (avoid "without" or "without a trump"); "double" (avoid stating the number of tricks or the denomination doubled); "6 Spades" (avoid "little slam").

n] Playing a card with special emphasis;

o] Playing with undue delay when the play does not need consideration;

p] Preparing to gather a trick before all four hands have played to it;

q] Detaching a card from his hand before it is his turn to lead or play;

r] Failing to keep the tricks in correct order and distinct from one another, or allowing some to be placed on the opposite side of the table;

s] Watching the place in a player's hand from which he draws a card, and drawing any inference therefrom;

t] Making gratuitous comments during the play as to the auction, the adequacy of the contract or the nature of the hand.

4] It is improper to attempt to conceal a revoke by revoking again, or to conceal a revoke card if a hand is not played out, but there is no obligation to call attention to an established revoke or other irregularity committed by self or partner.

5] It is improper to play out of turn, carelessly or otherwise.

6] While it is reprehensible to allow partner's hesitation, remark or manner to influence a call, lead or play, it is proper to draw inferences from an opponent's gratuitous hesitation, remark or manner, but such inferences are drawn at one's own risk.

7] It is proper to warn partner against infringing a law of the game (e. g., against revoking, or against calling, leading or playing out of turn).

8] All four players are responsible to see that each hand plays a card, and but one, to each trick, and should forthwith correct such an irregularity.

9] Declarer should play out all hands in which there is any doubt as to the eventual outcome.

10] Bystanders or members not playing should refrain from making gratuitous remarks. They should not call attention to any irregularity or mistake, or speak on any question of fact or law except when requested to give an opinion.

11] It is improper to employ, without explaining its meaning to the opponents, a convention in calling or an unusual convention in play, the significance of which may not be clear to them. When applied to a call, the term convention covers a call designed to convey an arbitrary or artificial meaning, or used by a player with the assurance that his partner will not accept it in its natural sense. Such a call is not subject to penalty as an improper remark. It is necessary that a convention so used should be fully understood by the other side, and players using convention calls should be ready to reply fully to a proper inquiry by an opponent as to their meaning or use. Should it be necessary to make such an inquiry during the auction, the partner of the player who has made the convention call should reply. The committee of any Association, Tournament or Club, or a group of persons playing Contract Bridge, may prohibit or restrict the use of conventions which are both generally unrecognized and sufficiently intricate to cause unreasonable delay.

RULES FOR CLUB PROCEDURE

The following rules, governing membership in new and existing tables, have proved satisfactory in club use over a long period of years:

Definitions

MEMBER   An applicant who has acquired the right to play at a table either immediately or in his turn.

COMPLETE TABLE   A table with six members.

INCOMPLETE TABLE   A table with four or five members.

Time limit on right to play

A] An applicant may not play in a rubber unless he has become a member of a table before a card is duly drawn for the selection of players or partners.

Newly formed tables

B] If there are more than six applicants, the six highest-ranking ones become members. The four highest-ranking members play the first rubber. Those who have not played, ranked in their order of entry into the room, take precedence over those who have played. The latter rank equally, except that players leaving existing tables to join the new table rank lowest.*

Existing tables

C] An application establishes membership in a table either forthwith or (if the table is complete) as soon as a vacancy occurs, unless applications in excess of the number required to complete a table are made at the same time, in which case precedence between applicants is established as in the preceding rule.

D] After each rubber place must be made, by the member who has played the greatest number of consecutive rubbers at that table, for any member who did not play the last rubber, except that a member who has left another existing table must draw cards for the right to play his first rubber with the member who would otherwise have played.

E] If a member breaks up a game by leaving three players at a table, he is not entitled to compete against them for entry at another table.

Membership limited to one table

F] No one can be a member of more than one table at the same time, unless a member consents, on request, to make a fourth at another table and announces his intention of returning to his former table as soon as his place can be filled. Failure to announce such intention results in loss of membership at his former table.

* Precedence between those of equal rank is determined by drawing cards, the drawer of the higher-ranking card obtaining precedence.

INDEX

Page numbers in regular type, as 410, refer to the Goren System for bidding and play. Page numbers in italics, as 505, refer to the International Laws of Contract Bridge.

CREDITS

Drawings of kings are by Jerome Snyder

This book was set by Kingsport Press, Inc., Kingsport, Tennessee, in Primer, a new type face designed by Rudolf Ruzicka. The four-color pages were printed by Case-Hoyt, Inc., Rochester, New York, the body pages by Rand McNally & Company, Skokie, Illinois. Bound by Rand McNally & Company, Hammond, Indiana. Paper by Crocker, Burbank Papers Inc., Fitchburg, Mass.